The Time-Life Holiday Cookbook

HOME REPAIR AND IMPROVEMENT
THE TIME-LIFE LIBRARY OF BOATING
HUMAN BEHAVIOR
THE ART OF SEWING
THE OLD WEST
THE EMERGENCE OF MAN
THE AMERICAN WILDERNESS
THE TIME-LIFE ENCYCLOPEDIA OF GARDENING
LIFE LIBRARY OF PHOTOGRAPHY
THIS FABULOUS CENTURY
FOODS OF THE WORLD
TIME-LIFE LIBRARY OF AMERICA
TIME-LIFE LIBRARY OF ART
GREAT AGES OF MAN
LIFE SCIENCE LIBRARY
THE LIFE HISTORY OF THE UNITED STATES
TIME READING PROGRAM
LIFE NATURE LIBRARY
LIFE WORLD LIBRARY
FAMILY LIBRARY:
   HOW THINGS WORK IN YOUR HOME
   THE TIME-LIFE BOOK OF THE FAMILY CAR
   THE TIME-LIFE FAMILY LEGAL GUIDE
   THE TIME-LIFE BOOK OF FAMILY FINANCE

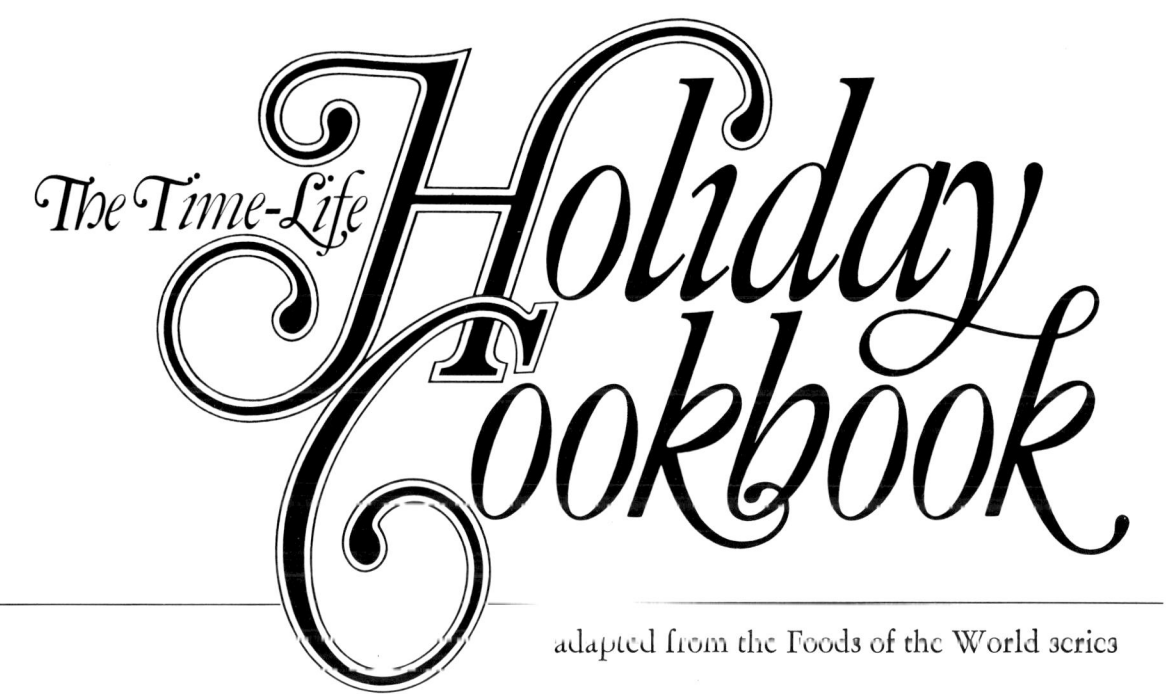

adapted from the Foods of the World series

by the Editors of TIME-LIFE BOOKS

TIME-LIFE BOOKS, NEW YORK

TIME-LIFE BOOKS

FOUNDER: Henry R. Luce 1898-1967

Editor-in-Chief: Hedley Donovan
Chairman of the Board: Andrew Heiskell
President: James R. Shepley

Vice Chairman: Roy E. Larsen

MANAGING EDITOR: Jerry Korn
Executive Editor: David Maness
Assistant Managing Editors:
Ezra Bowen, Martin Mann
Planning Director: Oliver E. Allen
Art Director: Sheldon Cotler
Chief of Research: Beatrice T. Dobie
Director of Photography: Melvin L. Scott
Senior Text Editors: Diana Hirsh, William Frankel
Assistant Planning Director: Carlotta Kerwin
Assistant Art Director: Arnold C. Holeywell
Assistant Chief of Research: Myra Mangan

PUBLISHER: Joan D. Manley
Associate Publisher: John D. McSweeney
General Manager: John Steven Maxwell
Assistant Publisher, North America: Carl G. Jaeger
Assistant Publisher, International: David J. Walsh
Business Manager: Peter B. Barnes
Promotion Director: Paul R. Stewart
Mail Order Sales Director: John L. Canova
Public Relations Director: Nicholas Benton

THE TIME-LIFE HOLIDAY COOKBOOK
EDITOR: Fred R. Smith
Designer: Elaine Zeitsoff
Staff Writer: Sue Hillaby
Researchers: Lea G. Gordon, Cinda Siler

EDITORIAL PRODUCTION
Production Editor: Douglas B. Graham
Assistant Production Editor: Feliciano Madrid
Operations Manager: Gennaro C. Esposito
Quality Director: Robert L. Young
Assistant Quality Director: James J. Cox
Associate: Serafino J. Cambareri
Copy Staff: David Harrison (chief),
Eleanore W. Karsten, Barbara Quarmby,
Florence Keith, Pearl Sverdlin
Picture Department: Dolores A. Littles,
Carolyn Turman Chubet
Traffic: Carmen McLellan

© 1976 Time Inc. All rights reserved.
First printing.
Published simultaneously in Canada.
Library of Congress catalogue card
number 76-10075.

The index for this book was prepared by Gail Liss. The editors also acknowledge the assistance of Mrs. Florence Lin for her advice on the Chinese New Year's feast.

Valuable help was given by the following departments and individuals of Time Inc.: Editorial Production, Norman Airey; Library, Benjamin Lightman; Picture Collection, Doris O'Neil; Photographic Laboratory, George Karas; TIME-LIFE News Service, Murray J. Gart.

Introduction

This is a cookbook for a year of celebrations. The more than 300 festive recipes, illustrated with more than 100 pages of color photographs, have been compiled from one of the most complete guides to cooking ever published, the 27 volumes that make up TIME-LIFE BOOKS' Foods of the World series. The recipes, all exactingly tested in the TIME-LIFE kitchens, are so detailed and explicit that even a cook with a limited experience will find them easy to follow.

The recipe ideas are as varied as the holidays that inspired them. Thus, in addition to England's classic plum pudding for Christmas, there are breads and cakes that are a part of the Christmas tradition in a half dozen other countries. For a New Year's open house, there are a Smithfield ham and a casserole of Hopping John to bring good luck, and also a Scandinavian smörgåsbord table to serve a crowd. For Mardi Gras, there are the delicious Creole favorites of New Orleans hostesses, and also England's Shrove Tuesday buns and Russia's pre-Lenten extravagance of bliny, sour cream and caviar. St. Patrick's Day means corned beef and cabbage, but also boxty pancakes and Irish coffee. A Passover menu might encompass a casserole of chicken, dill and matzos or potato, onion and matzo pancakes. Easter brings glazed ham, spring lamb and a galaxy of traditional breads and cakes from Rumania, Greece, Russia and Poland.

Every family has its own special celebrations—a wedding perhaps, when the rehearsal supper might end with a luscious dessert of *bavarois Clermont;* or a birthday when the candlelit cake could be one layered with peach filling and topped with maple icing. The Fourth of July is cookout time—lobsters and steaks, shish kabob and barbecued spareribs, clambakes and outdoor picnics of chili or fried chicken and fresh summer salads.

And so *The* TIME-LIFE *Holiday Cookbook* goes through the year's happy occasions. In the fall it's Octoberfest and sauerbraten and beer, and then Columbus Day and pasta and pizza. Roast chicken with kumquats decorates a Succoth harvest table, and 16 different cookies and doughnuts are served up for Halloween treats. The book ends with America's national feast—38 different recipes for the Thanksgiving table, from pumpkin soup to toasted nuts.

Contents

The Spirit of Christmas — 9
Cocktail Party Fare — 11
Holiday Dinners — 21
Christmas Breads, Cakes and Desserts — 34
The Cheerful Glass — 63

Saluting the New Year — 67
The Open House — 69
Punch, Fizzes and Cocktails — 89
The Chinese Celebration — 96

Winter Revels — 107
Sweets for Valentines — 109
Mardi Gras Time — 116
On Washington's Birthday — 127
Traditional Purim Delights — 132
St. Patrick's Day Specials — 134

The Rites of Spring — 141
Easter Favorites — 143
The Passover Seder — 159
Derby Day Partying — 164

Family Celebrations — 171
- Special Luncheon Parties — 173
- Gala Occasion Entrées — 188
- Dramatic Desserts — 200

The Fourth of July — 213
- Cookouts and Picnics — 213
- Cold Soups and Garden Salads — 235
- All-American Desserts — 241

October Festivals — 251
- An Autumn Beer Fest — 253
- Columbus Day Dishes — 263
- Succoth—the Harvest Holiday — 272
- Treats for Halloween — 278

The Thanksgiving Table — 281
- America's National Feast — 283

Picture Credits — 316
Index — 316

The Spirit of Christmas

Of all the holidays in the year, Christmas is the one that most challenges the adventurous cook. Other festivities may come and go in a day, but the Christmas season often means a month of celebrating, with the oven hardly cooling off from December 1 to year's end. Christmas cookies and gingerbread houses are as much a part of Yuletide flavor as caroling and eggnog, *Jingle Bells* and hot spiced wine. But making these traditional favorites is just part of the Christmas challenge. At this partying time, hostesses search for new hors d'oeuvre ideas, festive main courses, special holiday desserts.

The 60 Christmas recipes that appear on the following pages have been selected to expand the repertoire of cooking and baking into the traditions of many countries. Instead of the standard American turkey, there is a Christmas goose, stuffed with apples and prunes, Danish style. In addition to an Old South fruit cake, there are the Christmas breads and cakes of England, Ireland, Germany and Poland. And such spectacular desserts as *bûche de Noël* or *gâteau Saint-Honoré* end a Christmas feast with as much of the spirit of the season as a flaming English plum pudding.

Flaming cognac forms a soft halo around a plum pudding decorated with holly. In England, this rich dessert is so firmly identified with the holiday season that it is called Christmas pudding.

Holiday fondue

Seven savory hors d'oeuvre

A buffet centerpiece—galantine of duck

Roast goose and all the trimmings

Christmas Eve borscht

Festive pheasant

Roast beef and Yorkshire pudding

Fruit-filled breads and cakes

Decorated cookies and candies

An ornamental gingerbread house

Flaming plum pudding and other desserts

Traditional Southern eggnog

Hot spiced drinks—glögg, grog and Glühwein

Christmas Recipes
Cocktail Party Fare

Fondue Neuchâteloise

In a large bowl, toss together the cheeses and cornstarch until thoroughly combined. Pour the wine into a 2-quart fondue dish (or any 2-quart flameproof enameled casserole), drop in the garlic, and bring to a boil over high heat. Let the wine boil briskly for 1 or 2 minutes, then with a slotted spoon remove and discard the garlic. Lower the heat so that the wine barely simmers. Stirring constantly with a table fork, add the cheese mixture a handful at a time, letting each handful melt before adding another. When the fondue is creamy and smooth, stir in the kirsch, nutmeg, salt and a few grindings of black pepper, and taste for seasoning.

To serve, place the fondue dish or casserole over an alcohol or gas table burner, regulating the heat so that the fondue barely simmers. Set a basketful of the bread cubes alongside the fondue. Traditionally, each guest spears a cube of bread on a fork (preferably a long-handled fondue fork), swirls the bread about in the fondue until it is thoroughly coated, then eats it immediately.

To serve 15 to 20

½ pound grated Swiss Gruyère cheese (about 2 cups)
½ pound imported Swiss Emmentaler cheese, coarsely grated (about 2 cups)
1 tablespoon cornstarch
2 cups dry white wine, preferably Neuchâtel
1 medium-sized garlic clove, peeled and bruised
2 tablespoons imported kirsch
⅛ teaspoon grated nutmeg
⅛ teaspoon salt
Freshly ground black pepper
1 large loaf French bread with the crust left on, cut into 1-inch cubes

Benne-Seed Cocktail Biscuits

Preheat the oven to 350°. Spread the benne seeds evenly in a shallow baking dish and, stirring occasionally, toast them in the middle of the oven until golden brown. Remove from the oven and set the seeds aside.

Combine the flour, baking powder and salt and sift them into a large chilled bowl. Add the butter bits and, with your fingertips, rub the fat and flour together until they resemble flakes of coarse meal. Pour in the milk and mix with your hands or a spoon until the dough is smooth. Then blend in the benne seeds, wrap the dough in wax paper and refrigerate for at least 1 hour before using.

Preheat the oven to 350°. Cut the chilled dough in half and shape each half into a rectangle. Place one half at a time between two sheets of lightly floured wax paper and roll out the dough paper thin. Gently peel off the top sheet of wax paper and, with a biscuit cutter or the rim of a glass, cut the dough into 1½-inch rounds. Using a metal spatula, carefully transfer the rounds to ungreased baking sheets. Gather the scraps into a ball, shape it into a rectangle and roll it out between sheets of wax paper as before; then cut as many more biscuits as you can.

Bake the biscuits in the middle of the oven for 10 to 12 minutes, or until they are a pale golden color. Slide them onto wire racks and at once sprinkle the tops lightly with the coarse salt. Serve the biscuits at room temperature. The benne-seed cocktail biscuits can safely be kept in a tightly covered jar or tin for 2 or 3 weeks. Before serving, warm and crisp them for a few minutes in a low oven (250°).

To make about 8 dozen 1½-inch biscuits

½ cup benne seeds (sesame seeds)
2 cups flour
1 teaspoon double-acting baking powder
½ teaspoon salt
8 tablespoons butter, chilled and cut into ¼-inch bits
4 tablespoons milk
Coarse (kosher) salt

A perfect blending of food and drink for a holiday party matches a hot cheese fondue with a cool, delicate Swiss Neuchâtel wine.

Caraway Twists

Place the flour, cheese, caraway seeds and table salt in a deep mixing bowl. Add the butter and shortening bits and, with your fingertips, rub the flour and fat together until the mixture resembles flakes of coarse meal. Pour in 3 tablespoons of ice water all at once and mix with your fingers or a fork until the dough can be gathered into a compact ball. If the dough seems crumbly, add up to 1 tablespoon more ice water by drops until all the particles adhere. Divide the dough into two balls, wrap the balls in wax paper, and refrigerate for at least 1 hour.

Preheat the oven to 375°. On a lightly floured surface, roll out one ball of the dough into a 12-inch square about ¼ inch thick. With a ruler and a pastry wheel or sharp knife, cut the square in half crosswise and then lengthwise into ½-inch-wide strips to make about 4 dozen 6-by-½-inch strips. With a pastry brush, spread about half of the beaten egg lightly but evenly over the top of the strips, and sprinkle the entire surface with 1 tablespoon of the coarse salt. Repeat the entire process with the second ball of dough. When you finish you should have a total of 8 dozen strips of prepared dough.

To shape each caraway twist, press two strips of dough together, salt sides out. Pinch the strips tightly at one end and, with your fingers, gently wind the two strips together lengthwise to form a long loose spiral.

With a large metal spatula, carefully arrange the caraway twists on two ungreased baking sheets and bake them in the middle of the oven for 8 to 10 minutes, or until they are crisp and golden brown. Slide the twists onto wire racks to cool to room temperature before serving them. In a tightly covered jar or tin, they can safely be kept for a week or two.

To make about 4 dozen twists

1½ cups unsifted flour
½ cup freshly grated Swiss cheese
1 tablespoon caraway seeds
¼ teaspoon table salt
6 tablespoons butter, chilled and cut into ¼-inch bits
2 tablespoons vegetable shortening, cut into ¼-inch bits
3 to 4 tablespoons ice water
1 egg, lightly beaten
2 tablespoons coarse (kosher) salt

Ham Balls

Soak the bread crumbs in the milk for about 5 minutes, then combine them with the ground pork and ham in a large mixing bowl. Add the mustard, parsley, lightly beaten egg and a few grindings of black pepper, and with a large spoon mix them thoroughly together. Form the mixture into small balls about 1 inch in diameter and chill for at least ½ hour.

Preheat the oven to 350°. Over high heat, melt the butter with the oil in a large, heavy skillet. When the foam subsides, add the ham balls. To help keep their shape as they brown, roll the balls around in the hot fat by shaking the pan back and forth over the burner. When the ham balls are well browned on all sides (this should take about 5 minutes), transfer them with a slotted spoon to a 2-quart casserole. Pour off all but a thin film of fat from the skillet and pour in the wine. Bring it to a boil over high heat, scraping and stirring into it any brown bits clinging to the bottom and sides of the pan. Cook briskly for about a minute, then pour the wine into the casserole. Cover tightly and bake in the middle of the oven for about 30 minutes, basting the ham balls after 15 minutes with the wine. Serve either directly from the casserole or arrange the balls on a heated platter and pour the sauce over them. Or, place the ham balls and sauce in a chafing dish and serve, speared with decorative tooth picks, as an accompaniment to cocktails.

To make 32 ham balls

1 cup fresh bread crumbs
3 tablespoons milk
1 pound fresh lean pork, finely ground, combined with ½ pound cooked smoked ham, finely ground
1 tablespoon prepared mustard
1 tablespoon finely chopped fresh parsley
1 egg, lightly beaten
Freshly ground black pepper
2 tablespoons butter
2 tablespoons vegetable oil
¾ cup dry red wine

14 CHRISTMAS RECIPES

To make 3 dozen

36 small white mushrooms, each about 1 inch in diameter (about 1 pound)
An 8-ounce package of cream cheese, softened to room temperature
2 tablespoons anchovy paste
1 teaspoon lemon juice
1 teaspoon finely grated onion
2 tablespoons finely cut fresh chives

Mushroom Caps Stuffed with Anchovy Cream Cheese

One at a time, remove the stems from the mushrooms by holding their caps securely, and gently bending back the stems until they snap free. With a small sharp knife, cut away any part of the stem that adheres to the center of the mushroom. It is not necessary to wash the mushrooms; merely wipe them clean with a damp cloth.

In a small mixing bowl, beat the cream cheese with a large spoon until smooth. Beat in the anchovy paste, lemon juice and grated onion. Taste for seasoning. Then spoon the mixture into a pastry bag fitted with a small star tip and pipe it into the mushroom caps. Or, if you prefer, use a small spoon to fill the mushrooms with the cheese mixture, mounding it slightly. Sprinkle lightly with the chives and refrigerate the mushrooms until ready to serve.

To make 12 croustades

1 tablespoon soft butter
12 thin slices fresh white bread
1 small tomato, peeled, seeded and coarsely chopped (about 2 tablespoons)
1 teaspoon fresh basil, finely chopped or ½ teaspoon dried, crumbled basil
½ teaspoon salt
Freshly ground black pepper
¼ cup grated Swiss cheese, preferably Gruyère
2 tablespoons butter, cut into ¼-inch bits

Tomato Cheese Croustades

Preheat the oven to 400°. To make the little bread cases called *croustades*, you will need a muffin tin composed of 12 tiny cups, each about 2 inches in diameter. With a pastry brush, lightly coat each cup with the soft butter. Cut 2½-inch rounds from the centers of the bread slices using a cookie cutter or the rim of a wine glass. Fit the rounds in the tins, molding them gently to form little cups. Don't fuss with them too much. Bake the *croustades* in the middle of the oven for 10 to 12 minutes until golden brown, then remove them from the tin and cool. The *croustades* may be prepared as much as a day in advance, or a large supply may be frozen for later use.

Fill the *croustades* just before baking or hours earlier, if you wish. Preheat the oven to 400°. In a small bowl, combine the tomato, basil, salt and a few grindings of black pepper, and taste for seasoning. Fill each *croustade* with 1 teaspoon of grated cheese and spread about ½ teaspoon of the tomato mixture on top. Then dot with butter. Arrange the *croustades* on a cookie sheet or jelly-roll pan and bake for about 10 minutes. Slide under the broiler for a few seconds to brown the tops, and serve hot.

To make about 3 dozen

8 tablespoons butter (1 quarter-pound stick), softened
½ pound Cheddar cheese, grated (about 2 cups)
¾ cup sifted flour
½ teaspoon salt
⅛ teaspoon cayenne
½ teaspoon powdered mustard

Cheese Pennies

Cream the butter by beating it against the sides of a bowl with a wooden spoon until it is light and fluffy. Then beat in the cheese. Still beating, add the flour, ¼ cup at a time, then the salt, cayenne and mustard. (The entire process may be done more easily in an electric mixer equipped with a paddle or pastry arm attachment.) In either case, the mixture should be dense enough to be formed into a compact ball. If it is too soft to hold together, beat in additional flour by the tablespoonful, testing the dough for density after each addition. On a lightly floured surface, shape the ball into a sausagelike roll about 10 inches long and 1¼ inches wide, wrap it in wax paper and refrigerate for at least an hour, until firm.

Preheat the oven to 350°. With a sharp, thin knife, carefully slice the chilled dough into ¼-inch rounds and arrange them ½ inch apart on an ungreased cookie sheet. Bake in the middle of the oven for 8 to 10 minutes, or until the pennies are firm and golden brown. Watch carefully; they burn easily. Transfer them with a metal spatula to a rack to cool. The cheese pennies may be served at once at room temperature, or stored in an airtight container or frozen for future use.

Steak Tartare Balls

To make about 2 dozen

- 1 pound ground top round beef, free of all fat, and of the best quality
- 1 tablespoon Worcestershire sauce
- ½ teaspoon salt
- Freshly ground black pepper
- ¼ cup finely chopped chives, or the green stems of scallions, finely chopped
- 2 tablespoons (1 ounce) black caviar

In a small mixing bowl, thoroughly combine the beef, Worcestershire sauce, ½ teaspoon of salt and a few grindings of pepper. Taste for seasoning, then shape the mixture into balls about 1 inch in diameter. Make a small indentation in each ball with the tip of a small spoon or your finger, and one by one, roll the balls in the chopped chives or scallions so that the herbs adhere to the surface of the meat. Fill the indentations of each ball with about ¼ teaspoon of caviar, arrange them caviar side up on an attractive platter and chill before serving.

More easily, if less impressively, the steak balls may be served without the caviar, in which case simply roll the balls in the herbs without indenting them.

Cheese Balls

To make about 2 dozen 1-inch balls

- 1 cup freshly grated Monterey Jack cheese plus 1 cup freshly grated Cheddar or longhorn cheese, or 2 cups any combination of these cheeses
- 2 tablespoons flour
- 1 cup fresh cracker crumbs, made from saltines pulverized in a blender or wrapped in wax paper and finely crushed with a rolling pin
- 3 egg whites
- 1½ teaspoons prepared mustard
- Vegetable oil for deep frying
- Salt

Combine the grated cheese and flour in a deep mixing bowl and toss them together with a spoon. Spread the cracker crumbs on a piece of wax paper and set aside.

With a wire whisk or a rotary or electric beater, beat the egg whites until they are stiff enough to stand in unwavering peaks on the whisk or beater when it is lifted from the bowl. Scoop the egg whites over the cheese mixture with a rubber spatula, add the mustard, and fold the ingredients together gently but thoroughly.

To make each cheese ball, scoop up a heaping tablespoonful of the cheese mixture and mold it into a ball by placing a second tablespoon on top. Slide the cheese ball off the spoon onto the cracker crumbs and roll it about to coat it evenly. Transfer the cheese ball to a piece of wax paper and set it aside while you proceed to shape and coat the remaining balls. (At this stage, the cheese balls can be draped with wax paper and refrigerated for up to 12 hours or overnight if you like.)

Pour vegetable oil into a deep fryer or large heavy saucepan to a depth of about 3 inches and heat the oil until it reaches a temperature of 375° on a deep-frying thermometer.

Deep-fry the cheese balls, four or five at a time, turning them about with a slotted spoon for about 3 minutes, or until they are crisp and golden brown. As they color, transfer them to paper towels to drain.

Arrange the cheese balls attractively on a heated platter, season them lightly with a sprinkling of salt, and serve them while they are still warm as an accompaniment to drinks.

Galantine de Canard

To serve 15 to 20

2 five-pound ducks

Following the diagrams below, bone and skin both ducks. Try not to pierce the skins of the birds while you remove the meat and bones; wrap both skins in a damp kitchen towel and refrigerate until ready to use. Set the duck bones and the carcasses aside. Save the livers, gizzards and hearts, but discard any large globules of fat. Cut the breast meat of the ducks lengthwise into neat strips about ½ inch wide. Then coarsely chop any scraps of breast and all the rest of the duck meat and reserve.

How to Bone a Chicken or Duck in the French Manner

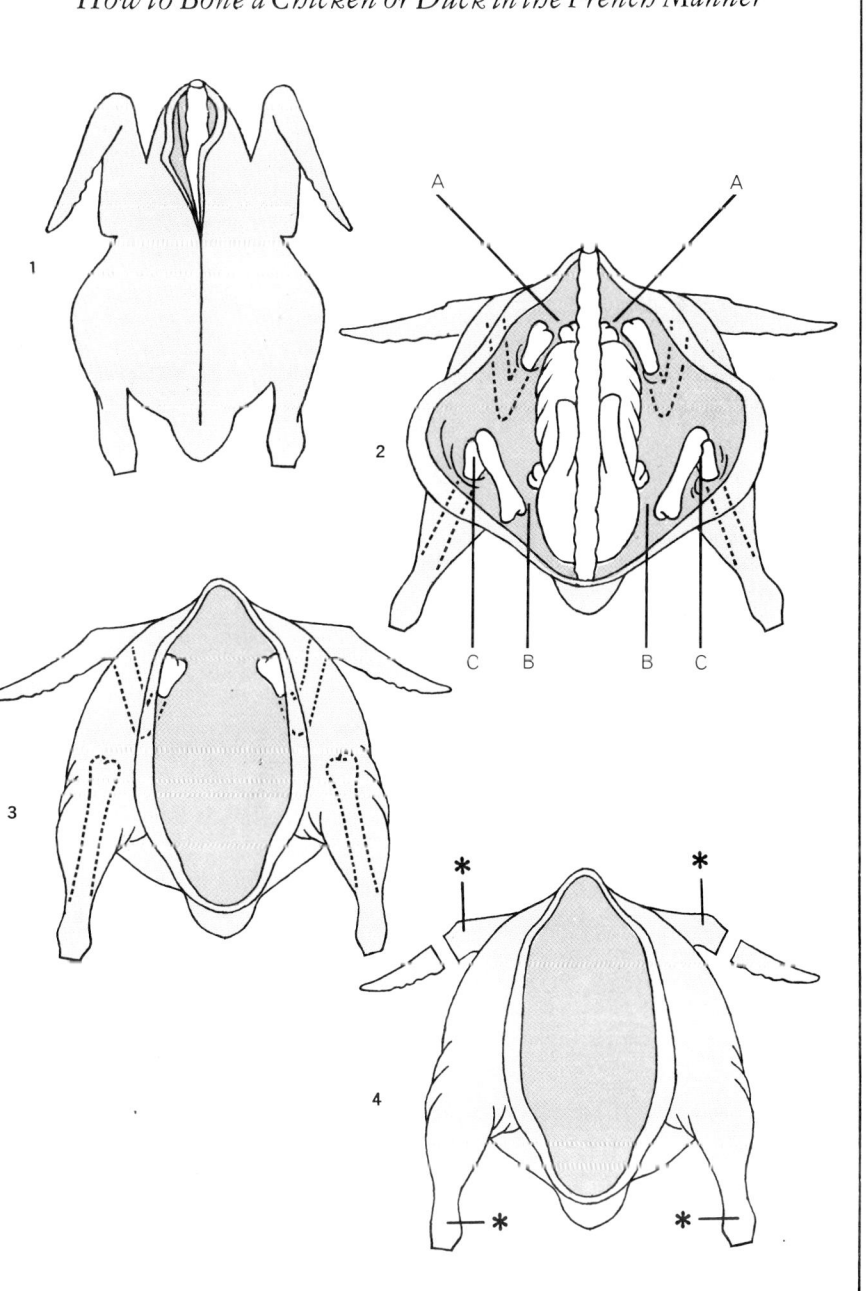

The first step in boning a duck or chicken is to place the bird on its breast and slit the skin along the backbone from neck to tail (1). With tiny cuts of a sharp, thin boning knife, free the meat around the neck cavity from the backbone. Then, folding the skin and flesh back as you proceed, continue to cut and scrape the meat away from the carcass. Work from neck to tail, turning the carcass when necessary.

Always cut as close to the bones as you can and try not to pierce the bird's skin. Wiggle each wing to find where the joint meets the carcass, then with knife or scissors cut through the joint to detach the wingbone (2A). Free the meat around each thighbone and cut the joints attaching the thighbones to the carcass (2B). With the knife separate the thighbones from the drumsticks (2C). Then lift out the carcass (3). Working from the cavity, free the meat from the two large bones of each wing and the drumsticks without piercing the skin (4). With a kitchen mallet or the side of a heavy cleaver, strike the wing tips and drumstick joints on the outside (at the points starred in number 4). Remove the bones. Next carefully remove all the meat from the bird, without piercing the skin. Finally, spread the skin out, breast side down. It is now ready to be filled. (If you are making a galantine, the wing tips are cut off after the galantine is cooked.)

For centuries the galantine has provided a festive touch for classic dinners and parties. The eye-catching version shown here is a galantine of duck. Flecked with truffles, fresh pork fat, pistachio nuts and ham, this ground mixture of duck with pork and veal is garnished with a realistic tomato rose.

MARINADE

A 7-ounce can black truffles, thinly peeled and cut into neatly squared-off strips about ¼ inch wide and ½ inch thick

The liquid from the truffles

¼ teaspoon ground allspice

The breast meat of the 2 ducks

¼ pound lean cooked ham, cut into neatly squared-off strips about 4 inches long, ½ inch wide and ¼ inch thick

5 ounces fresh pork fatback, cut into neatly squared-off strips the size of the ham strips

The livers of the 2 ducks, each cut into halves

4 strips fresh pork fatback (or side pork) sliced parallel to the rind, each about 8 inches long, 2½ to 3 inches wide, and ⅛ inch thick, then pounded as thin as possible between 2 sheets of wax paper

FOND

The carcasses, gizzards and hearts of the two ducks

4 to 5 quarts cold water

1 large onion, peeled and pierced with 2 whole cloves

1 large carrot, scraped

1 large leek, including 2 inches of the green top, trimmed, slit lengthwise in half and thoroughly washed to remove any sand

1 large bay leaf

4 fresh parsley sprigs

2 fresh thyme sprigs or ½ teaspoon crumbled dried thyme

8 whole black peppercorns

1 tablespoon salt

MARINADE: In a glass loaf dish or deep bowl, combine the truffles, truffle liquid and ¼ teaspoon ground allspice, and stir together gently. Add the duck breast, ham, 4-inch-long fatback strips and the duck livers, and turn them carefully about with a spoon until they are evenly moistened. Cover with the 8-inch slices of fatback and then with plastic wrap or foil and marinate in the refrigerator for 2 or 3 days.

FOND (STOCK): Place the duck bones, carcasses, gizzards and hearts in a heavy 6- to 8-quart casserole. Pour in 4 quarts of water; add more if necessary to cover the bones by at least 2 inches. Bring to a simmer over moderate heat, skimming off the foam and scum as they rise to the surface.

Add the onion, carrot, leek, bay leaf, parsley, thyme, peppercorns and 1 tablespoon salt, and reduce the heat to low. Simmer partially covered for 3 hours, or until the stock has developed an intense and definite flavor. With a slotted spoon, pick out and discard the duck pieces and vegetables. Then strain the stock through a fine sieve lined with a double thickness of dampened cheesecloth and set over a deep bowl.

When the stock has cooled to room temperature, refrigerate uncovered until the surface is coated with a layer of solidified fat. Sealed with the fat, the stock may safely be kept in the refrigerator for 3 or 4 days. Before using it, carefully lift off and discard all the fat.

FARCE (STUFFING): Put the chopped duck meat, chopped ham, pork fat, lean pork, veal and shallots through the finest blade of a meat grinder 3 or 4 times and then beat in the white wine. Or grind the meat and shallots once, then purée them in an electric blender, about 1 cup at a time, using ¼ cup of the wine with each cup of meat. Transfer the purée to a deep bowl and mix thoroughly.

Add the Madeira, the egg yolks, 1 teaspoon of ground allspice, ¼ teaspoon saltpeter, 5 teaspoons salt and ½ teaspoon freshly ground black pepper to the purée. Knead vigorously with both hands, then beat with a wooden spoon until the *farce* is light and fluffy. To check the seasoning, drop a spoonful of the *farce* into a small pan of simmering water. Poach it for 3 to 4 minutes, taste, and add more salt and pepper to the raw *farce* if necessary. Cover the bowl tightly with foil or plastic wrap and marinate in the refrigerator for 2 or 3 days.

ASSEMBLY: Coat a double thickness of dampened cheesecloth about 36 inches long and 22 inches wide with the softened butter. Spread out the more perfect of the two duck skins with the outside surface down on the cheesecloth. If there are any punctures in the surface of the duck skin, cut oversized square patches out of the second skin and set them outside surface down over the holes to conceal them. Discard the remainder.

With a spatula, spread a layer of *farce* about ¼ inch thick on the duck skin and stuff the wing and leg cavities. Place alternating rows of pistachios, marinated duck, ham, truffle and 4-inch-long fatback strips end to end lengthwise on top of the *farce,* spacing the rows about 1 inch apart. Cover the strips with a layer of *farce* about ½ inch thick. Then place one 8-inch slice of fatback lengthwise down the center and form a groove in it with the side of your hand. Lay the pieces of duck liver down the length of the groove and cover them with another 8-inch slice of fatback. Make sure the livers are completely and smoothly surrounded by the fatback. If you need more of these fatback slices to cover the livers, use the two remaining 8-inch slices or save them for another use.

Arrange alternate rows of meat strips and pistachios along both sides of the fat-wrapped livers, add another ½-inch layer of *farce* and place the remaining pistachios, marinated strips of truffles, meat and 4-inch-long fatback in lengthwise rows on top. Cover with the rest of the *farce*.

Carefully lift up the side edges of the duck skin and pull them together tightly over the filling, thus forming a thick compact roll, or galantine. Sew the seams together with a needle and heavy thread; turn the neck skin back over the seam and stitch it to the roll. (If you have used a bird with the legs left on, bend them forward, press them close against the body and tie them in place.)

Wrap the cheesecloth around the roll, twist the ends of the cheesecloth together and tie each one securely with kitchen cord close to the galantine. Then tie the cord loosely around the bird in 3 or 4 places to keep the galantine in shape.

Place the galantine in a 15-quart fish poacher or a casserole just large enough to hold it comfortably. Pour in the degreased stock and the 3 cups of white wine. The liquid should cover the galantine; if necessary, add canned chicken stock, or even water. If the galantine rises above the surface of the water, set a heatproof platter over it to submerge it.

Bring to a simmer over moderate heat, cover partially and reduce the heat to low. Poach the galantine for 1½ hours, then turn off the heat and let it cool to room temperature in the poaching liquid. Transfer the galantine to a large platter and, while it is still warm, remove the cheesecloth. Cover the galantine with foil or plastic wrap and refrigerate for 2 or 3 days before serving. Strain the poaching liquid into a deep bowl through a fine sieve lined with dampened cheesecloth. Let it cool to room temperature and refrigerate.

Remove and discard all the fat from the chilled poaching stock and make aspic, following the directions given below. Save the remaining stock for another use.

FARCE
The coarsely chopped meat of the 2 ducks
5 ounces lean cooked ham, coarsely chopped
¾ pound fresh pork fat, coarsely chopped
¾ pound lean pork, cut into 1-inch pieces
½ pound lean veal, cut into 1-inch pieces
½ cup finely chopped shallots
1 cup dry white wine
¼ cup dry Madeira
3 egg yolks
1 teaspoon ground allspice
¼ teaspoon saltpeter
5 teaspoons salt
½ teaspoon freshly ground black pepper
5 to 6 tablespoons butter, softened
½ cup shelled blanched unsalted pistachios
3 cups dry white wine

GELÉE (ASPIC): Pour 2 cups of the cool stock into a heavy 4- to 5-quart copper or enameled-iron saucepan and sprinkle the gelatin evenly over it. When the gelatin has softened for several minutes, add the vegetables, egg whites and egg shells and mix well. Pour in the remaining 6 cups of stock, set the pan over high heat and, stirring constantly, bring to a boil. Reduce the heat to low and simmer the stock undisturbed and uncovered for about 20 minutes, then strain it.

Set a saucepan containing the aspic in a large bowl or pot half-filled with crushed ice or ice cubes and water, and stir the aspic with a large metal spoon until it thickens enough to flow sluggishly off the spoon.

GELÉE
6 envelopes unflavored gelatin

Pour aspic to a depth of about ¼ inch into the large platter on which the galantine is to be served, and refrigerate. Set the galantine on a wire rack over a jelly-roll pan. Spoon more aspic from the saucepan over the galantine to cover the surface with a thin translucent glaze. Then refrigerate the galantine, still on the jelly-roll pan, until the glaze is firm. (Keep the remaining aspic in the saucepan at room temperature so that it stays liquid and ready to use; if it begins to set, warm briefly over low heat to soften it, then stir it over ice again until it reaches the same thick but still fluid consistency as before.)

NOTE: As an aid to decorating and presenting the galantine, refer to the photograph on page 16.

GARNITURE

2 or 3 large green leaves from the top of a leek or scallion
1 black truffle thinly peeled
2 small firm ripe tomatoes

GARNITURE: Meanwhile prepare the decoration for the garniture. Drop the leek or scallion leaves into boiling water and boil for 1 or 2 minutes. Drain the greens in a sieve, run cold water over them, then spread them on paper towels and pat them dry. Cut the leek or scallion leaves into bladelike leaf shapes and a dozen or more thin strips to use as stems. Slice the truffle thin and cut it into triangles and diamonds with truffle cutters or a small, sharp knife. Peel the tomatoes in a spiral fashion to make long continuous strips about ¾ inch wide. Shape one of the tomato strips into a roselike coil; cut the other strip into triangles, diamonds or other decorative shapes.

Carve a dozen slices, each about ¼ inch thick, off one end of the galantine, set them on a rack placed in a second jelly-roll pan and spoon a layer of aspic over them. Refrigerate until the aspic is firm and then coat and chill them once more. Arrange the slices in an overlapping circle at one end of the aspic-coated platter. Coat the tomato rose lightly with liquid aspic and chill until firm, then place it in the center of the circle of galantine slices. Return the platter to the refrigerator.

Dip the decorative pieces of leek or scallion top, truffle and tomato skin into the aspic remaining in the saucepan and arrange them attractively on the unsliced section of the galantine. Refrigerate until the garniture is anchored firmly, then carefully pour spoonfuls of aspic over the uncut galantine once or twice more, chilling it each time. When the galantine is well glazed transfer it to the serving platter.

Meanwhile, with a rubber spatula, scrape up the aspic from both jelly-roll pans and return it to the aspic remaining in the saucepan. Warm briefly over low heat to melt it, then pour the aspic into a small loaf pan. Refrigerate for at least 1 hour, or until firmly set. Remove the loaf pan from the refrigerator, dip the bottom in hot water, cover the top with an inverted plate. Grasping the loaf pan and plate firmly together, turn them over. The aspic should slide out easily. Cut the aspic into ¼-inch slices and then into ¼-inch dice. Scatter the dice around the galantine on the platter and refrigerate again until ready to serve.

Holiday Dinners

Roast Goose Stuffed with Apples and Prunes

Preheat the oven to 325°. To prepare this classic Danish Christmas dish, first wash the goose under cold running water. Pat it thoroughly dry with paper towels, then rub the bird inside and out with the cut side of half a lemon. Lightly salt and pepper the inside, and stuff the cavity with the coarsely chopped apples and prunes and the onion quarters. Close the opening by lacing it with skewers or by sewing it with heavy white thread. Fasten the neck skin to the back of the goose with a skewer and truss the bird securely so that it will keep its shape while cooking.

Roast the goose on a rack set in a shallow open pan for 3 to 3½ hours (about 20 to 25 minutes to the pound). As the goose fat accumulates in the pan, draw it off with a bulb baster or large kitchen spoon. Basting the goose itself is unnecessary.

To test whether the bird is done, pierce the thigh with the tip of a small, sharp knife. If the juice that runs out is still somewhat pink, roast another 5 to 10 minutes. If the juice is a pale yellow, set the finished bird in the turned-off oven with the door ajar for about 15 minutes to make it easier to carve.

Transfer the goose to a large heated platter and remove the string and skewers. Scoop out the stuffing and discard it. The fruits and onion will have imparted their flavor to the goose but will be far too fatty to serve.

Traditionally, poached apples stuffed with prunes *(page 23)* are served with the Christmas goose. Red cabbage and caramelized potatoes *(below and page 23)* complete the Christmas menu in Denmark.

To serve 8 to 10

- 8- to 10-pound young goose
- ½ lemon
- Salt
- Freshly ground black pepper
- 2 cups apples, peeled, cored and coarsely chopped
- 2 cups presoaked dried prunes, pitted and chopped
- 1 large onion, peeled and quartered

Braised Red Cabbage

Wash the head of cabbage under cold running water, remove the tough outer leaves, and cut the cabbage in half from top to bottom. Lay the flat sides down on the chopping board, cut away the core and slice the cabbage very finely. There should be approximately 9 cups of shredded cabbage when you finish.

Preheat the oven to 325°. Combine the butter, sugar, salt, water and vinegar in a heavy stainless-steel or enameled 4- to 5-quart casserole. When it comes to a boil and the butter has melted, add the shredded cabbage and toss thoroughly with two wooden spoons or forks. Bring to a boil again, cover tightly and place in the center of the oven to braise for 2 hours. There is little danger that the cabbage will dry out during the cooking, but it is a good idea to check on the liquid level occasionally. Add a little water if it seems necessary.

About 10 minutes before the cabbage is finished, stir in the jelly and grated apple, replace the cover and complete the cooking.

The piquant taste of red cabbage will improve if, after it has cooled, it is allowed to rest for a day in the refrigerator and then reheated either on top of the stove or in a 325° oven. Serve hot, as an accompaniment to goose to complete the traditional Danish Christmas dinner.

To serve at least 6

- 1 medium head red cabbage, 2 to 2½ pounds
- 4 tablespoons butter, cut into small pieces
- 1 tablespoon sugar
- 1 teaspoon salt
- ⅓ cup water
- ⅓ cup white vinegar
- ¼ cup red currant jelly
- 2 tablespoons grated apple

Caramelized Potatoes

Drop the unpeeled potatoes into a pan of boiling water and cook 15 to 20 minutes, or until they offer no resistance when pierced with the tip of a sharp knife. Let them cool slightly; then peel them.

Melt the ½ cup of sugar in a heavy 10- to 12-inch skillet over low heat. Cook slowly for 3 to 5 minutes, until the sugar turns to a light-brown caramel. Stir constantly with a wooden spoon and watch the sugar closely; the syrup changes color very rapidly and burns easily. It must not become too dark or it will be bitter. Stir in the melted butter, and add as many potatoes as possible without crowding the pan. Shake the pan almost constantly to roll the potatoes and coat them on all sides with the caramel. Remove the hot, caramelized potatoes to a heated serving bowl and repeat the procedure until all the potatoes are coated.

To serve 8

24 small new potatoes
½ cup sugar
8 tablespoons (1 quarter-pound stick) unsalted butter, melted

Apple Halves Stuffed with Prunes in Port Wine

In an enameled, stainless-steel or ovenproof glass bowl, combine the wine, sugar and prunes. Marinate the prunes in this mixture for at least 6 hours, then preheat the oven to 350°. Bake the prunes in their bowl, uncovered, for about 30 minutes, or until they are tender but not falling apart.

Meanwhile, prepare the poached apples. Pare the apples and cut them in half vertically. Scoop out the cores as neatly as possible with a small, sharp knife. In a 2- to 3-quart enameled or stainless-steel saucepan, combine the sugar and water, bring to a boil, and boil steadily for 2 or 3 minutes. Then lower the heat and add the apple halves, 8 at a time. Simmer for 10 minutes, until they are tender but not too soft. Transfer the poached apples to a heated platter with a slotted spoon and poach the remaining apples. Drain the baked prunes of all of their liquid and place 1 prune in each apple half.

To prepare these in advance, cover with plastic wrap and refrigerate. Just before serving, place the prune-filled apples on a lightly buttered cookie sheet, cover with foil and bake 10 minutes in a preheated 400° oven. Serve with roast goose, or duck, as part of the traditional Danish Christmas dinner.

To serve 8

16 medium prunes
2 teaspoons sugar
⅔ cup port wine
8 baking apples, ½ pound each
1 cup sugar
1 quart cold water

Rice and Almond Dessert

Bring the milk to a boil in a 2-quart saucepan and add the sugar and rice. Stir once or twice, then lower the heat and simmer uncovered about 25 minutes, or until the rice is quite soft but not mushy. (Cooking time for rice varies, but a sure test is to rub a grain between the thumb and forefinger; if there is no hard kernel in the center, the rice is done.) Pour the finished

To serve 6 to 8

1 quart milk
3½ tablespoons sugar
¾ cup long-grain white rice
¾ cup blanched and chopped almonds
¼ cup sherry
2 teaspoons vanilla
½ pint chilled heavy cream

The Danish holiday dinner depicted here can be prepared from the recipes on these pages. On the bottom shelf are red cabbage and sugar-browned potatoes; on the middle shelf, a roast goose stuffed and garnished with prunes and apples. On the top, at center, is a rice and almond dessert, a light, fluffy rice pudding, blended with chopped almonds and decorated with cherries; and last, but not least, a trayful of the sweet, crisp cookies known as *brune kager* and *Jødekager* —little brown cakes and Jewish cookies. The Christmas tree is decorated with traditional Danish ornaments of glass and paper under a shower of tinsel.

rice immediately into a shallow bowl to cool it quickly, and then add the chopped almonds, sherry and vanilla.

Whip the heavy cream in a chilled bowl with a wire whisk or hand or electric beater until it thickens and holds its shape softly. Fold it into the tepid rice mixture, turn the pudding into a serving dish and chill before serving.

A cold cherry or raspberry sauce or a spoonful of cherry liqueur is often served on top of this modern version of an ancient Christmas porridge.

Jewish Cookies

To make about 3 dozen cookies

16 tablespoons (2 quarter-pound sticks) unsalted butter
¾ cup sugar
1 egg
2½ cups flour
½ teaspoon salt
1 teaspoon baking powder
1 egg white, lightly beaten
¼ cup cinnamon and ¼ cup granulated sugar combined

Cream the butter and sugar together by using an electric mixer set at medium speed or by beating them with a wooden spoon until light and fluffy. Beat in the egg. Sift together the flour, salt and baking powder and beat into the creamed butter, ½ cup at a time. Continue to beat until thoroughly mixed. Then form into a ball, wrap in wax paper and chill for several hours.

Preheat the oven to 400°. Divide the chilled dough in thirds. On a lightly floured pastry board, roll out each third of dough into a circle about ⅛ inch thick. Using a 2- or 3-inch cookie cutter, cut the dough into rounds. Gather up the excess dough, roll it out again, and cut out additional rounds. Lay the rounds side by side on a lightly greased cookie sheet, and, with a pastry brush, spread the tops lightly with the beaten egg white. Then sprinkle with the cinnamon-sugar mixture. Bake 2 sheets of cookies at a time in the center of the oven for about 8 minutes. Remove from the oven and, with a spatula, immediately transfer the cookies to a cake rack. Let them cool thoroughly before storing them in airtight tins.

Little Brown Cakes

To make about 6 dozen cookies

½ cup dark corn syrup
5 tablespoons dark brown sugar
4 tablespoons unsalted butter
½ teaspoon baking soda
1½ cups flour
1 teaspoon powdered cloves
1¼ teaspoons ground cardamom
1¼ teaspoons grated lemon peel
3 ounces whole blanched almonds

Heat the corn syrup, brown sugar and butter in a heavy saucepan until the sugar is thoroughly dissolved. Do not let it boil. Remove from the heat and let it cool. Meanwhile, sift the baking soda, flour and powdered cloves together into a large bowl. Add the cardamom, grated lemon peel and the lukewarm syrup and knead the dough well by pressing it down with the heel of your hand, turning it, folding it over and pressing again. Continue kneading for 5 to 10 minutes, until the dough is smooth and shiny. Wrap in wax paper and set aside in a cool place for at least 2 hours.

Preheat the oven to 400°. On a lightly floured surface, roll the dough into a sheet ⅛ inch thick, then with a cookie cutter or small wine glass cut it into 2-inch rounds. Grease a cookie sheet and lay the cookies on it about an inch apart. Lightly press 1 almond into the center of each and bake 5 or 6 minutes, or until they are a light gold. Cool the little cakes on the cookie sheet. The cookies can be stored for several weeks in tightly sealed tins.

Roast goose, stuffed with sauerkraut and surrounded by bread dumplings, is a festive special-occasion bird in Czechoslovakia.

Roast Goose with Sauerkraut

Preheat the oven to 325°. Pull out all the loose fat from inside the goose and dice it into ½-inch chunks. In a small saucepan simmer the fat with a cup of water, covered, for about 20 minutes. Uncover the pan and boil the liquid completely away. The fat will then begin to sputter. Continue to cook until the sputtering stops. Strain the fat into a bowl and reserve. Discard the browned fat particles.

Drain the sauerkraut, wash it well under cold running water, then, to reduce its sourness, soak it in cold water for 10 to 20 minutes. Squeeze it dry by the handful. Heat 6 tablespoons of the goose fat in a heavy 10- or 12-inch skillet and add the onions and sauerkraut. Stirring occasionally, cook uncovered for about 10 minutes. Transfer the sauerkraut mixture to a large mixing bowl. Add the apples, potato, ½ teaspoon salt, caraway seeds and a few grindings of pepper.

Wash the goose inside and out with cold running water, pat it dry with paper towels and sprinkle the cavity generously with salt and a few grindings of pepper. Fill the goose with the sauerkraut stuffing, sew up the openings with needle and thread, and truss the legs with cord. Set the goose, breast up, on a rack in a large roasting pan. Cook it in the middle of the oven for 2 to 2½ hours, or 20 to 25 minutes a pound. With a bulb baster, occasionally remove the grease that drips into the pan. The goose is done when the juice from a punctured thigh runs pale yellow.

When the goose is done, remove it to a serving platter and cut away the thread and cords. Transfer the stuffing to a serving dish. Let the goose rest on the platter for at least 15 minutes before carving it.

To serve at least 6

An 8- to 10-pound goose
1 cup water
4 pounds fresh, canned or packaged sauerkraut
2 cups finely chopped onions
2 cups finely chopped apples
1 cup grated raw potato
½ teaspoon salt
1 tablespoon caraway seeds
Freshly ground black pepper
Salt

Bread Dumplings

To make about 12 dumplings

4 tablespoons butter
3 cups bread cubes, cut in ½-inch chunks
3 tablespoons finely chopped onions
10 tablespoons flour
2 tablespoons finely chopped parsley
½ teaspoon salt
⅛ teaspoon nutmeg
¼ cup milk

Melt 3 tablespoons of the butter in a heavy skillet. When the foam subsides, add the bread cubes. Toss them about in the butter until they are brown on all sides, then set them aside.

Add the rest of the butter to the skillet and when it has melted, stir in the onions. Cook them 3 or 4 minutes, until they are lightly colored, then scrape them into a large mixing bowl. Stir in the flour, parsley, salt and nutmeg, and moisten with the milk. Knead lightly to form a dough. Gently fold in the bread cubes and let the mixture stand for about 30 minutes.

Divide the dough in half and, with your hands, knead and form it into 2 long, sausagelike rolls about 2 inches in diameter. (They will each be 5 to 7 inches long.)

Carefully place the rolls in an 8-inch saucepan half full of boiling salted water. Cook them gently over medium heat for 20 to 25 minutes, turning them once with a large spoon or 2 slotted spoons. Remove them to paper towels to drain. Cut them into ½-inch slices while they are still hot. Serve them immediately with roast goose *(page 25)* or any meat dish that has a gravy or sauce.

Brussels Sprouts with Walnuts

To serve 4 to 6

3 cups (about 10 ounces) firm fresh Brussels sprouts
1 quart water
2 teaspoons salt
4 tablespoons butter
1 tablespoon flour
¾ cup chicken stock, fresh or canned
Freshly ground black pepper
1 cup coarsely chopped walnuts
½ cup bread crumbs

With a small sharp knife, trim the base of each Brussels sprout and cut off or pull away any wilted or yellowed leaves. Wash the sprouts thoroughly under cold running water.

In a heavy 2- to 3-quart saucepan, bring the water and 1 teaspoon of the salt to a boil over high heat. Add the sprouts and boil gently, uncovered, for about 10 minutes, or until they are tender when pierced with the tip of a knife. Drain the sprouts and set them aside.

Melt 2 tablespoons of the butter in the saucepan and, when the foam subsides, stir in the flour. Gradually pour in the chicken stock and bring to a boil, stirring constantly with a whisk or spoon until the sauce is slightly thickened and smooth. Sprinkle with the remaining teaspoon of salt and a few grindings of black pepper and taste for seasoning. Stir in the walnuts and sprouts and simmer, partially covered, for 10 minutes.

In a small skillet, melt the remaining 2 tablespoons of butter over moderate heat. Stir in the bread crumbs and, stirring constantly, cook for 3 or 4 minutes, or until they are golden brown.

Transfer the contents of the saucepan to a heated serving bowl and sprinkle with the browned bread crumbs. Serve at once.

Christmas Eve Borscht

To serve 4

MUSHROOM STOCK
3 ounces imported European dried mushrooms, preferably dried Polish mushrooms
4 cups boiling water

Place the mushrooms in a 2- to 3-quart enameled or stainless-steel saucepan and pour the boiling water over them. Let them soak at room temperature for at least 2 hours. Then place the pan over high heat and bring the soaking water to a boil. Lower the heat and simmer uncovered for about 2 hours, or until the liquid is reduced to ½ cup. Drain the stock through a fine sieve set over a bowl and set aside.

CHRISTMAS RECIPES 27

Meanwhile, in a 3- to 4-quart enameled or stainless-steel saucepan, bring the grated beets and 5 cups of cold water to a boil over high heat. Reduce the heat to moderate and cook uncovered for 10 minutes. Then reduce the heat to low, stir in the vinegar and 2 teaspoons of salt, and simmer partially covered for 30 minutes. Strain the beet stock through a fine sieve into a bowl, pressing down hard on the beets with the back of a spoon to extract all their juice before discarding them.

Return the beet stock to the saucepan in which it cooked, add the reserved mushroom stock, ½ teaspoon of salt, the sugar and lemon juice, and bring to a boil over high heat. Taste for seasoning and serve at once.

BEET STOCK
2½ pounds medium-sized firm young beets, peeled and coarsely grated
5 cups cold water
2 tablespoons red wine vinegar
2 teaspoons salt

½ teaspoon salt
¼ teaspoon sugar
1 tablespoon strained fresh lemon juice

Roast Pheasant

Preheat the oven to 350°. Wash the pheasant quickly under cold running water and pat it thoroughly dry inside and out with paper towels. Rub the inside of the bird with the salt and a few grindings of pepper and place the ground beef in the cavity. Close the opening by lacing it with skewers or sewing it with heavy white thread.

Fasten the neck skin to the back of the pheasant with a skewer, and, using a pastry brush, coat the skin of the bird evenly with the 2 tablespoons of softened butter. Drape the bacon slices side by side over the breast and wrap them around the bird, pressing the slices snugly against the body to keep them in place.

Place the pheasant, breast side up, on a rack in a shallow roasting pan just large enough to hold the bird comfortably. Roast undisturbed in the middle of the oven for 20 minutes, then increase the oven heat to 400°. Remove and discard the bacon slices. Using a pastry brush, baste the pheasant with 2 tablespoons of melted butter and roast it for about 20 minutes longer, basting generously every 5 minutes or so with a few tablespoons of the remaining melted butter.

To test whether the bird is done, pierce the thigh with the tip of a small, sharp knife. The juice should spurt out a clear yellow; if it is still pink, roast the pheasant for another 5 to 10 minutes.

Transfer the pheasant to a heated platter and let it rest for 10 minutes for easier carving. Discard the ground beef, which is used to keep the bird moist during the cooking and is not intended as a stuffing.

The roast pheasant is traditionally served with bread sauce and game chips *(recipes, page 30),* and may be decorated with bunches of watercress and its own tail feathers before serving.

To serve 4 to 6

A 3½- to 4-pound oven-ready pheasant
½ teaspoon salt
Freshly ground black pepper
4 ounces ground beef
2 tablespoons butter, softened, plus ½ cup butter, melted
4 slices lean bacon

Overleaf: Soaring, black-marked brown plumes, added for decoration after the bird has been cooked, make this dish of roast pheasant a particularly festive one. Garnished with watercress and surrounded with crisp, homemade game chips—a variety of potato chips—the pheasant will be carved and served and then the bread sauce *(at right of the platter)* will be passed.

Game Chips

To serve 4 to 6

4 cups vegetable oil or shortening
6 medium-sized baking potatoes (about 2 pounds), peeled
2 teaspoons salt

Preheat the oven to 250°. Line a jelly-roll pan or large, shallow roasting pan with a double thickness of paper towels, and set it aside. In a deep-fat fryer or large, heavy saucepan, heat the oil to 360° on a deep-frying thermometer, or until a haze forms above it.

With a large knife or a vegetable slicer, cut the potatoes into slices 1/16 inch thick and drop them directly into cold water to remove the starch and prevent them from discoloring. When ready to use, drain them in a colander, spread them out in a single layer on paper towels, and pat them thoroughly dry with more towels.

Drop about 1/2 cup of the potatoes at a time into the hot fat and, turning the slices about with a slotted spoon, fry for 2 or 3 minutes, or until they are crisp and golden brown. Transfer the chips to the paper-lined pan and keep them warm in the oven while you proceed with the remaining batches.

To serve, heap the chips in a heated bowl and sprinkle them with the salt. Game chips are traditionally served with roasted birds, such as pheasant, in which case they may be arranged in a circle around the bird and served on the same platter.

Bread Sauce

To make about 2 cups

2 cups milk
5 tablespoons butter
1 small white onion, studded with 2 whole cloves
1 small bay leaf
1/2 teaspoon salt
1/4 teaspoon white pepper
3 cups fresh soft crumbs, made from white bread, trimmed of crusts and pulverized in a blender
1 tablespoon heavy cream

In a heavy 2- to 3-quart saucepan, bring the milk, 4 tablespoons of the butter, onion, bay leaf, salt and pepper to a boil over moderate heat, stirring until the butter is completely melted. Set the pan aside off the heat and let the onion steep for 20 minutes, then discard it. Return the pan to moderate heat and bring the sauce to a boil. Gradually stir in the crumbs and cook, mashing them against the sides of the pan, until the sauce thickens and is somewhat smooth. Stir in the remaining 1 tablespoon of butter and the cream, and taste for seasoning. Serve at once. Bread sauce is traditionally served as an accompaniment to roast game birds such as pheasant or partridge, and hot or cold roast chicken or turkey.

Broccoli Purée

To serve 6 to 8

3 pounds firm fresh broccoli
8 tablespoons butter, cut into 1/2-inch bits and softened
1/4 teaspoon ground nutmeg, preferably freshly grated
1 teaspoon salt
Freshly ground black pepper
1 hard-cooked egg, finely chopped

With a small sharp knife, cut the broccoli flowerets from their stalks. Trim off and discard the tough woody ends of the stalks, then peel each of them deeply enough with the knife to expose the pale green flesh. Slice the stalks into 2-inch lengths.

Drop the stalks and flowerets into enough lightly salted boiling water to cover them by at least 2 inches. Boil briskly, uncovered, for 8 to 10 minutes, or until a piece of the stalk can be easily mashed against the side of the pan with the back of a fork. Thoroughly drain the broccoli in a large sieve or colander, shaking it from side to side to remove any clinging water. Then purée the broccoli through the coarse blade of a food mill or rub it through a coarse sieve with the back of a spoon.

Return the purée to the saucepan and, stirring constantly, cook over low heat until almost all of its moisture has evaporated. Stir in the softened butter bits, the nutmeg, salt and a few grindings of pepper. Taste for seasoning. Mound the broccoli purée in a heated serving dish, garnish the top with the chopped egg and serve at once.

Roast Beef

To serve 6 to 8

An 8-pound standing 3-rib roast

Preheat the oven to 450° (it will take about 15 minutes for most ovens to reach this temperature). For the most predictable results, insert a meat thermometer into the thickest part of the beef, being careful not to let the tip of the thermometer touch any fat or bone.

Place the beef, fat side up, in a large shallow roasting pan. (It is unnecessary to use a rack, since the ribs of the roast form a natural rack.)

Roast the beef undisturbed in the middle of the oven for 20 minutes. Reduce the heat to 325° and continue to roast, without basting, for about 90 minutes, or until the beef is cooked to your taste. A meat thermometer will register 130° to 140° when the beef is rare, 150° to 160° when medium, and 160° to 170° when it is well done. If you are not using a thermometer, start timing the roast after you reduce the heat to 325°. You can estimate approximately 12 minutes per pound for rare beef, 15 minutes per pound for medium, and 20 minutes per pound for well done.

Transfer the beef to a heated platter and let it rest for at least 15 minutes for easier carving. If you plan to accompany the beef with Yorkshire pudding *(below)*, increase the oven heat to 400° as soon as the beef is cooked. Transfer the roast from the oven to a heated platter, drape foil loosely over it, and set aside in a warm place while the pudding bakes. If you have two ovens, time the pudding to finish cooking during the 15 minutes that the roast rests.

To carve, first remove a thin slice of beef from the large end of the roast so that it will stand firmly on this end. Insert a large fork below the top rib and carve slices of beef from the top, separating each slice from the bone as you proceed. Traditionally, roast beef is served with its own juices and with a horseradish sauce *(page 32)*.

NOTE: Bringing meat to room temperature before cooking it is unnecessary. Roasts may go directly from the refrigerator to the oven.

Yorkshire Pudding

To serve 6 to 8

2 eggs
½ teaspoon salt
1 cup all-purpose flour
1 cup milk
2 tablespoons roast beef drippings, or substitute 2 tablespoons lard

To make the batter in a blender, combine the eggs, salt, flour and milk in the blender jar, and blend at high speed for 2 or 3 seconds. Turn off the machine, scrape down the sides of the jar, and blend again for 40 seconds. (To make the batter by hand, beat the eggs and salt with a whisk or a rotary or electric beater until frothy. Slowly add the flour, beating constantly. Then pour in the milk in a thin stream and beat until the mixture is smooth and creamy.) Refrigerate for at least 1 hour.

Preheat the oven to 400°. In a 10-by-15-by-2½-inch roasting pan, heat the fat over moderate heat until it splutters. Briefly beat the batter again and pour it into the pan. Bake in the middle of the oven for 15 minutes, reduce the heat to 375°, and bake for 15 minutes longer, or until the pudding has risen over the top of the pan and is crisp and brown. With a sharp knife, divide the pudding into portions, and serve immediately.

Yorkshire pudding is always served with roast beef.

Horseradish Sauce

To make about 1 cup

¼ cup bottled horseradish, drained and squeezed dry in a towel
1 tablespoon white wine vinegar
1 teaspoon sugar
¼ teaspoon dry English mustard
½ teaspoon salt
½ teaspoon white pepper
½ cup chilled heavy cream

In a small bowl, stir the horseradish, vinegar, sugar, mustard, salt and white pepper together until well blended. Beat the cream with a whisk or a rotary or electric beater until stiff enough to form unwavering peaks on the beater when it is lifted from the bowl. Pour the horseradish mixture over the cream and, with a rubber spatula, fold together lightly but thoroughly. Taste for seasoning. Serve the sauce from a sauceboat as an accompaniment to roast beef (*opposite*) or to such fish as smoked trout, smoked eel and grilled salmon.

Glazed Onions

To serve 4

12 firm white onions, each about 1½ inches in diameter
4 tablespoons butter
2 tablespoons honey
½ teaspoon salt

Preheat the oven to 400°. Drop the onions into enough boiling water to immerse them completely and cook briskly, uncovered, for about a minute. Drain the onions in a sieve or colander. With a small, sharp knife trim the stem ends, slip off the white parchmentlike skins, and cut the tops from the onions. Arrange the onions side by side in a baking-serving dish just large enough to hold them in one layer.

In a small skillet, melt the butter over moderate heat. When the foam begins to subside, add the honey and salt and stir until it is hot and fluid. Pour the honey mixture over the onions, turning them about with a spoon to coat them evenly.

Basting the onions occasionally with the cooking liquid, bake them in the middle of the oven for about 45 minutes, or until they are golden brown and show no resistance when pierced deeply with the point of a small knife. Serve at once, directly from the baking dish.

Britain's deservedly long-reigning favorite, a rib roast of beef, served with the classic accompaniments of Yorkshire pudding and horseradish sauce, is displayed against the coat of arms of the British Crown. This Dickensian meal makes a perfect Christmas feast.

Christmas Breads, Cakes and Desserts

Polish Christmas Poppy-Seed Roll

To make 1 roll

FILLING
¾ cup black poppy seeds
1 tablespoon unsalted butter
3 tablespoons sugar
3 tablespoons honey
2 tablespoons seedless raisins
¼ cup blanched almonds, pulverized in a nut grinder or with a mortar and pestle
1 egg white

DOUGH
¾ cup lukewarm milk (110° to 115°)
1 package active dry yeast
¼ cup confectioners' sugar
2¼ cups all-purpose flour
3 egg yolks
2 tablespoons rum
½ teaspoon vanilla extract
1½ teaspoons finely grated fresh orange peel
6 tablespoons unsalted butter, softened

1 tablespoon unsalted butter, softened
1 egg white, lightly beaten
1 egg, lightly beaten

Place the poppy seeds in a small heatproof bowl, pour in enough boiling water to cover them by at least 1 inch, and let them soak for 3 hours.

Drain the poppy seeds in a fine sieve and spread them out on paper towels to dry. Then pulverize them in a blender or with mortar and pestle.

In a small skillet, melt 1 tablespoon of butter over moderate heat. When the foam begins to subside, stir in the poppy seeds, sugar and honey. Reduce the heat to low and, stirring frequently, simmer for about 10 minutes, or until all the liquid in the pan has evaporated and the mixture is thick enough to hold its shape almost solidly in a spoon. With a rubber spatula, scrape the entire contents of the skillet into a deep bowl. Cool to room temperature, then add the raisins and almonds, and stir until well mixed.

Beat the egg white with a wire whisk or a rotary or electric beater until it forms unwavering peaks on the beater when it is lifted from the bowl. Scoop the egg white over the poppy-seed mixture and, with a spatula, fold them together gently but thoroughly. Cover the bowl with foil or plastic wrap and refrigerate for at least 1 hour.

To make the dough: Pour the milk into a small bowl and sprinkle it with the yeast and ½ teaspoon of the confectioners' sugar. Let the mixture stand for 2 or 3 minutes, then stir to dissolve the yeast completely. Set the bowl aside in a warm, draft-free place (such as an unlighted oven) for 10 minutes, or until the mixture almost doubles in volume.

Sift 2 cups of the flour and the remaining confectioners' sugar into a deep bowl and make a well in the center. Pour in the yeast mixture, egg yolks, rum and vanilla and, with a large spoon, gradually stir the flour into the liquid ingredients. Continue to stir until well mixed, then stir in the orange peel and beat in the 6 tablespoons of softened butter a few tablespoonfuls at a time. The dough should be just firm enough to be gathered into a ball. If necessary, stir in up to ¼ cup more flour, adding it by the tablespoon.

On a lightly floured surface, knead the dough by pushing it down with the heels of your hands, pressing it forward, and folding it back on itself. Repeat—pushing, pressing and folding—for about 10 minutes, or until the dough is smooth and elastic. Gather it into a ball, place it in a lightly buttered bowl, and dust the top with flour. Drape the bowl with a towel and set it aside in the draft-free place for about 1 hour, or until the dough doubles in volume.

With a pastry brush, spread 1 tablespoon of softened butter evenly on an 11-by-16-inch jelly-roll pan. Punch the dough down with a single blow of your fist and, on a lightly floured surface, roll it out into a rectangle about 15 inches long and 10 inches wide and no more than ¼ inch thick. Brush the dough with the beaten egg white and then, with a metal spatula, spread the poppy-seed filling over the surface to within about ½ inch of the edges. Starting at one of the 15-inch-long sides, roll the dough jelly-roll fashion into a tight cylinder. Carefully transfer the roll, seam side down, to the buttered jelly-roll pan. Let it rise in the draft-free place for about 20 minutes, then brush the top and sides of the roll with the beaten egg.

While the roll is rising, preheat the oven to 325°. Bake the poppy-seed roll in the middle of the oven for about 30 minutes, or until it is golden brown. Transfer the roll to a wire cake rack and let it cool to room temperature before slicing and serving.

Czech Christmas Sweet Bread

Pour the water into a small bowl and sprinkle with the yeast and 1 teaspoon of the sugar. Let it rest for 2 or 3 minutes, then stir. Set the bowl aside in a warm, draft-free place (such as an unlighted oven) for 5 to 8 minutes, or until the mixture almost doubles in volume.

Combine 4½ cups of flour, the remaining sugar, and the salt, lemon rind and mace in a large mixing bowl and make a well in the center. Pour in the yeast mixture, milk, eggs and egg yolk, and 4 tablespoons of the butter. With a large spoon, stir the dry ingredients into the liquid. Beat until the dough can be gathered into a medium-soft ball. Place on a lightly floured surface and knead, pushing the dough down with the heels of your hands, pressing it forward and folding it back on itself. Sprinkle flour over the ball by the tablespoonful, adding up to ¼ cup more flour if necessary to prevent the dough from sticking to your hands. Knead for about 10 minutes longer, or until the dough is smooth and elastic.

With a pastry brush, spread 1 tablespoon of the softened butter over the inside of a large bowl. Drop in the dough and turn it about to butter the entire surface. Drape the bowl with a kitchen towel and set it aside in the draft-free place for 1 hour, or until the dough doubles in volume. Punch the dough down with a blow of your fist and knead in the nuts and raisins. Cut the dough into five equal parts and braid as shown.

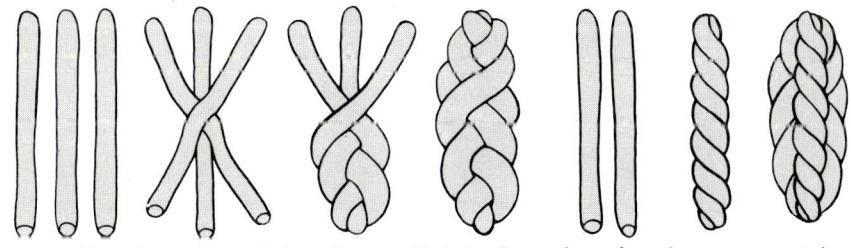

Roll each section of dough on a lightly floured surface into a rope 16 inches long and 2 inches wide. Brush a large cookie sheet with the remaining tablespoon of softened butter and set three of the ropes of dough side by side on the sheet. Starting at the center of the ropes and working toward each end, braid the dough loosely. Twist the remaining two ropes of dough together and set them lengthwise along the top of the braided dough. Tuck the ends under, drape with a towel and set aside in the draft-free place for 45 minutes, or until the dough almost doubles in volume.

Preheat the oven to 350°. Brush the loaf with the egg-and-milk mixture and bake in the center of the oven for 30 to 35 minutes, or until golden brown. Transfer to a wire rack to cool to room temperature.

To make one 16-inch loaf

¼ cup lukewarm water (110° to 115°)
1 package active dry yeast
1 teaspoon plus ½ cup sugar
4½ to 4¾ cups all-purpose flour
2 teaspoons salt
1 teaspoon grated lemon rind
¼ teaspoon mace
1 cup lukewarm milk (110° to 115°)
2 eggs plus 1 egg yolk
6 tablespoons unsalted butter, softened
½ cup finely chopped walnuts or pecans
1 cup seedless raisins
1 egg beaten with 1 tablespoon milk

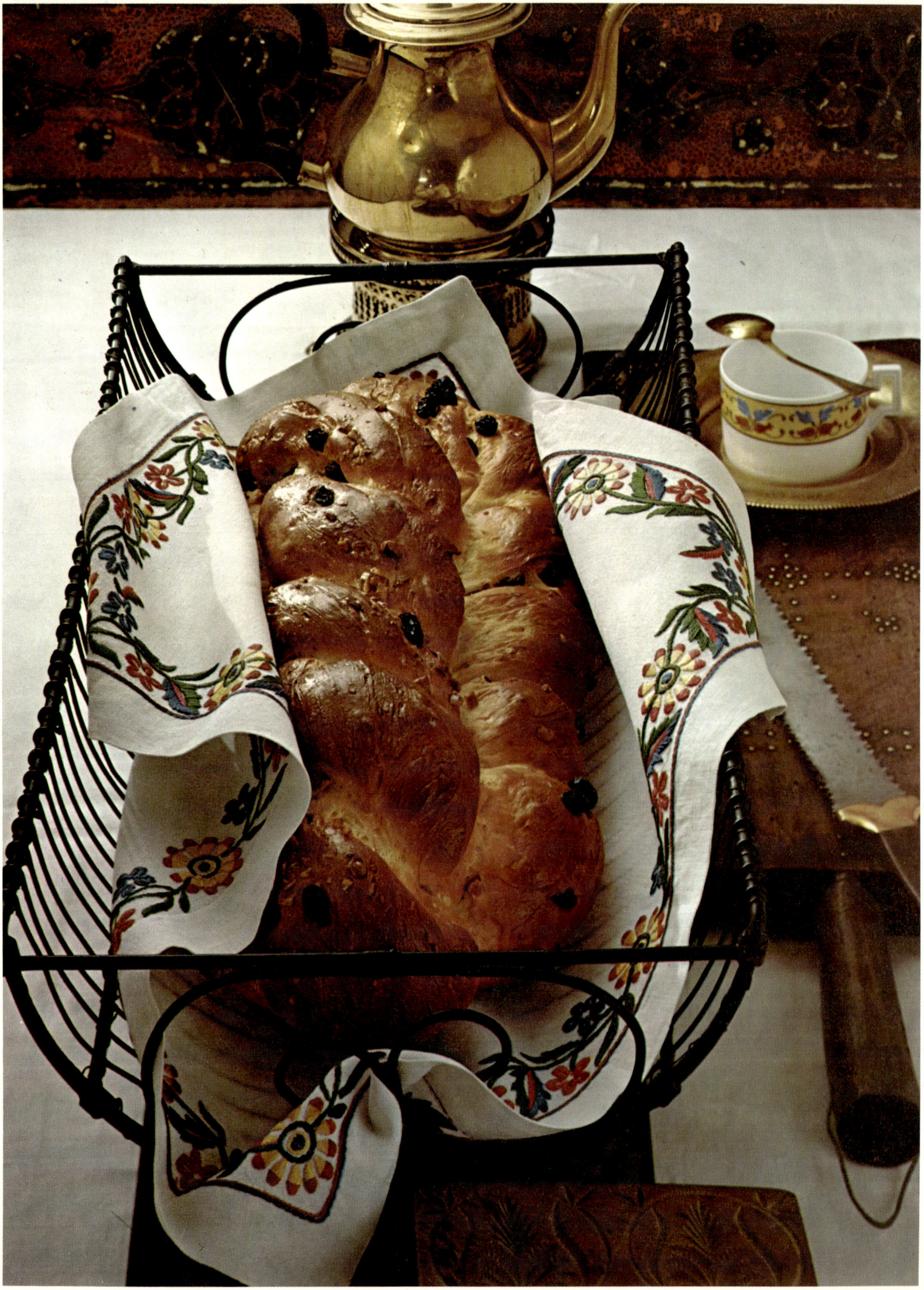

Danish Christmas Fruit Loaf

Sprinkle the yeast and 1 tablespoon of the sugar over the lukewarm milk. Let the mixture stand in the cup for 2 or 3 minutes, then stir gently to dissolve them. Set in a warm place, perhaps in an unlighted oven. When the yeast begins to bubble in about 8 to 10 minutes, stir it gently, and with a rubber spatula, transfer it to a large mixing bowl. Stir in the salt, vanilla, lemon rind, eggs, cardamom and the remaining sugar. Then add 3 cups of flour, a little at a time, stirring at first and then kneading with your hands until the dough becomes firm enough to be formed into a ball.

Shake the candied fruits in a small paper bag with 1 tablespoon of flour. (The flour will prevent the fruits from sticking together and enable them to disperse evenly throughout the dough.) Now add the fruits and the softened butter to the dough and knead for about 10 minutes, adding more flour, if necessary, to make the dough medium-soft. The finished dough should be shiny and elastic, and its surface blistered. Shape into a ball and place in a large buttered bowl. Dust the top lightly with flour, cover with a kitchen towel and set it in a warm, draft-free spot (again, an unlighted oven is ideal). In 45 minutes to 1 hour the dough should double in bulk and leave a deep depression when two fingers are pressed into the center.

After removing the dough, preheat the oven to 350°. Punch the dough down with your fists and knead again quickly. Shape it into a fat loaf and put it into a lightly buttered 1½-quart loaf pan. Cover again with the towel and let the dough rise in a warm spot for 15 to 20 minutes until it is almost double in bulk.

Bake the Christmas loaf in the center of the oven for 45 minutes. Remove the loaf from the pan and let it cool on a cake rack. It will keep well for 2 or 3 weeks if tightly wrapped in aluminum foil and refrigerated.

To make 1 large loaf

2 packages active dry yeast
¼ cup sugar
½ cup lukewarm milk (110° to 115°)
¼ teaspoon salt
½ teaspoon vanilla
½ teaspoon grated lemon rind
2 eggs, lightly beaten
½ teaspoon ground cardamom
3 to 4 cups flour, all-purpose
1 cup mixed candied fruits (lemon, orange, cherry, pineapple)
1 tablespoon flour
8 tablespoons (1 quarter-pound stick) unsalted butter, softened

Dundee Cake

Preheat the oven to 300°. Using a pastry brush, coat the bottom and sides of an 8-by-3-inch springform cake pan with 1 tablespoon of the softened butter. Sprinkle in 2 tablespoons of the flour, tipping the pan to spread the flour evenly. Invert the pan, and rap it sharply to remove the excess.

In a large mixing bowl, cream the remaining ½ pound of butter and the sugar together by mashing and beating them against the sides of the bowl with a spoon until they are light and fluffy. Beat in one of the eggs, then ½ cup of flour and so on alternately until all the eggs and the 2½ cups of flour have been added. Beat in the currants, raisins, candied peel, cherries, pulverized almonds, grated peel and salt, and continue beating until well combined. Stir in the dissolved soda, pour the batter into the pan, and arrange the split almonds on top in concentric circles. Bake in the middle of the oven for 1½ hours, or until a cake tester inserted in the center comes out clean. Let the cake cool in the pan for 4 or 5 minutes, then cool it thoroughly on a rack before serving.

To make one 8-inch round cake

1 tablespoon plus ½ pound butter, softened
2 tablespoons plus 2½ cups all-purpose flour
1 cup sugar
5 eggs
¾ cup dried currants
¾ cup seedless raisins
¾ cup coarsely chopped mixed candied fruit peel
8 candied cherries, cut in half
½ cup almonds, pulverized in a blender or with a nut grinder or mortar and pestle
2 tablespoons finely grated orange peel
A pinch of salt
1 teaspoon baking soda dissolved in 1 teaspoon milk
⅓ cup blanched almonds, split lengthwise into halves

This intricately braided sweet bread laden with raisins and chopped nuts is traditionally a Christmas-time feature in Czech households.

To make two 13-inch loaves

½ cup seedless raisins
½ cup dried currants
1 cup mixed candied citrus peel
¼ cup candied angelica, cut into ¼-inch dice
½ cup candied cherries, cut in half
½ cup rum
¼ cup lukewarm water (110° to 115°)
2 packages active dry yeast
¾ cup plus a pinch of sugar
5½ cups plus 2 tablespoons all-purpose flour
1 cup milk
½ teaspoon salt
½ teaspoon almond extract
½ teaspoon finely grated fresh lemon peel
2 eggs, at room temperature
¾ cup unsalted butter, cut into ¼-inch bits and softened
8 tablespoons melted unsalted butter
1 cup blanched slivered almonds
¼ cup confectioners' sugar, sifted

Dresdner Stollen

Combine the raisins, currants, candied citrus peel, angelica and cherries in a bowl. Pour the rum over them, tossing the fruit about to coat the pieces evenly. Soak for at least 1 hour.

Pour the lukewarm water into a small bowl and sprinkle it with the yeast and a pinch of sugar. Let the mixture stand for 2 or 3 minutes, then stir to dissolve the yeast completely. Set the bowl in a warm, draft-free place (such as a turned-off oven) for about 5 minutes, or until the mixture almost doubles in volume.

Meanwhile, drain the fruit, reserving the rum, and carefully pat the pieces completely dry with paper towels. Place the fruit in a bowl, sprinkle it with 2 tablespoons of the flour, and turn it about with a spoon until the flour is completely absorbed. Set aside.

In a heavy 1½- to 2-quart saucepan, combine the milk, ½ cup of the sugar and the salt. Heat to lukewarm (110° to 115°), stirring constantly until the sugar dissolves. Off the heat, stir in the reserved rum, the almond extract and fresh lemon peel, and finally the yeast mixture.

Place 5 cups of the flour in a large bowl and with a fork stir in the yeast mixture, a cup or so at a time. Beat the eggs until frothy and stir them into the dough, then beat in the bits of softened butter. Gather the dough into a ball and place it on a board sprinkled with the remaining ½ cup of flour. Knead the dough, by pushing it down with the heels of your hands, pressing it forward and folding it back on itself. Continue the kneading for about 15 minutes, or until all the flour is incorporated and the dough is smooth and elastic. Flour your hands lightly from time to time. Now press the fruit and almonds into the dough, ⅓ cup or so at a time, but do not knead or handle it too much or the dough will discolor. Coat a deep bowl with 1 teaspoon of melted butter and drop in the dough. Brush the top of the dough with another 2 teaspoons of melted butter, drape a towel over the bowl and set it in a warm, draft-free place for 2 hours, or until the dough doubles in bulk.

Punch the dough down and divide it into two equal pieces. Let them rest for 10 minutes, then roll the pieces out into strips about 12 inches long, 8 inches wide and ½ inch thick. Brush each strip with 2 tablespoons of the remaining butter and sprinkle each with 2 tablespoons of the remaining sugar. Fold each strip lengthwise in the following fashion: bring one long side over to the center of the strip and press the edge down lightly. Then fold the other long side across it, overlapping the seam down the center by about 1 inch. Press the edge gently to keep it in place. With lightly floured hands, taper the ends of the loaf slightly and pat the sides gently together to mound it in the center. The finished loaf should be about 3½ to 4 inches wide and 13 inches long.

With a pastry brush, and 1 tablespoon of melted butter, coat the bottom of an 11-by-17-inch jelly-roll pan. Place the loaves on the pan and brush them with the remaining 2 tablespoons of melted butter. Set the loaves aside in a warm draft-free place for about 1 hour, or until doubled in bulk. Preheat the oven to 375°. Then bake the bread in the middle of the oven for 45 minutes, or until golden brown and crusty. Transfer the loaves to wire racks to cool completely. Just before serving, sprinkle the loaves with the sifted confectioners' sugar.

Crisp German Christmas Cookies

Preheat the oven to 375°. With a pastry brush, coat a baking sheet with 1 tablespoon of the softened butter. Set aside.

In a large mixing bowl, cream the remaining ½ pound of butter and the ¾ cup of sugar together by mashing them against the side of the bowl with a wooden spoon until the mixture is light and fluffy. Beat in the egg yolks, one at a time, and when they are well incorporated beat in the vanilla and almond extracts. Beat in 1½ cups of the flour, ½ cup at a time, and gather the dough into a ball. Transfer the dough to a lightly floured surface, and knead it by pressing it down with the heel of your hand, pushing it forward, and folding it back on itself, meanwhile sprinkling it with the remaining cup of flour. When all of the flour is incorporated and the dough is smooth, roll it out into a rough circle about ⅛ inch thick. With a 2½-inch round cookie cutter or with cookie cutters shaped like stars, Christmas trees or Santa Clauses, cut out as many cookies as you can. Gather together all the scraps, roll out the dough again, and cut out additional cookies. Repeat until you have used all of the dough.

Place the cookies on the prepared baking sheet and sprinkle with the colored decorating sugar. Bake in the center of the oven for about 8 minutes, or until they are a light gold. With a metal spatula, transfer the cookies to wire cake racks, and cool to room temperature.

To make about 2 dozen

1 tablespoon plus ½ pound unsalted butter, softened
¾ cup sugar
3 egg yolks
½ teaspoon vanilla extract
¼ teaspoon almond extract
2½ cups all-purpose flour
Colored decorating sugar

The fruit-filled *Dresdner Stollen*, which improves with age, is a Christmas cake exchanged throughout Germany as a season's gift.

Gingerbread House

GINGERBREAD

1 tablespoon butter, softened
6¼ cups all-purpose flour
6 tablespoons double-acting baking powder
1½ teaspoons ground cinnamon
1 teaspoon ground cloves
¼ teaspoon ground nutmeg
¼ teaspoon ground cardamom
⅛ teaspoon salt
¾ cup honey
1¾ cups sugar
¼ cup butter
⅓ cup fresh lemon juice
1 tablespoon finely grated lemon peel
1 egg
1 egg yolk

DECORATION

2 egg whites
2½ cups confectioners' sugar
Candies and cookies for decorating the house
1 to 2 cups sugar for decorating the base

NOTE: This recipe makes enough dough for one 11-by-17-inch gingerbread cake. You will need three of these cakes to make the house shown on the opposite page and in the diagrams on pages 42-43. You may bake the cakes in three batches (they become firmer and easier to handle as they age, so it is possible to do the baking over a period of several days as long as you cut them as soon as they are baked). Or you may double or triple this recipe and make the cakes in one or two batches; in that event, you will need a very large mixing bowl and extra pans. The icing recipe is intended to make enough for the whole house, but generous decorations may require more.

Cut out the cardboard templates for the house and its base as shown in the diagrams on page 42. Set them aside. With a pastry brush or paper towel, lightly coat an 11-by-17-inch jelly-roll pan with 1 tablespoon of soft butter. Sprinkle ¼ cup of flour into the pan, and tip it from side to side to coat it evenly. Then turn it over and knock out the excess. Set the pan aside.

Sift 6 cups of flour, baking powder, cinnamon, cloves, nutmeg, cardamom and salt together into a large mixing bowl and set them aside.

Preheat the oven to 325°. In a heavy 4- to 5-quart saucepan, bring the honey, sugar and butter to a boil over high heat, stirring with a large spoon until the sugar is dissolved and the butter melted. Remove the pan from the heat, mix in the lemon juice and lemon peel, and cool to room temperature. Beat in 2 cups of the flour-and-spice mixture, add the egg and egg yolk, and then beat in the remaining 4 cups of flour-and-spice mixture. Flour your hands lightly and knead until the dough is smooth, pliable and still slightly sticky. If it is too moist to handle, beat in more flour by the tablespoon.

Place the dough in the jelly-roll pan, and with a lightly floured pin, press and roll it out as evenly as possible, forcing it into the corners with your fingers. Bake for 35 minutes, or until the cake is firm and the top brown. Let the cake cool in the pan for 4 or 5 minutes, then using the templates as your guide, cut it into the requisite shapes with a pastry wheel or small knife. Do not be tempted to cut the house pieces freehand; they must fit together precisely to make a stable structure. Set the pieces aside on wax paper until they cool completely. Bake and cut the remaining cakes in the same fashion.

In a large bowl, beat the egg whites with a whisk or a rotary or electric beater until they are frothy and slightly thickened. Sift the confectioners' sugar into the whites ½ cup at a time, beating thoroughly after each addition. Continue to beat for about 5 minutes, or until a stiff icing is formed. Fill a pastry bag fitted with a round decorative tip with a cup of the icing.

While the pieces of gingerbread are still spread out flat, decorate the front, back and sides of the house with windows, shutters, doors and the like to approximate the gingerbread house shown on the cover, or to suit your own fancy. When the icing is completely dry, assemble the base and walls of the house according to the directions on page 43, using the icing as cement to hold the pieces together. Let the walls stand undisturbed until the icing is completely set. With the remaining icing, cement the roof and chimney pieces in place, and after the icing is set, decorate the roof and chimney. Make more icing if necessary. For more elaborate decoration, coat candies and cookies on one side with the icing and press them gently onto the walls and roof. As a final touch, sift a snowlike coating of sugar over the base.

This decorative gingerbread house makes a fine holiday project for the whole family. Once made, the house can be used for years.

A Gingerbread House That Can Stand for Years

A gingerbread house like the one on page 41 is as much fun to make as it is to look at, and you may be as whimsical as you like with its decoration. But to make a house that will stand proudly through the Christmas holidays for years to come, the gingerbread must be cut with precision and the pieces fitted firmly together.

The first step is to make patterns for the pieces from stiff cardboard, following the dimensions and shapes in the diagrams at right. (Where pieces are identical, one pattern will do.) Now bake three 11-by-17-inch gingerbread cakes according to the recipe on page 40. While the cakes are still in the pans, lay the patterns on the cakes and cut the warm gingerbread with a pastry wheel or a small, sharp knife. If you like, cut out a door and a window or two as well. With a wide metal spatula, slide the cakes onto wax paper to cool. (There will be gingerbread left over, including one piece big enough to be cut into gingerbread figures.) Then outline door and window frames, shutters and other trim on the walls with the egg-white-and-sugar icing described on page 40.

After the wall trim decorations are dry, set the base on a cutting board or a large piece of heavy cardboard to enable you to move the house from place to place when it is finished. Assemble the house, using icing to cement the pieces together.

First ice the bottom of one end wall—the back of the house—and the bottom and one end of a side wall; fit them together and place them carefully on the base. Ice the bottom and two sides of a corner post and place it between them. Hold the pieces upright for 3 or 4 minutes, until the icing has set. Ice the opposite end of the side wall and the bottom of the other end wall, and fit that wall onto the house for

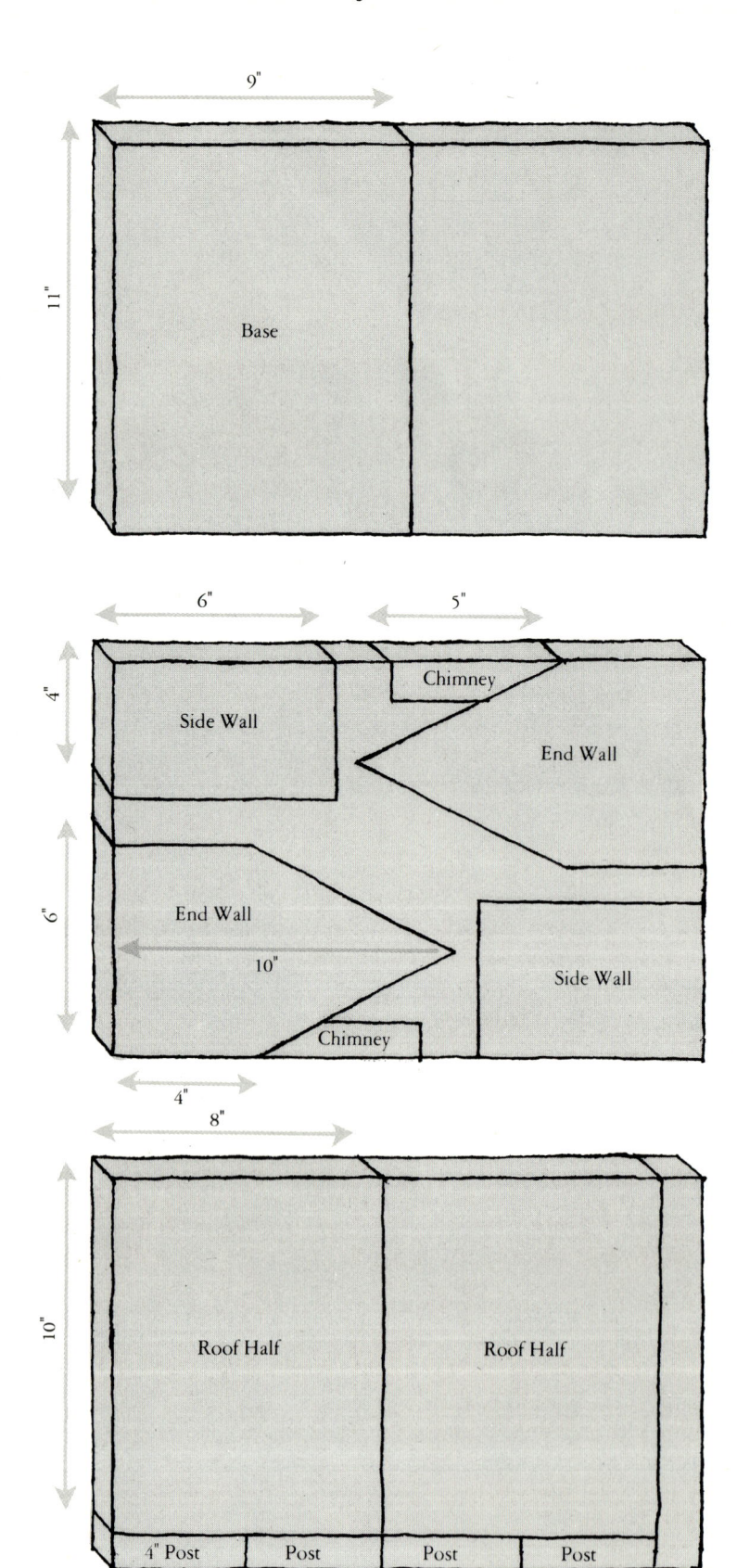

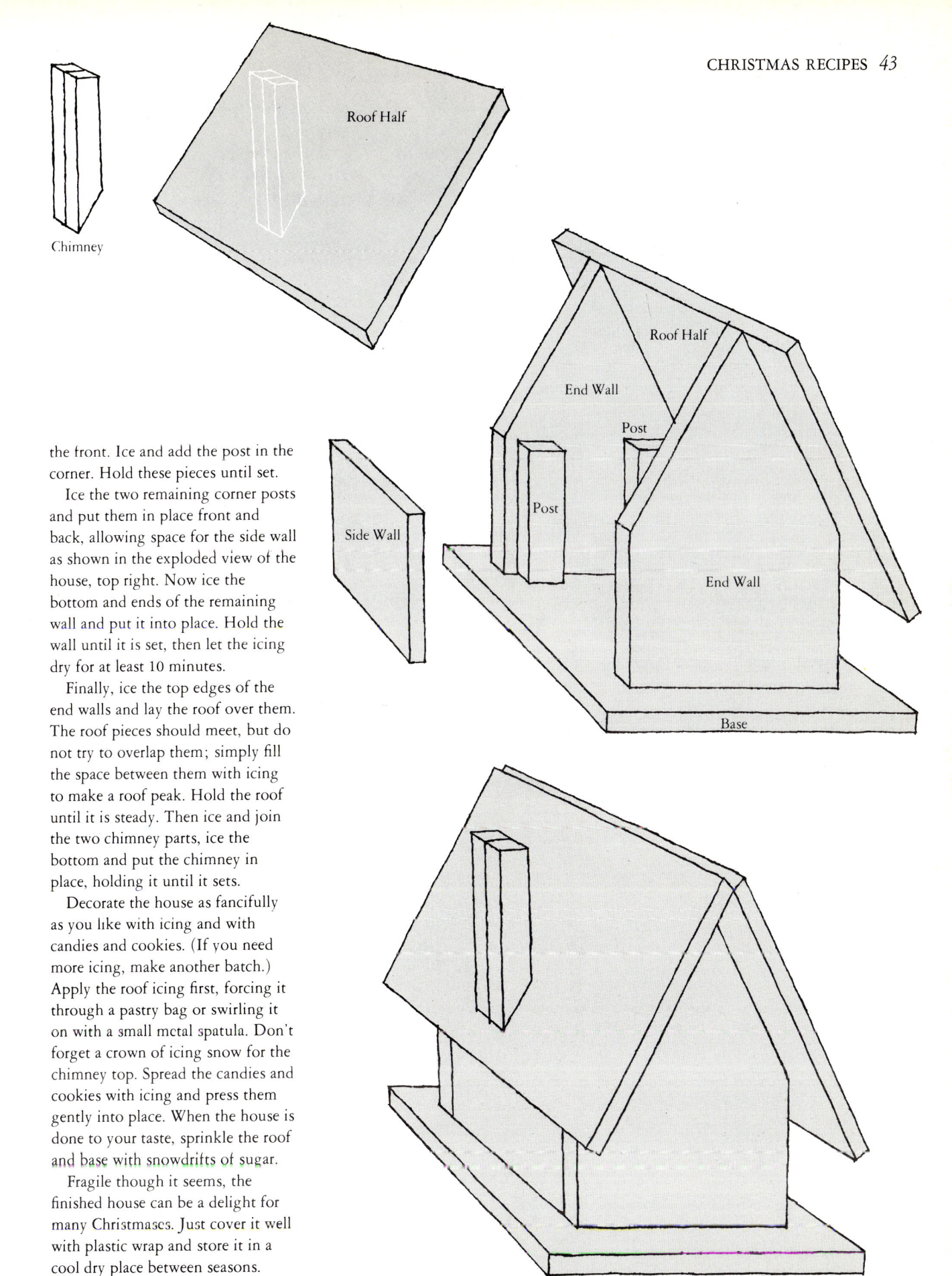

CHRISTMAS RECIPES 43

the front. Ice and add the post in the corner. Hold these pieces until set.

Ice the two remaining corner posts and put them in place front and back, allowing space for the side wall as shown in the exploded view of the house, top right. Now ice the bottom and ends of the remaining wall and put it into place. Hold the wall until it is set, then let the icing dry for at least 10 minutes.

Finally, ice the top edges of the end walls and lay the roof over them. The roof pieces should meet, but do not try to overlap them; simply fill the space between them with icing to make a roof peak. Hold the roof until it is steady. Then ice and join the two chimney parts, ice the bottom and put the chimney in place, holding it until it sets.

Decorate the house as fancifully as you like with icing and with candies and cookies. (If you need more icing, make another batch.) Apply the roof icing first, forcing it through a pastry bag or swirling it on with a small metal spatula. Don't forget a crown of icing snow for the chimney top. Spread the candies and cookies with icing and press them gently into place. When the house is done to your taste, sprinkle the roof and base with snowdrifts of sugar.

Fragile though it seems, the finished house can be a delight for many Christmases. Just cover it well with plastic wrap and store it in a cool dry place between seasons.

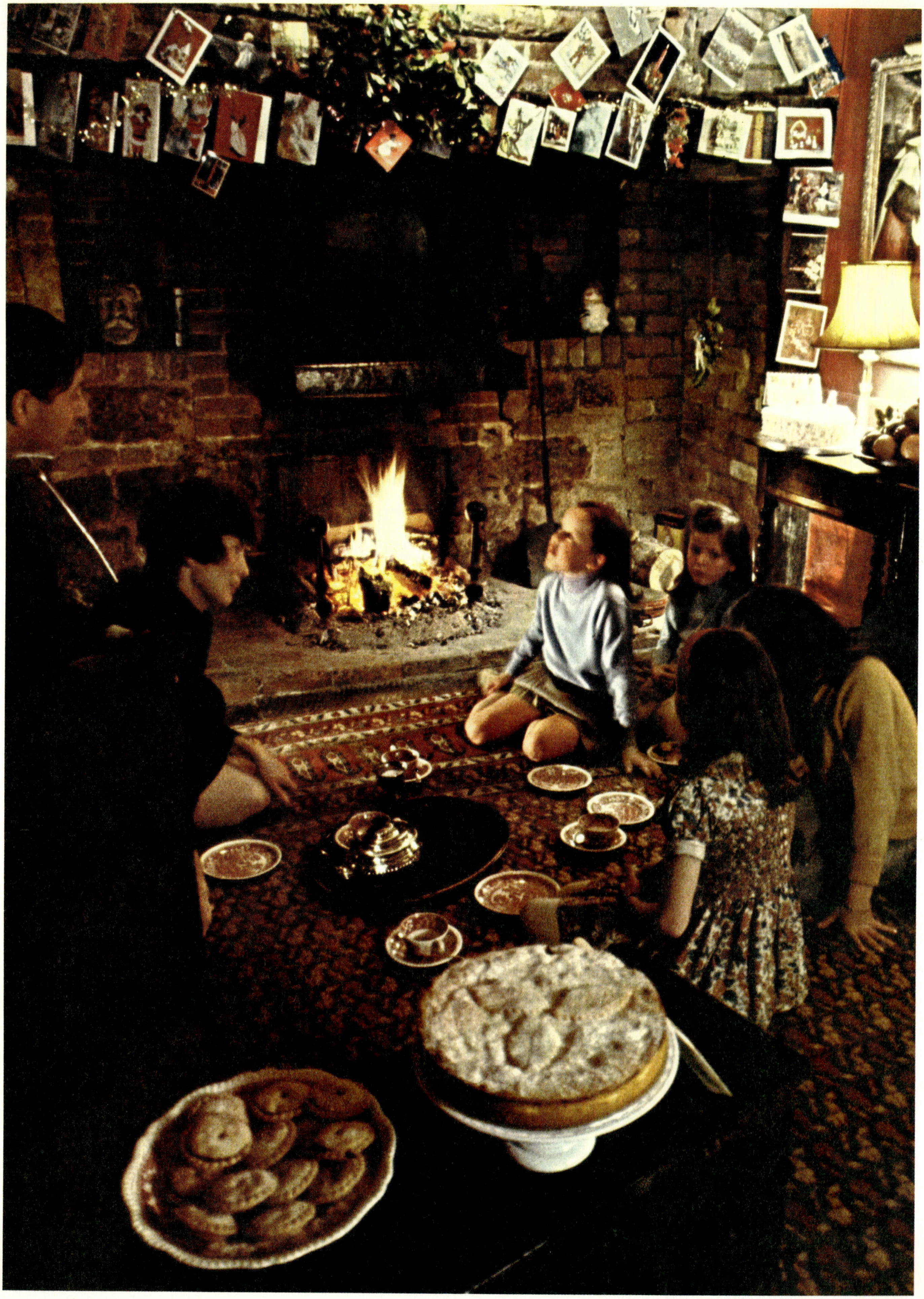

Individual Mince Pies

Preheat the oven to 375°. With a pastry brush, coat the bottom and sides of eight 2½-inch tart tins with the softened butter, allowing 1 teaspoon of butter for each tin. (These mince pies are most successful baked in specialized tart tins, available in well-stocked housewares stores; check the size by measuring the diameter of the bottom, not the top.)

On a lightly floured surface, roll out the pastry into a circle about ⅛ inch thick. With a cookie cutter or the rim of a glass, cut sixteen 3½-inch rounds of pastry. Gently press 8 of the rounds, 1 at a time, into the tart tins. Then spoon about 3 tablespoons of mincemeat into each pastry shell. With a pastry brush dipped in cold water, lightly moisten the outside edges of the pastry shells and carefully fit the remaining 8 rounds over them. Crimp the edges of the pastry together with your fingers or press them with the tines of a fork. Trim the excess pastry from around the rims with a sharp knife, and cut two ½-inch long parallel slits about ¼ inch apart in the top of each of the pies.

Arrange the pies on a large baking sheet, and bake them in the middle of the oven for 10 minutes. Reduce the heat to 350° and bake for 20 minutes longer, or until the crust is golden brown. Run the blade of a knife around the inside edges of the pies to loosen them slightly, and set them aside to cool in the pans. Then turn out the pies with a narrow spatula and serve.

NOTE: Mince pies are traditional Christmas fare, often served with whipped cream, Cumberland rum butter or brandy butter *(page 46)*.

To make eight 2½-inch pies

8 teaspoons butter, softened
Short-crust pastry
1½ cups mincemeat

Mincemeat

Combine the suet, raisins, currants, almonds, citron, dried figs, candied orange peel, candied lemon peel, apples, sugar, nutmeg, allspice, cinnamon and cloves in a large mixing bowl and stir them together thoroughly. Pour in the brandy and sherry, and mix with a large wooden spoon until all the ingredients are well moistened. Cover the bowl and set the mincemeat aside in a cool place (not the refrigerator) for at least 3 weeks. Check the mincemeat once a week. As the liquid is absorbed by the fruit, replenish it with sherry and brandy, using about ¼ cup at a time. Mincemeat can be kept indefinitely in a covered container in a cool place, without refrigeration, but after a month or so you may refrigerate it if you like.

To make about 3 quarts mincemeat

½ pound fresh beef suet, chopped fine
4 cups seedless raisins
2 cups dried currants
1 cup coarsely chopped almonds
½ cup coarsely chopped candied citron
½ cup coarsely chopped dried figs
½ cup coarsely chopped candied orange peel
¼ cup coarsely chopped candied lemon peel
4 cups coarsely chopped, peeled and cored cooking apples
1¼ cups sugar
1 teaspoon ground nutmeg
1 teaspoon ground allspice
1 teaspoon ground cinnamon
½ teaspoon ground cloves
2½ cups brandy
1 cup pale dry sherry

Short-Crust Pastry

In a large, chilled bowl, combine the butter, lard, flour, salt and sugar. With your fingertips rub the flour and fat together until they look like coarse meal. Do not let the mixture become oily. Pour 3 tablespoons of ice water over the mixture all at once, toss together lightly, and gather the dough into a ball. If the dough crumbles, add up to 1 tablespoon more ice water by drops until the particles adhere. Dust the pastry with a little flour and wrap it in wax paper. Refrigerate for at least 1 hour before using.

NOTE: If you are not making a sweet pastry, substitute ½ teaspoon salt for the ¼ teaspoon salt and the 1 tablespoon sugar in the recipe above.

6 tablespoons unsalted butter, chilled and cut into ¼-inch bits
2 tablespoons lard, chilled and cut into ¼-inch bits
1½ cups all-purpose flour
¼ teaspoon salt
1 tablespoon sugar
3 to 4 tablespoons ice water

The individual mincemeat pies on the table in the foreground are a special Christmas afternoon teatime treat enjoyed by an English family.

To make about ¾ cup

4 tablespoons unsalted butter, softened
½ cup light-brown sugar, rubbed through a sieve
¼ cup light rum
⅛ teaspoon ground nutmeg

Cumberland Rum Butter

Combine the butter, sugar, rum and nutmeg in a bowl, and beat with an electric beater until smooth and well blended. (By hand, cream the butter by beating and mashing it against the sides of a mixing bowl with a spoon until it is light and fluffy. Beat in the sugar, a few tablespoons at a time, and then the rum and nutmeg.) Refrigerate for at least 4 hours, or until firm. Cumberland rum butter is traditionally served with plum pudding.

To make about ¾ cup

4 tablespoons unsalted butter, softened
½ cup superfine sugar
3 tablespoons brandy
½ teaspoon vanilla extract

Brandy Butter

Combine the butter, sugar, brandy and vanilla in a bowl, and beat with an electric beater until the mixture is smooth and well blended. (By hand, cream the butter by beating and mashing it against the sides of a mixing bowl with a spoon until it is light and fluffy. Beat in the sugar, a few tablespoons at a time, and continue beating until the mixture is very white and frothy. Beat in the brandy and vanilla.) Refrigerate at least 4 hours, or until firm. Brandy butter is traditionally served with plum pudding, and may be sprinkled with ground nutmeg before serving.

To make one 12-inch round fruitcake

CAKE

½ pound (2 sticks) plus 4 tablespoons butter, softened
2 cups finely chopped mixed candied fruit peel (about 10 ounces)
2 cups white raisins (about 10 ounces)
1½ cups dried currants (about 8 ounces)
1 cup seedless raisins (about 5 ounces)
½ cup candied cherries, cut in half (about 4 ounces)
½ cup finely chopped candied angelica (about 4 ounces)
2 cups all-purpose flour
½ teaspoon double-acting baking powder
½ teaspoon salt
1 cup dark-brown sugar
1 cup shelled almonds (about 6 ounces), pulverized in a blender or with a nut grinder or mortar and pestle
4 eggs
¼ cup pale dry sherry, rum or brandy

GLAZE

¼ cup red currant jelly

English Christmas Cake

Preheat the oven to 275°. Using a pastry brush, coat the bottom and sides of a 12-by-3-inch springform cake pan with 2 tablespoons of the softened butter. Coat one side of a 20-inch strip of wax paper with 2 tablespoons of butter, and fit the paper, greased side up, inside the pan.

In a large bowl, combine the fruit peel, white raisins, currants, seedless raisins, cherries and angelica. Sprinkle the fruit with ½ cup of the flour, tossing it about with a spoon to coat the pieces evenly. Set aside. Then sift the remaining 1½ cups of flour with the baking powder and salt. Set aside.

In another large bowl, cream the remaining ½ pound of butter with the brown sugar by mashing and beating them against the sides of the bowl until they are light and fluffy. Add the pulverized almonds, then beat in the eggs one at a time. Add the flour-and-baking-powder mixture, a half cup or so at a time, then beat the fruit mixture into the batter. Finally, add the sherry and pour the batter into the springform pan. It should come to no more than an inch from the top. If necessary, remove and discard any excess.

Bake in the middle of the oven for 2 hours, or until a cake tester inserted in the center of the cake comes out clean. Let the cake cool for about 30 minutes before removing the sides of the springform pan, then slip the cake off the bottom of the pan onto a cake rack to cool completely. Then carefully peel off the strip of wax paper.

Heat the currant jelly in a small saucepan over moderate heat until it reaches a temperature of 225° on a candy thermometer or is thick enough to coat a wooden spoon lightly. With a small metal spatula, spread the hot glaze evenly over the top and sides of the cake.

To make the marzipan, use an electric mixer, preferably one equipped with a paddle. Crumble the almond paste in small pieces into the bowl, add the almond extract and ½ teaspoon of salt, and beat at medium speed until well blended. Gradually add the corn syrup in a thin stream, beating constantly until the mixture is smooth. Then beat in the 7 cups of confectioners' sugar, ½ cup at a time. As soon as the mixture becomes so stiff that it clogs the beater, knead in the remaining sugar with your hands. From time to time it will be necessary to soften the marzipan as you add the sugar by placing it on a surface and kneading it for a few minutes. Press the ball down, push it forward, and fold it back on itself, repeating the process as long as necessary to make it pliable.

On a clean surface, roll out half the marzipan into a circle about ½ inch thick. Using a 12-inch pan or plate as a pattern, cut a 12-inch disc out of the circle with a pastry wheel or small, sharp knife. Roll and cut the remaining marzipan into a 36-by-3-inch strip. Gently set the disc of marzipan on top of the cake and press it lightly into place. Wrap the strip of marzipan around the cake, pressing it gently to secure it. If the strip overlaps the top, fold the rim down lightly.

Wrap the cake in foil or plastic, and let it stand at room temperature for at least 48 hours before icing. The cake may be stored for longer periods; it improves with age, and can be kept for several months.

Just before serving, ice the cake. Combine the 6 cups of confectioners' sugar, egg whites, lemon juice and ⅛ teaspoon salt in a large mixing bowl. With a whisk or a rotary or electric beater, beat until the mixture is fluffy but firm enough to stand in soft peaks on the beater when it is lifted out of the bowl. With a small metal spatula, spread the icing evenly over the sides and top of the cake. Then decorate the cake to your taste with swirls of icing, fresh or artificial holly and artificial mistletoe, candied fruits, or even small china reindeer, people and houses.

MARZIPAN

2 cups almond paste
1 teaspoon almond extract
½ teaspoon salt
1 cup light corn syrup
7 cups confectioners' sugar (2 pounds), sifted

ICING

6 cups confectioners' sugar, sifted
4 egg whites
1 tablespoon strained fresh lemon juice
⅛ teaspoon salt

Irish Christmas Cake

Preheat the oven to 275°. Using a pastry brush, coat the bottom and sides of a 9-by-3-inch springform cake pan with 2 tablespoons of the softened butter. Sprinkle 2 tablespoons of the flour into the pan, tip it from side to side to spread the flour evenly, then invert the pan and rap it sharply on the bottom to remove excess flour. Combine the cherries, seedless and white raisins, currants, candied peel and angelica in a bowl, add ¼ cup of the flour, and toss the fruit about with a spoon to coat the pieces evenly. Set aside.

In a large bowl, cream ¾ pound of softened butter and the sugar and 2 more tablespoons of the flour together by mashing and beating them against the sides of the bowl until they are light and fluffy. Beat in the eggs, one at a time, then slowly beat in the remaining flour, the allspice and the salt. Combine the nuts with the fruit mixture and add the mixture to the batter, about ½ cup at a time, beating well after each addition. Pour the batter into the prepared pan, spreading it out with a spatula. Bake in the middle of the oven for 2 hours, or until the top of the cake is light golden in color or a cake tester inserted in the center comes out clean. Cool the cake completely before removing it from the pan.

To make one 9-inch round white fruitcake

¾ pound (3 sticks) plus 2 tablespoons butter, softened
1¼ cups plus 2 tablespoons all-purpose flour
⅔ cup coarsely chopped candied cherries
1¼ cups seedless raisins
1¼ cups white raisins
1¼ cups dried currants
¼ cup finely chopped mixed candied fruit peel
2 tablespoons finely chopped candied angelica
1¼ cups sugar
7 eggs
1 teaspoon ground allspice
1 tablespoon salt
1 cup finely chopped walnuts

To serve 8 to 10

½ cup finely diced mixed glacéed fruit
¼ cup imported kirsch
1 envelope plus 1 teaspoon unflavored gelatin
¼ cup water
Vegetable oil
½ cup uncooked long-grain white rice (not the converted variety)
2½ cups milk
1 cup sugar
2 tablespoons unsalted butter
1 vanilla bean
5 egg yolks
¼ cup apricot jam, rubbed through a fine sieve
2 cups heavy cream
Angelica and assorted thinly sliced candied fruits

Riz à l'Impératrice

Combine the glacéed fruit and the kirsch in a small bowl, stir well and marinate at room temperature for at least 45 minutes. Sprinkle the gelatin over ¼ cup of water and set it aside to soften. Brush the inside of a 2-quart charlotte mold with vegetable oil, then rub it with paper towels to remove the excess.

In a heavy 2- to 3-quart saucepan, bring 1 quart of water to a boil over high heat, drop in the rice and cook briskly for 5 minutes. Pour the rice into a sieve, rinse it under cold water and drain.

Pour 1 cup of the milk into the top of a double boiler, add ¼ cup of the sugar, the butter and vanilla bean. Stirring occasionally, cook over moderate heat until the sugar and butter are dissolved and small bubbles appear around the edge of the pan. Set the pan above simmering (not boiling) water and stir the rice into the mixture. Cover tightly and cook for 25 to 30 minutes, or until the rice is soft. Check from time to time and if the milk seems to be evaporating too rapidly, add a few spoonfuls more. When the rice is finished, however, the milk should be absorbed. To remove any excess moisture, drain the rice in a fine sieve. Remove and discard the vanilla bean.

In a 2- to 3-quart enameled or stainless-steel saucepan, heat the remaining 1½ cups of milk over moderate heat until bubbles form around the edge of the pan. Set aside off the heat and cover.

With a wire whisk or a rotary or electric beater, beat the egg yolks and the remaining ¾ cup of sugar together in a deep bowl for 3 or 4 minutes, or until the yolks form a slowly dissolving ribbon when the beater is lifted from the bowl. Whisking constantly, pour in the milk in a slow, thin stream. When thoroughly blended, return the mixture to the saucepan. Cook over low heat, stirring constantly, until the custard is as thick as heavy cream. Do not let the custard come near a boil or it will curdle. Mix in the softened gelatin and continue to mix until it is dissolved.

Strain the custard through a fine sieve set over a bowl. Stir in the glacéed fruits, kirsch and the apricot jam, then gently mix in the rice.

With a wire whisk, rotary or electric beater, whip the cream in a large chilled bowl until it forms soft peaks. Set aside. Place the bowl of custard in a pot filled with crushed ice or ice cubes and water, and stir for 4 or 5 minutes, or until the custard is cool and begins to thicken very slightly.

Remove the bowl from the ice and scoop the whipped cream over the custard. With a rubber spatula, fold the custard and cream gently together, using an over-under cutting motion rather than a stirring motion until no trace of white remains. Ladle the mixture into the mold, cover with foil, and refrigerate for 6 hours until it is completely firm.

To unmold the *riz à l'impératrice,* run a sharp knife around the sides of the mold and dip the bottom in hot water for a few seconds. Then wipe the mold dry, place a chilled serving platter upside down over the mold and, grasping plate and mold firmly, invert them. Rap the platter on a table and the *riz à l'impératrice* should slide out of the mold.

Decorate this dessert *(photograph, pages 50-51)* with the angelica and candied fruit, pressing the slices gently in place. Refrigerate the *riz à l'impératrice* until ready to serve. Before serving pour some raspberry sauce around the edge of the platter, and present the rest in a small bowl.

SAUCE DE FRAMBOISES: Wash the raspberries quickly under a spray of cold water, remove the hulls, and discard any badly bruised or discolored berries. (Frozen raspberries need only to be thoroughly defrosted and well drained in a sieve.)

Combine the raspberries, sugar and kirsch in the jar of an electric blender and blend at high speed for 10 seconds. Turn off the machine, scrape down the sides of the jar with a rubber spatula, and blend again for a minute. Then, with the back of a spoon, rub the purée through a fine sieve set over a small bowl. Cover tightly with foil or plastic wrap and refrigerate until ready to use. (The sauce may be kept for 3 to 4 days.)

SAUCE DE FRAMBOISES
2 cups fresh raspberries, or substitute 4 ten-ounce packages frozen whole raspberries
¾ cup sugar
¼ cup imported kirsch

Plum Pudding

In a large, deep bowl, combine the currants, seedless raisins, white raisins, candied fruit peel, cherries, almonds, apple, carrot, orange and lemon peel, and beef suet, tossing them about with a spoon or your hands until well mixed. Stir in the flour, bread crumbs, brown sugar, allspice and salt.

In a separate bowl, beat the eggs until frothy. Stir in the 1 cup of brandy, the orange and lemon juice, and pour this mixture over the fruit mixture. Knead vigorously with both hands, then beat with a wooden spoon until all the ingredients are blended. Drape a dampened kitchen towel over the bowl and refrigerate for at least 12 hours.

Spoon the mixture into four 1-quart English pudding basins or plain molds, filling them to within 2 inches of their tops. Cover each mold with a strip of buttered foil, turning the edges down and pressing the foil tightly around the sides to secure it. Drape a dampened kitchen towel over each mold and tie it in place around the sides with a long piece of kitchen cord. Bring two opposite corners of the towel up to the top and knot them in the center of the mold; then bring up the remaining two corners and knot them similarly.

Place the molds in a large pot and pour in enough boiling water to come about three fourths of the way up their sides. Bring the water to a boil over high heat, cover the pot tightly, reduce the heat to its lowest point and steam the puddings for 8 hours. As the water in the steamer boils away, replenish it with additional boiling water.

When the puddings are done, remove them from the water and let them cool to room temperature. Then remove the towels and foil and re-cover the molds tightly with fresh foil. Refrigerate the puddings for at least 3 weeks before serving. Plum puddings may be kept up to a year in the refrigerator or other cool place; traditionally, they were often made a year in advance.

To serve, place the mold in a pot and pour in enough boiling water to come about three fourths of the way up the sides of the mold. Bring to a boil over high heat, cover the pot, reduce the heat to low and steam for 2 hours. Run a knife around the inside edges of the mold and place an inverted serving plate over it. Grasping the mold and plate firmly together, turn them over. The pudding should slide out easily.

Christmas pudding is traditionally accompanied by Cumberland rum butter or brandy butter *(page 46)*. In England, small paper-wrapped coins (such

To make 4 puddings

1½ cups dried currants
2 cups seedless raisins
2 cups white raisins
¾ cup finely chopped candied mixed fruit peel
¾ cup finely chopped candied cherries
1 cup blanched slivered almonds
1 medium-sized tart cooking apple, peeled, quartered, cored and coarsely chopped
1 small carrot, scraped and coarsely chopped
2 tablespoons finely grated orange peel
2 teaspoons finely grated lemon peel
½ pound finely chopped beef suet
2 cups all-purpose flour
4 cups fresh soft crumbs, made from homemade-type white bread, pulverized in a blender or shredded with a fork
1 cup dark-brown sugar
1 teaspoon ground allspice
1 teaspoon salt
6 eggs
1 cup brandy
⅓ cup fresh orange juice
¼ cup fresh lemon juice
½ cup brandy, for flaming (optional)

A Rice Dessert Fit for an Empress

The richly colorful *riz à l'impératrice* is a molded Bavarian cream with rice and glacéed fruits, named after Napoleon III's consort, the Empress Eugénie. The dessert is decorated with glacéed fruits and encircled by raspberry sauce.

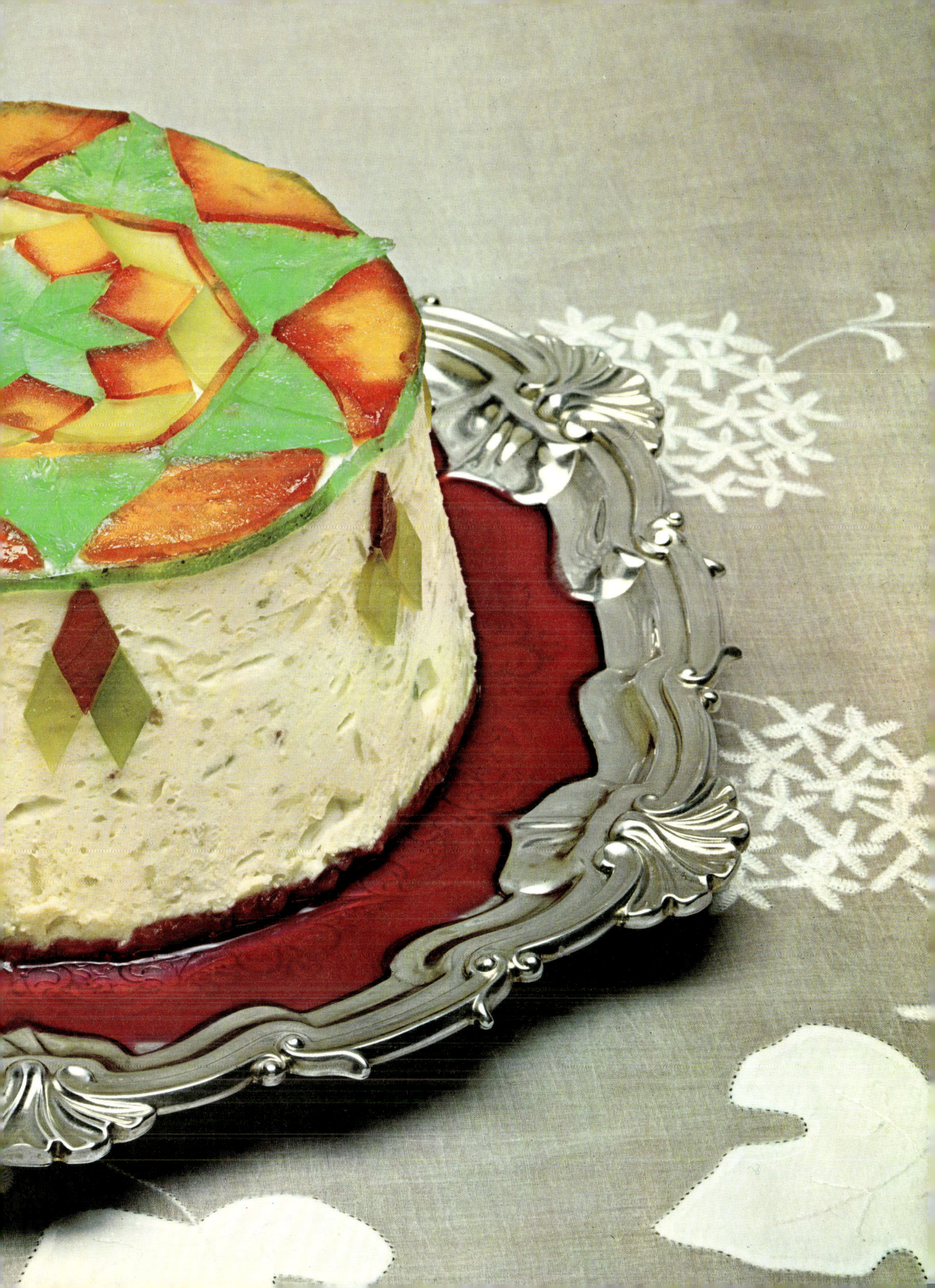

as sixpences and threepenny bits) are sometimes pressed into the pudding as good-luck pieces just before it is served.

If you would like to set the pudding aflame before you serve it, warm the ½ cup of brandy in a small saucepan over low heat, ignite it with a match and pour it flaming over the pudding.

Gâteau Saint-Honoré

To serve 10

PÂTE SUCRÉE
1 cup plus 2 tablespoons all-purpose flour
1 tablespoon sugar
¼ teaspoon salt
6 tablespoons unsalted butter, chilled and cut into ½-inch bits plus 1 tablespoon butter, softened
2 tablespoons vegetable shortening, chilled and cut into ½-inch bits
3 to 4 tablespoons ice water

PÂTE SUCRÉE (SWEET PASTRY): In a large mixing bowl combine 1 cup of flour, 1 tablespoon of sugar, ¼ teaspoon of salt, the 6 tablespoons of butter bits and the vegetable shortening. With your fingertips rub the flour and fat together until they look like flakes of coarse meal. Do not overblend or let the mixture become oily.

Pour 3 tablespoons of ice water over the mixture all at once, toss together lightly and gather the dough into a ball. If the dough crumbles, add up to 1 tablespoon more ice water by drops until the particles adhere. Dust the pastry dough with a little flour and wrap it in wax paper. Refrigerate for at least 30 minutes before using.

With a pastry brush, spread the tablespoon of softened butter over a large baking sheet. Sprinkle 2 tablespoons of flour over the butter, tipping the sheet to coat it evenly. Then invert the sheet and rap it sharply to remove the excess flour.

On a lightly floured surface, pat the dough into a rough circle about 1 inch thick. Dust a little flour over and under it and roll it out, from the center to within an inch of the far edge of the pastry. Lift the dough and turn it clockwise about 2 inches; roll again from the center to within an inch or so of the far edge. Repeat—lifting, turning, rolling—until you have created a rough circle about 10 to 11 inches in diameter and no more than ¼ inch thick.

Roll the dough loosely over the rolling pin, lift it and unroll it carefully on the buttered baking sheet. With a pastry wheel or sharp knife, and using a pie tin or plate as a guide, cut the dough into a 9-inch round. Remove and discard the excess dough, then prick the pastry all over with the tines of a table fork, but do not pierce through it completely. Refrigerate the pastry while you make the *pâte à choux*.

PÂTE À CHOUX
6 eggs
1½ cups water
12 tablespoons unsalted butter, cut into ½-inch bits plus 1 tablespoon butter, softened
1 tablespoon sugar
¼ teaspoon salt
1½ cups plus 2 tablespoons all-purpose flour

PÂTE À CHOUX (PUFF PASTE): Break one egg into a small bowl, beat lightly with a fork and set aside. In a heavy 2-quart saucepan, bring 1½ cups of water, 12 tablespoons of butter bits, 1 tablespoon of sugar and ¼ teaspoon of salt to a boil over high heat, stirring occasionally. As soon as the butter has completely melted, pour in the 1½ cups of flour all at once, remove the pan from the heat, and beat vigorously with a wooden spoon for 2 or 3 minutes until the paste moves freely with the spoon and pulls away from the bottom and sides of the pan in a mass.

Use the spoon to make a well in the center of the paste. Break an egg into the well and beat it into the paste. When this egg has been completely absorbed, add the 4 remaining eggs, one at a time—beating well after each egg is added. The finished paste should be smooth, shiny and just thick enough to fall slowly from the spoon in a thick strand when it is lifted out of the pan. To achieve this consistency, add as much of the reserved beaten egg as necessary, beating it in by the tablespoonful. (The paste, covered with plastic wrap, may be safely kept at room temperature for several hours before baking if you like.)

When you are ready to bake the *pâte à choux,* preheat the oven to 425°. Brush a large baking sheet with the tablespoon of softened butter. Sprinkle 2 tablespoons of flour over the sheet, invert and rap the sheet sharply to remove the excess flour.

Spoon the *pâte à choux* into a pastry bag fitted with a ½-inch plain tip and pipe the paste onto the *pâte sucrée* base, creating a ring about ½ inch wide and ¼ inch or so from the outside edges of the base. Pipe the remaining *pâte à choux* onto the buttered baking sheet into puffs about 1½ inches in diameter and 1 inch high, spacing them approximately 2 inches apart. (There should be about 15.)

Place the baking sheets side by side on the middle shelf of the oven if it is wide enough to accommodate them. If the oven is too narrow, bake the *pâte sucrée* base first, then bake the individual cream puffs later. Keep the puffs at room temperature while waiting. In either case use the following sequence of oven temperatures. Bake at 425° for 8 minutes, reduce the heat to 350° and, with the point of a small knife, prick the bubbles that have formed in the *pâte sucrée*. Continue baking for 15 to 20 minutes longer, or until the crust base is golden brown and the ring and puffs are firm and dry to the touch. Turn off the oven and let the pastry rest for 15 minutes to allow it to become dry and crisp. With a wide metal spatula, carefully slide the crust base and the individual puffs onto wire cake racks to cool to room temperature.

CARAMEL: When the base and puffs have cooled completely, prepare the caramel. In a 1- to 1½-quart enameled cast-iron or copper saucepan, bring the 2 cups of sugar, ½ cup of water and cream of tartar to a boil over moderate heat, stirring until the sugar dissolves. Boil the syrup briskly until it turns a rich golden tealike color. This may take 10 minutes or more. Watch carefully and do not let the sugar burn; it colors very quickly. (As the syrup bubbles up around the sides of the pan, brush the sugar crystals back down with a hair bristled [not nylon] pastry brush that has been dipped into cold water.)

As soon as the syrup reaches the proper color, remove the pan from the heat and place it in a wide pot half filled with hot water. This will keep the caramel fluid and warm.

Working quickly but carefully, pick up one puff at a time with tongs and submerge the top in the caramel. Hold the puff in place over the ring on the pastry crust and let the excess caramel drip off the puff onto the ring. When the caramel stops flowing freely, carefully set it glazed side up over the drops of caramel on the ring. (The whole procedure is somewhat like anchoring a candle in hot wax.) Place the glazed puffs side by side completely around the ring. There should be several puffs left over; glaze one of the extra puffs to decorate the center of the cake and set it aside on a plate. The cake may now be kept at room temperature for 3 or 4 hours.

CRÈME SAINT-HONORÉ (SAINT-HONORÉ PASTRY CREAM): In a 2- to 3-quart enameled cast-iron or copper saucepan, heat the milk and vanilla

CARAMEL
2 cups sugar
½ cup water
⅛ teaspoon cream of tartar

CRÈME SAINT-HONORÉ
2 cups milk
1 whole vanilla bean, or substitute 2 teaspoons vanilla extract
6 egg yolks
½ cup sugar
⅓ cup flour
A pinch of salt
6 egg whites
¼ cup Grand Marnier or other orange-flavored liqueur
1 envelope unflavored gelatin
⅓ cup water
1½ cups heavy cream, chilled
½ cup confectioners' sugar

bean over moderate heat until small bubbles appear around the edge of the pan. Remove the pan from the heat and cover to keep the milk warm.

With a wire whisk or a rotary or electric beater, beat the egg yolks and ½ cup of sugar together until the yolks are thick enough to fall in a ribbon when the beater is lifted from the bowl. Beating constantly, gradually sift in ⅓ cup of flour. When the flour is absorbed, remove the vanilla bean from the milk and pour in the warm milk in a thin stream, beating all the while. Immediately pour the mixture back into the saucepan.

Stirring deeply along the sides and into the bottom of the pan with a whisk or a wooden spoon, bring to a simmer over moderate heat. Do not let the pastry cream come near a boil at any point, but simmer it long enough to remove any taste of raw flour, about 5 minutes. Remove the pan from the heat and strain the hot pastry cream into a large bowl.

Then, working quickly, add a pinch of salt to the egg whites in another bowl and, with a wire whisk or a rotary or electric beater, beat until

Threads of spun sugar wreathe the candle-decked *gâteau Saint-Honoré (below)*—itself a fanciful composition of caramel-coated cream puffs, liqueur-laced pastry cream and whipped cream ribbons assembled on a crisp pastry base.

they are just stiff enough to form unwavering peaks on the beater when it is lifted from the bowl. Scoop about ¼ of the egg whites at a time over the hot pastry cream, stirring after each addition until no trace of white shows. Stir in the Grand Marnier and set the pastry cream aside to cool to room temperature.

Complete the pastry cream no more than an hour before you plan to serve the cake. Sprinkle the gelatin into a heatproof measuring cup or small bowl filled with ⅓ cup of cold water. When the gelatin has softened for 2 or 3 minutes, set the cup or bowl in a small pan of simmering water and, stirring constantly, cook over low heat until the gelatin dissolves completely. Remove the pan from the heat but leave the cup or bowl of gelatin in the water to keep it warm.

With a wire whisk or a rotary or electric beater, whip 1½ cups of chilled heavy cream until it begins to thicken. Sprinkle in the ½ cup of confectioners' sugar and continue beating until the cream is stiff enough to form soft peaks on the beater when it is lifted from the bowl. Beat in the dissolved gelatin.

Scoop the whipped-cream mixture over the pastry cream and, with a rubber spatula, fold them together gently but thoroughly, using an over-under cutting motion rather than stirring. Taste for flavoring and refrigerate for at least 30 minutes.

CRÈME CHANTILLY (CHANTILLY CREAM): In a large chilled bowl, beat ½ cup of chilled heavy cream with a wire whisk or a rotary or electric beater until it begins to thicken. Sprinkle the top with 1 tablespoon of confectioners' sugar and ½ teaspoon of vanilla extract, and continue beating until the cream is very stiff and stands in firm peaks on the beater when it is lifted from the bowl. Refrigerate until ready to use.

FINAL ASSEMBLY: Carefully slide the puff-topped cake onto a serving plate with a large metal spatula.

With the point of a skewer gently make a hole near the base of each individual cream puff from the inside edge of the ring. Spoon one third of the pastry cream into a pastry bag fitted with a ¼-inch plain tip and carefully fill each puff with a little of the cream. To prevent the puffs from crushing or loosening at this stage, hold each one lightly with one hand while filling it with the other. (Fill the reserved glazed cream puff with *crème Saint-Honoré* and set it aside.)

Fill the center of the cake with the remaining *crème Saint-Honoré*, smoothing it evenly with a spatula and mounding the center slightly.

Decorate the top of the cake as fancifully as you like with the *crème Chantilly* piped through a pastry bag fitted with a star tip. Set the reserved cream puff in the center. If you like, surround the edge of the cake with spun sugar.

CRÈME CHANTILLY
½ cup heavy cream, chilled
1 tablespoon confectioners' sugar
½ teaspoon vanilla extract

Sucre filé

Before making the syrup, prepare a place in your kitchen to spin it. Place two wooden spoons at least 12 inches long parallel to one another and 18 to 24 inches apart on top of wax paper, with the bowls of the spoons weighted down on a counter or table and the handles projecting from the

1 cup sugar
½ cup water
A pinch of cream of tartar

edge of the surface by 8 or more inches. (If you have no long wooden spoons, use long metal skewers instead.) Cover all the nearby floor and counter space with wax paper or newspapers to catch any drippings of syrup when you spin the sugar.

In a heavy 1- to 1½-quart saucepan, bring the sugar and water to a boil over moderate heat, stirring until the sugar dissolves. Cook briskly, uncovered and undisturbed, until the syrup reaches a temperature of 290° on a candy thermometer, or a few drops spooned into ice water immediately separate into flexible, but not brittle, threads. The syrup should remain absolutely clear. Remove the pan from the heat immediately.

Working quickly, grasp two table forks in one hand so the tines form a fairly straight row. Dip the tines of the fork into the hot syrup and let the excess drip off into the pan. Then, using a figure-eight motion, swirl the syrup over the protruding handles of the spoons. The syrup will quickly harden into glossy threads and cling to the handles. Let the threads accumulate on the handles to the desired thickness, and then sweep them up with both hands and lay them on a plate. Repeat the entire procedure until you have spun all of the syrup into threads. Spun sugar is used as nests for desserts or to veil them.

NOTE: To produce even longer strands of spun sugar, place the spoon handles farther apart—or instead of spoons use thin 3-foot-long wooden poles. Rather than using two forks to spin the sugar, you may make a shaker by cutting the loops from a sauce whisk, leaving a cluster of straight wires 3 or 4 inches in length. Many professional confectioners prefer to use a shaker made of wood studded with nails.

Bûche de Noël

To serve 10

2 tablespoons butter, softened, plus 8 tablespoons unsalted butter, softened and cut into ½-inch bits
2 tablespoons plus 1 cup flour
4 teaspoons cornstarch
1¼ teaspoons double-acting baking powder
¼ teaspoon salt
6 egg whites
1 cup sugar
½ teaspoon vanilla extract
4 egg yolks
3 tablespoons cold water
¾ cup crab-apple jelly
¾ cup maple syrup
1 ounce unsweetened baking chocolate, coarsely grated
Candied cherries
Candied green citron

Preheat the oven to 350°. Brush 1 tablespoon of softened butter over the bottom and sides of a 10½-by-15½-inch jelly-roll pan. Line the pan with a 20-inch strip of wax paper and let the extra paper extend over the ends. Brush 1 tablespoon of softened butter on the paper and sprinkle it with 2 tablespoons of flour, tipping the pan from side to side. Turn the pan over and rap it sharply to remove the excess flour. Combine the 1 cup of flour, cornstarch, baking powder and salt and sift them onto a plate.

With a wire whisk or a rotary or electric beater, beat 4 of the egg whites until they begin to thicken. Slowly add ½ cup of the sugar, beating continuously until the whites are stiff enough to form unwavering peaks on the beater when it is lifted from the bowl. Beat in the vanilla.

In another bowl and with the unwashed whisk or beater, beat the egg yolks, the remaining ½ cup of sugar and the water together. When the yolk mixture thickens enough to fall from the beater in a slowly dissolving ribbon, beat in the sifted flour mixture a few tablespoons at a time. Make sure each addition is completely incorporated before beating in more. Stir ½ cup of the beaten egg whites into the yolk mixture, then scoop it over the whites and fold the two together gently but thoroughly.

Pour the batter into the lined pan and spread it evenly into the corners with a spatula. Bake in the middle of the oven for 20 minutes, or until the sides of the cake have begun to shrink away from the pan and the cake springs back instantly when pressed lightly with the tip of a finger.

Carefully turn the cake out on wax paper, peel the layer of paper from the top, and let it rest for 5 minutes, then spread the surface with crabapple jelly. Starting at one long edge, roll the cake into a cylinder. Cut a 1-inch-thick slice from each end of the cake and trim each slice into a round about 1½ inches in diameter. Set the cake aside to cool.

To prepare the icing, bring the maple syrup to a boil over moderate heat in a 3- to 4-quart saucepan. Cook uncovered and undisturbed, regulating the heat to prevent the syrup from boiling over. When the syrup reaches a temperature of 238° on a candy thermometer, or when a drop spooned into ice water immediately forms a soft but compact mass, remove the pan from the heat. Add the chocolate and stir to dissolve it.

In a large bowl, beat the two remaining egg whites with a wire whisk or a rotary or electric beater until they are stiff enough to stand in unwavering peaks on the beater when it is lifted from the bowl. Beating the egg whites constantly, pour in the maple syrup-and-chocolate mixture in a slow, thin stream and continue to beat until the mixture has cooled to room temperature. Then beat in the butter bits a few pieces at a time.

When the icing is smooth and thick, spread most of it over the top, sides and ends of the cake roll with a metal spatula or knife. With fork tines, make irregular lines the length of the roll to give the icing a barklike look and the cake the appearance of a log. Ice one side and the edges of the reserved rounds and set one on top of the log and the other on a side to resemble knotholes. Decorate the cake with holly berries made from the cherries and with leaf shapes cut from the citron.

Coconut Cake with Lemon Filling

Preheat the oven to 350°. With a pastry brush, spread the 2 tablespoons of softened butter over the bottom and sides of two 9-inch layer-cake pans. Add 1 tablespoon of flour to each pan and, one at a time, tip the pans from side to side to distribute the flour evenly. Then invert each pan and rap it sharply to remove the excess flour.

Combine the 2 cups of sifted flour, the teaspoon of baking powder and ⅛ teaspoon of salt and sift them together on a plate or on a sheet of wax paper. Set aside.

In a deep bowl, beat the egg yolks and 2 cups of sugar with a wire whisk or a rotary or electric beater for 4 to 5 minutes, or until the mixture is thick enough to fall back on itself in a slowly dissolving ribbon when the beater is lifted from the bowl. Beat in the ¼ cup lemon juice and 2 teaspoons lemon peel. Then add the flour mixture, about ½ cup at a time, beating well after each addition.

With a whisk or a rotary or electric beater, beat the 8 egg whites in another bowl until they are stiff enough to stand in unwavering peaks on the beater when it is lifted up out of the bowl. Scoop the egg whites over the batter and, with a rubber spatula, fold them gently but thoroughly together until no trace of white shows.

Pour the batter into the buttered and floured pans, dividing it equally between them and smoothing the tops with the spatula. Bake in the mid-

To make one 9-inch 4-layer cake

CAKE

2 tablespoons butter, softened
2 tablespoons plus 2 cups flour, sifted before measuring
1 teaspoon double-acting baking powder
⅛ teaspoon salt
8 egg yolks
2 cups sugar
¼ cup strained fresh lemon juice
2 teaspoons finely grated fresh lemon peel
8 egg whites

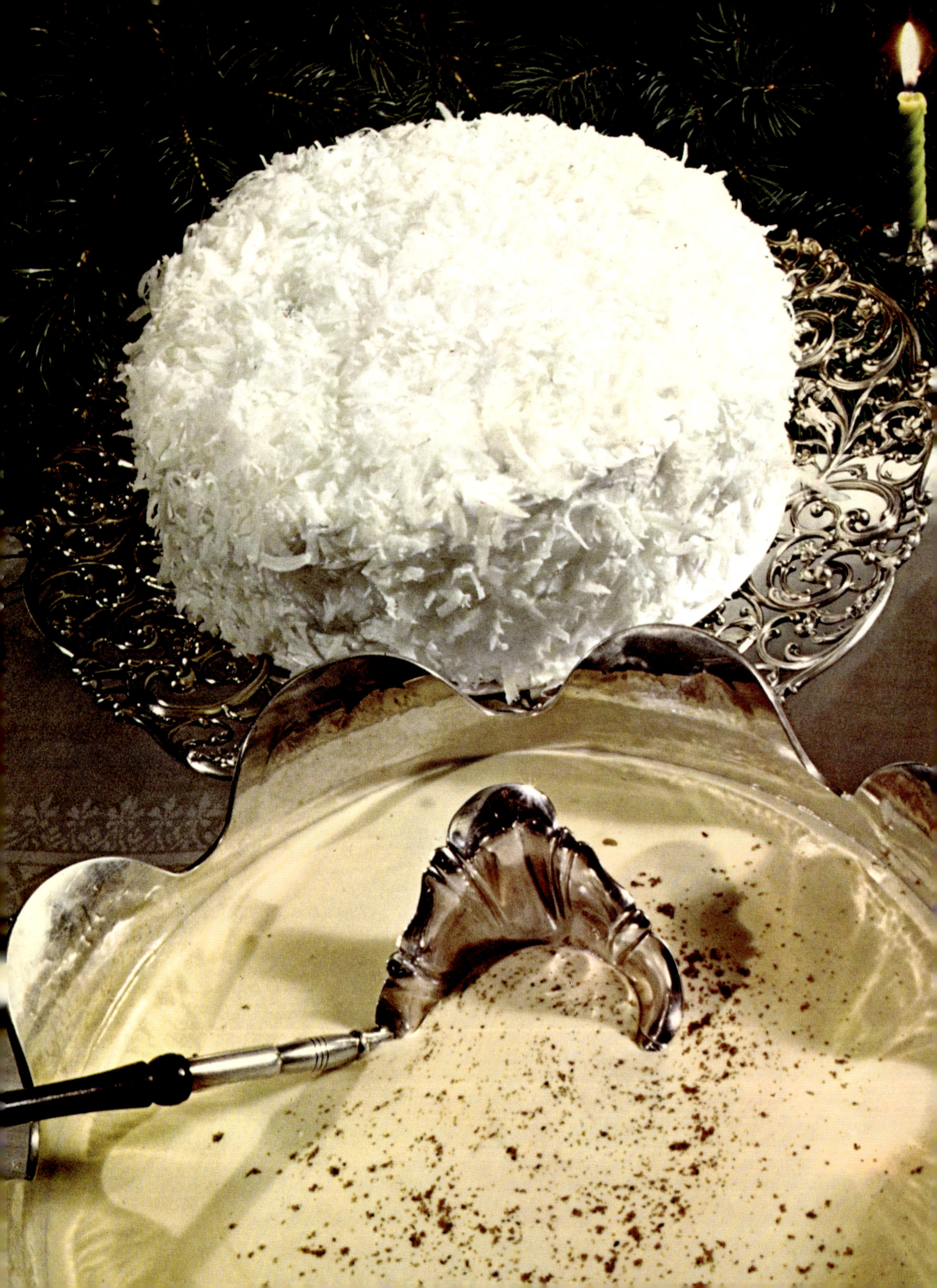

Christmas in the South means a creamy bowl of rum-and-bourbon-based eggnog *(bottom left)* and a rich array of cakes and candies: coconut cake *(top left)*; white fruitcake *(top right)*; bourbon-ball candies *(bottom right)*; and sugary divinity candies topped with pecans *(center)*.

FILLING

1½ cups sugar
¼ cup cornstarch
⅛ teaspoon salt
2 eggs, lightly beaten
2 tablespoons butter, cut into ¼-inch bits
2 tablespoons finely grated fresh lemon peel
⅔ cup strained fresh lemon juice
1 cup water

ICING

4 egg whites
½ cup confectioners' sugar
1 teaspoon vanilla extract
1½ cups white corn syrup
2 cups freshly grated, peeled coconut meat

dle of the oven for about 20 minutes, or until a toothpick or cake tester inserted in the center of the cake comes out clean and dry. Let the cakes cool in the pans for about 5 minutes, then turn them out on wire racks to cool to room temperature.

Meanwhile, prepare the filling in the following fashion: Combine the 1½ cups sugar, the cornstarch, ⅛ teaspoon salt and the 2 beaten eggs in a heavy 1½- to 2-quart saucepan and mix well with a wire whisk or wooden spoon. Stir in the butter bits, 2 tablespoons lemon peel, ⅔ cup lemon juice and 1 cup water and, when all the ingredients are well blended, set the pan over high heat.

Stirring the filling mixture constantly, bring to a boil over high heat. Immediately reduce the heat to low and continue to stir until the filling is smooth and thick enough to coat the spoon heavily. Scrape the filling into a bowl with a rubber spatula, and let it cool to room temperature.

When the cake and filling are cool, prepare the icing: With a wire whisk or a rotary or electric beater, beat the 4 egg whites until they are stiff enough to stand in soft peaks on the uplifted beater. Sprinkle them with the confectioners' sugar and vanilla and continue to beat until the egg whites are stiff and glossy.

In a small saucepan, bring the corn syrup to a boil over high heat and cook briskly until it reaches a temperature of 239° on a candy thermometer, or until a drop spooned into ice water immediately forms a soft ball. Beating the egg white mixture constantly with a wooden spoon, pour in the corn syrup in a slow, thin stream and continue to beat until the icing is smooth, thick and cool.

To assemble, cut each cake in half horizontally, thus creating four thin layers. Place one layer, cut side up, on an inverted cake or pie tin and, with a small metal spatula, spread about ⅓ of the lemon filling over it. Put another cake layer on top, spread with filling, and cover it with the third layer. Spread this layer with the remaining filling, and place the fourth layer on top.

Smooth the icing over the top and sides of the cake with the spatula. Then sprinkle the coconut generously on the top and, with your fingers, pat it into the sides of the cake. Carefully transfer the coconut cake to a serving plate and serve at once. If the cake must wait, drape waxed paper around the top and sides to keep the icing moist.

White Fruit Cake

Preheat the oven to 250°. With a pastry brush, spread 1 tablespoon of the softened butter over the bottom and sides of a 9-by-3-inch springform tube cake pan. Coat two strips of wax paper with another tablespoon of the butter and fit the strips around the tube and the sides of the pan, with the greased surfaces toward the center. Set aside.

Combine the flour, baking powder, nutmeg and salt and sift them together into a deep bowl. Add the raisins, lemon peel, orange peel, pineapple and citron, and toss the fruit about with a spoon until the pieces are evenly coated.

In another deep bowl, cream the remaining 12 tablespoons of butter and the sugar together, beating and mashing them against the sides of the bowl with the back of a large wooden spoon until the mixture is light and fluffy. Stir in the flour-and-fruit mixture a cup or so at a time. Then add ¾ cup of the bourbon and, when it is completely incorporated, stir in the slivered almonds.

With a wire whisk or a rotary or electric beater, beat the egg whites until they are stiff enough to stand in unwavering peaks on the beater when it is lifted from the bowl. Scoop the egg whites over the batter and, with a rubber spatula, fold them together gently but thoroughly.

Pour the batter into the paper-lined pan, filling it about three quarters full, and smooth the top with the spatula. Bake in the middle of the oven for 2½ to 3 hours, or until a toothpick or cake tester inserted in the center of the cake comes out clean.

Let the cake cool overnight before removing the sides of the springform. Then slip it off the bottom of the pan and carefully peel away the paper. Place the cake on a serving plate and sprinkle it evenly with the remaining ½ cup of bourbon. Wrap in cheesecloth and set the cake aside at room temperature for at least 24 hours before serving. Securely wrapped in foil or plastic, it can be kept for several months, and its flavor will improve with age.

Bourbon Balls

In a small heavy skillet, melt the chocolate over low heat, stirring almost constantly to prevent the bottom from scorching. Remove the pan from the heat and let the chocolate cool to lukewarm.

Combine the pulverized vanilla wafers, pecans and ⅔ cup of sugar in a deep bowl. Pour in the chocolate, bourbon and corn syrup and stir vigorously with a wooden spoon until the ingredients are well combined.

To shape each bourbon ball, scoop up about a tablespoon of the mixture and pat it into a ball about 1 inch in diameter. Roll the balls in the remaining cup of sugar and, when they are lightly coated on all sides, place them in a wide-mouthed 1-quart jar equipped with a securely fitting lid. Cut two rounds from a double thickness of paper towels to fit inside the lid of the jar. Moisten the paper rounds with a little additional bourbon and press them tightly into the lid.

Seal the jar with the paper-lined lid and set the bourbon balls aside at room temperature for 3 or 4 days before serving. Tightly covered, the bourbon balls can safely be kept for 3 to 4 weeks.

Divinity Candies

Combine the sugar, water and corn syrup in a heavy 1½- to 2-quart saucepan and bring to a boil over high heat, stirring until the sugar dissolves. Then cook briskly, uncovered and undisturbed, for 10 to 15 minutes, until the syrup reaches a temperature of 255° on a candy thermometer, or until a drop spooned into ice water immediately forms a compact and almost brittle ball.

Meanwhile, in a deep bowl, beat the egg whites with a wire whisk or a

---

To make one 6-pound cake

14 tablespoons butter, softened
3 cups flour
2 teaspoons double-acting baking powder
½ teaspoon ground nutmeg, preferably freshly grated
¾ teaspoon salt
2 cups golden raisins
¾ cup finely slivered candied lemon peel (about 6 ounces)
¾ cup finely slivered candied orange peel (about 6 ounces)
¾ cup finely slivered candied pineapple (about 6 ounces)
¾ cup finely chopped candied citron (about 6 ounces)
1 cup sugar
1¼ cups bourbon
1½ cups slivered blanched almonds (about 6 ounces)
8 egg whites

To make about 60 one-inch candies

8 one-ounce squares semisweet chocolate, coarsely chopped
60 vanilla wafers, pulverized in a blender or wrapped in a towel and finely crushed with a rolling pin (about 3 cups)
1 cup finely chopped pecans
1⅔ cups sugar
½ cup bourbon
¼ cup light corn syrup

To make about 24

2 cups sugar
½ cup water
⅓ cup light corn syrup
2 egg whites
½ teaspoon vanilla extract
1½ cups coarsely chopped pecans

Rum is a traditional ingredient of wintertime holiday cheer. The three classic hot drinks shown below are *(from right)* Glühwein, a spiced and sweetened mulled red wine; hot buttered rum *(page 64);* and Tom and Jerry *(page 64),* a blend of rum, brandy and milk, enriched with butter and beaten eggs.

rotary or electric beater until they are stiff enough to stand in unwavering peaks on the beater when it is lifted from the bowl.

As soon as the syrup reaches the proper temperature, remove the pan from the heat. Whipping the egg whites constantly with the whisk or beater, pour in the syrup in a very slow, thin stream. (Do not scrape the saucepan; the syrup that clings to it is likely to be too sugary.) Add the vanilla and continue to beat for about 10 minutes longer, or until the candy begins to lose its gloss and is thick enough to hold its shape almost solidly in a spoon. Immediately stir in the pecans.

Without waiting a moment, drop the divinity by the tablespoon onto wax paper, letting each spoonful mound slightly in the center. Allow the candy to stand undisturbed until it is firm.

The Cheerful Glass

Traditional Southern Eggnog

In a deep bowl, beat the egg yolks and sugar together with a wire whisk or a rotary or electric beater until the mixture is thick enough to fall back on itself in a slowly dissolving ribbon when the beater is lifted from the bowl. Then with a wooden spoon, beat in the whiskey, rum and milk. Cover the bowl with foil or plastic wrap and refrigerate the mixture for at least 2 hours or, even better, overnight.

Just before serving the eggnog, whip the cream in a large chilled bowl with a wire whisk or a rotary or electric beater until it is stiff enough to stand in unwavering peaks on the beater when it is lifted from the bowl.

Then beat the egg whites in a separate large bowl with a clean beater. When they are firm enough to stand in peaks on the beater, scoop the whipped cream over the whites and fold gently but thoroughly together with a rubber spatula.

Pour the egg-yolk mixture into a large chilled punch bowl, add the egg-white mixture and, using an over-under cutting motion rather than a stirring one, fold together with the spatula until no trace of white remains. Sprinkle with nutmeg and serve at once from chilled punch cups.

To serve 12

12 egg yolks
½ cup superfine sugar
1 fifth (about 26 ounces) blended whiskey or bourbon
1½ cups dark Jamaica rum
2 cups milk
1 quart heavy cream, chilled
12 egg whites
1 tablespoon ground nutmeg

Swedish Glögg

In a 6- to 8-quart enameled or stainless-steel pot, mix together the dry red wine, muscatel, sweet vermouth, bitters, raisins, orange peel and the slightly crushed cardamoms, whole cloves, ginger and cinnamon. Cover and let the mixture stand at least 12 hours so that the flavors will develop and mingle. Shortly before serving, add the aquavit and the sugar. Stir well and bring it to a full boil over high heat. Remove at once from the heat, stir in the almonds and serve the hot *glögg* in mugs. In Sweden, a small spoon is placed in each mug to scoop up the almonds and raisins.

ALTERNATE: To make a simpler *glögg*, divide the quantities of spices in half and mix them with 2 bottles of dry red wine. Leave it overnight, then stir in ¾ cup of sugar and bring almost to a boil. Remove from the heat, stir in 1 cup of whole, blanched and peeled almonds, and serve hot.

To serve 20 to 25

2 quarts dry red wine
2 quarts muscatel
1 pint sweet vermouth
2 tablespoons Angostura bitters
2 cups raisins
Peelings of 1 orange
12 whole cardamoms, bruised in a mortar with a pestle or by covering with a towel and crushing with a rolling pin
10 whole cloves
1 piece (about 2 inches) fresh ginger
1 stick cinnamon
1½ cups (12 ounces) aquavit
1½ cups sugar
2 cups whole almonds, blanched and peeled

Vin Chaud (or Glühwein)

Stud each lemon slice with 2 cloves and combine them with the sugar and cinnamon sticks in a 1-quart enameled, copper or stainless-steel skillet, casserole or chafing dish. Place over moderate heat, stir occasionally with a wooden spoon until the sugar has melted, then pour in the red wine. Continue to stir until the wine has almost reached the boiling point. Remove from the heat immediately, scoop out the lemon slices and cinnamon with a spoon or spatula, and pour the hot wine into mugs.

To serve 2

2 slices lemon
4 whole cloves
2 tablespoons superfine sugar
1½ sticks cinnamon
2 cups (1 pint) claret or Burgundy

Two 8-ounce mugs

Tom and Jerry

To serve 2

¾ cup milk
2 tablespoons unsalted butter
2 eggs
2 teaspoons sugar
⅛ teaspoon vanilla extract
3 ounces brandy
3 ounces Jamaica rum
Ground nutmeg

Three 6- to 8-ounce mugs

Combine the milk and butter in a saucepan and place over low heat until the butter is melted and the milk is hot. Meanwhile, separate the eggs. Place the egg whites in a small bowl and beat them with a wire whisk or a rotary or electric beater until they are frothy. In another bowl, beat the yolks until they thicken slightly and are well combined. Pour the egg whites into the bowl with the yolks and beat in the sugar and vanilla.

Remove the milk from the heat and pour the eggs into the pan, whisking constantly. Return the pan to the heat, add the brandy and rum, and continue to whisk while the ingredients warm. Do not let them boil or the drink will curdle.

Pour about half of the contents of the pan into a mug, then pour back and forth from one mug to another to make sure the drink is well combined and froths. Continue pouring back and forth with the other 2 mugs until a second mug has been filled. Sprinkle the top of each drink with ground nutmeg and serve hot.

Hot Buttered Rum

To make 1 hot drink

1½ teaspoons superfine sugar
A 1-inch piece cinnamon stick
3 ounces rum
1 cup hot milk
1 tablespoon unsalted butter
Ground nutmeg

A 12-ounce mug

Wash the mug with very hot water and shake it dry. Place the sugar, piece of cinnamon stick and rum in the mug, and stir to dissolve the sugar. Pour in the hot milk, top with the tablespoon of butter, and sprinkle with ground nutmeg.

Hot Toddy

To make 1 toddy

Pinch of superfine sugar
1 strip lemon peel stuck with 1 whole clove
Pinch of cinnamon, or substitute a 1-inch piece cinnamon stick
3 ounces bourbon, blended whiskey or brandy
Boiling water

An old-fashioned glass or a 6- to 8-ounce mug

Warm the glass or mug by washing it with very hot water and shaking it dry. Place the pinch of sugar, lemon peel stuck with a clove, cinnamon and spirits in the glass or mug, fill with boiling water, and stir.

The hot toddy is a very popular cold remedy, but there is a less familiar drink, known as the toddy, which is simply whiskey, ice cubes and a strip of lemon peel.

Grog

To make 1 hot drink

1 slice lemon
2 whole cloves
1 teaspoon superfine sugar
A 1-inch piece cinnamon stick
3 ounces Jamaica rum
4 ounces boiling water

An 8-ounce glass, preferably with handle

Stud the slice of lemon with the 2 cloves. Wash a glass with very hot water and shake it dry. Place the sugar, piece of cinnamon and slice of lemon in the warm glass, and add the rum. Stir with a spoon to dissolve the sugar, leave the spoon in the glass so that the glass will not crack, and fill with boiling water. Stir briefly and serve.

Claret Cup

Place the fruits of your choice in the pitcher or bowl first, then add the blackberry brandy, maraschino liqueur and curaçao. Place the vessel in the refrigerator (or freezer) for at least 1 hour (½ hour if you use the freezer). Remove and fill with ice cubes. A solid block of ice cut to fit the pitcher or bowl is even better, since it will not melt as quickly and dilute the drink. Pour in the claret and sparkling water, stir briefly, and serve in chilled wine glasses or punch cups.

Kentucky Christmas Champagne Punch

Place the fruit of your choice in a large punch bowl, then stir in the cherries, lemon juice, brandy, maraschino liqueur and curaçao. Refrigerate the bowl for at least 1 hour, then remove and add the block of ice. (Ice cubes can be used, but they will dilute the drink by melting too quickly.)

Just before serving, pour in the champagne and club soda. Stir briefly with a glass stirring rod or bar spoon and serve at once in chilled punch cups or wine glasses.

To serve 4

Approximately 1 cup of fruits of the season: peeled orange and/or grapefruit sections, lemon slices, fresh or frozen strawberries, cucumber peel
4 ounces blackberry brandy
4 ounces maraschino liqueur
4 ounces curaçao
12 to 16 ice cubes or a block of ice
1 bottle claret (Bordeaux)
6 ounces cold Perrier water or club soda

A 1½- to 2-quart pitcher or punch bowl
4 wine glasses or punch cups, chilled

To make about 2 quarts

1 orange, peeled, with all of the white outer pith removed, and the orange separated into sections
6 maraschino cherries
1 cup strained fresh lemon juice (from about 6 medium-sized lemons)
1 cup brandy
½ cup maraschino liqueur
½ cup curaçao
A block of ice or ice cubes
1 quart champagne, chilled
1 pint club soda, chilled

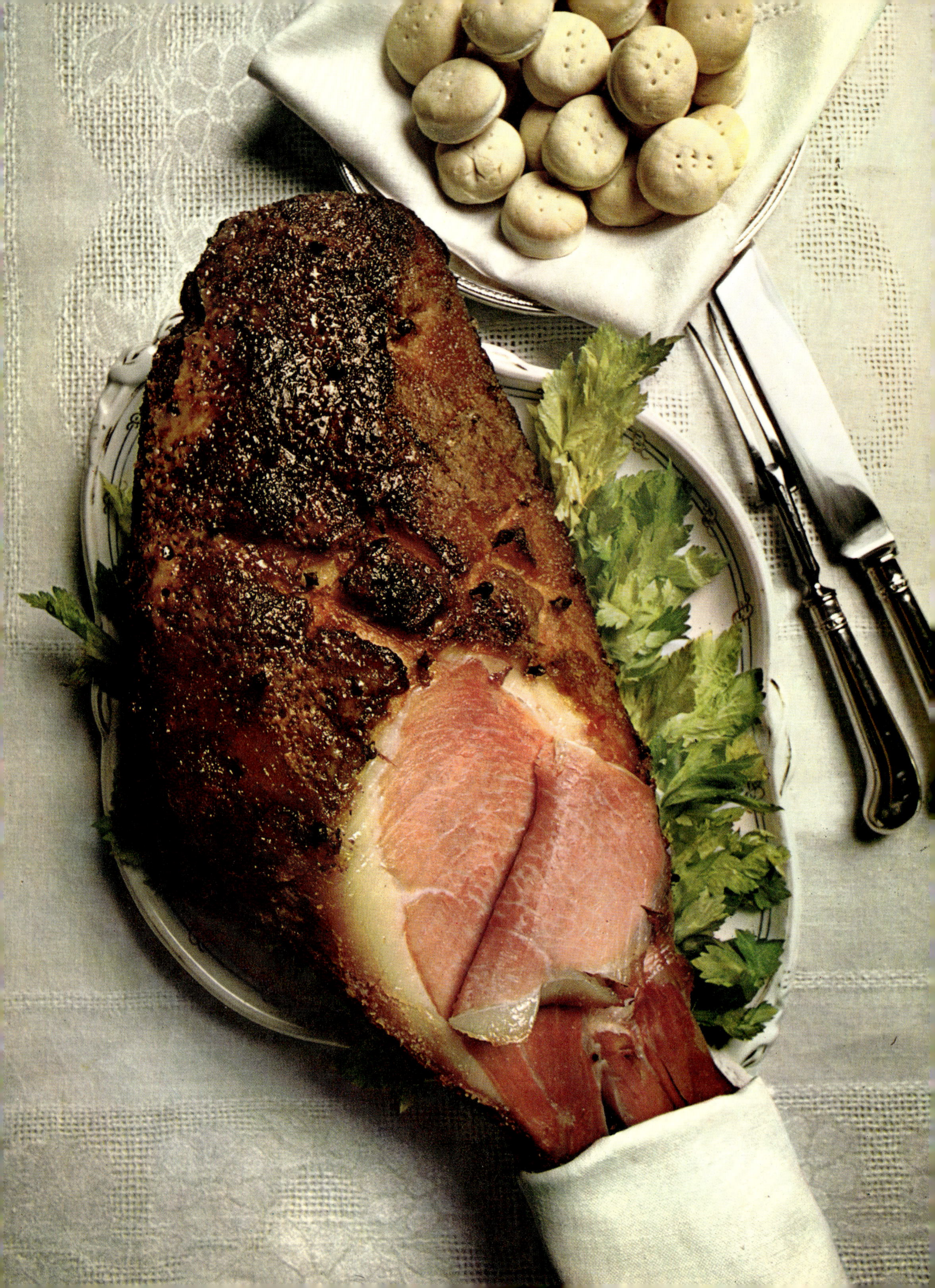

Saluting the New Year

It is an old and honored custom to welcome friends and neighbors at home over the New Year's holiday. Martha Washington served punch and cakes to all the Philadelphia citizens who dropped by on New Year's afternoon to wish the President the compliments of the season.

The food today is likely to mean a laden buffet, which in many homes traditionally includes Smithfield ham and beaten biscuits, accompanied by Hopping John, a Southern dish of black-eyed peas and rice, in promise of good luck for the coming year. A smörgåsbord table, filled with smoked and marinated fish dishes, pâté, cheeses and breads, is a delectable solution to open-house entertaining borrowed from the Scandinavians. New Year's Day also means toasting one's friends, and this chapter includes a recipe for Fish House punch, a colonial Philadelphia favorite, as well as other more contemporary toasting potions.

In any city with a Chinese population, the New Year is celebrated a second time. The Chinese New Year's feast, falling between January 20 and February 20, is a multicourse affair featuring such delicacies as Peking duck or bird's nest soup. Recipes for a Chinese New Year's meal begin on page 96.

Sugar-glazed Smithfield ham, Virginia's proudest gift to gastronomy, baked, then carved thin and served with beaten biscuits, has always been a New Year's Day ritual in homes in the South.

Ham and Hopping John for luck

Cassoulet for a crowd

After-midnight onion soup

New Year's Day smörgåsbord

A galaxy of Viennese tortes

Fish House punch and other drinks

Chinese appetizers to bring good fortune

Bird's nest soup

Peking duck with Mandarin pancakes

A fish dish that promises prosperity

New Year's Recipes

The Open House

Baked Ham with Brown-Sugar Glaze

Starting a day ahead, place the ham in a pot large enough to hold it comfortably and pour in enough water to cover the ham by at least 1 inch. Let the ham soak for at least 12 hours (for 24 hours if possible), changing the water 2 or 3 times. Remove the ham from the pot and discard the soaking water. Then, under lukewarm running water, scrub the ham vigorously with a stiff brush to remove any traces of pepper or mold.

With a dampened kitchen towel wipe the ham and return it to the pot. Pour in enough water to cover the ham by at least 1 inch and bring to a simmer over high heat. Reduce the heat to low and simmer partially covered for 3 to 4 hours, allowing 15 to 20 minutes to the pound. When the ham is fully cooked, you should be able to move and easily pull out the small bone near the shank.

Transfer the ham to a platter and, if you wish, set the cooking water aside to be used for cooking greens. When the ham is cool enough to handle remove the rind with a small sharp knife, leaving only a ⅛-inch-thick layer of fat. If you intend to stud the ham with cloves, make crisscrossing cuts about 1 inch apart on the fatty side, slicing down through the fat to the meat.

Preheat the oven to 400°. With your fingers, press enough of the bread crumbs into the fatty side of the ham to coat it thoroughly. Then sift the brown sugar evenly over the crumbs. If you are using cloves, insert them where the scoring lines intersect. Place the ham on a rack set in a shallow roasting pan and bake it uncovered in the middle of the oven for about 20 minutes, or until the glaze is richly browned.

Set the ham on a large platter and let it cool to room temperature. Smithfield or country ham is carved into paper-thin slices and often served with beaten biscuits. Tightly covered with foil or plastic wrap, the ham can safely be kept in the refrigerator for at least one month.

A 12- to 16-pound Smithfield ham or a 12- to 16-pound Virginia, Kentucky, Tennessee or Georgia country ham
½ to ¾ cup fine dry bread crumbs
1 cup dark-brown sugar
¼ cup whole cloves (optional)

Beaten Biscuits

Preheat the oven to 400°. With a pastry brush, spread the softened butter evenly on a large baking sheet and set aside.

Combine the flour, sugar and salt, and sift them into a deep bowl. Drop in the lard and, with your fingers, rub the flour and fat together until they resemble flakes of coarse meal. Add the milk-and-water mixture, about 2 tablespoonfuls at a time, rubbing and kneading after each addition until the liquid is completely absorbed. Knead the dough vigorously in the bowl until it is smooth. Then put it through the coarsest blade of a food grinder four times, or until the dough is pliable and elastic.

To shape beaten biscuits the Maryland way, take a handful of the

To make about 2 dozen 1½ inch biscuits

1 teaspoon butter, softened
2 cups flour
1½ teaspoons sugar
1 teaspoon salt
2 tablespoons lard, cut into ¼-inch bits
¼ cup milk combined with ¼ cup water

dough and squeeze your fingers into a fist, forcing the dough up between your thumb and forefinger. When it forms a ball about the size of a walnut, pinch it off and gently pat the dough into a flat round about ½ inch thick. To shape the biscuits as they do in Virginia, gather the dough into a ball and roll it out ½ inch thick on a lightly floured surface. With a biscuit cutter or the rim of a glass, cut the dough into 1½-inch rounds. Collect the scraps into a ball again, roll it out as before and cut as many more biscuits as you can.

Place the biscuits about 1 inch apart on the buttered baking sheet. Then prick the top of each one lightly with a three-tined fork to make a pattern of two or three parallel rows. Bake in the middle of the oven for about 20 minutes, or until the biscuits are a delicate golden color. Serve them at once with butter.

New Year's Day Hopping John

To serve 8 to 10

2 cups (1 pound) dried black-eyed peas
6 cups cold water
1 pound salt pork (rind removed), cut into strips about 2 inches long and ½ inch wide
1 cup finely chopped onions
2½ cups uncooked long-grain white rice, not the converted variety

Place the black-eyed peas in a sieve or colander and run cold water over them until the draining water is clear. Transfer the peas to a 3- to 4-quart casserole, add 6 cups of cold water, and bring to a boil over high heat. Then lower the heat and simmer, partially covered, for 30 minutes.

Meanwhile, drop the salt pork strips into a pot of boiling water and bring the water back to a boil. Immediately drain the strips, pat them dry with paper towels, then place them in a 10- to 12-inch skillet. Fry uncovered over moderately high heat for 10 to 12 minutes, turning the strips frequently with a large spoon and adjusting the heat if necessary to prevent the pork from burning. When the strips are brown and crisp and have rendered all their fat, transfer them with tongs to paper towels to drain, and set aside.

Add the chopped onions to the fat remaining in the skillet and cook over moderate heat for 3 to 5 minutes, stirring frequently, until the onions are soft but not yet browned. Remove from the heat and set aside.

In a fine sieve, wash the rice under cold running water until the draining water is clear.

After the peas have cooked their allotted time, stir in the salt pork, onions and the rice and brink back to a boil. Cover the casserole tightly, reduce the heat to low, and simmer 20 to 30 minutes, or until the peas are tender and the rice is dry and fluffy. Taste for seasoning and serve at once.

Quiche au Fromage

To make an 8- to 9-inch *quiche*

PÂTE BRISÉE (pastry dough or pie crust)
6 tablespoons chilled butter, cut in ¼-inch bits
2 tablespoons chilled vegetable shortening
1½ cups all-purpose flour
¼ teaspoon salt
3 to 5 tablespoons ice water

PÂTE BRISÉE: In a large, chilled mixing bowl, combine butter, vegetable shortening, flour and salt. Working quickly, use your fingertips to rub the flour and fat together until they blend and look like flakes of coarse meal. Pour 3 tablespoons of ice water over the mixture all at once, toss together lightly and gather the dough into a ball. If the dough seems crumbly, add up to 2 tablespoons more ice water by drops. Dust the pastry with a little flour and wrap it in wax paper or a plastic bag. Refrigerate it for at least 3 hours or until it is firm.

Remove the pastry from the refrigerator 5 minutes before rolling it. If it seems resistant and hard, tap it all over with a rolling pin. Place the ball on a floured board or table and, with the heel of one hand, press it into a flat circle about 1 inch thick. Dust a little flour over and under it and roll it out—from the center to within an inch of the far edge. Lift the dough and turn it clockwise, about the space of two hours on a clock; roll again from the center to the far edge. Repeat—lifting, turning, rolling—until the circle is about 1/8 inch thick and 11 or 12 inches across. If the pastry sticks to the board or table, lift it gently with a metal spatula and sprinkle a little flour under it.

Butter the bottom and sides of an 8- to 9-inch false-bottomed *quiche* or cake pan no more than 1 1/4 inches deep. Roll the pastry over the pin and

The *quiche*, with its shell removed from the baking pan, comes to the table a flaky, fragrant round of pastry filled with golden custard.

unroll it over the pan, or drape the pastry over the rolling pin, lift it up and unfold it over the pan. Gently press the pastry into the bottom and around the sides of the pan, being careful not to stretch it. Roll the pin over the rim of the pan, pressing down hard to trim off the excess pastry. With a fork, prick the bottom of the pastry all over, trying not to pierce all the way through. Chill for 1 hour.

Preheat the oven to 400°. To keep the bottom of the pastry from puffing up, spread a sheet of buttered aluminum foil across the pan and press it gently into the edges to support the sides of the pastry as it bakes. Bake on the middle shelf of the oven for 10 minutes, then remove the foil. Prick the pastry again, then return it to the oven for 3 minutes or until it starts to shrink from the sides of the pan and begins to brown. Remove it from the oven and set it on a wire cake rack to cool.

CHEESE-CUSTARD FILLING

1 teaspoon butter
6 slices lean bacon, cut in ¼-inch pieces
2 eggs plus 2 extra egg yolks
1½ cups heavy cream
½ teaspoon salt
Pinch of white pepper
¾ cup grated imported Swiss cheese or Swiss and freshly grated Parmesan cheese combined
2 tablespoons butter, cut in tiny pieces

CHEESE-CUSTARD FILLING: Preheat the oven to 375°. In a heavy 8- to 10-inch skillet, melt the butter over moderate heat. When the foam subsides, cook the bacon until it is lightly browned and crisp. Remove from the skillet with a slotted spoon and drain on paper towels. With a wire whisk, rotary or electric beater, beat the eggs, extra egg yolks, cream and seasonings together in a large mixing bowl. Stir in the grated cheese. Place the cooled pastry shell on a baking sheet. Scatter the bacon over the bottom of the shell and gently ladle the egg-cheese custard into it, being sure the custard does not come within ⅛ inch of the rim of the shell. Sprinkle the top with dots of butter and bake in the upper third of the oven for 25 minutes or until the custard has puffed and browned and a knife inserted in the center comes out clean. To remove the *quiche* from the pan, set the pan on a large jar or coffee can and slip down the outside rim. Run a long metal spatula under the *quiche* to make sure it isn't stuck to the bottom of the pan, then slide the *quiche* onto a heated platter. Serve hot or warm.

After-Midnight Onion Soup

To serve 6 to 8

4 tablespoons butter
2 tablespoons vegetable oil
2 pounds onions, thinly sliced (about 7 cups)
1 teaspoon salt
3 tablespoons flour
2 quarts beef stock, fresh or canned, or beef and chicken stock combined

CROÛTES
12 to 16 one-inch-thick slices of French bread
2 teaspoons olive oil
1 garlic clove, cut
1 cup grated, imported Swiss cheese or Swiss and freshly grated Parmesan cheese combined

In a heavy 4- to 5-quart saucepan or a soup kettle, melt the butter with the oil over moderate heat. Stir in the onions and 1 teaspoon salt, and cook uncovered over low heat, stirring occasionally, for 20 to 30 minutes, or until the onions are a rich golden brown. Sprinkle flour over the onions and cook, stirring, for 2 or 3 minutes. Remove the pan from the heat. In a separate saucepan, bring the stock to a simmer, then stir the hot stock into the onions. Return the soup to low heat and simmer, partially covered, for another 30 or 40 minutes, occasionally skimming off the fat. Taste for seasoning, and add salt and pepper if needed.

While the soup simmers, make the *croûtes*. Preheat the oven to 325°. Spread the slices of bread in one layer on a baking sheet and bake for 15 minutes. With a pastry brush, lightly coat both sides of each slice with olive oil. Then turn the slices over and bake for another 15 minutes, or until the bread is completely dry and lightly browned. Rub each slice with the cut garlic clove and set aside.

To serve, place the *croûtes* in a large tureen or individual soup bowls and ladle the soup over them. Pass the grated cheese separately.

ALTERNATIVE: To make onion soup *gratinée,* preheat the oven to 375°.

Ladle the soup into an ovenproof tureen or individual soup bowls, top with *croûtes*, and spread the grated cheese on top. Sprinkle the cheese with a little melted butter or olive oil. Bake for 10 to 20 minutes, or until the cheese has melted, then slide the soup under a hot broiler for a minute or two to brown the top if desired.

Cassoulet

THE BEANS AND SAUSAGE: In a heavy 6- to 8-quart pot or soup kettle, bring the chicken stock to a bubbling boil over high heat. Drop the beans in and boil them briskly for 2 minutes. Remove the pot from the heat and let the beans soak for 1 hour. Meanwhile, simmer the salt pork and optional pork rind in 1 quart of water for 15 minutes; drain and set aside.

With the point of a sharp knife, pierce 5 or 6 holes in the sausage; then add the sausage, salt pork and pork rind to the beans. Bring to a boil over high heat, skimming the top of scum. When the stock looks fairly clear, add the whole onions, garlic, thyme, *bouquet garni*, salt and a few grindings of black pepper. Reduce the heat and simmer uncovered for 45 minutes, adding stock or water if needed. With tongs, transfer the sausage to a plate and set it aside. Cook the beans and salt pork for another 30 to 40 minutes, or until the beans are tender, drain and transfer the salt pork and rind to the plate with the sausage; discard the onions and *bouquet garni*. Strain the stock through a large sieve or colander into a mixing bowl. Skim the fat from the stock and taste for seasoning. Then set the beans, stock and meats aside in separate containers. If they are to be kept overnight, cool, cover and refrigerate them.

THE BROILED DUCK: Preheat the oven to 350°. Cream the butter by beating it vigorously against the sides of a small bowl with a wooden spoon until it is fluffy, then beat in the oil. Dry the duck with paper towels, and coat the quarters with creamed butter and oil. Lay them skin side down on the broiler rack, and broil them 4 inches from the heat for 15 minutes, basting them once with pan juices, and broil 5 minutes more. Then increase the heat to 400° and broil for 15 minutes, basting the duck once or twice. With tongs, turn the quarters over, baste, and broil skin side up for 10 minutes. Increase the heat to 450°, baste again, and broil for 10 minutes more. Remove the duck to a plate and pour the drippings from the broiler into a bowl, scraping in any browned bits that cling to the pan. Let the drippings settle, then skim the fat from the top and save it in a small bowl. Pour the degreased drippings into the bean stock. When the duck is cool, trim off the excess fat and gristle, and use poultry shears to cut the quarters into small serving pieces. If they are to be kept overnight, cool and cover the duck and bowl of fat and refrigerate them.

THE PORK AND LAMB: Preheat the oven to 325°. In a heavy 10- to 12-inch skillet, sauté the diced pork fat over moderate heat, stirring constantly, until crisp and brown. Remove the dice and reserve. Pour all but 2 or 3 tablespoons of rendered fat into a small mixing bowl. Heat the fat remaining in the skillet almost to the smoking point, and in it brown the pork and the lamb, 4 or 5 chunks at a time, adding more pork fat as needed. When the

To serve 10 to 12

THE BEANS AND SAUSAGE

4 quarts chicken stock, fresh or canned
2 pounds or 4 cups dry white beans (Great Northern, marrow, or navy)
1 pound lean salt pork, in one piece
½ pound fresh pork rind (optional)
1 quart water
1 pound uncooked plain or garlic pork sausage, fresh or smoked (French, Italian or Polish)
3 whole peeled onions
1 teaspoon finely chopped garlic
1 teaspoon dried thyme, crumbled
Bouquet garni, made of 4 parsley sprigs, 3 celery tops, white part of 1 leek, and 2 bay leaves, wrapped and tied in cheesecloth
Salt
Freshly ground black pepper

THE DUCK

4 tablespoons soft butter
1 tablespoon vegetable oil
A 4- to 5-pound duck, quartered

THE PORK AND LAMB

½ pound fresh pork fat, diced
1 pound boned pork loin, cut in 2-inch chunks
1 pound boned lamb shoulder, cut in 2-inch chunks
1 cup finely chopped onions
½ cup finely chopped celery
1 teaspoon finely chopped garlic
1 cup dry white wine
1½ pounds firm ripe tomatoes, peeled, seeded and coarsely chopped (about 2 to 2½ cups) or substitute 2 cups chopped, drained, canned whole-pack tomatoes
1 bay leaf
½ teaspoon salt
Freshly ground black pepper

THE GRATIN TOPPING

1½ cups fine, dry bread crumbs
½ cup finely chopped fresh parsley

Crusty and golden brown, the *cassoulet* should look moist when the surface is broken and the meat and bean flavors should be well blended. Although time-consuming to prepare, the *cassoulet* can be cooked in easy stages, assembled and refrigerated for a day or so before final baking. Among the most famous of French provincial dishes—it originated in Languedoc—the *cassoulet* can be the main feature of an open-house buffet. The one shown here is a fairly complex dish, calling as it does for duck, lamb, pork and sausage. But many housewives in France create delicious *cassoulets* with only two or three meats.

75

chunks are a rich brown on all sides, transfer them with tongs to a 4-quart Dutch oven or heavy flameproof casserole.

Now discard all but 3 tablespoons of fat from the skillet and cook the chopped onions over low heat for 5 minutes. Scrape in any browned bits clinging to the pan. Stir in the celery and garlic and cook for 2 minutes. Then pour in the wine, bring to a boil and cook over high heat until the mixture has been reduced to about half. With a rubber spatula, scrape the contents of the skillet into the casserole. Gently stir the tomatoes, bay leaf, salt and a few grindings of pepper into the casserole. Bring to a boil on top of the stove, cover, and bake on the middle shelf of the oven (adding a little stock or water if the meat looks dry) for 1 hour, or until the meat is tender. With tongs, transfer the meat to a bowl. If it is to be kept overnight, cool, cover and refrigerate. Skim the fat from the juices in the casserole, then strain the juices into the bean stock and discard the vegetables.

ASSEMBLING THE CASSOULET: Preheat the oven to 350°. Peel the sausage and cut it into ¼-inch slices; cut the salt pork and pork rind into 1-inch squares. In a heavy flameproof 6- to 8-quart casserole at least 5 inches deep spread an inch-deep layer of beans. Arrange half of the sausage, salt pork, pork rind, diced pork fat, duck, braised pork and lamb on top. Cover with another layer of beans, then the rest of the meat, finally a last layer of beans, with a few slices of sausage on top. Slowly pour in the bean stock until it almost covers the beans. (If there isn't enough stock, add fresh or canned chicken stock.) Spread the bread crumbs in a thick layer on top and sprinkle them with 3 or 4 tablespoons of duck fat. Bring the casserole to a boil on top of the stove, then bake it uncovered in the upper third of the oven for 1¼ hours, or until the crumbs have formed a firm, dark crust. If desired, the first gratin, or crust, can be pushed gently into the *cassoulet,* and the dish baked until a new crust forms. This can be repeated two or three times if you wish. Serve directly from the casserole, sprinkled with parsley.

To serve 4

4 tablespoons butter

2 pounds gray, lemon or petrale sole fillets or 2 pounds flounder fillets, cut into serving pieces

2 tablespoons fresh lemon juice

½ teaspoon salt

2 medium-sized onions, peeled, thinly sliced and separated into rings

3 tablespoons tomato purée

1 tablespoon white wine vinegar or cider vinegar

½ teaspoon grated fresh horseradish or 1 teaspoon bottled horseradish, thoroughly drained and squeezed dry in a towel

2 medium-sized dill pickles, cut lengthwise into thin wedges

German Fish Dish for a Hangover

Preheat the oven to 375°. With 1 tablespoon of the butter, coat the bottom and sides of a shallow baking dish or casserole large enough to hold the fish in a single layer. Set the dish aside. Spread the fillets on wax paper, sprinkle them with lemon juice and salt, and let the fillets marinate for 10 minutes. In a heavy 8- to 10-inch skillet, melt 2 tablespoons of butter over moderate heat. When the foam subsides, drop in the onion rings and cook them, turning them frequently, for 5 minutes, or until the rings are soft and transparent but not brown.

Arrange the fish fillets side by side in the prepared baking dish. Beat the tomato purée, vinegar and horseradish together in a bowl, and spread the mixture evenly over the fillets. Scatter the onion rings and pickle wedges over the fish. Cut the remaining 1 tablespoon of butter into small pieces and dot the fish with them. Bake in the middle of the oven for about 15 minutes, or until the fillets are opaque and firm to the touch. Do not overcook. Serve at once, directly from the baking dish.

Herring Plate

Arrange the herring fillets side by side on a long chilled platter. With a sharp, heavy knife, make diagonal cuts ½ inch apart through the fillets. Spread the sour cream (or sour cream and mayonnaise) in a circle around the herring fillets. On the border of the platter, arrange alternate mounds of chopped egg white, egg yolk, sliced radishes and parsley.

3 or more fillets of canned *matjes* or pickled herring, drained
½ cup sour cream, or ¼ cup sour cream combined with ¼ cup mayonnaise
2 hard-cooked eggs, the whites and yolks finely chopped separately
¼ cup finely chopped parsley
4 sliced radishes

Pickled Beets

In a stainless-steel or enameled 1½- to 2-quart saucepan, combine the vinegar, water, sugar, salt and pepper, bring to a boil and boil briskly for 2 minutes. Meanwhile, place the sliced beets in a deep glass, stainless-steel or enamel bowl. Pour the hot marinade over the beets and let them cool uncovered to room temperature. Cover the bowl with plastic wrap and refrigerate for at least 12 hours, stirring every few hours to keep the slices moist.

Makes 2 cups

½ cup white vinegar
½ cup water
⅓ cup sugar
1 teaspoon salt
⅛ teaspoon freshly ground black pepper
2 cups thinly sliced freshly cooked or canned beets

Pickled Cucumber Salad

Scrub the wax coating (if any) off the cucumbers and dry them. Score the cucumbers lengthwise with a fork and cut them in the thinnest possible slices; ideally, the slices should be almost translucent. Arrange them in a thin layer in a shallow china or glass dish and sprinkle with salt. Place 2 or 3 china plates on top of the cucumbers (to press out excess water and bitterness) and let them rest at room temperature for a couple of hours.

Remove the plates, drain the cucumbers of all their liquid, and spread them out on paper towels. Gently pat the cucumbers dry with paper towels and return them to their dish. In a small bowl, beat together the vinegar, sugar, salt and pepper. Pour over the cucumbers and strew them with the chopped dill. Chill for 2 or 3 hours and just before serving, drain away nearly all of the liquid.

To serve 4

2 large (8-inch) or 3 medium (6-inch) cucumbers
1 tablespoon salt
¾ cup white vinegar
1 tablespoon sugar
1 teaspoon salt
¼ teaspoon white pepper
2 tablespoons chopped fresh dill

Overleaf: The smörgåsbord spread is a perfect Scandinavian solution for a New Year's Day open house anywhere. The dishes include herring plate (1); cucumber salad (2); chopped chives for garnish (3); herring salad with sliced eggs (4); pink sour-cream sauce (5); egg yolk with chopped parsley, beets, capers, onions and anchovies (6); hard-cooked eggs topped with red cod roe or caviar (7); mustard sauce for salmon (8); dill-marinated salmon (9); Swedish liver pâté (10); sliced cucumber to garnish the liver pâté (11); a selection of Swedish cheeses, including Fontina and Herrgård (12); Scandinavian breads and rye crisps (13); Jansson's Temptation—a potato, onion, anchovy and cream casserole (14); Swedish meatballs (15); and onion rolls stuffed with meatballs (16). Smörgåsbord recipes begin on this page and continue through page 82.

A Smörgåsbord Sampler

16

15

7

14

Herring Salad with Sour-Cream Sauce

To serve 8 to 10

1 cup finely chopped herring (salt, *matjes*, pickled, Bismarck)
½ pound finely chopped cooked tongue or veal (optional)
½ cup diced cold boiled potatoes
3 cups finely chopped cold beets, freshly cooked or canned
½ cup finely chopped apple, cored and peeled
⅓ cup finely chopped onion
½ cup finely chopped dill pickle
4 tablespoons finely chopped fresh dill
2 tablespoons white wine vinegar
Salt
Freshly ground black pepper

DRESSING
3 chilled hard-cooked eggs
1 tablespoon prepared mustard
2 tablespoons white wine vinegar
¼ cup vegetable oil
2 to 4 tablespoons heavy cream

SAUCE
3 tablespoons beet juice
½ teaspoon lemon juice
1 cup sour cream

In a large mixing bowl, combine the finely chopped herring, optional meat, potatoes, beets, apple, onion and pickle. Mix three tablespoons of the dill with the vinegar, and add salt and pepper to taste. Pour over the salad ingredients and toss gently with a wooden spoon.

DRESSING: Remove the yolks from the hard-cooked eggs. Mince the whites and set them aside. Force the yolks through a sieve into a small bowl with the back of a large spoon, then mash them to a paste with the tablespoon of prepared mustard. Gradually beat in the vinegar and oil, then the cream, a tablespoon at a time, until the sauce has the consistency of heavy cream. Pour over the salad, mix lightly but thoroughly, cover, and chill for at least 2 hours.

Just before serving, transfer the salad to a large serving bowl or platter and sprinkle it with the minced egg whites and the remaining chopped dill.

SAUCE: Stir the beet and lemon juice into the sour cream until it is smooth and well blended. Pass this sauce separately.

Gravlax—Salmon Marinated in Dill

To serve 8 to 10

3 to 3½ pounds fresh salmon, center cut, cleaned and scaled
1 large bunch dill
¼ cup coarse (kosher) salt, or if unavailable, substitute regular salt
¼ cup sugar
2 tablespoons white peppercorns (or substitute black), crushed

Ask the fish dealer to cut the salmon in half lengthwise and to remove the backbone and the small bones as well.

Place half of the fish, skin side down, in a deep glass, enamel or stainless-steel baking dish or casserole. Wash and then shake dry the bunch of dill, and place it on the fish. (If the dill is of the hothouse variety and not very pungent, chop the herb coarsely to release its flavor and sprinkle it over the fish instead.) In a separate bowl, combine the salt, sugar and crushed peppercorns. Sprinkle this mixture evenly over the dill. Top with the other half of the fish, skin side up. Cover the fish with aluminum foil and on it set a heavy platter slightly larger than the salmon. Pile the platter with 3 or 4 cans of food; these make convenient weights that are easy to distribute evenly. Refrigerate for 48 hours (or up to 3 days). Turn the fish over every 12 hours, basting it with the liquid marinade that accumulates, and separating the halves a little to baste the salmon inside. Replace the platter and weights each time.

When the *gravlax* is finished, remove the fish from its marinade, scrape away the dill and seasonings, and pat it dry with paper towels. Place the separated halves skin side down on a carving board and slice the salmon halves thinly on the diagonal, detaching each slice from the skin.

Mustard-and-Dill Sauce for Salmon

To make about ¾ cup

4 tablespoons dark, highly seasoned prepared mustard
1 teaspoon powdered mustard
3 tablespoons sugar
2 tablespoons white vinegar
⅓ cup vegetable oil
3 tablespoons fresh chopped dill

In a small, deep bowl, mix the two mustards, sugar and vinegar to a paste. With a wire whisk, slowly beat in the oil until it forms a thick mayonnaise-like emulsion. Stir in the dill. The sauce may be kept refrigerated in a tightly covered jar for several days, but will need to be shaken vigorously or beaten with a whisk to remix the ingredients before serving with *gravlax*.

Swedish Liver Pâté

Melt the butter in a saucepan, remove from the heat, and stir in the flour. Add the milk and cream and bring to a boil, beating constantly with a whisk until the sauce is smooth and thick. Let it simmer for a minute, then set aside to cool. Cut the liver into chunks. Roughly chop the pork fat and mix both with the onion and anchovies. Divide the mixture into thirds. Purée each batch in an electric blender set at high speed, adding enough sauce to keep the mixture from clogging the blender. Transfer each completed batch to a large bowl and beat in any remaining cream sauce. (To make by hand, put the liver, pork fat, onion and anchovies through the finest blade of a meat grinder twice, then combine with the cream sauce, beating them together thoroughly.) Beat the eggs with the salt, pepper, allspice and cloves and mix thoroughly into the liver mixture. The blender mixture will be considerably more fluid than the one made by hand.

Preheat the oven to 350°. Line a 1-quart loaf pan or mold with the strips of pork fat. Arrange the strips lengthwise or crosswise; they should overlap slightly and cover the bottom and sides of the pan. If long enough, let them hang over the sides; otherwise, save enough strips to cover the top. Spoon the liver mixture into the loaf pan and fold the overhanging strips (or extra strips) of fat over the top. Cover with a double sheet of aluminum foil, sealing the edges tightly, and place in a large baking pan. Pour into the baking pan enough boiling water to reach at least halfway up the side of the loaf pan and bake in the center of the oven for 2 hours. Remove from the oven and lift off the foil. When cool, re-cover with foil and chill thoroughly.

To serve 12 to 16

2 tablespoons butter
2 tablespoons flour
1 cup milk
1 cup heavy cream
1 pound fresh pork liver
¾ pound fresh pork fat
1 onion, coarsely chopped (½ cup)
3 flat anchovy fillets, drained
2 eggs
1½ teaspoons salt
¾ teaspoon white pepper
½ teaspoon ground allspice
¼ teaspoon ground cloves
¾ pound fresh pork fat, sliced into long, ⅛-inch-thick strips or sheets

Small Swedish Meatballs

In a small frying pan, melt the tablespoon of butter over moderate heat. When the foam subsides, add the onions and cook for about 5 minutes, until they are soft and translucent but not brown.

In a large bowl, combine the onions, mashed potato, bread crumbs, meat, cream, salt, egg and optional parsley. Knead vigorously with both hands or beat with a wooden spoon until all of the ingredients are well blended and the mixture is smooth and fluffy. Shape into small balls about 1 inch in diameter. Arrange the meatballs in one layer on a baking sheet or a flat tray, cover them with plastic wrap and chill for at least 1 hour before cooking.

Over high heat, melt the 2 tablespoons of butter and 2 tablespoons of oil in a heavy 10- to 12-inch skillet. When the foam subsides, add the meatballs, 8 to 10 at a time. Reduce the heat to moderate and fry the balls on all sides, shaking the pan almost constantly to roll the balls around in the hot fat to help keep their shape. In 8 to 10 minutes the meatballs should be brown outside and show no trace of pink inside when one is broken open with a knife. Add more butter and oil as needed, and transfer each finished batch to a casserole or baking dish and keep warm in a 200° oven.

You may want to make a sauce with the pan juice. Remove from the heat, pour off all but a thin film of fat from the pan, and stir in 1 tablespoon

To make about 50 meatballs

1 tablespoon butter
4 tablespoons finely chopped onion
1 large boiled potato, mashed (1 cup)
3 tablespoons fine dry bread crumbs
1 pound lean ground beef
⅓ cup heavy cream
1 teaspoon salt
1 egg
1 tablespoon finely chopped fresh parsley (optional)
2 tablespoons butter
2 tablespoons vegetable oil
1 tablespoon flour
¾ cup light or heavy cream

of flour. Quickly stir in ¾ cup of light or heavy cream, scraping up any browned bits clinging to the pan. Boil the sauce over moderate heat for 2 or 3 minutes, stirring constantly, until it is thick and smooth. Pour over the meatballs and serve.

Stuffed Onion Rolls

To serve 4 to 6

½ Swedish meatball recipe
3 large yellow onions (½ pound each), peeled
3 tablespoons butter
2 tablespoons fresh bread crumbs

Place the peeled onions in a 2- to 3-quart pot, add enough cold water to cover, and bring to a boil over moderate heat. Lower the heat and simmer the onions, uncovered, for 40 minutes. Remove the onions from the pot with a slotted spoon, drain them and let them cool on a platter while you make the meat stuffing.

Pull off each onion layer separately. They should slide off quite easily. Cut the largest outer layers of the onions in half, but remember to leave them large enough to enclose the stuffing. Discard the inner part of the onions (or use them for some other purpose) if the leaves are too small to stuff. Put a heaping teaspoon of the meat stuffing in the middle of each onion leaf and enclose it by folding over the edges of the leaf. (At this point they may be covered with plastic wrap and refrigerated for up to 2 days before cooking.)

Preheat the oven to 400°. In a shallow 1- to 1½-quart flameproof baking dish, melt 3 tablespoons of butter over low heat. Remove the dish from the heat and place the onion rolls, sealed side down, side by side in the butter, first rolling each in the butter to coat it. Bake 15 minutes, then baste with the butter in the dish, sprinkle with the bread crumbs, and bake another 15 minutes, until the onions are lightly browned and the crumbs are crisp.

Jansson's Temptation

To serve at least 6

7 medium boiling potatoes, peeled and cut into strips 2 inches long and ¼ inch thick
2½ tablespoons butter
2 tablespoons vegetable oil
2 to 3 large yellow onions, thinly sliced (4 cups)
16 flat anchovy fillets, drained
White pepper
2 tablespoons fine dry bread crumbs
2 tablespoons butter, cut into ¼-inch bits
½ cup milk
1 cup heavy cream

Preheat the oven to 400°. Place the potato strips in cold water to keep them from discoloring. Heat 2 tablespoons of butter and 2 tablespoons of oil in a 10- to 12-inch skillet; when the foam subsides, add the onions and cook 10 minutes, stirring frequently, until they are soft but not brown.

With a pastry brush or paper towel, spread a 1½- to 2-quart soufflé dish or baking dish with the remaining half tablespoon of butter. Drain the potatoes and pat them dry with paper towels. Arrange a layer of potatoes on the bottom of the dish and then alternate layers of onions and anchovies, ending with potatoes. Sprinkle each layer with a little white pepper. Scatter bread crumbs over the top layer of potatoes and dot the crumbs with the bits of butter. In a small saucepan, heat the milk and cream until the mixture barely simmers, then pour it slowly down the sides of the dish. Bake in the center of the oven for 45 minutes, or until the potatoes are tender when pierced with the tip of a sharp knife and the liquid is nearly absorbed.

Dutch New Year's Eve Fritters

In a small bowl, sprinkle the yeast and a pinch of the sugar over the lukewarm milk. Let the mixture stand for 2 or 3 minutes, then stir to dissolve the yeast. Set the bowl in a warm, draft-free place such as an unlighted oven for about 5 minutes, or until the yeast bubbles up and the mixture almost doubles in volume.

Sift 2 cups of flour, the remaining sugar and the salt into a deep mixing bowl. Make a well in the center, pour in the yeast-and-milk mixture, and with a large spoon gradually incorporate the flour into the liquid ingredients. Drop in the eggs and beat until all of the flour has been absorbed. The dough should hold its shape lightly in the spoon; if the dough is too fluid, beat in up to ½ cup more flour, a few tablespoons at a time. Cover the bowl with a dampened kitchen towel and set it aside in the draft-free spot for about 1 hour, or until it doubles in bulk.

Pour vegetable oil into a deep fryer or large, heavy saucepan to a depth of about 3 inches and heat the oil until it reaches a temperature of 345° on a deep-frying thermometer.

Punch the dough down with a blow of your fist and gently but thoroughly stir in the currants, raisins, orange peel and lemon peel. For each of the fritters, scoop up about ¼ cup of the dough and drop it into the hot oil. Deep-fry 3 or 4 balls at a time, turning them with a slotted spoon, for about 10 minutes. As they brown, transfer the fritters to paper towels to drain.

Serve the fritters warm or at room temperature; they will stay crisp for 2 to 3 hours. Just before serving, dust the balls lightly with confectioners' sugar.

To make about 18 fritters

1 package active dry yeast
2 tablespoons sugar
1½ cups lukewarm (110° to 115°) milk
2 to 2½ cups all-purpose flour
½ teaspoon salt
2 eggs
Vegetable oil for deep frying
¼ cup dried currants
¼ cup seedless raisins
¼ cup coarsely chopped candied orange peel
2 tablespoons finely grated fresh lemon peel
Confectioners' sugar

Haselnusstorte

Preheat the oven to 275°. In a large bowl, beat the egg yolks and the whole egg together with a wire whisk, or rotary or electric beater, continuing to beat until the mixture is thick and light yellow in color. Gradually beat in ½ cup of the sugar, then the nuts and the bread crumbs. Continue to beat until the mixture forms a dense, moist mass.

In another bowl, beat the egg whites with the wire whisk or rotary or electric beater until they begin to foam, then add ¼ cup of the sugar, 1 tablespoon at a time. Continue to beat until the whites form stiff, unwavering peaks when the beater is lifted from the bowl. With a rubber spatula, mix about ¼ of the whites into the hazelnut mixture, then sprinkle the flour over it and gently fold in the rest of the whites. Continue to fold until no trace of the whites remains. Be careful not to overfold.

Butter and flour a 10-inch springform pan. Turn the pan over and strike it on the table to remove excess flour. Pour the batter into the pan, smooth the top with a spatula and bake in the middle of the oven for 45 to 50 minutes, or until it shrinks away slightly from the sides of the pan. Remove the upper part of the pan as soon as you take it from the oven. Let the cake cool, then slice it into two equal layers, using a long, sharp, serrated

To make 1 ten-inch cake

6 eggs, separated
1 whole egg
1 cup ground hazelnuts
¾ cup sugar
⅓ cup bread crumbs
1 teaspoon flour

THE FILLING
1½ cups heavy cream
1 tablespoon sugar
1 teaspoon vanilla extract

THE DECORATION
⅓ cup ground hazelnuts

Four Fabulous Viennese Cakes

In Vienna a cake is more than just a cake. It is a creation that allows free rein to the cook's creativity. Four that would enrich a New Year's buffet are: *Haselnusstorte (left)*, made with beaten eggs and ground hazelnuts; *Doboschtorte (center bottom)*, a many-layered spongecake filled with chocolate cream and glazed with caramel sugar; *Rehrücken (center top)*, a mock saddle of venison with almonds and unsweetened chocolate; and *Linzertorte (far right)*.

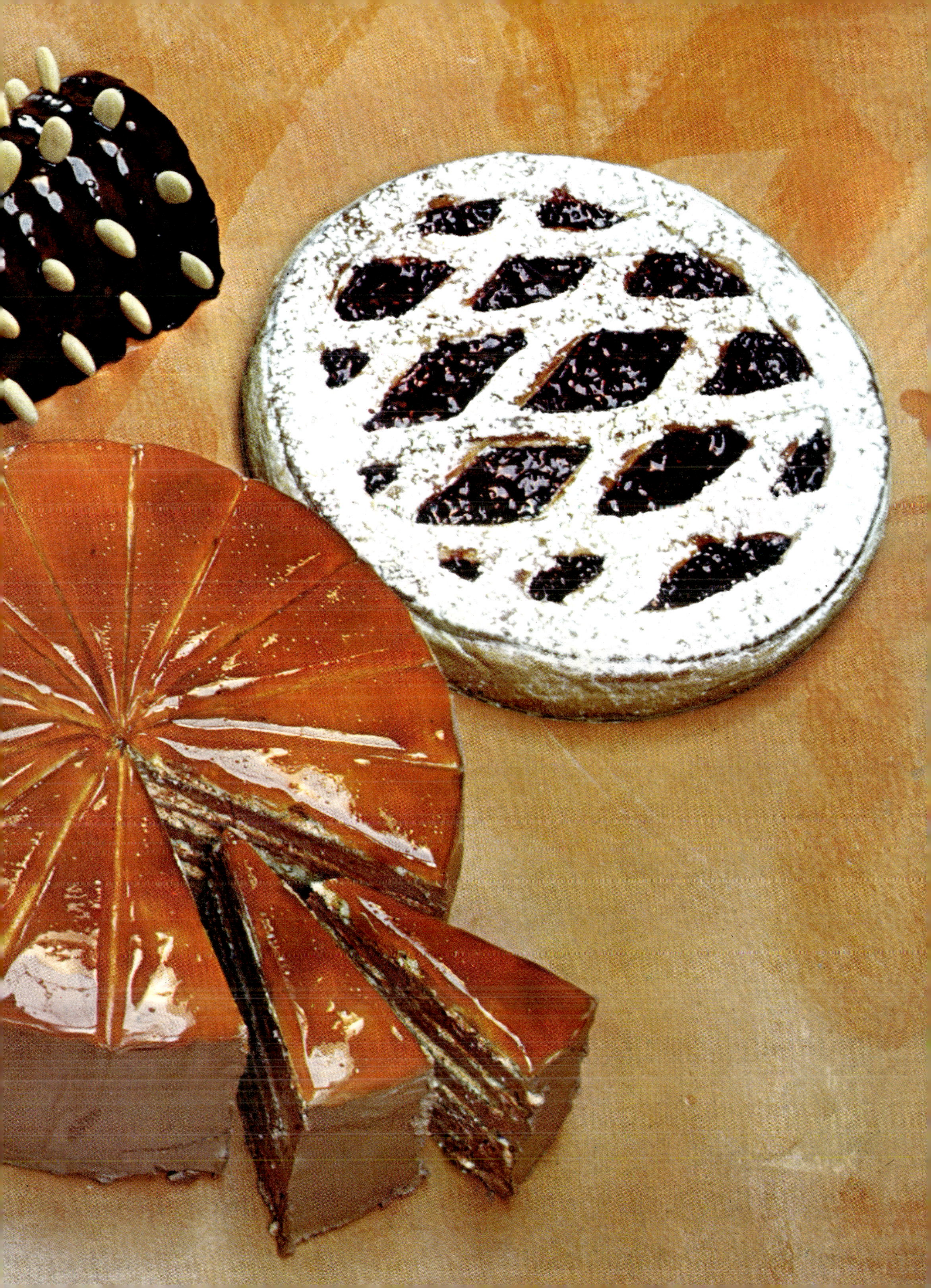

knife. (The cake will fall somewhat after it is removed from the oven.)

THE FILLING: Whip the chilled cream with a wire whisk or rotary or electric beater until it begins to thicken. Add the sugar and vanilla and continue to whip until the cream holds its shape firmly.

Reconstruct the cake by first placing the bottom layer on a sheet of wax paper at least 18 inches square. Spread whipped cream on top to a thickness of ½ inch and place the other layer over it. With a spatula, completely mask the cake with the rest of the whipped cream.

THE DECORATION: Scatter the ⅓ cup of hazelnuts on the wax paper around the cake. Then lift a small portion of the paper and toss the nuts on to the cake. Repeat until all the nuts are used. Serve at once.

Doboschtorte

To make 16 slices

THE CAKE
½ pound unsalted butter, softened
1 cup granulated sugar
4 eggs, lightly beaten
1½ cups all-purpose flour
1 teaspoon vanilla extract

THE FILLING
1⅓ cups sugar
¼ teaspoon cream of tartar
⅔ cup water
8 egg yolks
½ cup dark unsweetened cocoa
2 teaspoons vanilla extract
2 cups (1 pound) unsalted butter, softened

THE GLAZE
⅔ cup sugar
⅓ cup water

THE CAKE: Preheat the oven to 350°. Cream the butter and sugar by beating them together against the side of a mixing bowl with a wooden spoon. Beat in the eggs, then stir in the flour and the vanilla extract. Continue to stir until the mixture becomes a smooth, firm batter.

With a pastry brush or paper towel, butter the underside of a 9-inch layer-cake pan, then dust it with flour. Strike the pan against the edge of a table to knock off the excess flour. With a metal spatula spread the batter as evenly as possible over the underside of the pan to a thickness of ⅛ inch. Bake in the middle of the oven 7 to 9 minutes, or until the layer is lightly browned around the edges.

Remove from the oven and scrape off any batter that has dribbled down the sides of the pan. Loosen the layer from the pan with a spatula, put a cake rack over it and invert. Wipe the pan with a paper towel, butter and flour it again and repeat the baking process with more batter. (You may, of course, bake as many layers at a time as you have 9-inch cake pans.) Continue until all the batter is used. You should have 7 exactly matching layers.

THE FILLING: In a small saucepan, combine the sugar, cream of tartar and water. Stir over low heat until the sugar is completely dissolved, then turn the heat to moderately high and boil the syrup without stirring until, if tested, it registers 238° on a candy thermometer, or until a drop of the syrup in cold water forms a soft ball.

Meanwhile, in a mixer, or by hand with a rotary or electric beater, beat the 8 egg yolks for 3 or 4 minutes, or long enough to thicken them and lighten them somewhat in color.

Pour the hot syrup into the eggs, continuing to beat as you pour in the syrup in a slow, steady stream. If you are using a mixer, beat at medium speed until the mixture cools to room temperature and changes to a thick, smooth cream. This usually takes from 10 to 15 minutes.

If you are beating by hand, set the mixing bowl in a pan of cold water to hasten the cooling and add the syrup a little at a time. Continue to beat until the cream is cool, thick and smooth, then beat in the cocoa and vanilla extract. Last, beat in the butter, adding it in small pieces until it is all absorbed. Refrigerate while you make the glaze.

THE GLAZE: First, place the most attractive of the cake layers on a cake rack set on a jelly-roll pan, then mix the sugar and water together in a small heavy saucepan. Without stirring, cook until the sugar dissolves, boils and begins to darken in color. Swirling the pan, continue to boil until the caramel becomes a golden brown, then pour it over the layer. With a buttered knife, quickly mark the glaze into 16 equal wedges, cutting nearly, but not quite, through to the bottom of the glaze. This mirrorlike layer will be the top of the *Torte*.

ASSEMBLING THE TORTE: Place a cake layer on a serving plate and, with a metal spatula, spread chocolate filling over it to a thickness of 1/8 inch, then top with another cake layer. Continue with the other layers, finishing with a layer of filling and the glazed top. Use the rest of the chocolate filling to cover the sides of the cake, smoothing it on with a spatula and refrigerate. To serve, slice along the lines marked in the glaze.

Rehrücken

To make the cake, preheat the oven to 350°, then with a paper towel or pastry brush, lightly butter a 4-by-12-inch loaf pan or a *Rehrücken* mold and dust it heavily with bread crumbs. Invert the pan and shake it to remove the bread crumbs that do not adhere to the butter.

With a wire whisk or rotary or electric beater, beat the egg whites until they foam, then beat in 1/4 cup of the sugar, 1 tablespoon at a time. Continue beating until the whites form stiff, unwavering peaks when the beater is lifted from the bowl.

Combine the yolks, the whole eggs and the rest of the sugar in a large mixing bowl. With the same beater you used before, beat until the mixture is pale yellow and quite thick. Then beat in the cinnamon, citron, almonds and chocolate. Continue beating until all the ingredients are thoroughly blended.

With a rubber spatula, mix about 1/4 of the egg whites into the batter, then reverse the process and pour the batter over the rest of the whites. Using an over-and-under cutting motion instead of a mixing motion, fold them together until no trace of the whites remains.

Pour the batter into the prepared loaf pan or *Rehrücken* mold and bake it in the middle of the oven for 25 to 30 minutes, or until the cake shrinks slightly away from the sides of the pan, is golden brown and is springy to the touch.

Remove the cake from the oven and let it cool for 2 or 3 minutes. (In cooling, this very delicate cake may shrink slightly or fall a bit in the center, but in neither event will its final shape be affected.) Turn the cake out on a rack, set the rack on a jelly-roll pan and let the cake cool further while you make the chocolate icing.

THE CHOCOLATE GLAZE: In a small heavy saucepan, combine the cream, butter, salt, cocoa and sugar. Cook the mixture over very low heat, stirring constantly, for about 5 minutes, or until the icing is smooth and thick. Remove it from the heat and stir in the vanilla extract. Let the icing cool for about 5 minutes, then holding the saucepan about 2 inches above the cake, pour the icing over it evenly.

Press the almonds upright into the icing about an inch apart, in a regular

To serve 10

1/4 cup bread crumbs
5 egg whites
1/2 cup sugar
5 egg yolks
2 whole eggs
1/2 teaspoon cinnamon
2 1/2 tablespoons finely chopped citron
1/4 pound grated almonds (about 3/4 cup)
1/3 cup grated unsweetened chocolate (about 2 1/4 ounces)

THE CHOCOLATE GLAZE
2/3 cup heavy cream
5 tablespoons unsalted butter
Pinch of salt
1 cup sifted dark, unsweetened cocoa
1 1/3 cups sugar
1 teaspoon vanilla extract
1 cup blanched almonds

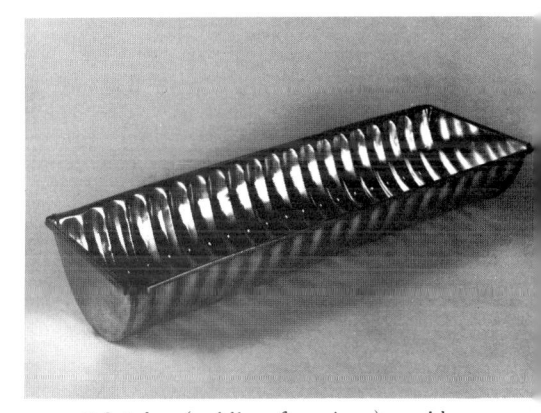

Rehrücken (saddle of venison) molds are available in sizes from 10 to 14 inches.

pattern. (Try rows of 5 or 6 almond halves across and 10 lengthwise.) Let the cake cool completely (for about 45 minutes) before serving. Slice *Rehrücken* so that one of the shorter rows of almond halves decorates each serving.

Linzertorte

To make 1 nine-inch cake

1½ cups all-purpose flour
⅛ teaspoon ground cloves
¼ teaspoon cinnamon
1 cup finely ground unblanched almonds
½ cup sugar
1 teaspoon grated lemon peel
2 hard-cooked egg yolks, mashed
1 cup unsalted butter (2 quarter-pound sticks), softened
2 raw egg yolks, lightly beaten
1 teaspoon vanilla extract
1½ cups thick raspberry jam
1 egg, lightly beaten
2 tablespoons light cream
Confectioners' sugar

Sift the flour, cloves and cinnamon together into a deep mixing bowl, then add the almonds, sugar, lemon peel and mashed egg yolks. With a wooden spoon, beat in the butter, raw egg yolks and vanilla extract. Continue to beat until the mixture is smooth and doughy. Form the dough into a ball, wrap it in wax paper or plastic wrap, and refrigerate it for at least 1 hour, or until it is firm.

Remove about ¾ of the dough from the wrapping and return the rest to the refrigerator.

With a paper towel or pastry brush, lightly butter a round 9-by-1- or 1½-inch false-bottomed cake pan. Add the dough (if it is too firm, let it soften a bit) and, with your fingers, press and push it out so that it covers the bottom and sides of the pan, making a shell about ¼ inch thick. Spoon in the raspberry jam and spread it evenly over the bottom of the shell with a spatula. On a floured surface with a floured rolling pin, roll out the rest of the dough into a 6-by-9-inch rectangle ¼ inch thick.

With a pastry cutter or sharp knife, cut the dough into strips ½ inch wide, 2 of them 9 inches long and the rest 8 inches long. Lay one of the 9-inch strips across the center of the jam and flank that strip on each side with one of the 8-inch strips placed halfway between the center and sides of the pan. Rotate the pan about ¼ of the way to your left and repeat the pattern with the other 3 strips, so that they create Xs with the first 3 in a latticelike effect.

Run a sharp knife around the top of the pan to loosen the part of the bottom dough that extends above the strips. Press this down with your fingers into a border about ¼ inch thick. Lightly beat the whole egg with the cream and, with a pastry brush, coat all the exposed pastry. Refrigerate for ½ hour.

Meanwhile preheat the oven to 350°.

Bake the *Torte* in the middle of the oven for 45 to 50 minutes, or until it is lightly browned. Set the pan on a large jar or coffee can and slip down the outside rim. Let the *Torte* cool for 5 minutes on the bottom of the pan, then sprinkle it with confectioners' sugar. *Linzertorte* should cool to room temperature before being served.

Scottish New Year's Black Bun Cake

To make one 8-inch cake

PASTRY

½ pound (2 sticks) unsalted butter, chilled and cut into ¼-inch bits
2½ cups all-purpose flour
6 to 8 tablespoons ice water
1 tablespoon butter, softened

In a large, chilled bowl, combine the ½ pound of chilled butter and 2½ cups of the flour and rub them together with your fingers until they look like flakes of coarse meal. Do not allow the mixture to become oily. Pour 6 tablespoons of ice water over the flour all at once; then shape the dough into a ball. If the dough crumbles, add more ice water by the teaspoonful until the particles adhere. Dust the pastry lightly with flour and wrap it in wax paper. Refrigerate for at least 2 hours.

Preheat the oven to 350°. With a pastry brush and 1 tablespoon of soft butter, coat the bottom and sides of a round baking dish about 8 inches in diameter and 3 inches deep.

To make the filling, sift 4 cups of the flour, the sugar, baking soda, cinnamon, mace, cloves, salt and pepper together into a mixing bowl. Add the seedless raisins, white raisins, almonds and candied peel a cup or so at a time, tossing them constantly with a spoon until the fruit and nuts are coated with the flour. Beat the eggs until frothy, stir in the buttermilk and brandy, and pour the mixture over the flour and fruit. Stir until all the ingredients are well combined.

Break off about two thirds of the chilled dough and place it on a lightly floured board. Pat it into a flat circle about 1 inch thick, and roll it out into a circle 15 to 16 inches in diameter and about ¼ inch thick. Drape the pastry over the pin and unroll it loosely over the baking dish. Gently press it into the bottom and around the sides of the dish, being careful not to stretch it. With scissors or a sharp knife, trim off the excess dough around the rim, and spoon the filling into the dish. Then roll the remaining pastry into a circle 9 to 10 inches in diameter and unroll it over the top of the dish. Cut off the excess and seal the edges of the circle securely to the dish by crimping it with your fingers or by pressing it down firmly with the tines of a fork. With a fork, prick the pastry all over the surface and, with a small knife, cut two 1-inch-long parallel slits about ½ inch apart in the center.

Bake in the center of the oven for 1½ hours, then reduce the heat to 275° and bake for another 1½ hours, or until the top is golden brown. Cool and then cover tightly with foil or plastic wrap and let stand at room temperature for at least a week before serving. In Scotland this dish is traditionally served on New Year's Eve. (It will keep for 3 or 4 weeks.)

FILLING

4 cups all-purpose flour
½ cup sugar
1 teaspoon baking soda
1 teaspoon ground cinnamon
½ teaspoon mace
⅛ teaspoon ground cloves
¼ teaspoon salt
½ teaspoon freshly ground black pepper
6 cups seedless raisins (about 2 pounds)
6 cups white raisins (about 2 pounds)
2 cups coarsely chopped blanched almonds (about 12 ounces)
1½ cups finely chopped, mixed candied fruit peel (about 8 ounces)
3 eggs
½ cup buttermilk
1 cup brandy

Punch, Fizzes and Cocktails

Fish House Punch

Place the sugar and lemon juice in the punch bowl and stir with a muddler or bar spoon to dissolve the sugar thoroughly. Add the rum, water, peach brandy and cognac, stir to combine the ingredients, and allow the punch to "ripen" at room temperature for at least 2 hours, stirring occasionally. Put the solid block of ice in the bowl and garnish, if you like, with sliced peaches. Serve in punch cups.

To make 1½ gallons

1½ cups superfine sugar
1 quart fresh lemon juice
2 quarts 80-proof light or dark rum
2 quarts cold water
4 ounces peach brandy
1 quart cognac
A block of ice
1 cup sliced, peeled peaches, fresh, frozen or canned (optional)

Fish House punch, a New Year's tradition that originated in 18th Century Pennsylvania, is a potent mix of rum and peach brandy.

To make 1 cocktail

8 to 12 ice cubes
2 teaspoons fresh lemon juice
4 ounces full-bodied tomato juice
3 ounces vodka
2 drops Worcestershire sauce
2 drops Tabasco
Freshly ground black pepper
A dash of celery salt (optional)

Bloody Mary

Fill a mixing glass with ice cubes and add the lemon juice, tomato juice, vodka, Worcestershire sauce and Tabasco. Season with a few grindings of black pepper. Place a shaker on top of the mixing glass and, grasping them firmly together with both hands, shake vigorously. Remove the shaker, place a strainer on top of the mixing glass, and strain into a wine or cocktail glass. Sprinkle the top with a dash of celery salt if you wish.

To serve the Bloody Mary "on the rocks," prepare as directed above and strain into an 8-ounce highball glass filled with 2 or 3 ice cubes.

Gimlet

Place the vodka in a 6-ounce glass and add the ice cubes. Top with lime juice and garnish with a slice of lime.

You may, if you wish, substitute fresh lime juice for the bottled juice. In that case, add ½ teaspoon of sugar to the vodka in the glass and stir with a bar spoon to dissolve.

To make 1 cocktail

3 ounces vodka
2 ice cubes
2 ounces Rose's sweetened lime juice
1 slice lime

Green Dragon

Combine the vodka, green crème de menthe and ice cubes in a mixing glass and stir gently with a bar spoon to combine and chill the ingredients. Place a strainer on top of the mixing glass and pour into a cocktail glass

To make 1 cocktail

2 ounces vodka
1 ounce green crème de menthe
2 to 3 ice cubes

Bullshot

Combine the ice, vodka and beef bouillon in a mixing glass, add salt and pepper to taste, and stir with a bar spoon. Place a strainer on top of the mixing glass and pour into a chilled wine glass.

To make 1 cocktail

3 to 4 ice cubes
3 ounces vodka
4 ounces strong, cold beef bouillon
Salt
Freshly ground pepper

Screwdriver

Combine the orange juice, vodka, sugar if you wish, and the ice cubes in a mixing glass. Place a shaker on top of the glass and, grasping them firmly together with both hands, shake well. Remove the shaker, place a strainer on top of the glass, and strain into a cocktail glass.

To make 1 cocktail

1½ ounces fresh orange juice
2½ ounces vodka
Pinch of superfine sugar (optional)
3 to 4 ice cubes

Black Russian

Combine the Kahlúa and vodka in a mixing glass, add the ice cubes, and stir gently to combine. Place a strainer over the mixing glass and pour into a chilled cocktail glass.

To make 1 cocktail

1 ounce Kahlúa (coffee liqueur)
3 ounces vodka
2 to 3 ice cubes

Silver Fizz

Combine the lemon juice, vodka and sugar in a mixing glass and stir with a bar spoon to dissolve the sugar. Add the egg white, dash of heavy cream and ice cubes. Place a shaker on top of the mixing glass and, grasping them firmly together with both hands, shake vigorously 6 or 7 times. Remove the shaker, place a strainer on top of the mixing glass, and pour into a chilled glass. Rinse the shaker with the cold club soda and pour into the drink.

To make 1 cocktail

1½ ounces fresh lemon juice
3 ounces vodka
1 teaspoon superfine sugar
1 egg white
A dash of heavy cream
3 to 4 ice cubes
2 ounces cold club soda

Overleaf: Surrounding a clear glass of vodka with a lemon peel in it is a sampling of varicolored vodka cocktails. Moving clockwise from the red Bloody Mary at the top, the drinks include: a Bull Shot, a Green Dragon, a gimlet, a screwdriver, a Black Russian and a vodka silver fizz.

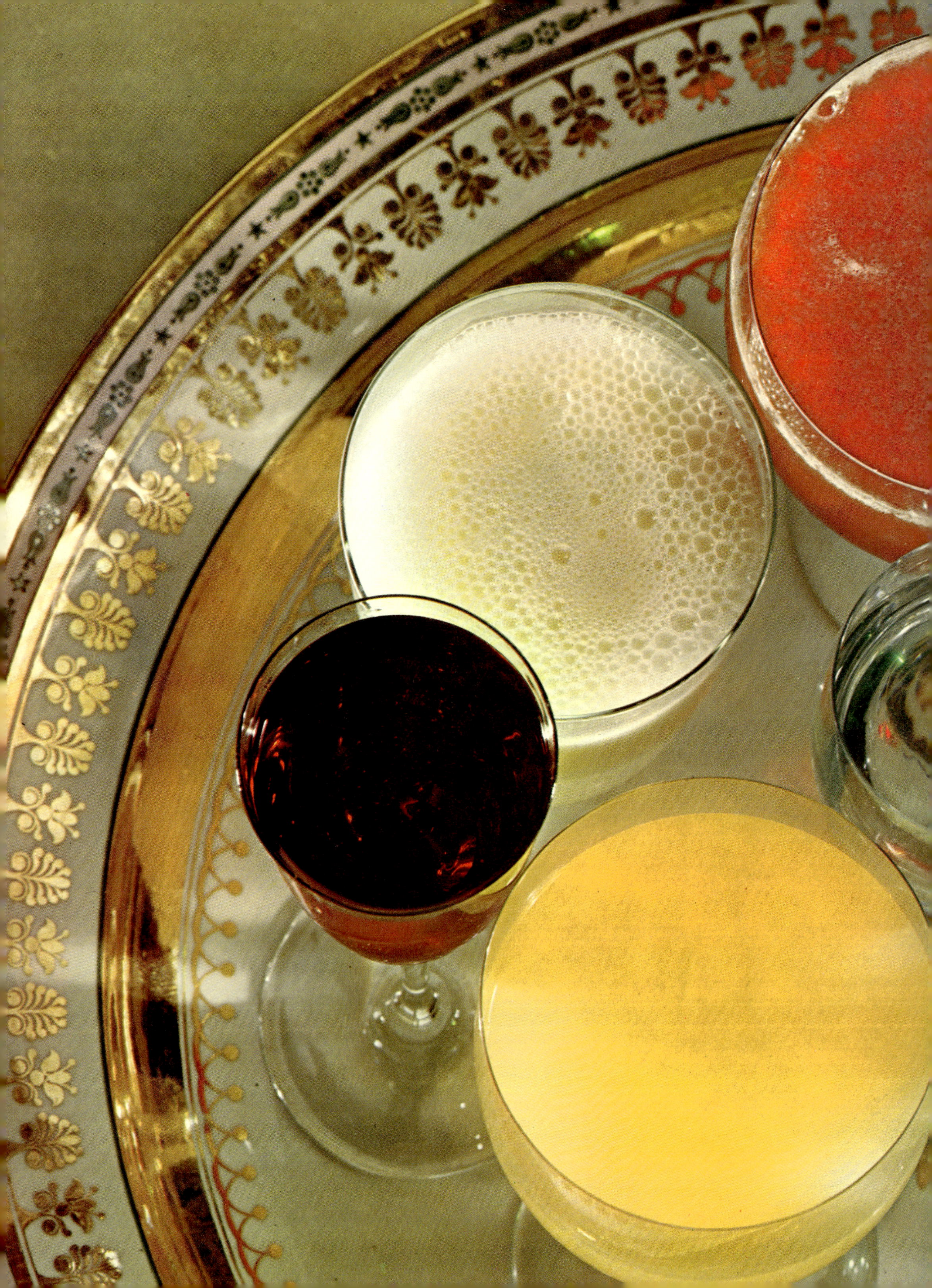

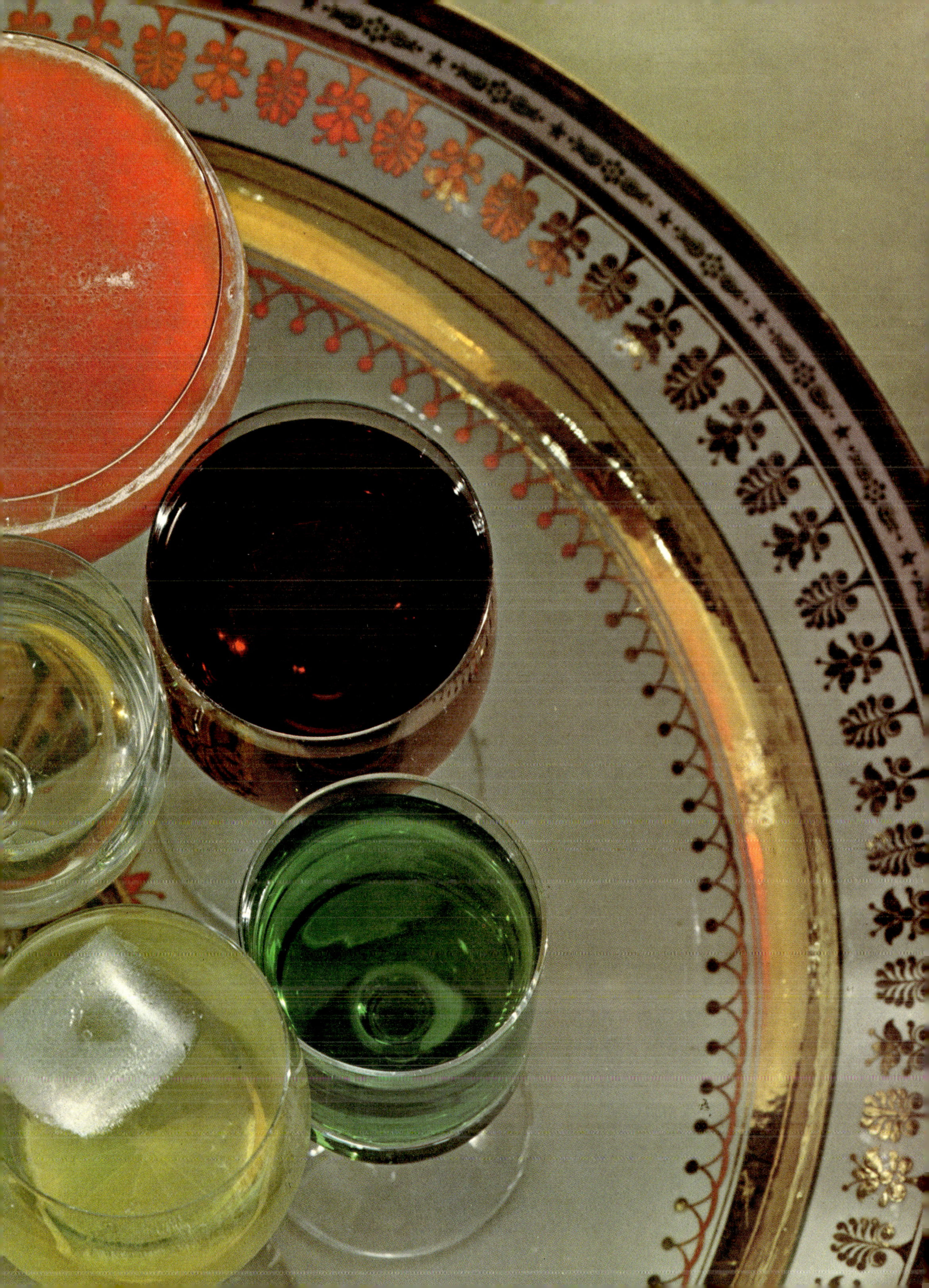

Champagne Pick-Me-Up

To make 1 pick-me-up

1 ounce fresh orange juice
½ ounce fresh lemon juice
1 teaspoon grenadine
2 ounces brandy
3 to 4 ice cubes
4 ounces cold champagne

Combine the orange and lemon juices, grenadine, brandy and ice cubes in a mixing glass. Place a shaker on top of the mixing glass and, grasping them firmly together with both hands, shake vigorously. Remove the shaker, place a strainer on top of the mixing glass, and pour into a large wine glass. Rinse the shaker with champagne and pour it slowly into the wine glass.

Milk Punch

To make 1 serving

⅓ cup light cream
2 ounces bourbon
2 teaspoons confectioners' sugar
⅛ teaspoon vanilla extract
3 or 4 ice cubes
Ground nutmeg, preferably freshly grated

Combine the cream, bourbon, sugar, vanilla extract and ice cubes in a mixing glass and place a bar shaker on top. Firmly grasp the glass and shaker together with both hands and shake vigorously 9 or 10 times. Remove the shaker, place a strainer over the mixing glass and pour the milk punch into a chilled old-fashioned glass. Sprinkle the top lightly with nutmeg and serve at once.

Absinthe Suissesse

To make 1 cocktail

1½ ounces Herbsaint, Pernod or Ojen
2 tablespoons light cream
1 egg white
1 tablespoon orgeat syrup
½ cup shaved or finely cracked ice

Combine the Herbsaint, Pernod or Ojen, cream, egg white, orgeat syrup and ice in the jar of an electric blender and blend at high speed for 5 seconds. Pour the absinthe *suissesse*, unstrained, into a chilled glass and serve at once with a short straw.

Gin Fizz

To make 1 tall drink

2 egg whites
4 teaspoons superfine sugar
½ cup light cream
2 ounces gin
4 teaspoons strained fresh lemon juice
½ teaspoon orange-flower water
¼ teaspoon vanilla extract
3 to 4 ice cubes

Combine the egg whites and sugar in a mixing glass and stir with a bar spoon until the sugar dissolves. Add the cream, gin, lemon juice, orange-flower water, vanilla extract and ice cubes.

Place a bar shaker on top of the mixing glass and, grasping the glass and shaker firmly together with both hands, shake vigorously 9 or 10 times. Remove the shaker, place a strainer over the mixing glass and pour the gin fizz into a chilled Tom Collins glass.

Light cream enriches a milk punch, an absinthe *suissesse* and a gin fizz, gentle concoctions to serve to guests on New Year's Day.

The Chinese Celebration

A Chinese New Year's dinner can comprise a dozen or more courses, include such festive dishes as Peking duck, bird's nest soup, sweet-and-sour pork, asparagus with mushroom sauce, chicken with broccoli or fried rice. It also traditionally includes egg rolls—representing gold bars, for riches—and something round, like shrimp balls, symbolizing freedom and happiness. The feast ends with fish, such as a steamed bass, since fish promises abundance in the year to come. A few of the ingredients of the recipes that follow are available only where Chinese specialties are sold. They can be ordered from the stores listed on page 105.

Egg Rolls with Shrimp and Pork

To make 16 egg rolls

THE FILLING

½ pound fresh bean sprouts or substitute a 1-pound can of bean sprouts
½ pound raw shrimp in their shells
3 tablespoons oil
½ pound lean boneless pork, finely ground
4 cups finely chopped celery
2 to 3 medium fresh mushrooms, cut in ¼-inch slices (about ½ cup)
1 tablespoon soy sauce
1 tablespoon Chinese rice wine, or pale dry sherry
2 teaspoons salt
½ teaspoon sugar
1 tablespoon cornstarch dissolved in 2 tablespoons cold chicken stock, fresh or canned, or cold water

THE WRAPPERS
2 cups flour
½ teaspoon salt
¾ cup cold water
1 egg, lightly beaten

Note: 1 pound ready-made egg-roll wrappers may be substituted for these homemade wrappers

3 cups peanut oil, or flavorless vegetable oil

PREPARE AHEAD: 1. Rinse the fresh bean sprouts in a pot of cold water and discard any husks that float to the surface. Drain and pat them dry with paper towels. To crisp canned bean sprouts, rinse them under running water and refrigerate them in a bowl of cold water for at least 2 hours. Drain and pat them dry before using.

2. Shell the shrimp. With a small, sharp knife, devein them by making a shallow incision down their backs and lifting out the black or white intestinal vein with the point of the knife. Using a cleaver or large knife, cut the shrimp into fine dice.

3. TO MAKE THE FILLING: Set a 12-inch wok or 10-inch skillet over high heat for 30 seconds. Pour in 1 tablespoon of oil, swirl it about in the pan and heat for another 30 seconds, turning the heat down to moderate if the oil begins to smoke. Add the pork and stir-fry for 2 minutes, or until it loses its reddish color. Then add the wine, soy sauce, sugar, shrimp and mushrooms, and stir-fry for another minute, or until the shrimp turn pink. Transfer the entire contents of the pan to a bowl and set aside.

Pour the remaining 2 tablespoons of oil into the same wok or skillet, swirl it about in the pan and heat for 30 seconds, turning the heat down to moderate if the oil begins to smoke. Add the celery and stir-fry for 5 minutes, then add the salt and bean sprouts, and mix thoroughly together. Return the pork and shrimp mixture to the pan, and stir until all the ingredients are well combined. Cook over moderate heat, stirring constantly, until the liquid starts to boil.

There should be about 2 or 3 tablespoons of liquid remaining in the pan. If there is more, spoon it out and discard it. Give the cornstarch mixture a quick stir to recombine it, and add it, stirring until the cooking liquids have thickened slightly and coated the mixture with a light glaze. Transfer the entire contents of the pan to a bowl and cool to room temperature before using.

4. TO MAKE THE WRAPPERS: Sift the flour and salt into a large mixing bowl. With a large spoon or your hands, gradually combine the flour and salt with the water, mixing until a stiff dough is formed. Knead the dough in the bowl for 5 minutes, or until it is smooth, then cover the

Marchers in a Chinese New Year's Eve parade *(right, top)* frolic through New York's Chinatown on the night of one of the year's most elaborate feasts. In San Francisco *(right, bottom)* demon-dispelling lions cavort on New Year's Day.

RATHSKELLER
RICE BOWL
BAR
FREE PARKING
PELL ST
WON FONG WO CO.

bowl with a dampened cloth and let it rest for 30 minutes. Turn the dough out on a lightly floured surface and firmly roll it out until it is no more than 1/16 inch thick. With a cookie cutter, pastry wheel or sharp knife, cut the dough into 7-inch squares. When you have finished, there should be 16 squares.

TO ASSEMBLE: For each egg roll, shape about 1/4 cup of filling with your hands into a cylinder about 4 inches long and an inch in diameter, and place it diagonally across the center of a wrapper. Lift the lower triangular flap over the filling and tuck the point under it, leaving the upper point of the wrapper exposed. Bring each of the two small end flaps, one at a time, up to the top of the enclosed filling and press the points firmly down. Brush the upper and exposed triangle of dough with lightly beaten egg and then roll the wrapper into a neat package. The beaten egg will seal the edges and keep the wrapper intact.

Place the filled egg rolls on a plate and cover them with a dry kitchen towel. If they must wait longer than about 30 minutes before being fried, cover them with plastic wrap and place them in the refrigerator.

TO COOK: Set a 12-inch wok or heavy deep-fryer over high heat, add 3 cups of oil and heat it until a haze forms above it or it reaches a temperature of 375° on a deep-frying thermometer. Place 5 or 6 egg rolls in the hot oil and deep-fry them for 3 to 4 minutes, or until they have become golden brown and are crisp. Transfer the egg rolls to a double thickness of paper towels and let the oil drain off while you deep-fry another batch of 5 or 6.

Serve the rolls as soon as possible, arranged attractively on a large heated platter. If necessary, the egg rolls can be kept warm for an hour or so in a preheated 250° oven, or they can be reheated for about 10 minutes in a 450° oven.

Deep-fried Shrimp Balls

To make about 2 dozen

1 slice fresh white bread

2 tablespoons cold chicken stock, fresh or canned, or cold water

1 pound uncooked shrimp in their shells

2 ounces fresh pork fat (1/4 cup)

4 peeled and washed fresh water chestnuts, finely chopped, or 4 drained canned water chestnuts, finely chopped

1 teaspoon salt

1/2 teaspoon finely chopped, peeled fresh ginger root

1 egg yolk

1 egg white

3 cups peanut oil, or flavorless vegetable oil

Roasted salt and pepper, prepared according to the following recipe

PREPARE AHEAD: 1. Trim crust from the bread and tear bread into small pieces. Place them in a bowl and sprinkle with the stock or water.

2. Shell the shrimp. With a small, sharp knife, make a shallow incision down their backs and lift out the intestinal vein with the point of the knife. Wash the shrimp under cold water and pat them dry with paper towels. With a cleaver or sharp knife, chop the shrimp and pork fat together until they form a smooth paste.

3. In a bowl, combine the soaked bread, shrimp mixture, water chestnuts, salt, ginger and egg yolk, and mix thoroughly. Beat the egg white to a froth with a fork or whisk, and stir it into the shrimp mixture.

4. Have the shrimp mixture, a bowl of cold water, a baking pan lined with a double thickness of paper towels, and the oil within easy reach.

TO COOK: Preheat the oven to its lowest setting. Pour 3 cups of oil into a 12-inch wok or large deep-fat fryer and heat until a haze forms above it or it reaches 350° on a deep-frying thermometer. Take a handful of the shrimp mixture and squeeze your fingers into a fist, forcing the mixture up between your thumb and forefinger. When it forms a ball about the size of a walnut, use a spoon to scoop off the ball and drop it in the hot oil. Repeat until you have made 6 to 8 balls, dipping the spoon into the bowl of cold water each time to prevent sticking. Turn them with a Chinese strainer or slotted spoon to keep the balls apart as they fry. They should become golden in 2 to 3 minutes. Transfer the fried balls to the paper-lined baking pan to drain and keep warm in the oven while you fry the rest. Transfer the finished shrimp balls to a heated platter and serve with roasted salt and pepper dip.

Roasted Salt and Pepper

To make about ¼ cup

Set a heavy 5- or 6-inch skillet over high heat, and pour in the salt and all the peppercorns. Turn the heat down to moderate and cook, stirring constantly, for 5 minutes, or until the mixture browns lightly. Be careful not to let it burn. Crush it to a fine powder with a mortar and pestle or wrap the mixture in wax paper and crush it with a kitchen mallet. Shake the crushed salt and pepper mixture through a fine sieve or strainer into a small bowl and serve it as a dip for deep-fried shrimp *(above)*.

5 tablespoons salt
1 tablespoon whole Szechwan peppercorns
½ teaspoon whole black peppercorns

Sweet-and-sour Pork

To serve 4 to 6

PREPARE AHEAD: 1. Trim the pork of any excess fat and, with a cleaver or sharp knife, cut the meat into 1-inch cubes.

2. In a large bowl, mix together the egg, ¼ cup cornstarch, ¼ cup flour, ¼ cup chicken stock and salt. Set aside.

3. For the sauce, have the oil, garlic, green pepper, carrot, chicken stock, sugar, vinegar, soy sauce and cornstarch mixture within easy reach.

TO COOK: Just before cooking, add the pork cubes to the egg and flour mixture, and stir until each piece of meat is well coated. Preheat the oven to 250°. Pour the 3 cups of oil into a 12-inch wok or deep-fat fryer and set it over high heat. When the oil almost begins to smoke or reaches 375° on a deep-frying thermometer, drop in half of the coated pork cubes one by one. Fry for 5 to 6 minutes, regulating the heat so that the pork turns a crisp, golden brown in that period without burning. Remove the pork with a strainer or slotted spoon to a small baking dish and keep it warm in the oven. Fry the other half and add to the first batch.

To make the sauce, use a 10-inch skillet. Set the pan over high heat for about 30 seconds. Pour in the tablespoon of oil, swirl it about in the pan and heat for another 30 seconds, turning the heat down to moderate if the oil begins to smoke. Add the garlic, then the green pepper and carrot, and stir-fry for 2 to 3 minutes until the pepper and carrot darken somewhat in color. Be careful not to let them burn. Pour in the ½ cup of chicken stock, the sugar, vinegar and soy sauce.

Bring to a boil, and boil rapidly for about 1 minute, or until the sugar has thoroughly dissolved. Immediately give the cornstarch mixture a quick stir to recombine it and add it to the pan. Cook a moment longer, stirring constantly. When the sauce is thick and clear, pour the entire contents of the pan over the fried pork and serve at once.

1 pound lean boneless pork, preferably butt
1 egg, lightly beaten
1 teaspoon salt
¼ cup cornstarch
¼ cup flour
¼ cup chicken stock, fresh or canned
3 cups peanut oil, or flavorless vegetable oil

SAUCE
1 tablespoon peanut oil, or flavorless vegetable oil
1 teaspoon finely chopped garlic
1 large green pepper, seeded, deribbed and cut into ½ inch squares
1 medium carrot, scraped and sliced into 2-inch strips ¼ inch wide and ¼ inch thick
½ cup chicken stock, fresh or canned
4 tablespoons sugar
4 tablespoons red-wine vinegar
1 teaspoon soy sauce
1 tablespoon cornstarch dissolved in 2 tablespoons cold water

Bird's Nest Soup

To serve 6

1 cup loosely packed dried bird's nest
1 whole chicken breast, about ¾ pound
¼ cup cold water
1 teaspoon cornstarch
1 teaspoon salt
2 egg whites
1 quart chicken stock, fresh or canned
⅛ teaspoon ground white pepper
2 tablespoons cornstarch dissolved in 3 tablespoons cold chicken stock, or cold water
A ⅛-inch-thick slice cooked Smithfield ham, minced

PREPARE AHEAD: 1. Place the bird's nest in a medium-sized bowl, add enough warm water to cover and soak the nest for 3 hours. Then, with a pair of tweezers, carefully remove any protruding feathers. Wash the nest thoroughly under running water. Place the bird's nest in a small saucepan, cover it with cold water and bring to a boil over high heat. Boil it uncovered for 5 minutes, then drain and discard the water.

2. Make chicken velvet in the following fashion: Lay the whole unsplit chicken breast on its side on a chopping board. Holding the breast firmly in place with one hand, cut it lengthwise along the curved breastbone with a cleaver or sharp knife. Carefully cut away all the meat from the bones, following the side of the breastbone and the outside of the ribs. Then grasp the meat in one hand and pull it off the bones and away from the skin—using the cleaver to free the meat if necessary. Turn the breast over and repeat on the other side. Remove each tube-shaped fillet from the rest of the breast meat, and pull out and discard the white tendons in each fillet. Slice the fillets lengthwise into thin strips. Holding the front of one main breast section, scrape the meat away from its membrane with repeated light strokes of the cleaver. Repeat with the other side of the breast.

Combine the breast meat with the fillets and then mince finely, adding about ¼ cup of water—a little at a time—as you work. Place the minced chicken in a mixing bowl, sprinkle it with the cornstarch and salt, and stir together gently but thoroughly with your hand or a large spoon. In a separate bowl, beat the egg whites with a fork or whisk until they are frothy, then pour them into the chicken mixture and mix thoroughly. The finished chicken velvet should be light and fluffy.

3. Have the bird's nest, chicken velvet, chicken stock, white pepper, cornstarch mixture and ham within easy reach.

TO COOK: In a 3- to 4-quart saucepan, bring the chicken stock to a boil over high heat. Drop in the bird's nest, bring to a boil again, then reduce the heat to low and simmer covered for 5 minutes. Add 1 teaspoon of salt and the white pepper. Give the cornstarch mixture a quick stir to recombine it and add it to the pan, stirring constantly and gently until the mixture thickens. Add the chicken velvet, stir once or twice to disperse it evenly through the soup and remove the pan from the heat. Pour the soup into a tureen, sprinkle the top with ham and serve at once.

Peking Duck

To serve 6

A 5-pound duck
6 cups water
¼ cup honey
4 slices peeled fresh ginger root, about 1 inch in diameter and ⅛ inch thick.
2 scallions, including the green tops, cut into 2-inch lengths

THE SAUCE
¼ cup *hoisin* sauce
1 tablespoon water
1 teaspoon sesame-seed oil
2 teaspoons sugar

12 scallions
Mandarin pancakes, prepared according to the recipe on page 102

PREPARE AHEAD: 1. Wash the duck under cold water, then pat dry inside and out with paper towels. Tie one end of a 20-inch length of white cord around the neck skin. If the skin has been cut away, loop the cord under the wings. Suspend the bird from the string in a cool, airy place for 3 hours to dry the skin, or train a fan on it for 2 hours.

2. In a 12-inch wok or large flameproof casserole, combine 6 cups water, ¼ cup honey, ginger root and cut scallions, and bring to a boil over high heat. Holding the duck by its string, lower it into the boiling liquid. With string in one hand and a spoon in the other, turn the duck from side to side until all of its skin is moistened with the liquid. Re-

The skin and meat of Peking duck are served separately, accompanied by scallion brushes, *hoisin* sauce and thin sesame-flavored pancakes.

move the duck (discarding the liquid) and hang it again in the cool place, setting a bowl beneath it to catch any drippings; the duck will dry in 1 hour with the fan trained upon it or 2 to 3 hours without it.

3. Make the sauce by combining *hoisin* sauce, water, sesame-seed oil and sugar in a small pan, and stirring until sugar dissolves. Bring to a boil, then reduce heat to its lowest point and simmer uncovered for 3 minutes. Pour into a small bowl, cool and reserve until ready to use.

4. To make scallion brushes, cut scallions down to 3-inch lengths and trim off roots. Standing each scallion on end, make four intersecting cuts 1 inch deep into its stalk. Repeat at other end. Place scallions in ice water and refrigerate until cut parts curl into brushlike fans.

TO COOK: Preheat oven to 375°. Untie the duck and cut off any loose neck skin. Place duck, breast side up, on a rack and set in a roasting pan just large enough to hold the bird. Roast the duck in the middle of the oven for one hour. Then lower the heat to 300°, turn the duck on its breast and roast for 30 minutes longer. Now raise the heat to 375°, return the duck to its original position and roast for a final half hour. Transfer the duck to a carving board.

With a small, sharp knife and your fingers, remove the crisp skin from the breast, sides and back of duck. Cut skin into 2-by-3-inch rectangles and arrange them in a single layer on a heated platter. Cut the wings and drumsticks from the duck, and cut all the meat away from breast and carcass. Slice meat into pieces 2½ inches long and ½ inch wide, and arrange them with the wings and drumsticks on a different heated platter.

To serve, place the platters of duck, the heated pancakes, the bowl of sauce and the scallion brushes in the center of the table. Traditionally, each guest spreads a pancake flat on his plate, dips a scallion in the sauce and brushes the pancake with it. The scallion is placed in the middle of the pancake with a piece of duck skin and a piece of meat on top. The pancake is folded over the scallion and duck, and tucked under. One end of the package is then folded over about 1 inch to enclose the filling, and the whole rolled into a cylinder that can be picked up with the fingers and eaten.

Mandarin Pancakes

To make 2 dozen pancakes

2 cups sifted all-purpose flour
3/4 cup boiling water
1 to 2 tablespoons sesame-seed oil

Sift flour into a mixing bowl, make a well in the center and pour into it the 3/4 cup of boiling water. With a wooden spoon, gradually mix flour and water together until a soft dough is formed; on a lightly floured surface, knead it gently for 10 minutes, or until smooth and elastic. Cover with a damp kitchen towel and let it rest for 15 minutes. On a lightly floured surface, roll dough into a circle about 1/4 inch thick. With a 2½-inch cookie cutter or a glass, cut as many circles of dough as you can. Knead scraps together, roll out again and cut more circles. Arrange circles side by side, brush half of them lightly with sesame-seed oil and, sandwich-wise, place the unoiled ones on top. With a rolling pin, flatten each pair into a 6-inch circle, rotating the sandwich an inch or so in a clockwise direction as you roll so that the circle keeps its shape, and turning it once to roll both sides. Cover the pancakes with a dry towel.

Set a heavy 8-inch skillet over high heat for 30 seconds. Reduce heat to moderate and cook the pancakes, one at a time, in the ungreased pan, turning them over as they puff up and little bubbles appear on the surface. Regulate the heat so that the pancakes become specked with brown after cooking about 1 minute on each side. As each pancake is finished, gently separate the halves and stack them on a plate. Serve them at once or wrap them in foil and refrigerate for later use. Or they may be wrapped and frozen, if you like. Reheat them (frozen pancakes need not be defrosted first) either by steaming them in a steamer for 10 minutes, or warming them, still wrapped in their foil, in a preheated 350° oven for about 10 minutes.

Chicken and Ham with Broccoli

To serve 6

A 4-pound roasting chicken, preferably freshly killed
3 slices cooked Smithfield ham, 1/8 inch thick, cut into 2-by-1-inch pieces
A 2-pound bunch broccoli
2 quarts chicken stock, fresh or canned, or 2 quarts cold water, or a combination of both
1 scallion, including the green top, cut into 2-inch pieces
4 slices peeled fresh ginger root, about 1 inch in diameter and 1/8 inch thick
1/4 teaspoon salt
1 teaspoon cornstarch dissolved in 1 tablespoon cold water

PREPARE AHEAD: 1. Wash the chicken inside and out under cold running water. Dry the chicken thoroughly with paper towels.

2. Cut off the broccoli flowerettes. Peel the stalks by cutting 1/8 inch deep into the skin and stripping it as if you were peeling an onion. Slice the stalks diagonally into 1-inch pieces, discarding the woody ends.

3. Have the chicken, ham, broccoli, chicken stock (or water), scallion, ginger and cornstarch mixture within easy reach.

TO COOK: In a heavy flameproof casserole or pot just large enough to hold the chicken snugly, bring the stock or water to a boil. Add the scallions and ginger, and place the chicken in the pot. The liquid should cover the chicken; add more boiling stock or water if it doesn't. Bring to a boil again, cover the pan, reduce the heat to low and simmer for 15 minutes. Then turn off the heat and let the chicken cool in the covered pot for 2 hours. The residual heat in the pot will cook the chicken through.

Transfer the chicken to a chopping board. (Reserve stock.) With a cleaver or knife, cut off wings and legs, and split the chicken in half lengthwise cutting through the breast and back bones. Cut the meat from the bones, leaving the skin in place. Then cut the meat into pieces about 2 inches long, 1 inch wide and ½ inch thick. Arrange the chicken and ham in alternating overlapped layers on a heated platter and cover with foil.

Pour 2 cups of the reserved stock into a 3-quart saucepan. Bring to a boil and drop in the broccoli. Return to a boil, turn off the heat, let it rest uncovered for 3 minutes, then remove the broccoli and arrange it around the chicken and ham. Or garnish the meat with only the flowerettes and serve the stems separately.

In a small saucepan, combine ½ cup of the stock with salt and bring to a boil. Give the cornstarch mixture a stir to recombine it and add it to the stock. When the stock thickens slightly and becomes clear, pour it over the chicken and ham. Serve at once.

Ham-and-Egg Fried Rice

To serve 3 to 4

½ cup shelled, fresh peas, or substitute thoroughly defrosted frozen peas
3 tablespoons peanut oil, or flavorless vegetable oil
2 eggs, lightly beaten
3 cups boiled rice
1 teaspoon salt
2 ounces boiled ham, sliced ¼ inch thick and cut into ¼-inch dice (about ½ cup)
1 scallion, including the green top, finely chopped

PREPARE AHEAD: 1. Blanch fresh peas by dropping them into 4 cups of boiling water and letting them boil uncovered for 5 to 10 minutes, or until tender. Then drain and run cold water over them to stop their cooking and set their color. Frozen peas need only be thoroughly defrosted.

2. Have the peas, oil, eggs, rice, salt, ham and scallions handy.

TO COOK: Set a 12-inch wok or 10-inch skillet over high heat for 30 seconds. Pour in 1 tablespoon of oil, swirl it about in the pan and immediately reduce the heat to moderate. Pour in the beaten eggs. They will form a film on the bottom of the pan almost at once. Immediately lift this film gently with a fork and push it to the back of the pan so that the still-liquid eggs can spread across the bottom of the pan to cook. As soon as the eggs are set, but before they become dry or begin to brown, transfer them to a small bowl and break them up with a fork. Pour the remaining 2 tablespoons of oil into the pan, swirl it around and heat it for 30 seconds. Add the rice and stir-fry for 2 to 3 minutes until all the grains are coated with oil. Add the salt, then the peas and ham, and stir-fry for 20 seconds. Return the eggs to the pan, add the scallions and cook only long enough to heat the eggs through. Serve at once.

Asparagus Tips with Chinese-Mushroom Sauce

To serve 4

2 ounces dried Chinese mushrooms
2 cups chicken stock, fresh or canned
¼ cup Chinese oyster sauce
2 tablespoons soy sauce
4 teaspoons sugar
2 tablespoons cornstarch combined with ¼ cup cold water
2 pounds firm fresh asparagus, or two 10-ounce packages frozen asparagus, thoroughly defrosted

Place the mushrooms in a small bowl, pour in enough warm water to cover them by at least 1 inch and let them soak for 30 minutes. Drain the mushrooms in a sieve and discard the water. Cut off and discard the mushroom stems, and cut each cap into eight pieces.

Combine the mushrooms, chicken stock, oyster sauce, soy sauce and

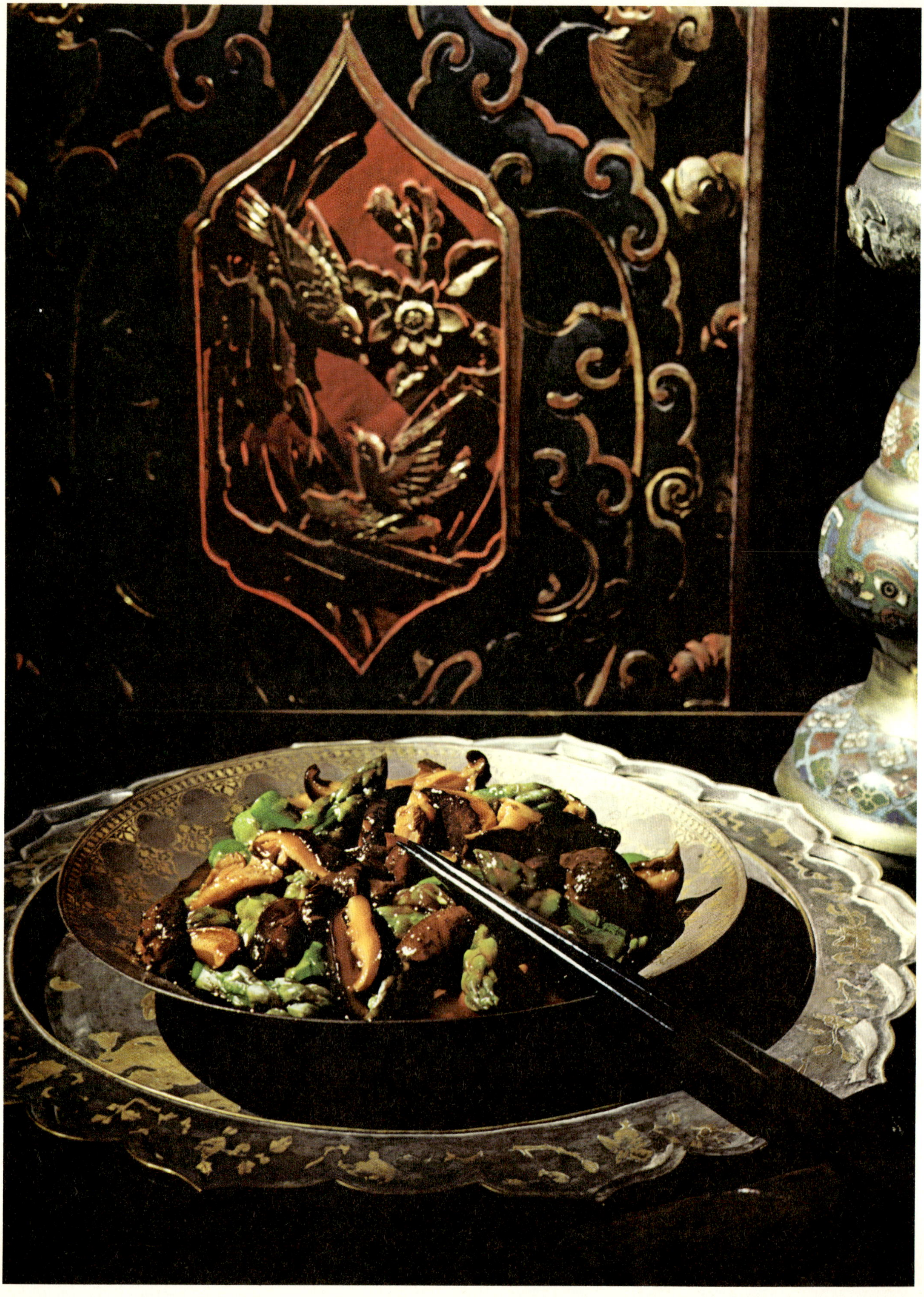

sugar in a 12-inch *wok* or heavy 8- to 10-inch skillet and, stirring constantly, bring to a boil over high heat. Reduce the heat to low, cover partially and simmer for about 45 minutes, or until the mushrooms are tender. Give the cornstarch-and-water mixture a quick stir to recombine it and, stirring constantly, pour it into the mushroom sauce in a slow, thin stream. Stir over moderate heat until the sauce comes to a boil, thickens lightly and is clear. Taste for seasoning.

Meanwhile, with a sharp knife, cut off the top 2 inches of each asparagus spear. Reserving the remaining pieces of asparagus for another use, drop the tips into enough lightly salted boiling water to cover them by at least 2 inches. Cook briskly, uncovered, for about 5 minutes, or until the tips are barely tender and show only slight resistance when pierced with the point of a small sharp knife.

Drain the asparagus tips in a colander, then transfer them to a heated bowl. Pour the mushroom sauce over the asparagus and serve at once.

Steamed Sea Bass with Fermented Black Beans

PREPARE AHEAD: 1. Wash the bass under cold running water and pat it dry inside and out with paper towels. With a sharp knife, lightly score the fish by making diagonal cuts ¼ inch deep at ½-inch intervals on both sides. Then sprinkle the fish, inside and out, with the salt.

2. With a cleaver or knife, coarsely chop the fermented beans, then combine them in a bowl with the soy sauce, wine, oil and sugar. Mix well.

3. Lay the fish on a heatproof platter ½ inch smaller in diameter than the pot you plan to steam it in. Pour the bowl of seasonings over the fish, and arrange the pieces of ginger and scallion on top.

TO COOK: Pour enough boiling water into the lower part of a steamer to come within an inch of the cooking rack, or make a steamer substitute by setting the plate on two small heatproof dishes set right side up in a large, tightly covered roasting pan. There must be enough space around the edge of the plate for the steam to circulate freely. Bring the water in the steamer to a rolling boil and place the platter of fish on the rack. Cover the pot securely. Keep the water in the steamer at a continuous boil and replenish it if it boils away. Steam the fish for about 15 minutes, or until it is firm to the touch. Serve at once on its own steaming platter placed on top of a serving dish.

To serve 4

A 1½-pound sea bass, cleaned but with head and tail left on (or substitute any other firm white fish)
1 teaspoon salt
2 teaspoons fermented black beans
1 tablespoon soy sauce
1 tablespoon Chinese rice wine, or pale dry sherry
1 tablespoon finely shredded, peeled fresh ginger root
1 scallion, including the green top, cut into 2-inch lengths
1 tablespoon peanut oil, or flavorless vegetable oil
½ teaspoon sugar

Tender tips of pale-green asparagus glisten under a silky coating of Chinese-mushroom sauce, which in turn has been sharpened with soy and oyster sauces.

The following stores will fill mail orders for hard-to-find Chinese recipe ingredients:

New Frontier Trading Corp.
2394 Broadway
New York, N.Y. 10024

Star Market
3349 North Clark Street
Chicago, Ill. 60657

Manley Produce
1101 Grant Avenue
San Francisco, Calif. 94133

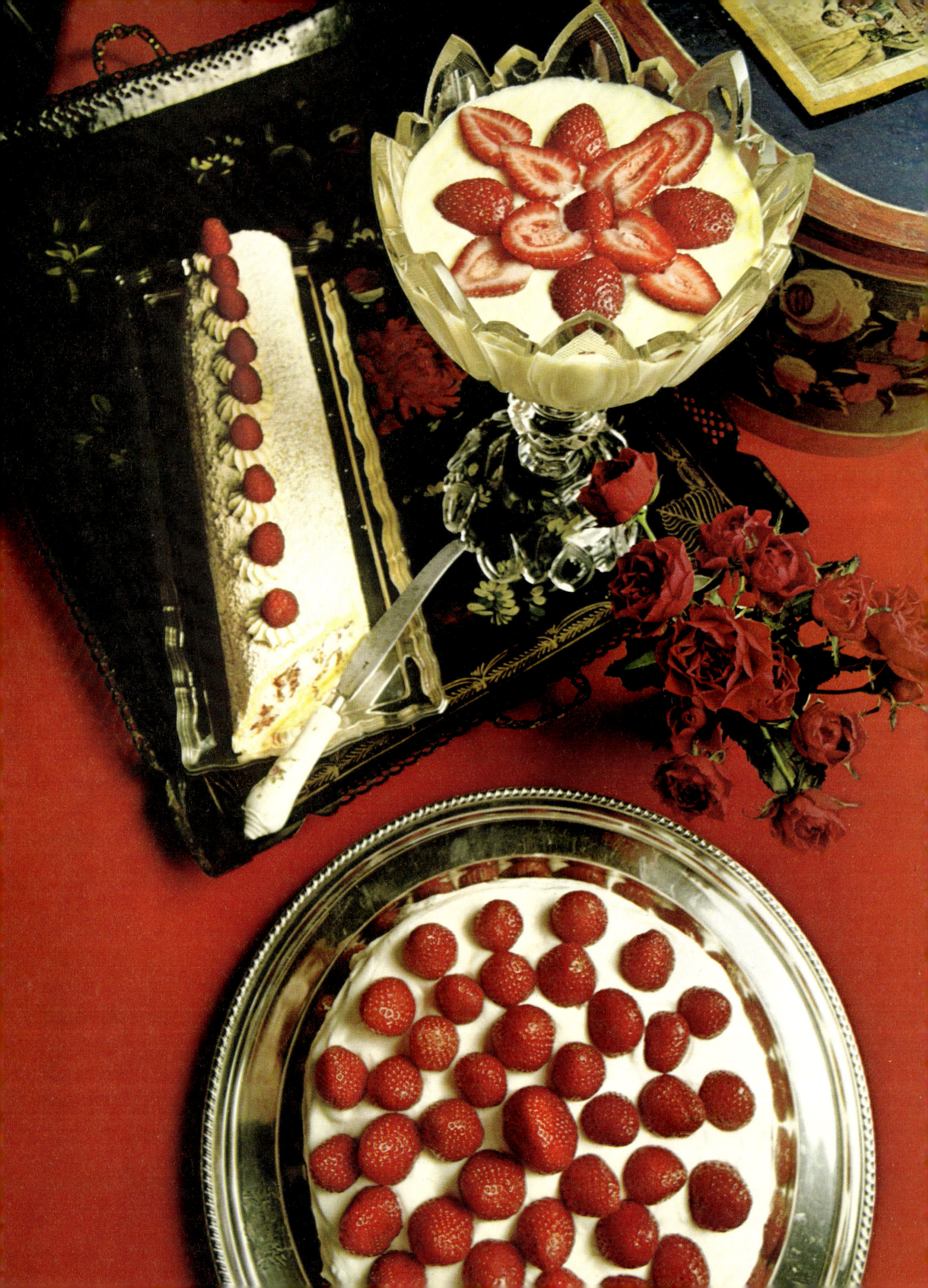

St. Valentine's Day
Mardi Gras
Washington's Birthday
Purim
St. Patrick's Day

Winter Revels

By the time chill, gray February comes, followed by blustery March, winter often seems to have outstayed its welcome. But a series of special holidays arrive—one dedicated to lovers, one to a patriot, plus two religious days and a pagan carnival—to lift the flagging spirit. St. Valentine's Day calls for homemade candies or a lovingly cooked February 14 dinner, crowned with a creamy dessert decorated with heart-shaped strawberries. Cherries in honor of Washington's Birthday are usually baked into a crusty pie, but they are equally delicious flamed in cherries jubilee or chilled with wine and cinnamon to make an exotic soup.

So eager are its celebrants to ban midwinter doldrums that the season of Mardi Gras begins right after the New Year, and the carnival spirit intensifies until the fasting time of Lent calls a stop. Mardi Gras is associated with New Orleans and glorious Creole dishes in the United States, but in other countries it means using up all the fat and the butter in the house before Lent—in doughnuts and pancakes and Russian bliny topped with caviar or jam. Purim's sweet cakes and St. Patrick's Day corned beef and Irish coffee also help to banish winter and set the stage for spring.

These three desserts are perfect endings for a St. Valentine's Day dinner. Heart-red strawberries decorate a whipped-cream roll, a delicate flummery custard and a four-layered spongecake.

Valentine strawberries and candies

Mardi Gras gumbo

Carnival Kings' cake

Russian festival bliny and caviar

Shrove Tuesday buns and Fasching doughnuts

Seven cherry recipes for Washington's Birthday

Purim cake and cookies

St. Patrick's Day corned beef

Irish stew and Irish coffee

Winter Recipes

Sweets for Valentines

Sweets for the sweet can be as heart-red as strawberries now that these berries are available almost everywhere in February. Maids-of-honor almond tarts and homemade candies also carry the message of love.

Strawberry Cream Roll

Preheat the oven to 400°. With a pastry brush, spread 1 tablespoon of the softened butter over the bottom and sides of a 16-by-11-inch jelly-roll pan. Line the pan with a 20-inch-long strip of wax paper and let the extra paper extend over the edges. Brush the remaining tablespoon of butter over the paper in the pan and sprinkle it with 2 tablespoons of the flour. Tip the pan from side to side to spread the flour evenly, then turn the pan over and rap it sharply to remove the excess flour. Combine the remaining ½ cup of flour with the salt and sift them together on a plate or piece of wax paper. Set aside.

With a wire whisk or a rotary or electric beater, beat the egg whites until they are stiff enough to stand in unwavering peaks on the beater when it is lifted from the bowl. In another bowl and with the same beater, beat the egg yolks, ¼ cup of the granulated sugar and the vanilla together for 4 or 5 minutes, until the mixture is thick.

Sprinkle the sifted flour on top of the egg whites, pour the yolk mixture over them and, with a rubber spatula, fold together lightly but thoroughly, using an over-under cutting motion rather than a stirring motion.

Pour the batter into the paper-lined pan, spread it into the corners with the spatula and smooth the top. Bake in the middle of the oven for 15 minutes, or until the cake begins to shrink from the sides of the pan and a cake tester or toothpick inserted in the center comes out clean.

Remove the pan from the oven and carefully turn the cake out onto a fresh sheet of wax paper. Gently peel off the layer of paper from the top of the cake and trim the edges of the cake with a sharp knife. Starting at one long edge, roll the cake into a loose cylinder. Set aside to cool to room temperature.

Wash the strawberries in a sieve or colander set under cold running water and pick out and discard any bruised or blemished berries. Spread the berries on paper towels to drain and pat them dry with paper towels.

In a chilled bowl, whip the cream with a wire whisk or a rotary or electric beater until the cream thickens lightly. Add the remaining ¼ cup of granulated sugar and continue to beat until the cream is stiff enough to form unwavering peaks on the beater when it is lifted from the bowl. Ladle about ⅓ cup of the cream into a pastry bag fitted with a star tube. With a rubber spatula, fold 1½ cups of the strawberries into the remaining cream.

To make one 15-inch cake roll

2 tablespoons butter, softened
2 tablespoons plus ½ cup unsifted flour
⅛ teaspoon salt
4 egg whites
4 egg yolks
½ cup granulated sugar
½ teaspoon vanilla extract
2 cups ripe fresh strawberries
2 cups heavy cream, chilled
3 tablespoons confectioners' sugar

To assemble the cake, unroll it and spread the top evenly with the strawberry cream. Carefully roll up the cake again and place it on a serving plate. Sprinkle the roll evenly with the confectioners' sugar and pipe rosettes of cream on top. Decorate each rosette with one of the reserved strawberries. Serve at once or refrigerate until ready to serve.

Strawberry Flummery

To serve 4 to 6

½ cup plus 2 tablespoons sugar
⅓ cup cornstarch
¼ teaspoon salt
3 cups milk
1 egg yolk, lightly beaten
1 teaspoon vanilla extract
1 pint firm ripe strawberries

Combine ½ cup of the sugar, the cornstarch and salt in a heavy 2- to 3-quart saucepan and, stirring the mixture constantly with a wire whisk, pour in the milk in a slow, thin stream. Whisking constantly, cook over moderate heat until the mixture comes to a boil and thickens heavily. Reduce the heat to its lowest setting.

Ladle several tablespoonfuls of the liquid into the beaten egg yolk, mix well and, still whisking, gradually pour the yolk into the simmering liquid. Simmer for 3 or 4 minutes longer to cook the egg yolk through, but do not let the mixture come anywhere near a boil.

Remove the pan from the heat and stir in the vanilla. Cool to room temperature, then pour the flummery into a serving bowl. Cover with wax paper and refrigerate for at least 2 hours, or until the flummery is thoroughly chilled.

Just before serving, pick over the strawberries, removing the hulls and discarding any blemished berries. Wash the strawberries briefly in a sieve or colander set under cold running water. Spread the berries on paper towels and pat them completely dry with fresh towels. Cut each berry in half lengthwise. Place the halves in a bowl, add the remaining 2 tablespoons of sugar, and toss gently together with a wooden spoon to coat the berries evenly. Arrange the strawberries attractively on top of the flummery and serve at once.

Strawberry Spongecake

To make one 9-inch 4-layer cake

1 quart firm ripe strawberries
¾ cup plus 2 tablespoons sugar
2 tablespoons butter, softened
2 tablespoons plus 1 cup unsifted flour
A pinch of salt
6 egg whites
6 egg yolks
2 teaspoons vanilla extract
2 cups heavy cream, chilled

Pick over the strawberries, removing the hulls and discarding any blemished berries. Wash the strawberries briefly in a large sieve or colander set under cold running water. Then spread them on paper towels to drain and pat them completely dry with fresh towels.

Select 2 cups of the most attractive berries and set them aside. Drop the remaining berries into a bowl, add ¼ cup of the sugar, and mash the berries to a thick purée by beating them against the sides of the bowl with the back of a spoon. Cover the bowl with foil or plastic wrap and let the puréed strawberries steep at room temperature until ready to serve.

Preheat the oven to 350°. With a pastry brush, spread the softened butter evenly over the bottom and sides of two 9-inch layer-cake pans. Add 1 tablespoon of the flour to each pan and tip it from side to side to spread the flour evenly. Invert the pans and rap their bottoms sharply to remove the excess flour.

Combine the remaining cup of flour and the salt and sift them together onto a plate or a sheet of wax paper. Set aside.

With a wire whisk or a rotary or electric beater, beat the egg whites until they are stiff enough to stand in unwavering peaks on the beater when it is lifted from the bowl. In another bowl and with the same beater, beat the egg yolks, ½ cup of the sugar, and 1 teaspoon of the vanilla together until they are thick and lemon-colored.

Sprinkle the sifted flour and salt over the egg whites, pour the egg-yolk mixture over them and, with a rubber spatula, fold together lightly but thoroughly, using an over-and-under cutting motion rather than a stirring motion.

Pour the batter into the buttered-and-floured pans, dividing it equally among them. Spread the batter and smooth the tops with the spatula. Bake in the middle of the oven for about 20 minutes, or until the cakes begin to shrink away from the sides of the pans and a cake tester or toothpick inserted in the centers comes out clean. Let the cakes cool in the pans for 4 or 5 minutes, then turn them out onto wire racks to cool completely to room temperature.

About half an hour before serving the cake, pour the cream into a large chilled bowl and whip it with a wire whisk or a rotary or electric beater. As soon as the cream becomes frothy, add the remaining 2 tablespoons of sugar and 1 teaspoon of vanilla. Continue to beat until the cream is stiff enough to stand in firm, unwavering peaks on the beater when it is lifted out of the bowl.

To assemble, slice each cake in half horizontally to make four thin layers. Place one of the layers, cut side up, on a serving plate and, with a metal spatula, spread it with about ½ cup of the puréed strawberries. Repeat two more times, spreading the third layer of the cake with all of the remaining puréed berries.

Carefully put the fourth layer on the top, cut side down. Then spread the whipped cream smoothly over the top and sides of the strawberry cake. Cut a dozen or so of the reserved 2 cups of whole strawberries in half lengthwise and set them on the plate, cut side up, in a ring around the cake. Arrange the remaining whole strawberries attractively on the top of the cake and serve at once.

Maids of Honor

Preheat the oven to 400°. With a pastry brush and the 2 tablespoons of softened butter, coat the inside surfaces of 2 medium-sized 12-cup muffin tins (each cup should be about 2½ inches across at the top). Sprinkle 4 tablespoons of the flour into the tins, tipping them to coat the bottoms and sides of the cups evenly. Then invert the tins and rap them sharply on a table to remove the excess flour.

On a lightly floured surface, roll the short-crust pastry into a circle about ¼ inch thick, and with a cookie cutter or the rim of a glass, cut it into 3-inch rounds. Gather the scraps together into a ball, roll it out into another circle, and cut out rounds as before. Gently fit the rounds into the cups of the muffin tins, pushing the pastry firmly into the sides. The pastry shells will be about 1 inch deep, and will not fill the cups completely.

In a mixing bowl, beat the egg yolks with a whisk to break them up.

To make about 18 tarts

2 tablespoons butter, softened
5 tablespoons flour
Short crust pastry *(page 45)*
2 egg yolks
½ cup sugar
½ cup blanched almonds, pulverized in a blender or with a nut grinder or a mortar and pestle
1 tablespoon finely grated lemon peel
2 tablespoons heavy cream

These gypsy creams are romantically named for a 19th Century Hungarian violinist who is reputed to have broken the hearts of princesses.

Then beat in the sugar, almonds, lemon peel and the remaining tablespoon of flour. Slowly add the cream and beat until the mixture is smooth. Ladle about 1 tablespoon of the mixture into each of the pastry shells, filling them to within ⅛ inch of the top.

Bake in the middle of the oven for 15 to 20 minutes, or until the filling is a light golden brown. Carefully remove the tarts from the tins and cool them to room temperature on cake racks. Maids of honor are traditionally served at afternoon tea.

NOTE: In some parts of England, jam or bread crumbs are added to the filling, and it is not uncommon to find the tarts topped with two crossed strips of the pastry.

Gypsy Creams

Preheat the oven to 350°. With a pastry brush or paper towel, butter an 11-by-17-inch jelly-roll pan and sprinkle the flour over the butter. Tap the edge of the pan on a table to knock out the excess flour.

Melt the chocolate over low heat in a heavy 1-quart saucepan or in the top of a double boiler placed over simmering water. Set the chocolate aside to cool to lukewarm. Cream the butter and ¼ cup of the sugar by beating them against the side of a mixing bowl with a wooden spoon, continuing to beat until the mixture is light and fluffy. Add the melted chocolate and beat in the egg yolks, one at a time.

In another mixing bowl preferably of unlined copper, beat the egg whites and a pinch of salt with a wire whisk or rotary beater until the whites cling to the beater; add the remaining ¼ cup of sugar and beat until the whites form stiff, unwavering peaks. With a rubber spatula, stir about ⅓ of the whites into the chocolate base, then pour the chocolate mixture over the rest of the whites. Sprinkle the flour lightly on top. Gently fold the flour into the mixture until no white streaks are visible.

Pour the batter into the prepared jelly-roll pan, spreading it evenly with a rubber spatula. Bake in the middle of the oven for 15 to 18 minutes, or until the cake shrinks slightly away from the sides of the pan and a knife inserted in the middle comes out clean. Remove the cake from the oven, loosen it from the pan by running a sharp knife around the sides, and turn it out on a rack to cool.

THE FILLING: In a heavy 1-quart saucepan, combine the cream and chocolate, and stir over medium heat until the chocolate dissolves. Then reduce the heat to very low and simmer, stirring almost constantly, until the mixture thickens into a heavy cream. Pour it into a bowl and refrigerate for at least 1 hour. When the mixture is very cold, pour in the rum and vanilla and beat with a wire whisk or a rotary or electric beater until the filling is smooth and creamy and forms soft peaks when the beater is lifted from the bowl. Do not overbeat or the cream will turn to butter.

Cut the cake in half to make two layers, each 8½ inches wide. Over one layer spread the filling, which will be about 2 inches thick. Set the other layer on top. Refrigerate on a rack for about 1 hour.

To make 35 cream slices

THE CAKE
2 tablespoons butter
2 tablespoons flour
3 ounces unsweetened chocolate
¾ cup (1½ quarter-pound sticks) unsalted butter, softened
½ cup sugar
4 eggs, separated
Pinch of salt
½ cup sifted all-purpose flour

THE FILLING
1½ cups heavy cream
10 ounces semisweet chocolate, broken or chopped into small chunks
4 tablespoons dark rum
1 teaspoon vanilla extract

THE GLAZE

1 cup fine granulated sugar
⅓ cup water
7 ounces semisweet chocolate, broken or chopped into small chunks

THE GLAZE: While the cake is refrigerating, make the glaze. In a heavy 1-quart saucepan, heat the sugar, water and chocolate over medium heat, stirring constantly, until the sugar and chocolate are dissolved. Remove the pan from the heat, cover and let the glaze cool for about 20 minutes.

Set the rack holding the cake on a jelly-roll pan and, holding the saucepan with the glaze 2 inches above the cake, pour the glaze over it. Refrigerate the cake on the rack 20 minutes longer, or until the glaze is firm.

Serve by cutting it into 35 small equal pieces, 5 in each row across and 7 in each row down. Use a sharp knife that has been dipped in warm water. Rinse the knife and dip it again in warm water before each cutting.

To make about 36 one-inch balls

1 teaspoon butter, softened
1 pound maple sugar
1 cup sugar
1 cup heavy cream
½ teaspoon cream of tartar
1 cup walnuts, pulverized in a blender or with a nut grinder

Maple-Walnut Fudge Balls

With a pastry brush, spread the softened butter evenly over the bottom and sides of an 8-by-6-by-2-inch baking dish.

If the maple sugar is moist, grate it on the finest side of a stand-up hand grater. If it is dry, grate it with a nut grinder. (There should be about 2 cups, packed, of grated maple sugar.) Combine the maple sugar, white sugar, cream and cream of tartar in a heavy 3- to 4-quart saucepan. Bring to a boil over high heat, stirring until the sugar dissolves. Reduce the heat and boil slowly, uncovered and undisturbed, until the syrup reaches a temperature of 240° on a candy thermometer, or until a few drops spooned into ice water immediately form a soft ball.

Pour the fudge into the buttered dish, cool to room temperature, then chill in the refrigerator for at least 3 hours. Transfer the fudge to a deep bowl and, with an electric beater or wooden spoon, beat it until light and creamy. Pinch off about 1 tablespoon of the fudge and roll it between the palms of your hands until it forms a ball about 1 inch in diameter. Roll it gently in the pulverized walnuts and when the entire surface is lightly coated set it aside on a platter. Refrigerate until ready to serve.

To make about 30 one-inch squares

2 cups light brown sugar, firmly packed
2 cups white sugar
2 cups light cream
1 teaspoon butter, softened
½ teaspoon vanilla extract

Penuche

Combine the brown sugar, white sugar and cream in a heavy 3- to 4-quart saucepan and stir over moderate heat until the sugar dissolves. Raise the heat and boil briskly, uncovered and undisturbed, until the candy reaches a temperature of 238° on a candy thermometer, or until a few drops spooned into ice water immediately form a soft but compact ball. Watch the candy carefully and when it begins to bubble up in the pan, reduce the heat for a few moments. If sugar crystals appear around the inside of the pan, brush them back into the candy with a natural bristled (not nylon) pastry brush that has been lightly moistened with water.

Remove the pan from the heat and let the candy cool for about 5 minutes. Meanwhile, with a dry pastry brush, spread the softened butter evenly over the bottom and sides of an 8-by-6-by-2-inch baking dish.

When the candy has cooled slightly, beat it with a wooden spoon until it is thick enough to hold its shape almost solidly in the spoon. Beat in the vanilla, then pour the penuche into the buttered dish, spreading it and smoothing the top with the spoon or a spatula. Cool to room temperature, then cut the candy into 1-inch squares.

Almond Nougat

Preheat the oven to 350°. Spread the almonds in one layer in a shallow baking dish and, stirring occasionally, toast them in the middle of the oven for about 5 minutes, or until they are delicately browned. Remove the dish from the oven and set the almonds aside. With a pastry brush, spread the tablespoon of softened butter evenly over a large baking sheet. Set the baking sheet aside.

Combine ½ cup of the granulated sugar and 1 cup of the corn syrup in a heavy 2- to 3-quart saucepan and stir over moderate heat until the sugar dissolves. Raise the heat and boil briskly, uncovered and undisturbed, until the syrup reaches a temperature of 248° on a candy thermometer, or until a few drops spooned into ice water immediately forms a firm but still slightly pliable ball.

Watch the syrup carefully and when it begins to bubble and rise in the pan, reduce the heat for a few moments. When sugar crystals appear inside the pan, brush them back into the syrup with a natural-bristle (not nylon) pastry brush that has been lightly moistened with water.

Meanwhile, in the large bowl of a stationary electric beater, beat the egg whites at medium speed until they are stiff enough to stand in soft peaks on the beater when it is lifted out of the bowl.

Beating constantly at medium speed, pour in the syrup in a slow, thin stream and continue to beat for 4 to 5 minutes, or until the mixture is thick and begins to stiffen. Turn off the machine and let the candy mixture stand at room temperature while you prepare a second batch of syrup.

In a heavy 3- to 4-quart saucepan, combine the remaining 2 cups of granulated sugar, the remaining ¾ cup of corn syrup and the water, and stir over moderate heat until the sugar dissolves. Raise the heat and boil briskly, uncovered and undisturbed, until the syrup reaches a temperature of 272° on a candy thermometer, or until a drop spooned into ice water immediately separates into hard, but not brittle, threads. Watch the syrup carefully and adjust the heat when necessary.

Beating constantly at medium speed, pour the second batch of syrup into the egg-white-and-syrup mixture in a slow, thin stream. Continue to beat for about 10 minutes longer, or until the candy becomes opaque and creamy, then beat in the 2 tablespoons of butter bits and the confectioners' sugar, vanilla extract and salt. With a wooden spoon, stir in the reserved toasted almonds.

Working quickly, spread the nougat mixture in the buttered baking dish. Pat it to a thickness of about ¾ inch with the palms of your hands and smooth the top with a rolling pin. When the nougat cools to room temperature, cover it with wax paper and set it aside in a cool place (not the refrigerator) for at least 12 hours.

Cut the nougat into 1¼-inch squares and serve at once. Or packet each piece in a square of foil or plastic wrap and store the nougat in a tightly covered jar or tin until ready to serve.

To make about eighty 1¼-inch squares

1½ cups coarsely chopped almonds (about ½ pound)
1 tablespoon butter, softened, plus 2 tablespoons butter, cut into ½-inch bits
2½ cups granulated sugar
1¾ cups light corn syrup
3 egg whites
⅓ cup water
¾ cup confectioners' sugar
1 teaspoon vanilla extract
½ teaspoon salt

Mardi Gras Time

The gayest midwinter revel of all is the one called Mardi Gras—Fat Tuesday—in French, Fasching in German. In England it is Shrove Tuesday, in Latin countries Carnival. Its festivities start on Twelfth Night, and continue until Ash Wednesday, when Lent begins, putting an end to the feasting and the partying.

Crab, Shrimp and Okra Gumbo

To serve 4

- 1 pound uncooked medium-sized shrimp (about 20 to 24 to the pound)
- 7 quarts water
- 5 dried hot red chilies, each about 2 inches long (*caution: see note at end of recipe*)
- 1 lemon, cut crosswise into ¼-inch-thick slices
- 3 large bay leaves
- 1½ teaspoons crumbled, dried thyme
- 1 tablespoon plus 1 teaspoon salt
- 10 live blue crabs, each about 8 ounces
- 4 tablespoons brown *roux (page 118)*
- ½ cup coarsely chopped onions
- 1½ teaspoons finely chopped garlic
- ½ pound fresh okra, trimmed, washed and cut into 1-inch chunks
- ¾ cup coarsely chopped green pepper
- 1 teaspoon ground hot red pepper (cayenne)
- ½ teaspoon Tabasco sauce
- 4 to 6 cups freshly cooked long-grain white rice

Shell the shrimp. Devein them by making a shallow incision down their backs with a small knife and lifting out the intestinal vein with the point of the knife. Wash the shrimp briefly and set them aside.

In a 10- to 12-quart pot, bring the water, chilies, lemon slices, 2 bay leaves, 1 teaspoon of thyme and 1 tablespoon of salt to a boil over high heat. Drop in the crabs and boil briskly, uncovered, for 5 minutes. Remove the crabs from the stock with tongs, and set them aside to cool.

Drop the shrimp into the stock remaining in the pot and cook uncovered for 3 to 5 minutes, or until they are pink and firm to the touch. With tongs, transfer the shrimp to a plate. Then boil the stock, uncovered, until it is reduced to 3 quarts. Strain the stock through a fine sieve set over a large pot, and discard the seasonings. Cover the pot to keep the stock warm until you are ready to use it.

When the crabs are cool enough to handle, shell them in the following fashion: Grasping the body of the crab firmly in one hand, break off the large claws and legs close to the body. With the point of a small sharp knife, pry off the pointed shell, or apron, and loosen the large bottom shell from around the meat and cartilage, cutting near the edges where the legs are joined to the shell. Lift the body of the crab, break it in half lengthwise, then with the knife pick out the firm white pieces of meat. Discard the gray featherlike gills and tough bits of cartilage but save the morsels of yellow liver and "fat" as well as any pieces of orange roe. Leave the large claws in their shells, but crack the legs lengthwise with a cleaver and pick out the meat. Reserve the meat, claws and roe (if any).

In a heavy 5- to 6-quart casserole, warm the *roux* over low heat, stirring constantly. Add the onions and garlic and stir for about 5 minutes, or until they are soft. Add the okra and green peppers and mix well.

Stirring constantly, pour in the reserved warm stock in a slow, thin stream and bring to a boil over high heat. (If the stock has cooled, reheat before adding it.) Add the red pepper, Tabasco, the remaining bay leaf, ½ teaspoon of thyme and 1 teaspoon of salt. Stir in the crabmeat and claws, reduce the heat to low and simmer, partially covered, for 1 hour.

Add the shrimp and simmer a few minutes longer, then taste for seasoning. The gumbo may require more Tabasco or red pepper.

Ladle the gumbo into a heated tureen and serve at once, accompanied by the rice in a separate bowl. Traditionally, a cupful of rice is mounded

During the afternoon of Mardi Gras, guests still clad in parade costumes gather at a New Orleans home for a late buffet lunch, featuring seafood gumbo, a dish as much associated with New Orleans as Mardi Gras itself.

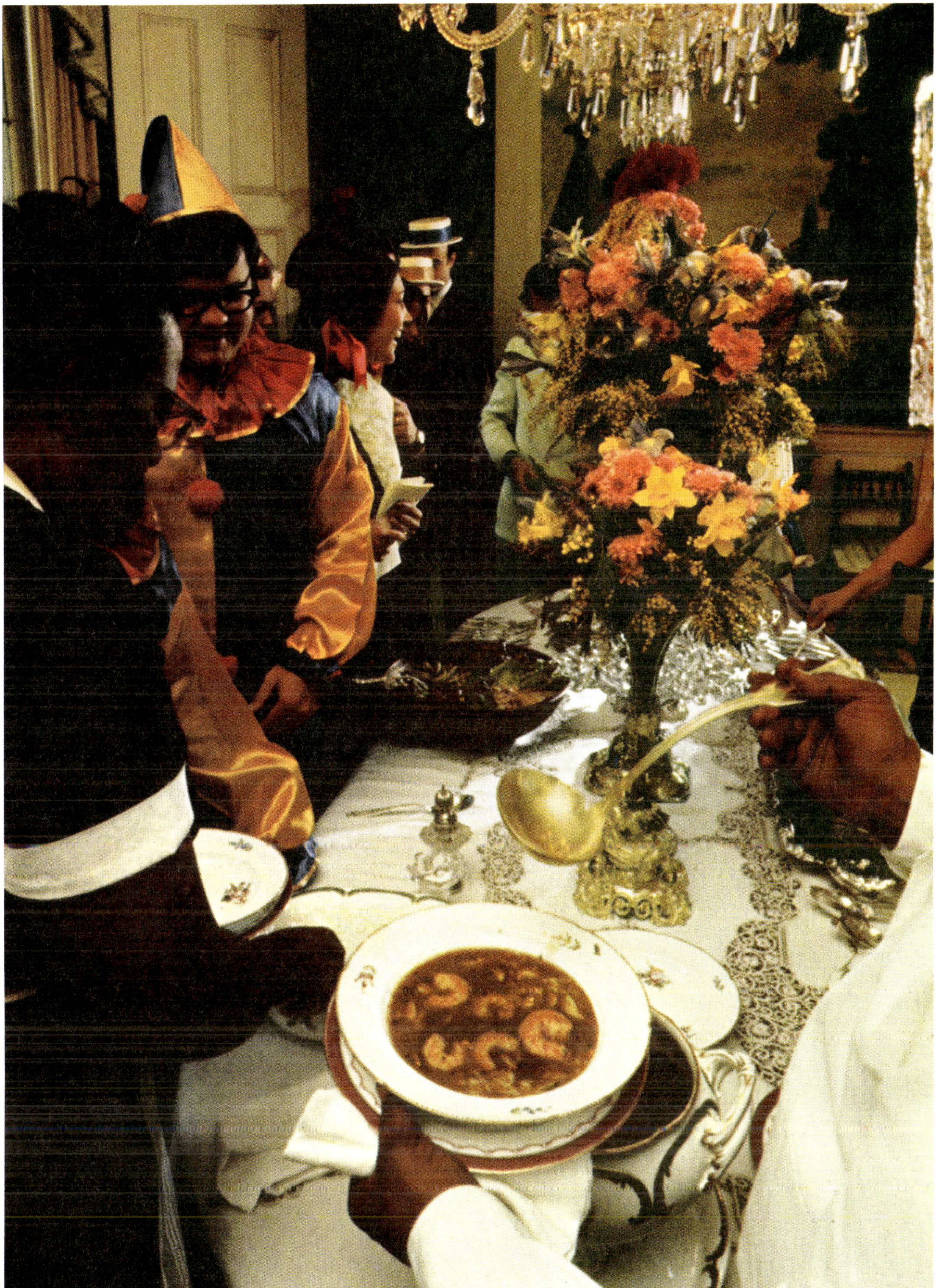

in a heated soup plate and the gumbo spooned around it. Give each diner a nutcracker so that the claws can be cracked easily at the table.

NOTE: Hot chilies require special handling. Their volatile oils may make your skin tingle and your eyes burn. While working with the chilies, wear rubber gloves if you can and be careful not to touch your face. To prepare chilies, rinse them clean under cold running water. (Hot water may cause fumes to rise from dried chilies, and even these fumes can irritate your nose and eyes.) After handling hot chilies it is essential that you wash your hands and gloves thoroughly with soap and water.

Louisiana Brown Roux

To make about 11 tablespoons

8 tablespoons unsifted all-purpose flour
8 tablespoons vegetable oil

Combine the flour and oil in a heavy 10-inch skillet (preferably cast-iron or enameled iron) and, with a large metal spatula, stir them to a smooth paste. Place the skillet over the lowest possible heat and, stirring constantly, simmer the *roux* slowly for 45 minutes to an hour.

After 5 minutes or so the mixture will begin to foam and this foaming may continue for as long as 10 minutes. After about half an hour, the *roux* will begin to darken and have a faintly nutty aroma. Continue to cook slowly, stirring with the spatula, until the *roux* is a dark rich brown. (During the last 5 minutes or so of cooking, the *roux* darkens quickly and you may want to lift the pan from the heat periodically to let it cool. Should the *roux* burn, discard it and make another batch.)

Immediately scrape the contents of the skillet into a small bowl. Let the *roux* cool to room temperature, then cover with foil or plastic wrap and refrigerate it until ready to use. (It can safely be kept for weeks.)

When it cools the *roux* will separate and the fat will rise to the surface. Before using the *roux*, stir it briefly to recombine it. Measure the desired amount into the pan and warm the *roux* slowly over low heat, stirring constantly. Whether added immediately or not, any liquid that is to be incorporated with the brown *roux* must be at least lukewarm or the mixture may separate. If it does, beat it together again with a whisk.

Kings' Cake

To make one 12-inch ring

CAKE
½ cup lukewarm water (110° to 115°)
2 packages active dry yeast
2 teaspoons plus ½ cup granulated sugar
3½ to 4½ cups unsifted flour
1 teaspoon ground nutmeg, preferably freshly grated
2 teaspoons salt
1 teaspoon finely grated fresh lemon peel
½ cup lukewarm milk (110° to 115°)
5 egg yolks
8 tablespoons butter (1 quarter-pound stick), cut into ½-inch bits and softened, plus 2 tablespoons butter, softened
½ cup finely chopped candied citron
1 shelled pecan half or uncooked dried bean
1 egg, lightly beaten with 1 tablespoon milk

To make the cake, pour the lukewarm water into a small shallow bowl and sprinkle the yeast and 2 teaspoons of the granulated sugar over it. Let the yeast and sugar rest for 2 to 3 minutes, then stir to mix the ingredients well. Set in a warm, draft-free place (such as an unlighted oven) for about 10 minutes, or until the yeast bubbles up and the mixture almost doubles in volume.

Combine 3½ cups of flour, the remaining ½ cup of granulated sugar, the nutmeg and the salt, and sift them into a deep mixing bowl. Stir in the lemon peel, then make a well in the center and into it pour the yeast mixture and the milk.

Add the egg yolks and, with a large wooden spoon, gradually incorporate the dry ingredients into the liquid ones. When the mixture is smooth, beat in the 8 tablespoons of butter bits, a tablespoonful at a time. Continue to beat for about 2 minutes longer, or until the dough can be gathered into a medium-soft ball.

Place the ball on a lightly floured surface and knead, pushing the dough down with the heels of your hands, pressing it forward and folding it back on itself. As you knead, incorporate up to 1 cup more flour, sprinkling it over the ball by the tablespoonful. When the dough is no longer sticky, knead it for about 10 minutes longer, or until it is smooth, shiny and elastic.

With a pastry brush, spread 1 tablespoon of softened butter evenly over the inside of a large bowl. Set the dough in the bowl and turn it about to butter the entire surface. Drape the bowl with a kitchen towel and put it in the draft-free place for 1½ hours, or until the dough doubles in volume.

Brush a large baking sheet with the remaining tablespoon of softened butter. Punch the dough down with a blow of your fist and place it on a lightly floured surface. Scatter the citron over the top, knead the dough until the citron is well distributed, then pat and shape it into a cylinder about 14 inches long. Loop the cylinder onto the buttered baking sheet and pinch the ends together to form a ring.

Press the pecan half or dried bean gently into the ring so that it is completely hidden by the dough. Drape the dough again and set it in the draft-free place to rise for about 45 minutes, until the ring doubles in volume.

Preheat the oven to 375°. (If you have used the oven to let the dough rise, transfer the ring to another warm place to rest while the oven heats.) Brush the top and sides of the ring with the egg-and-milk mixture and bake the Kings' cake in the middle of the oven for 25 to 30 minutes, or until it is golden brown.

Slide the cake onto a wire rack to cool to room temperature.

Meanwhile, prepare the colored sugars. Squeeze a dot of green coloring paste onto the center of the palm of one hand. Sprinkle 2 tablespoons of granulated sugar over the paste and rub your palms together briskly until the sugar is evenly green. Add more paste if the color is too light and rub the sugar a few minutes longer. Place the green sugar on a saucer or piece of wax paper and repeat the entire procedure again to color 2 more tablespoons of the sugar.

Wash your hands, squeeze a blob of purple food coloring paste on one palm and in a similar fashion color 4 tablespoons of the granulated sugar purple. Wash your hands again and, using the yellow food coloring paste, tint the remaining 4 tablespoons of granulated sugar yellow. Set the green, purple and yellow sugars aside.

When the cake has cooled, prepare the icing. Combine the confectioners' sugar, lemon juice and 3 tablespoons of the water in a deep bowl and stir until the icing mixture is smooth. If the icing is too stiff to spread easily, beat in up to 3 tablespoons more water, 1 teaspoonful at a time. With a small metal spatula, spread the icing over the top of the cake, allowing it to run irregularly down the sides.

Sprinkle the colored sugars over the icing immediately, forming a row of purple, yellow and green strips, each about 2 inches wide, on both sides of the ring as shown in the photograph overleaf. Arrange two

SUGARS
Green, purple and yellow food-coloring pastes
12 tablespoons granulated sugar

ICING
3 cups confectioners' sugar
¼ cup strained fresh lemon juice
3 to 6 tablespoons water
2 candied cherries, cut lengthwise into halves

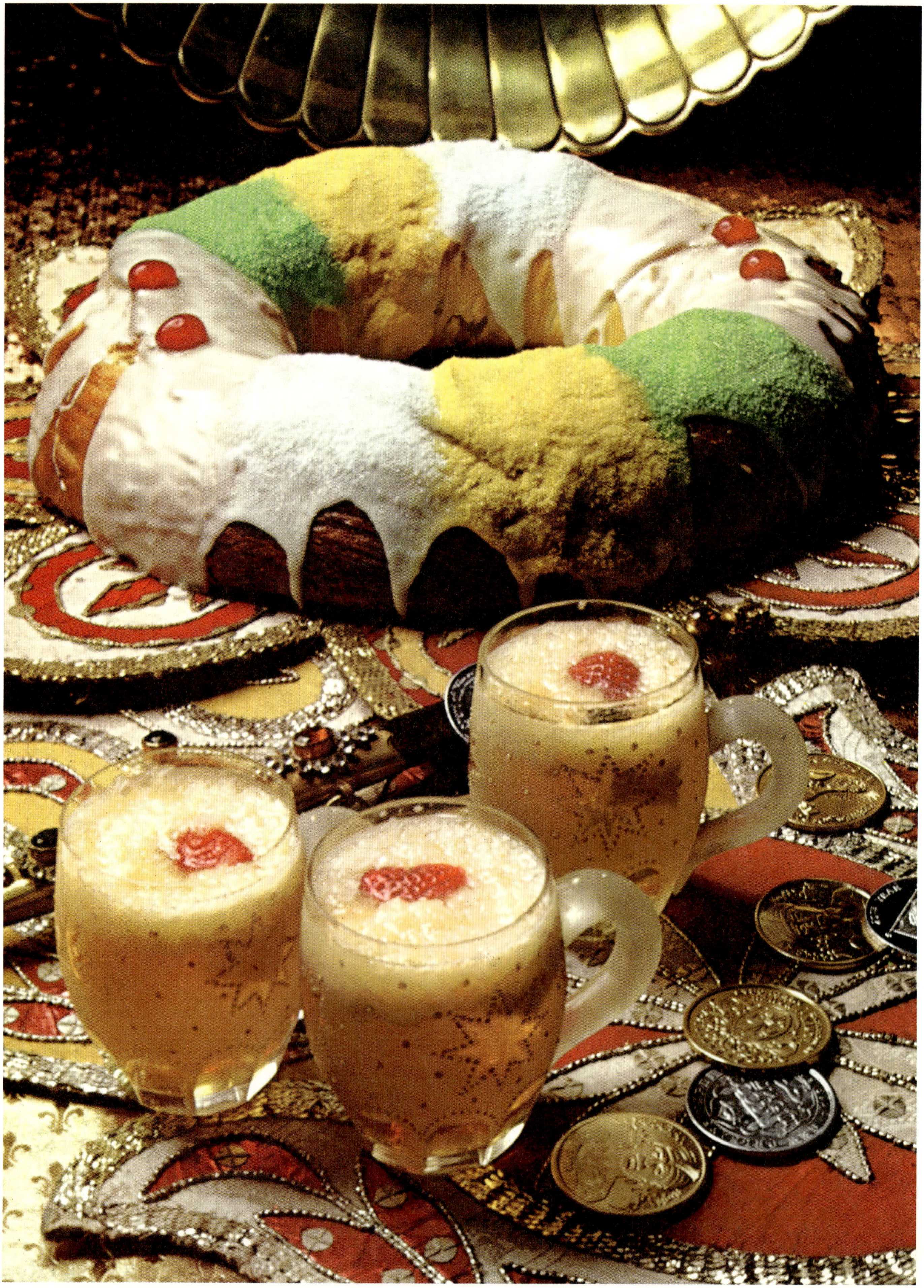

cherry halves at each end of the cake, pressing them gently into the icing cut side down.

NOTE: Food coloring pastes are available at bakers' supply stores. Do not use liquid food coloring, which makes the sugar dissolve and clump and does not color the granules evenly.

Creole Champagne Punch

Place the pineapple on its side on a cutting board and, grasping it firmly with one hand, slice off the leafy crown and the base with a large sharp knife. Stand the pineapple on end and slice off the prickly rind in seven or eight downward strokes, cutting deep enough each time to remove the eyes. Then divide the fruit lengthwise into quarters and cut the triangular section of core away from each quarter. Cut two of the quarters lengthwise in half and slice each of these crosswise into ½-inch-thick wedges. Grate the remaining two quarters of the pineapple on the teardrop-shaped holes of a stand-up hand grater. Set aside the pineapple wedges and grated pineapple.

Pick over the strawberries carefully, removing the stems and hulls and discarding any fruit that is badly bruised or shows signs of mold. Wash briefly in a sieve or colander set under cold running water, then spread the berries on paper towels to drain and pat them completely dry with fresh paper towels.

Just before serving, combine the superfine sugar, lemon and orange juice, and curaçao in the punch bowl and stir to dissolve the sugar completely. Stir in the champagne, wine and club soda. Carefully place the solid block of ice in the bowl, then stir the pineapple wedges, grated pineapple and strawberries into the punch.

To make about 5 quarts

1 large fresh ripe pineapple
1 pint firm fresh strawberries
1 pound superfine sugar
1 cup strained fresh lemon juice
1 cup strained fresh orange juice
½ cup curaçao or other orange-flavored liqueur
1 quart champagne, chilled
1 quart dry white wine, chilled
1½ quarts (6 cups) club soda, chilled

A 2- to 3-gallon punch bowl
A large solid block of ice

Shrove Tuesday Buns

Pour the lukewarm water into a small shallow bowl and sprinkle the yeast on top. Let the mixture stand for 2 or 3 minutes, then mix well. Set the bowl in a warm, draft-free place (such as an unlighted oven) for 5 minutes, or until the mixture bubbles and almost doubles in volume.

Combine 2½ cups of the flour with the sugar and salt, sift them into a deep bowl, and make a well in the center. Pour in the yeast mixture and the lukewarm cream and, with a large spoon, gradually incorporate the dry ingredients into the liquid ones. Beat until smooth, then add the 8 tablespoons of butter bits and continue to beat until the batter is absorbed.

Gather the dough into a ball and place it on a lightly floured surface. Knead it by pushing it down with the heels of your hands, pressing it for-

To make 12 buns

½ cup lukewarm water (110° to 115°)
1 package active dry yeast
2½ to 3½ cups flour
¼ cup sugar
⅛ teaspoon salt
½ cup heavy cream, heated to lukewarm (110° to 115°), plus ½ cup heavy cream, chilled
8 tablespoons butter, cut into ½-inch bits and softened, plus 2 tablespoons butter, softened
1 egg beaten with 2 tablespoons milk
½ cup blanched almonds
1 egg white
1 cup confectioners' sugar
⅛ teaspoon almond extract

Kings' cake, like the French *gâteau des Rois* it was inspired by, is served on Twelfth Night, at the start of the Mardi Gras season. Made of rich yeast dough and citron, the regal ring is decorated with sugar tinted in the classic carnival colors. Inside is a single bean or pecan half; whoever finds this treasure in his portion is declared the King or Queen of the Twelfth Night celebration. Cups of champagne punch, enriched by fresh strawberries, accompany the cake. The coins are souvenir "doubloons" tossed at carnival spectators from Mardi Gras floats by costumed parade participants.

ward, and folding it back on itself. Repeat for about 10 minutes, meanwhile sprinkling in up to 1 cup more flour, adding it by the tablespoonful and using only enough to make a smooth, elastic dough.

With a pastry brush, spread 1 tablespoon of the softened butter over the entire inside surface of a deep bowl. Place the dough in the bowl and turn it about to grease all sides evenly. Drape loosely with a kitchen towel and set aside in the warm, draft-free place for 1 to 1½ hours, or until the dough doubles in bulk.

Brush the remaining tablespoon of softened butter evenly on a large baking sheet. Punch the dough down with a single blow of your fist and divide it into 12 equal parts. On a lightly floured surface, pat and shape the dough into a dozen balls and arrange them 2 inches apart on the buttered baking sheet. Set the balls aside in the warm, draft-free place for 20 to 30 minutes, or until they double in volume.

Preheat the oven to 425°. Brush the top of the balls with the egg-and-milk mixture and bake them in the middle of the oven for 15 minutes, or until they are golden brown. Turn the buns out on wire racks, separate, and let them cool to room temperature.

Meanwhile, reduce the oven temperature to 350°. Spread the almonds in a baking dish and, stirring occasionally, toast them for 8 to 10 minutes, or until they are delicately browned. Pulverize the almonds in an electric blender or with a nut grinder.

Drop the egg white into a bowl and sift ¾ cup of the confectioners' sugar over it. Mix well, then add the pulverized almonds and the almond extract and stir to a smooth paste. Set aside.

In a chilled bowl, whip the remaining ½ cup of heavy cream with a wire whisk or a rotary or electric beater until the cream is stiff enough to stand in unwavering peaks on the beater when it is lifted from the bowl. Cover with foil or plastic wrap and refrigerate until ready to use.

Just before serving, cut a 1-inch slice off the top of each bun. Spread each bun with 1 tablespoon of the almond paste and spoon about 1 tablespoon of cream over the paste, then set the slice in place like a lid. Sprinkle the buns lightly with the remaining confectioners' sugar and serve at once.

Carnival Breakfast Griddle Cakes

To make 18 to 20 pancakes

2 cups all-purpose flour
2 teaspoons baking powder
2 teaspoons sugar
1 teaspoon salt
3 eggs, lightly beaten
2 cups milk
¼ cup melted butter
¼ cup vegetable oil

Sift the flour, baking powder, sugar and salt together into a large mixing bowl. Make a well in the center of the flour and pour into it the eggs and milk. With a large spoon mix together only long enough to blend, then stir in the melted butter. Do not overmix; the pancakes will be lighter if the batter is not too smooth. Heat a griddle or heavy skillet over moderate heat until a drop of water flicked onto it evaporates instantly. Grease the griddle or skillet very lightly with a pastry brush dipped in oil; continue to grease when necessary. Pour the batter from a pitcher or small ladle into the hot pan to form pancakes 4 inches in diameter. Cook 2 to 3 minutes until small, scattered bubbles have formed—but have not broken—on the surface . Immediately turn with a spatula and cook for a minute until the other side of the pancake is golden brown. Stack on a heated plate and serve with melted butter and maple syrup.

NOTE: One cup of thoroughly drained, fresh, canned or thoroughly defrosted and drained frozen fruit may be added to the batter before frying.

Russian Festival Bliny

To serve 6 to 8

½ cup lukewarm water (110° to 115°)
1½ packages active dry yeast
½ cup buckwheat flour
2 cups white all-purpose flour
2 cups lukewarm milk (110° to 115°)
3 egg yolks, lightly beaten
½ teaspoon salt
1 teaspoon sugar
½ pound butter, melted and cooled
2 cups sour cream (1 pint)
3 egg whites

16 ounces red or black caviar or substitute 1 pound thinly sliced smoked salmon, sturgeon or herring fillets

Pour the lukewarm water into a small, shallow bowl and sprinkle the yeast over it. Let the yeast stand 2 or 3 minutes, then stir to dissolve it completely. Set in a warm, draft-free spot (such as an unlighted oven) for 3 to 5 minutes, or until the mixture almost doubles in volume.

In a large mixing bowl, combine ¼ cup of the buckwheat flour and the 2 cups of white flour. Make a deep well in the center and pour in 1 cup of the lukewarm milk and the yeast mixture. Slowly stir the flour into the liquid ingredients with a large wooden spoon, then beat vigorously until the mixture is smooth. Cover the bowl loosely with a towel and set aside in the warm, draft-free spot for 3 hours, or until the mixture doubles in volume.

Stir the batter thoroughly and vigorously beat in the remaining ¼ cup of buckwheat flour. Cover with a towel and let the batter rest in the warm draft-free spot another 2 hours. Again stir the batter and gradually beat in the remaining cup of lukewarm milk and the 3 egg yolks, salt, sugar, 3 tablespoons of the melted butter and 3 tablespoons of the sour cream.

With a whisk or a rotary or electric beater, beat the egg whites in a large bowl until they form stiff, unwavering peaks on the beater when it is lifted from the bowl. With a rubber spatula, fold the egg whites gently but thoroughly into the batter, cover loosely with a towel, and let the batter rest in the warm, draft-free spot for 30 minutes.

Preheat the oven to 200°. With a pastry brush, lightly coat the bottom of a 10- to 12-inch skillet (preferably with a nonstick surface) with melted butter. Set the pan over high heat until a drop of water flicked across its surface evaporates instantly. Pour in about 3 tablespoons of the batter for each pancake (you will be able to make about 3 at a time, each about 3 or 4 inches wide) and fry 2 or 3 minutes, then brush the top lightly with butter. With a spatula or your fingers, turn the pancake over and cook another 2 minutes, or until golden brown. Transfer the pancakes to an ovenproof dish and keep them warm in the oven while you fry the remaining pancakes similarly, adding additional butter to the pan as needed.

Serve the *bliny* hot, accompanied by bowls of the remaining butter and the sour cream. Traditionally, the *bliny* are spread with melted butter and a mound of red caviar or slice of smoked fish, then topped with a spoonful of sour cream. If you are serving black caviar, omit the sour cream.

Overleaf: Bliny, pancakes as round as the sun, whose coming they celebrate, have been the highlight of the Russian festival of Maslenitsa (literally, Butter Festival) since Czarist days. In old Russia, seven weeks of Lenten fasting lay in the immediate future, and in consolation bliny were eaten with such soon-to-be-forbidden spreads as sour cream or melted butter, topped with pink sliced salmon, red salmon roe, sliced smoked sturgeon, black caviar or pickled herring.

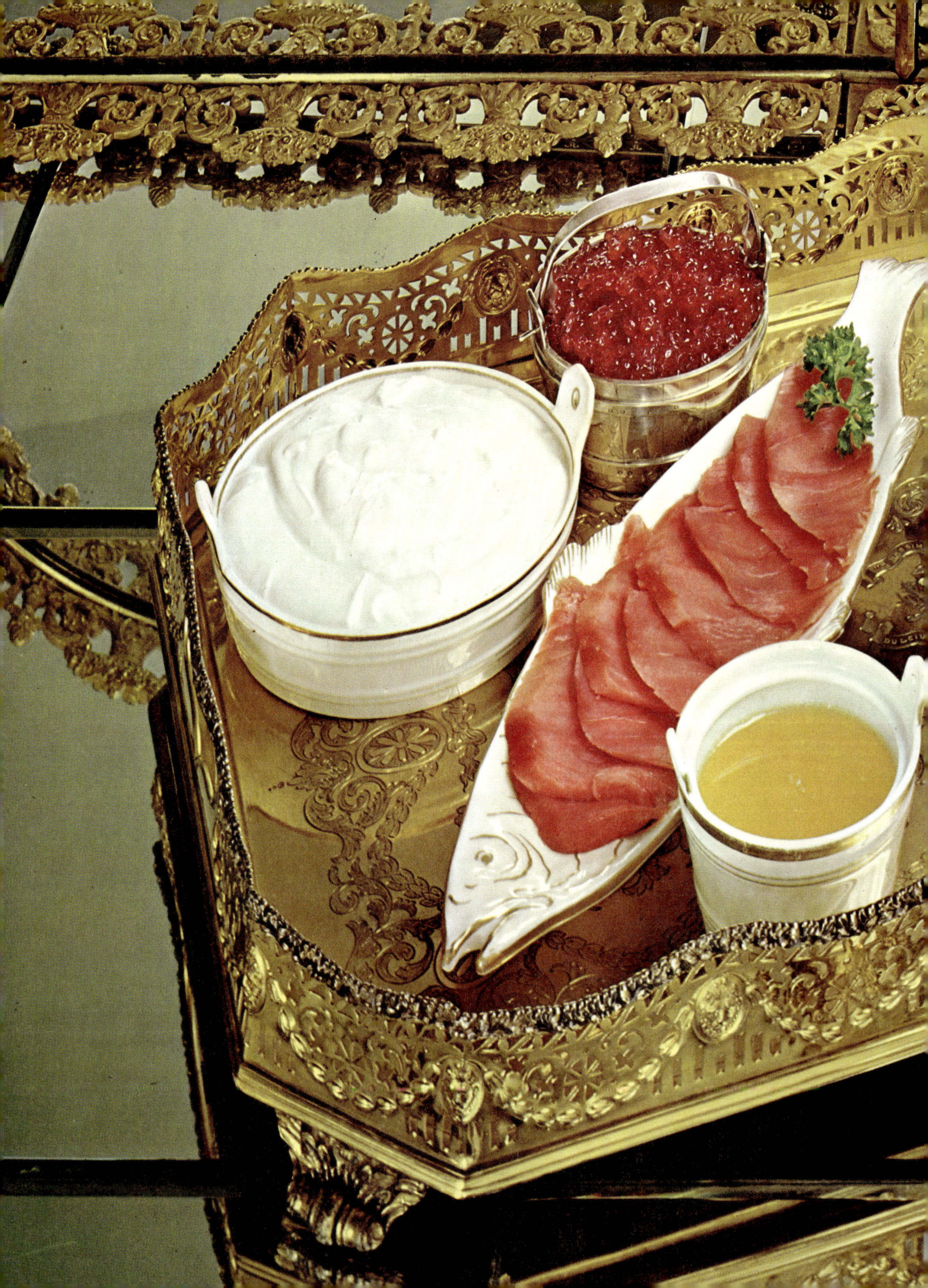

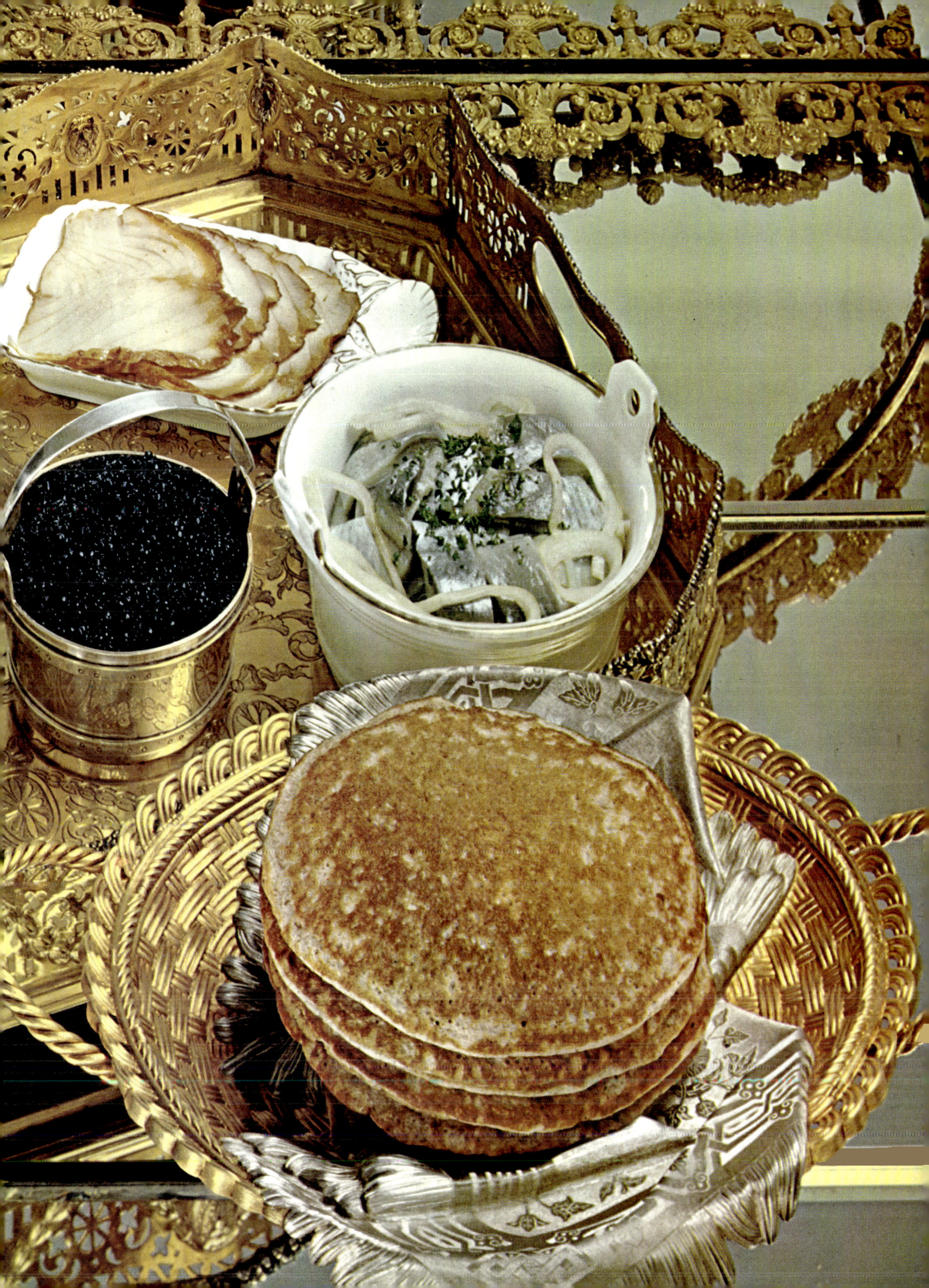

Fasching Doughnuts

To make about 2 dozen doughnuts

2 cups water
1 medium-sized boiling potato, peeled and quartered
4 tablespoons butter, cut into ½-inch bits and softened, plus 2 teaspoons butter, softened
1 package active dry yeast
1 teaspoon plus 2½ cups sugar
6 to 6½ cups unsifted flour
1 teaspoon salt
2 eggs
Vegetable oil for deep frying

In a small heavy saucepan, bring the water to a boil over high heat. Drop in the potato quarters and boil briskly, uncovered, until a quarter can be easily mashed against the side of the pan with the back of a fork.

Drain the potatoes in a sieve set over a bowl, pat them dry with a kitchen towel and return them to the pan. (Measure and reserve 1½ cups of the potato water.) Then mash the potatoes to a smooth purée with the back of a fork (you will need about ½ cup of the potato purée). Beat the 4 tablespoons of butter bits into the potatoes, and cover the pan to keep the purée warm.

When the reserved potato water has cooled to lukewarm (110° to 115°), pour ¼ cup of it into a shallow bowl. Add the yeast and 1 teaspoon of sugar. Let the mixture stand for 2 or 3 minutes, then stir well. Set the bowl in a warm, draft-free place, such as an unlighted oven, for about 5 minutes, or until the yeast bubbles up and the mixture almost doubles in volume.

Combine 6 cups of the flour, ½ cup of the sugar and the salt in a deep mixing bowl, and make a well in the center. Drop in the potato purée, the yeast mixture, the eggs and the remaining 1¼ cups of potato water. With a large wooden spoon, mix the ingredients together and stir until the dough is smooth and can be gathered into a soft ball.

Place the ball on a lightly floured surface and knead, pushing the dough down with the heels of your hands, pressing it forward and folding it back on itself.

As you knead, sprinkle flour over the ball by the tablespoonful, adding up to ½ cup more flour if necessary to make a firm dough. Then continue to knead for about 10 minutes longer, or until the dough is smooth, shiny and elastic.

With a pastry brush, spread the 2 teaspoons of softened butter evenly over the inside of a large bowl. Set the dough in the bowl and turn it about to butter the entire surface. Drape the bowl with a kitchen towel and put it in the draft-free place for about 1½ hours, or until the dough doubles in bulk.

Line one or two large baking sheets with wax paper. Place the dough on a lightly floured surface and roll it out into a rough rectangle about ½ inch thick. With a small sharp knife or a pastry wheel, cut the dough into 2-inch squares, and make a 1-inch slash in the center of each. Arrange the squares about 1 inch apart on the paper-lined baking sheet and return them to the draft-free place to rise for 30 to 45 minutes, or until doubled in bulk.

Pour vegetable oil into a deep fryer or large heavy saucepan to a depth of 3 inches and heat it to a temperature of 375° on a deep-frying thermometer. At the same time, place about ½ cup of the remaining sugar in a paper bag and set it aside.

Deep-fry the dough squares 4 or 5 at a time, turning them with a slotted spoon, for 3 minutes, or until they are puffed and brown. Drain the doughnuts briefly on paper towels, then drop two at a time into the bag and shake to coat them with sugar. (Add more sugar to the bag as needed.) Place the doughnuts on a platter to cool while you fry and sugar the remaining doughnuts.

On Washington's Birthday

To honor George Washington and the legend of the cherry tree, here are recipes using sweet cherries, sour cherries, black cherries, red cherries and candied cherries. There is even a recipe for cherry soup.

Cherries Jubilee

Pour the cherry liquid into a small saucepan and bring it to a simmer over moderate heat. Stirring constantly, add the cornstarch-and-water mixture and cook until the sauce comes to a boil, thickens lightly and is smooth. Remove the pan from the heat and let the sauce cool to room temperature, then cover tightly and set it aside.

Prepare and assemble the cherries jubilee at the dinner table, when you are ready to serve them. Light an alcohol burner or table-top stove and set a 12-inch copper *flambé* or crêpe suzette pan over the flame. Arrange the cherry sauce, cherries, kirsch and maraschino conveniently beside the pan. Place a scoop of ice cream in each of four chilled individual dessert bowls and set them to one side.

Drop the cherries into the *flambé* pan and stir until they are heated. Carefully pour the kirsch and maraschino into the pan, step back from the table and let the liqueurs warm for a few seconds. They may burst into flame spontaneously. If not, ignite them with a match.

Gently slide the pan back and forth over the heat until the flames die, basting the cherries all the while with the liqueurs. Then stir in the cherry sauce and cook briefly to heat it through.

Ladle the cherries and sauce over the ice cream and serve at once.

To serve 4

A 1-pound can pitted sweet Bing cherries, drained, with all their liquid reserved
1 tablespoon cornstarch mixed with 1 tablespoon cold water
¼ cup kirsch liqueur
¼ cup maraschino liqueur
1 pint vanilla ice cream

Cherry Cobbler

Preheat the oven to 425°. Sift the flour, 2 tablespoons of sugar, baking powder and salt together into a large mixing bowl. Add the chilled butter, and, with your fingertips, rub the dry ingredients and butter together until most of the lumps have disappeared and the mixture resembles coarse meal. Pour in the heavy cream and mix thoroughly until a soft dough is formed. Gather it into a compact ball and transfer it to a lightly floured board. Knead the dough for about a minute by folding it end to end and then pressing it down and pushing it forward several times with the heel of your hand. Now roll the dough out into a circle about ½ inch thick. With a 2½-inch cookie cutter, cut out 6 circles and set them aside. In a large mixing bowl, combine 1 tablespoon of the melted butter, sugar, the ¼ cup of cherry juice and arrowroot, and stir together until the arrowroot has dissolved. Add the cherries, stir again, then pour the entire contents of the bowl into a 6-by-8-by-2½-inch ovenproof baking dish. Spread the cherries out in the dish and arrange the circles of dough over them side by side. Brush the dough with the remaining 1 tablespoon of melted butter. Bake in the middle of the oven for 25 to 30 minutes, or until the biscuits are a golden brown. Serve warm or at room temperature directly from the dish.

To serve 6

1 cup all-purpose flour
2 tablespoons sugar
1½ teaspoons baking powder
½ teaspoon salt
2 tablespoons butter, chilled and cut into bits
⅔ cup heavy cream
2 tablespoons melted and cooled butter
½ cup sugar
2 one-pound cans pitted sour cherries, thoroughly drained, ¼ cup of juice reserved, or 2 pounds freshly cooked pitted cherries, with ¼ of their cooking liquid reserved
1 tablespoon arrowroot

A sour-cherry pie like this one is as American as apple pie. Cherry trees were among the first trees planted by early American settlers.

To make one 9-inch double-crust pie

1 tablespoon unsalted butter, softened, plus 2 tablespoons unsalted butter, cut into ¼-inch bits
Short-crust pastry (*double recipe on pages 241-242*)
6 cups pitted sour cherries (from about 3¾ pounds)
¼ cup quick-cooking tapioca
1 cup sugar
1½ tablespoons strained fresh lemon juice
¼ teaspoon almond extract

Sour-Cherry Pie

With a pastry brush, spread the tablespoon of softened butter over the bottom and sides of a 9-inch pie tin. Make pastry for a double-crust pie, divide it in half, and chill for at least one hour.

On a lightly floured surface, roll half of the dough into a rough circle about ⅛ inch thick and 12 to 13 inches in diameter. Drape the dough over the rolling pin, lift it up, and unroll it slackly over the pie tin. Gently press the dough into the bottom and sides of the tin. With a pair of scissors, cut off the excess dough from the edges, leaving a 1-inch overhang all around the outside rim. Refrigerate while you prepare the filling.

Combine the sour cherries, tapioca, sugar, lemon juice and almond extract in a large bowl, and toss together gently but thoroughly. Let the mixture rest uncovered and at room temperature for about 10 minutes. Then spoon the contents of the bowl into the unbaked pie shell and, with a rubber spatula, spread out the cherries as evenly as possible. Dot the top of the filling with the butter bits.

Preheat the oven to 450°. For the upper crust, roll the remaining half of the dough into a circle about ⅛ inch thick and 12 to 13 inches in diameter. With a pastry brush dipped in cold water, lightly moisten the outside edge of the pastry shell. Drape the dough over the rolling pin, lift it up and unroll it over the pie. Trim off the excess pastry from around the rim with scissors, then crimp the top and bottom pastry together firmly with your fingertips or press them with the tines of a fork. Cut a 1-inch hole in the center of the top of the pie. Bake in the center of the oven for 10 minutes, then lower the heat to 350° and bake another 40 to 45 minutes, or until the top is golden brown.

Spongecake with Cherries

Preheat the oven to 350°. With a pastry brush or paper towel, butter the bottom of a 9-inch layer-cake pan. Pour the cherries into a sieve or colander and let them drain while you prepare the batter.

In a mixing bowl, with a wire whisk or a rotary or electric beater, beat the egg whites with the salt until they foam, then beat in the sugar, a tablespoon at a time. Continue to beat until the whites form stiff, unwavering peaks when the beater is lifted from the bowl.

Beat the egg yolks lightly with a fork, then add the lemon peel, lemon juice and vanilla extract. Mix about ¼ of the beaten egg whites into the egg yolks, then reverse the process and pour the yolk mixture over the remaining whites and sprinkle the flour on top. With a rubber spatula, fold until no traces of the whites remains. Do not overfold.

Pour the batter into the pan and spread the cherries evenly over it. Bake in the middle of the oven 35 to 40 minutes, or until the cake is golden brown and springy to the touch. Cool in the pan before serving.

To make 1 nine-inch cake

1 cup canned pitted sweet black cherries
3 eggs, separated
Pinch of salt
½ cup sugar
½ teaspoon grated lemon peel
2 teaspoons lemon juice
½ teaspoon vanilla extract
½ cup sifted all-purpose flour

Cherry Cake

Preheat the oven to 350°. To make the batter in a blender, combine the milk, eggs, flour, sugar and vanilla in the blender jar, and whirl them at high speed for a few seconds. Turn the machine off and scrape down the sides of the jar with a rubber spatula, then blend again for about 40 seconds. To make the batter by hand, stir the flour and eggs together in a large mixing bowl, and slowly stir in the milk, sugar and vanilla extract. Beat with a whisk or a rotary or electric beater until the flour lumps disappear and the batter is smooth.

Pat the cherries completely dry with paper towels. Spread them evenly in a shallow, buttered baking dish or pan that holds 5 to 6 cups and is about 2 inches deep. Pour in the batter. Bake on the middle shelf of the oven for 1½ hours, or until the top is golden brown and firm to the touch. Dust lightly with confectioners' sugar, and serve the cake while it is still warm.

To serve 4 to 6

1½ cups milk
4 eggs
½ cup all-purpose flour
¼ cup sugar
2 teaspoons vanilla extract
2 to 3 cups fresh black sweet cherries, pitted; or drained, canned, pitted Bing cherries; or frozen sweet cherries, thawed and drained
Confectioners' (powdered) sugar

Cherry Twist

DOUGH: Pour the water into a small bowl and sprinkle the yeast and 1 teaspoon of the sugar over it. Let stand for 2 or 3 minutes, then stir well. Set in a warm, draft-free place (such as an unlighted oven) for about 10 minutes, or until the yeast bubbles up and the mixture almost doubles in volume. Meanwhile, combine the milk and 4 tablespoons of the butter and, stirring occasionally, cook over moderate heat until the butter has melted and bubbles begin to form around the edges of the pan. Then pour the mixture into a deep bowl and set aside to cool to lukewarm.

Add the yeast mixture, the salt, the remaining ⅓ cup of sugar and the lightly beaten egg and, with a wooden spoon, stir until all the ingredients

To make one 16-inch twist

DOUGH
¼ cup lukewarm water (110° to 115°)
1 package active dry yeast
1 teaspoon plus ⅓ cup sugar
¾ cup lukewarm milk (110° to 115°)
6 tablespoons unsalted butter, softened
1 teapoon salt
1 egg, lightly beaten
3 to 3½ cups flour

are well blended. Then add 3 cups of the flour, 1 cup at a time, and continue to stir until the dough can be gathered into a medium-soft ball.

Place the ball on a lightly floured surface and knead, pushing the dough down with the heels of your hands, pressing it forward and folding it back on itself. As you knead, incorporate as much of the remaining ½ cup of flour as is required to make a smooth, fairly dry dough. When the dough is shiny and elastic, reshape it into a ball. With a pastry brush, coat the inside of another large bowl with 1 tablespoon of the softened butter. Drop in the dough and turn it about to coat the entire ball with butter. Then drape the bowl with a towel and put it into the draft-free place for about 45 minutes, or until the dough doubles in volume. Meanwhile, brush a baking sheet with the remaining tablespoon of butter.

Punch the dough down with a single blow of your fist and place it on a lightly floured surface.

SHAPING AND TOPPING: Cut the dough in half and with your hands shape each half into a cylinder about 18 inches long and 1½ inches wide. Place the cylinders side by side on the baking sheet and pinch the tops together so that the cylinders form a narrow "V." Then shape the dough into a twist about 14 inches long. Set the twist aside to rise for 45 minutes, or until it doubles in bulk.

Preheat the oven to 375°. With a pastry brush, coat the twist with the combined egg yolk and milk, then mix the almonds, sugar and cinnamon, and sprinkle them over the top. Set the candied cherry halves in two rows along the length of the twist. Bake in the center of the oven for about 25 minutes, or until golden brown. Turn the cherry twist out on a wire rack to cool. Serve it warm or at room temperature.

TOPPING

1 egg yolk, lightly beaten and combined with 1 teaspoon milk
¼ cup blanched almonds, coarsely chopped
¼ cup sugar
1 teaspoon ground cinnamon
4 candied cherries, halved

To serve 6

3 cups cold water
1 cup sugar
1 cinnamon stick
4 cups pitted sour cherries or drained canned sour cherries
1 tablespoon arrowroot
¼ cup heavy cream, chilled
¾ cup dry red wine, chilled

Cold Cherry Soup

In a 2-quart saucepan, combine the water, sugar and cinnamon stick. Bring to a boil and add the cherries. Partially cover and simmer over low heat for 35 to 40 minutes if the cherries are fresh or 10 minutes if they are canned. Remove the cinnamon stick.

Mix the arrowroot and 2 tablespoons of cold water into a paste, then beat into the cherry soup. Stirring constantly, bring the soup almost to a boil. Reduce the heat and simmer about 2 minutes, or until clear and slightly thickened. Pour into a shallow glass or stainless-steel bowl, and refrigerate until chilled. Before serving—preferably in soup bowls that have been prechilled—stir in the cream and wine.

Ice-cold cherry soup, a delightful first course in Hungary, also makes a perfect dessert for a Washington's Birthday meal.

Traditional Purim Delights

Purim celebrates the deliverance of the ancient Jews from the Persian Prime Minister Haman, who had plotted their annihilation. Triangle-shaped cookies—reminders either of Haman's three-cornered hat or his pocket (no one is sure which)—are traditionally served on this day.

Hamantaschen Cookies

To make about 18

DOUGH
12 tablespoons (1½ quarter-pound sticks) butter, softened
½ cup sugar
3 cups sifted all-purpose flour
1 egg
¼ cup milk combined with ½ teaspoon vanilla extract

FILLING
1 cup *lekvar* (prune butter)
½ cup finely chopped blanched almonds
2 teaspoons grated orange rind
2 tablespoons sugar
2 tablespoons butter, softened
1 egg yolk, beaten lightly and combined with 2 tablespoons milk

DOUGH: In a deep bowl, cream 12 tablespoons of butter and ½ cup of sugar together by mashing them against the sides of the bowl with a large spoon until the mixture is light and fluffy. Beat in ¼ cup of the flour and, when it is completely incorporated, add the egg. Beating well after each addition, add 1 cup of flour, the 2 tablespoons of the milk-and-vanilla mixture, followed by another cup of flour, the remaining milk mixture, and the remaining flour. Gather the dough into a ball, cover it with wax paper, and refrigerate for at least 30 minutes.

FILLING: Meanwhile, prepare the filling. Place the *lekvar* in a large mixing bowl and beat in the almonds, orange rind and 2 tablespoons of sugar. When the ingredients are well combined, set the filling aside.

Preheat the oven to 350°. With a pastry brush, coat two large baking sheets with the remaining 2 tablespoons of butter.

On a lightly floured surface, roll the dough out into a rough circle about 1/16 inch thick. With a 4-inch round cookie cutter, cut the dough into as many rounds as you can. Gather the scraps of dough into a small ball, reroll, and cut out additional rounds. Continue the process until all the dough has been used.

Place a heaping tablespoon of the *lekvar*-and-nut filling in the center of a round of dough and lightly moisten the edges of the round with a finger dipped in water. Let the tips of your thumbs meet under the nearest edge of the round; slide each of your index fingers forward so that thumbs and index fingers form a triangle when they are brought up around the filling. Pinch the ends of the dough together, leaving the center of the filling exposed.

Place the cookies on the baking sheets, brush the tops with the beaten egg-and-milk mixture, and bake in the center of the oven for 20 to 25 minutes, or until they are lightly browned. With a spatula, transfer them to a cake rack to cool before serving.

Honey Cake

To make one 9-inch loaf cake

1 teaspoon plus ¼ cup vegetable oil
2¼ cups all-purpose flour
¼ cup seedless raisins
¼ cup chopped candied orange peel
3 egg yolks
¾ cup honey
⅓ cup sugar
2 teaspoons finely grated lemon peel
4½ teaspoons instant coffee dissolved in 1 tablespoon boiling water
1 teaspoon baking powder
¼ teaspoon baking soda
¼ teaspoon ground cinnamon
¼ teaspoon ground allspice
A pinch of ground cloves
¼ teaspoon salt
3 egg whites
½ cup sliced blanched almonds

Preheat the oven to 325°. With a pastry brush coat the bottom and sides of a 9-by-5-by-3-inch loaf pan with 1 teaspoon of the oil. Sprinkle the oiled pan with 2 tablespoons of the flour, tipping the pan from side to side to spread the flour evenly. Then invert the pan and rap the bottom sharply to remove the excess flour. Combine the raisins and orange peel in a bowl, add 2 tablespoons of the flour and turn the fruit about with a spoon until it is evenly and lightly coated. Set aside.

This almond-decorated honey cake, frequently served at Purim, contains one ingredient that shatters tradition—instant coffee.

In a deep bowl, beat the egg yolks with a whisk or a rotary or electric beater until frothy. Then beat in the remaining ¼ cup of oil, the honey, sugar, lemon peel, and the dissolved coffee. Combine the remaining 2 cups of flour, the baking powder, soda, cinnamon, allspice, cloves and salt and sift them into the egg-yolk batter, ¼ cup or so at a time, beating well after each addition. Stir in the raisins and orange peel.

Wash and dry the whisk or beater, and in a separate bowl beat the egg whites until they form unwavering peaks when the beater is lifted from the bowl. With a rubber spatula, gently but thoroughly fold the egg whites into the batter, using an over-under cutting motion rather than a stirring motion.

Pour the batter into the loaf pan and spread it out evenly. Decorate the top with the almonds, arranging the slices to make simple daisy shapes in the center of the cake and leaving enough almonds to make a small stripe at each end. Bake in the middle of the oven for 1 hour and 15 minutes, or until a cake tester or toothpick inserted in the center comes out clean. Cool in the pan for 4 or 5 minutes, then run a sharp knife around the edges and turn the cake out on a rack. Cool completely.

Honey cake is often served with unsalted butter.

St. Patrick's Day Specials

March 17 means Irish stew or corned beef plus a goodly helping of potatoes, an aromatic dish of cabbage, or colcannon, a mix of the two. Soused mackerel, boxty pancakes and soda bread also have the true Hibernian flavor. A holiday version of Irish coffee is flamed in a chafing dish.

Irish Stew

To serve 4 to 6

6 medium-sized peeled potatoes (about 2 pounds), cut crosswise into ¼-inch slices
4 large onions (about 1½ pounds), peeled and cut into ¼-inch slices
3 pounds lean boneless lamb neck or shoulder, trimmed of all fat and cut into 1-inch cubes
1 teaspoon salt
Freshly ground black pepper
¼ teaspoon thyme
Cold water

Spread half the potatoes on the bottom of a heavy 4- to 5-quart casserole or Dutch oven, and cover them with half the onion slices and then all the lamb. Sprinkle with ½ teaspoon of the salt, a few grindings of pepper and the thyme. Arrange the rest of the onions over the meat and spread the remaining potatoes on top. Sprinkle with ½ teaspoon of salt and a few grindings of pepper, then pour in enough cold water just to cover the potatoes.

Bring the stew to a boil over high heat, reduce the heat to its lowest possible point, and cover the casserole tightly. Simmer for 1½ hours. Check from time to time and add boiling water, a tablespoon or two at a time, if the liquid seems to be cooking away.

Serve the stew directly from the casserole or Dutch oven, ladling it into heated deep individual serving plates. Traditionally, Irish stew is accompanied by pickled red cabbage.

NOTE: If you prefer, you may cook the stew in a preheated 350° oven instead of on top of the stove. In that event, bring the casserole to a boil on top of the stove before placing it in the lower third of the oven.

Pickled Cabbage

To make about 4 pints

2 medium-sized red cabbages (about 6 pounds)
6 tablespoons coarse (kosher) salt
1 quart malt vinegar
¼ cup sugar
2 tablespoons mixed pickling spice
1 teaspoon whole black peppercorns

Wash the cabbages under cold running water, remove the tough outer leaves, and cut each head into quarters. Shred the cabbage by first cutting out the cores and then slicing the quarters crosswise into ⅛-inch-thick strips. In a large stainless-steel or enameled bowl or pot, arrange the cabbage in 3 layers, sprinkling 2 tablespoons of coarse salt evenly over each layer. Let the cabbage stand in a cool place for 2 days, turning it about and lifting it up from the bottom of the bowl with a large wooden spoon several times each day.

On the third day, combine the vinegar, sugar, pickling spice and peppercorns in a 2- to 3-quart saucepan, and bring to a boil over high heat, stirring until the sugar dissolves. Boil briskly, uncovered, for 5 minutes, then remove the pan from the heat and cool to room temperature. Meanwhile drain the cabbage in a large colander. Squeeze it as dry as possible, a handful at a time, and return it to the bowl or pot. Strain the vinegar mixture over it, turning the cabbage about with a fork to moisten it thoroughly.

Cover, refrigerate, and let the cabbage marinate for at least 3 days before serving. Stir it occasionally. Covered tightly and refrigerated, it will keep for about 2 weeks.

Colcannon

Drop the quartered potatoes into enough lightly salted boiling water to cover them by 2 inches, and boil briskly until they are tender but not falling apart. Meanwhile, place the cabbage in a separate pot, pour in enough water to cover it completely, and bring to a boil. Boil rapidly, uncovered, for 10 minutes, then drain thoroughly in a colander. Melt 2 tablespoons of the butter over moderate heat in a heavy 8- to 10-inch skillet. When the foam begins to subside, add the cabbage, and cook, stirring constantly, for a minute or two. Cover the skillet and set aside off the heat.

Drain the potatoes and return them to the pan. Shake over low heat until they are dry and mealy. Then mash them to a smooth purée with a fork, a potato ricer or an electric mixer. Beat into them the remaining 2 tablespoons of butter and then ½ cup of the milk, 2 tablespoons at a time. Use up to ½ cup more milk if necessary to make a purée thick enough to hold its shape in a spoon. Stir in the cooked cabbage and the scallions, and add the salt and a few grindings of pepper. Taste for seasoning. Then transfer the colcannon to a heated serving bowl, sprinkle with parsley, and serve at once.

To serve 4 to 6

6 medium-sized boiling potatoes (about 2 pounds), peeled and quartered
4 cups finely shredded green cabbage (about 1 pound)
4 tablespoons butter
1 cup lukewarm milk
6 medium-sized scallions, including 2 inches of the green tops, cut lengthwise in half and crosswise into ⅛-inch slices
1 teaspoon salt
Freshly ground black pepper
1 tablespoon finely chopped fresh parsley

Corned Beef and Cabbage Dinner

Place the brisket in a 5- to 6-quart casserole and add enough water to cover it by at least 1 inch. Bring to a boil over high heat, meanwhile skimming off the scum and foam as they rise to the surface. Reduce the heat to low and simmer partially covered for about 3 hours, or until the brisket is tender and shows no resistance when pierced deeply with the point of a skewer or small knife. (Check the pot from time to time. The water should cover the brisket throughout the entire cooking time; add boiling water to the casserole if needed.)

Meanwhile, in a heavy 2- to 3-quart saucepan, bring 1 quart of water to a boil over high heat. Drop in the dried beans and boil them for about 2 minutes. (The water should cover the beans by at least 2 inches; if necessary, add more.) Turn off the heat and let the beans soak for 1 hour. Then add the clove-pierced onion and the salt and bring to a boil again. Reduce the heat to low, and simmer partially covered for 1 hour, or until the beans are tender. (Check the beans occasionally; add more boiling water if needed.) Drain the beans and discard the onion.

With a small, sharp knife cut the tops from the beets, leaving about 1 inch of stem on each. Scrub the beets under cold running water, then place them in a 3- to 4-quart saucepan and pour in enough cold water to cover them by 2 inches. Bring to a boil over high heat, reduce the heat to low, cover the pan and simmer until the beets show no resistance when pierced with the point of a small skewer or knife. This may take from 30 minutes to 2 hours; add boiling water to the beets if necessary. Drain the beets and, when they are cool enough to handle, slip off their skins.

The potatoes, carrots and rutabaga may be cooked together in a large pan of lightly salted boiling water. Drop the vegetables into the pot and cook briskly, uncovered, for about 20 minutes, or until they are tender but not falling apart. Drain, then peel the potatoes with a small knife.

To serve 8

A 4- to 4½-pound corned beef brisket, preferably second cut
1 cup dried horticultural shell beans, such as cranberry beans, or substitute dried pink or pinto beans (½ pound)
1 medium-sized onion, peeled and pierced with 1 whole clove
1 teaspoon salt
16 small firm young beets
8 medium-sized boiling potatoes, scrubbed
8 medium-sized carrots, scraped
1 large rutabaga (about 1½ pounds), peeled and cut crosswise into ½ inch-thick slices
2 pounds firm green cabbage, trimmed, quartered and cored
1 bunch fresh parsley sprigs, trimmed, washed and thoroughly drained

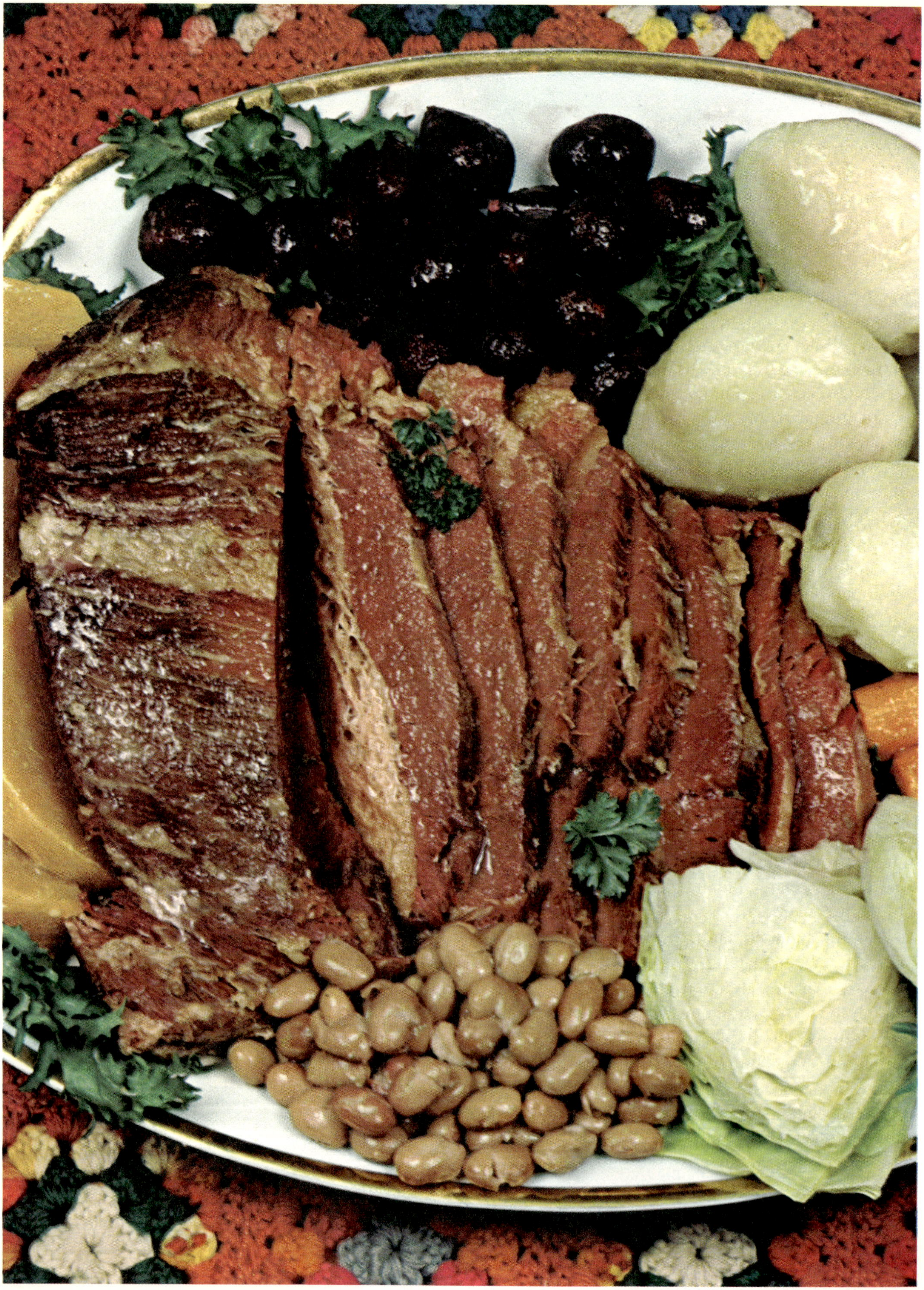

Cook the cabbage separately by dropping the quarters into enough salted boiling water to cover them completely. Reduce the heat to low and simmer partially covered for about 15 minutes, or until the cabbage is almost tender but still somewhat resistant when pierced with the point of a small sharp knife. Drain thoroughly and cut each quarter into halves.

To serve the boiled dinner, carve the beef and arrange the slices slightly overlapping attractively along the center of a large, heated platter. Surround the meat with mounds of individual vegetables and garnish the platter with the parsley. Horseradish, mustard and pickles are spicy accompaniments to a corned beef dinner.

Soused Mackerel

Preheat the oven to 325°. Wash the mackerel inside and out under cold running water and pat them dry with paper towels. Lay the fish side by side in a shallow flameproof ceramic, stainless-steel or enameled baking pan just large enough to hold them comfortably. Strew the onion rings, chopped parsley and bay leaves evenly over the fish and sprinkle them with the thyme, peppercorns and salt. Pour in the vinegar, water and lemon juice, and bring to a boil over high heat. Then bake uncovered in the middle of the oven for 15 minutes, or until the fish are firm to the touch, basting them two or three times with the cooking liquid. Do not overcook. Let the fish cool to room temperature and cover tightly with foil or plastic wrap. Marinate in the refrigerator for at least 6 hours. Brush the onions and seasonings off the fish and, with a slotted spatula, carefully transfer the mackerel to a platter.

To debone the mackerel for easier serving, divide the top layer into individual portions with a fish server without cutting through the spine. Leave the tail intact. Lift up the portions with the fish server and a fork, and arrange them on a serving dish. Lift out the backbone in one piece and divide the bottom layer of fish into portions. Garnish each serving with a sprig of parsley.

To serve 6

3 one-pound mackerel, eviscerated, with heads removed but tails left on
2 medium-sized onions, thinly sliced and separated into rings
¼ cup finely chopped parsley
2 small bay leaves
⅛ teaspoon thyme
12 whole black peppercorns
1½ teaspoons salt
1 cup malt or white wine vinegar
1 cup cold water
2 tablespoons fresh lemon juice
Parsley sprigs

Irish Soda Bread

Preheat the oven to 425°. With a pastry brush coat a baking sheet evenly with the tablespoon of softened butter.

Sift the flour, soda and salt together into a deep mixing bowl. Gradually add 1 cup of the buttermilk, beating constantly with a large spoon until the dough is firm enough to be gathered into a ball. If the dough crumbles, beat up to ½ cup more buttermilk into it by the tablespoon until the particles adhere.

Place the dough on a lightly floured board, and pat and shape it into a flat circular loaf about 8 inches in diameter and 1½ inches thick. Set the loaf on the baking sheet. Then with the tip of a small knife, cut a ½-inch-deep X into the dough, dividing the top of the loaf into quarters.

Bake the bread in the middle of the oven for about 45 minutes, or until the top is golden brown. Serve at once.

To make one 8-inch round loaf

1 tablespoon butter, softened
4 cups all-purpose flour
1 teaspoon baking soda
1 teaspoon salt
1 to 1½ cups buttermilk

This corned beef dinner includes dried shell beans among its vegetables, along with sliced rutabaga, beets, potatoes, carrots and cabbage.

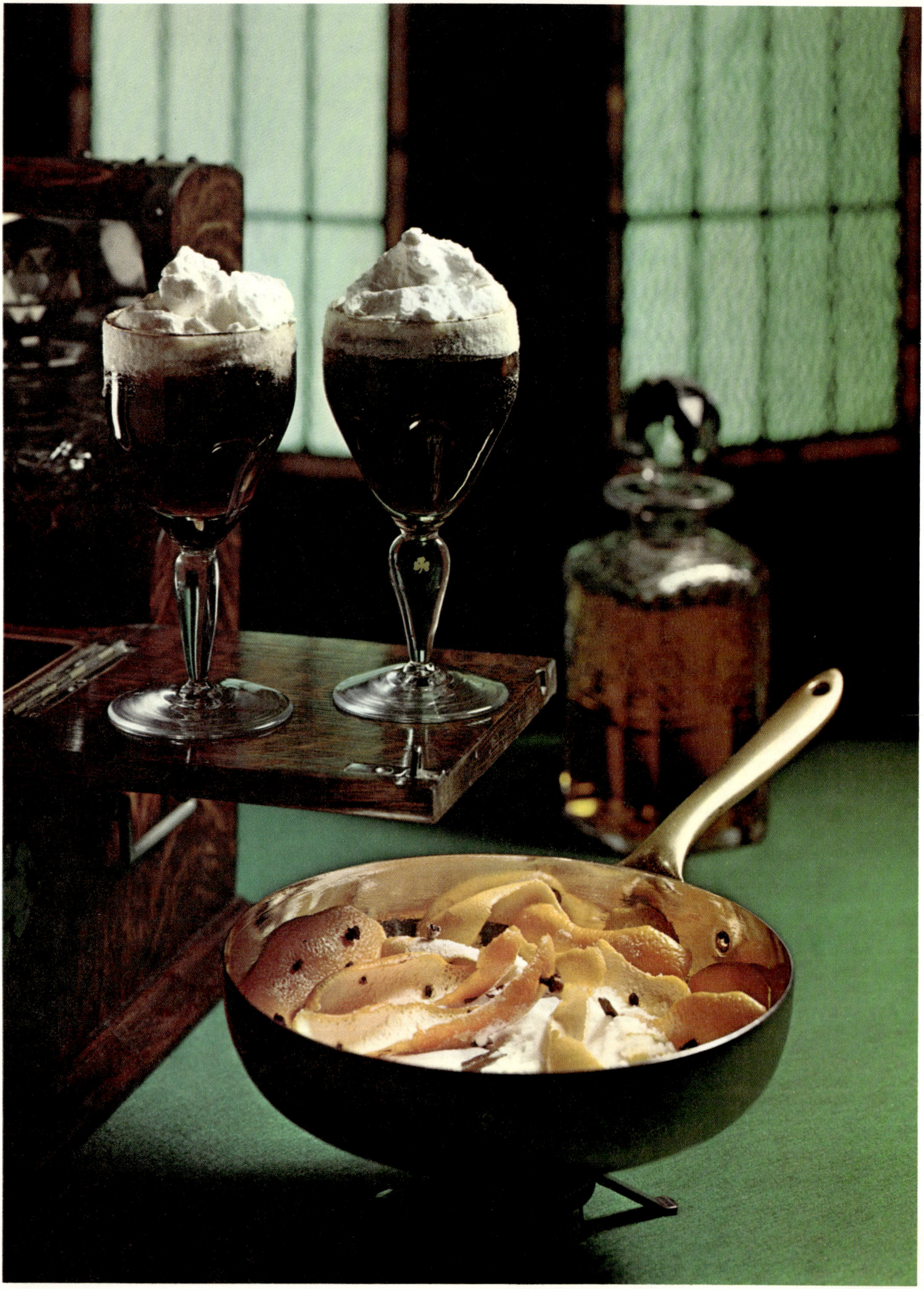

Boxty Pancakes

Peel the potatoes and drop them into a bowl of cold water to prevent their discoloring. In a large bowl, stir together the flour, salt and milk, and optional caraway seeds. One at a time, pat the potatoes dry and grate them coarsely into a sieve or colander. As you proceed, press each potato firmly down into the sieve with the back of a large spoon to remove its moisture, then immediately stir the gratings into the flour-and-milk mixture.

In a heavy 8- to 10-inch skillet, melt 2 tablespoons of the butter or fat over moderate heat. When the foam begins to subside, pour in about 1 tablespoon of batter for each pancake. Cook 3 or 4 pancakes at a time, leaving enough space between them so that they can spread into 3½- to 4-inch cakes. Fry them for about 3 minutes on each side, or until they are golden brown and crisp around the edges. Transfer the finished pancakes to a heated plate and drape foil over them to keep them warm while you cook the remaining cakes, adding fat to the pan when necessary. Serve the pancakes as soon as they are all cooked, accompanied if you wish by crisp bacon.

To make about 10 pancakes

3 medium-sized potatoes (about 1 pound), preferably baking potatoes
½ cup flour
½ teaspoon salt
¼ cup milk
½ teaspoon caraway seeds (optional)
3 to 4 tablespoons butter or rendered bacon fat
Crisp fried bacon (optional)

Irish Coffee

Stud the strips of orange and lemon peel with 2 cloves each and place them in a skillet or chafing dish with the stick of cinnamon and the 2 teaspoons of sugar. Set over moderate heat, stirring occasionally with a wooden spoon, until the sugar has melted; pour the Irish whiskey into the pan and light a match to the liquid. Be sure to step back since the flame will flare up instantly. Shake the pan back and forth slowly until the flame dies out; pour in the hot coffee all at once and let it come to a simmer. Remove from the heat.

Rub the cut edge of a strip of lemon peel around the inside of each glass or mug and dip the container into a dish of sugar so that the sugar adheres to the inside rim. Pour in the coffee, trying not to disturb the sugar. Top each serving with a dollop of whipped cream.

To serve 2

4 strips orange peel
4 strips lemon peel
16 whole cloves
1 stick cinnamon
2 teaspoons superfine sugar
5 ounces Irish whiskey
1½ cups strong hot coffee
A dish of superfine or confectioners' sugar
¼ cup whipped heavy cream

Two 8-ounce stemmed goblets, mugs or cups

These whipped-cream-topped servings of Irish coffee get their distinctive flavor from Irish whiskey that has been poured over clove-studded orange and lemon peel, cinnamon stick and sugar *(foreground),* and then set aflame.

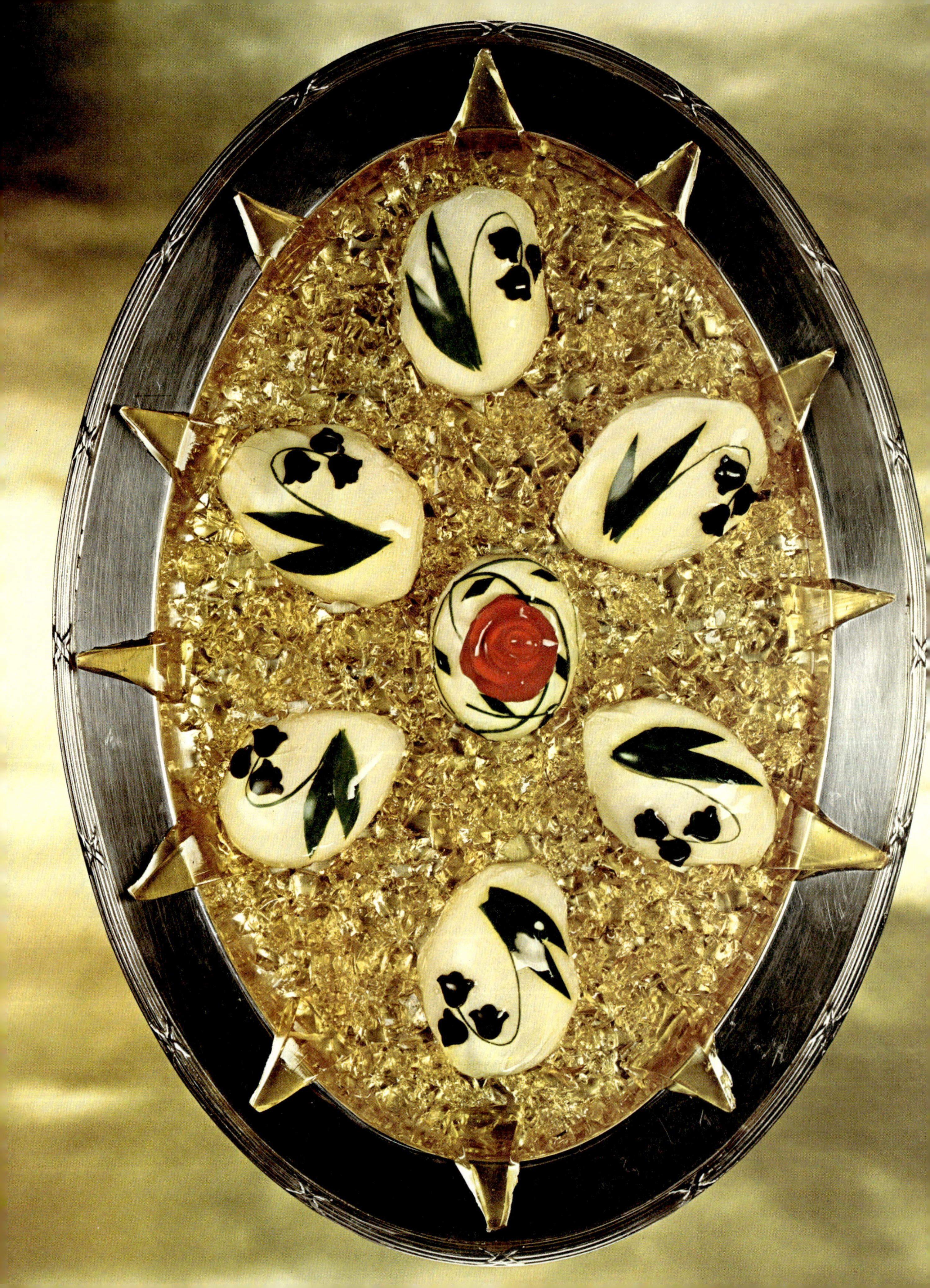

Easter
Passover
Derby Day

The Rites of Spring

"Spring, the sweet spring, is the year's pleasant king," exulted the Elizabethan poet Thomas Nash, and his delight in the season is shared by families around an Easter table or gathered for the Passover Seder, or by guests at elaborate Derby Day breakfasts.

This is the season when the simple egg, ancient symbol of rebirth and resurrection, comes into its own in such dishes as *oeufs en gelée,* decorated with spring-flower designs and set in a bed of trembling aspic. The egg vitalizes traditional soups and classic sauces; it can even be hard-cooked, then dyed red and baked inside a Greek Easter bread. Louisville racegoers may breakfast on eggs Derby, sauced with sweetbreads and mushrooms, or Kentucky scrambled eggs with corn and peppers.

Ham with a bourbon-and-orange glaze or a crown roast of spring lamb served with early garden vegetables would be a perfect choice for an Easter meal. The main dish at a Passover dinner might be a chicken-and-matzo casserole, subtly flavored with onions and dill.

A glittering version of *oeufs en gelée* features poached eggs with leeks and truffles forming lilies of the valley. This classic French dish makes a pretty beginning for a luncheon on Easter Day.

Oeufs en gelée printemps

Crown roast of spring lamb

Bourbon-glazed Easter ham

New potatoes, young peas, fresh asparagus

Rumanian and Greek Easter breads

Russian Easter cakes

Foods for the Passover Seder

Derby Day breakfasts

Turkey hash and batty cakes

Kentucky mint juleps

Spring Recipes

Easter Favorites

Oeufs en Gelée Printemps

OEUFS EN GELÉE (EGGS IN ASPIC): Pour cold water into a 12-inch sauté pan or skillet to a depth of about 2 inches, and add the vinegar. Bring to a simmer, then reduce the heat so that the surface of the liquid barely shimmers. Break 4 eggs into individual saucers. Gently slide one egg into the water, and with a large spoon, lift the white over the yolk. Repeat once or twice more to enclose the yolk in the white. One at a time, quickly slide the 3 other eggs from the saucers into the pan, enclosing them in their whites and spacing them at least 1 inch apart.

Poach the eggs for 3 or 4 minutes until the whites are set and the yolks still feel soft when prodded gently with the tip of your finger. With a slotted spoon, transfer the eggs to a bowl of cold water and let them cool completely. Repeating the procedure, poach the 4 remaining eggs. Then lift the eggs from the water and with scissors trim each egg into a smooth oval, being careful not to pierce the yolk. Place the eggs on a wire rack set in a jelly-roll pan and refrigerate for at least 2 hours.

Meanwhile prepare the decoration for the eggs. Drop the leek or scallion leaves into boiling water and boil for 1 or 2 minutes. Drain the greens in a sieve, run cold water over them, then spread them on paper towels and pat them dry. Cut the leek or scallion leaves into bladelike leaf shapes and a dozen or more thin strips to use as stems. Slice the truffle into rounds ⅛ inch thick. With a lily-of-the-valley truffle cutter, make truffle flowers and set them aside with the leaves and stems.

With a small, sharp knife, peel the skin of the tomato in spiral fashion to make a long continuous strip about ¾ inch wide. Shape the strip into a roselike coil and set aside. Coarsely chop the tomato and set aside.

GELÉE (ASPIC): Combine the chopped tomato, chopped leek, gelatin, egg whites, egg shells and tarragon in a heavy 2- to 3-quart enameled or stainless-steel saucepan and pour in the stock. Set the pan over moderate heat and, stirring constantly, bring the stock to a simmer.

When the mixture begins to froth and rise, remove the pan from the heat and let the stock rest for 10 minutes. Then pour the entire contents of the pan into a fine sieve lined with a double thickness of dampened cheesecloth and set over another enameled or stainless-steel pan. Allow the liquid to drain through undisturbed. Season with more salt if needed.

Set the pan in a large pot half-filled with crushed ice or ice cubes and water, and stir the aspic with a metal spoon until it thickens enough to flow sluggishly. Then spoon a little aspic over one of the eggs. It should cling and cover the surface with a thin translucent glaze. Coat the other eggs with aspic and return them to the refrigerator until the aspic is firm. (Keep the remaining aspic at room temperature so that it remains liquid

To serve 8 as a first course

POACHED EGGS
¼ cup tarragon vinegar
8 fresh eggs

DECORATION FOR THE EGGS
2 or 3 large green leaves from the top of a leek or scallion
1 black truffle
1 small firm ripe tomato

GELÉE
1 small firm ripe tomato, coarsely chopped
¼ cup coarsely chopped leeks, including 2 inches of the green tops, thoroughly washed
3 envelopes unflavored gelatin
¼ cup egg whites
2 egg shells, finely crushed
2 tablespoons finely cut fresh tarragon leaves or 1 tablespoon crumbled, dried tarragon
1 quart canned chicken stock, chilled, then degreased

and ready to use; if it begins to set, warm briefly over low heat to soften it, then stir it over ice again until it is thick but still fluid.)

Dip the truffle flowers and green leaf blades and stems one at a time into the aspic and arrange them fancifully on top of 7 of the eggs. Dip the tomato rose in aspic, place it in the center of the remaining egg and create a swirl of stems and leaves around it. Refrigerate again until the decorations are anchored firmly. Then carefully spoon aspic over the eggs two more times, chilling them to set the glaze after each coating.

With a rubber spatula, scrape up the aspic left in the jelly-roll pan and add it to the aspic remaining in the pan. Melt it over low heat, then pour a ⅛-inch layer of aspic over the bottom of a serving platter and pour the rest into a small loaf pan. Refrigerate the platter and pan until the aspic has firmly set. Remove the pan from the refrigerator, dip it in hot water, then place an inverted plate over it. Grasping pan and plate together firmly, turn them over. The aspic should slide out easily. Cut the aspic into ¼-inch slices, and then into diamonds or other shapes. Finely dice the scraps

Arrange the eggs decoratively on the chilled platter with the tomato-topped egg in the center. Use the aspic diamonds to ring the platter and scatter the dice between the eggs. Refrigerate until ready to serve.

Greek Egg-and-Lemon Soup

To serve 4 to 6

6 cups chicken stock, fresh or canned
⅓ cup uncooked long- or medium-grain rice
4 eggs
3 tablespoons fresh lemon juice
Salt
2 tablespoons finely cut fresh mint or 1 tablespoon dried mint

In a 3- to 4-quart saucepan, bring the chicken stock to a boil over high heat. Pour in the rice, reduce the heat to low and simmer partially uncovered for about 15 minutes, or until the grains are just tender but still slightly resistant to the bite. Reduce the heat to low.

Beat the eggs with a whisk or a rotary beater until frothy. Beat in the lemon juice and stir in about ¼ cup of the simmering chicken broth. Then slowly pour the mixture into the broth, stirring constantly. Cook over low heat for 3 to 5 minutes, or until the soup thickens enough to coat the spoon lightly. Do not let the soup come to a boil or the eggs will curdle. Add salt to taste and serve at once, garnished with mint.

Norwegian Spinach Soup

To serve 4 to 6

2 pounds fresh spinach, or 2 packages frozen chopped spinach
2 quarts chicken stock, fresh or canned
3 tablespoons butter
2 tablespoons flour
1 teaspoon salt
¼ teaspoon white pepper
⅛ teaspoon nutmeg
2 hard-cooked eggs, sliced

Wash the fresh spinach thoroughly under cold running water to remove any sand. Drain the spinach by shaking it vigorously by hand or in a lettuce basket, then chop it coarsely. If frozen spinach is used, thoroughly defrost and drain it.

Bring the 2 quarts of chicken stock to a boil in a 3- to 4-quart saucepan and add the fresh or frozen chopped spinach. Simmer uncovered about 6 to 8 minutes, then pour the entire contents of the pan into a sieve set over a large bowl. Press down hard on the spinach with the back of a wooden spoon to extract all of its juices. Set the liquid aside in the bowl and chop the cooked spinach very fine.

Melt the 3 tablespoons of butter in the saucepan. When the foam subsides, remove the pan from the heat and stir in the flour. With a wire whisk, beat the hot stock into this white *roux* a little at a time. Return the saucepan to the heat and, stirring it constantly, bring it to a boil. Then add the spinach. Season the soup with salt, pepper and nutmeg. Half cover the pan and simmer the soup over low heat about 5 minutes longer. Stir occasionally.

Garnish each serving of soup with a few slices of hard-cooked egg. On festive occasions, such as Easter, Norwegian spinach soup is often served with a stuffed egg half floating in each soup bowl. To make these, remove the yolks from 2 or 3 hard-cooked eggs (depending on how many people you plan to serve) and mash them to a paste with about 1 to 2 teaspoons of softened butter. Roll the mixture into little balls and nestle 2 or 3 into each halved egg white.

Marinated Leg of Lamb, Yugoslav Style

Rub the leg of lamb with the salt and put it in an earthenware or enameled casserole. In a saucepan, combine the vinegar, water, bay leaves, onions, peppercorns, parsley and thyme. Over high heat, bring to a boil, cool to lukewarm, then pour over the lamb. Marinate the lamb, uncovered, in the refrigerator for 6 to 24 hours, turning it every couple of hours.

Preheat the oven to 350°. Remove the lamb from the marinade and pat it dry with paper towels. Heat the lard in a heavy 12-inch skillet until a light haze forms over it, then add the lamb. Cook it for 15 to 20 minutes, or until it is brown, turning it every 5 minutes with two wooden spoons. Place it in a casserole or roasting pan just large enough to hold it. Strain the marinade into a bowl and add the contents of the strainer, 1½ cups of the marinade and the tomatoes to the casserole. Lay the bacon slices over the lamb. Bring the liquid to a boil on top of the stove, then cook, covered, in the middle of the oven for about 2 hours, checking occasionally to see that the liquid is barely bubbling. (Reduce the heat if necessary.) When the meat shows no resistance when pierced with the point of a small sharp knife, remove it to a platter. Strain the cooking juices through a sieve into a saucepan, pressing down hard on the vegetables before discarding them. Skim the surface fat and bring the juices to a boil on top of the stove. Taste for seasoning. To serve, slice the lamb, and arrange it on a serving platter. Mask the slices with some of the sauce and serve the rest in a sauceboat.

To serve 6 to 8

A 7-pound leg of lamb, boned and tied
1 teaspoon salt
1 cup vinegar
2 cups water
3 bay leaves
2 cups sliced onions
6 peppercorns
2 sprigs parsley
½ teaspoon thyme
2 tablespoons lard
4 large fresh tomatoes, coarsely chopped, or 1 large can tomatoes, drained
3 slices bacon
Salt

Crown Roast of Lamb with Peas and New Potatoes

Preheat the oven to 475°. With the point of a small, sharp knife make small incisions a few inches apart in the meaty portions of the lamb, and insert in them the slivers of garlic, if you are using it. Combine the salt, pepper and rosemary, and with your fingers pat the mixture all over the bottom and sides of the crown. To help keep its shape, stuff the crown with a crumpled sheet of foil and wrap the ends of the chop bones in strips of foil to prevent them from charring and snapping off. Place the crown of lamb on a small rack set in a shallow roasting pan just large enough to hold it comfortably and roast it in the center of the oven for about 20 minutes. Then turn down the heat to 400° and surround the crown with the new potatoes, basting them with the pan drippings and sprinkling them

To serve 6 to 8

A crown roast of lamb, consisting of 16 to 18 chops and weighing about 4½ pounds
1 clove garlic, cut into tiny slivers (optional)
2 teaspoons salt
1 teaspoon freshly ground black pepper
1 teaspoon crushed dried rosemary
16 to 18 peeled new potatoes, all about 1½ inches in diameter
3 cups cooked fresh or frozen peas
2 tablespoons melted butter
6 to 8 sprigs of fresh mint

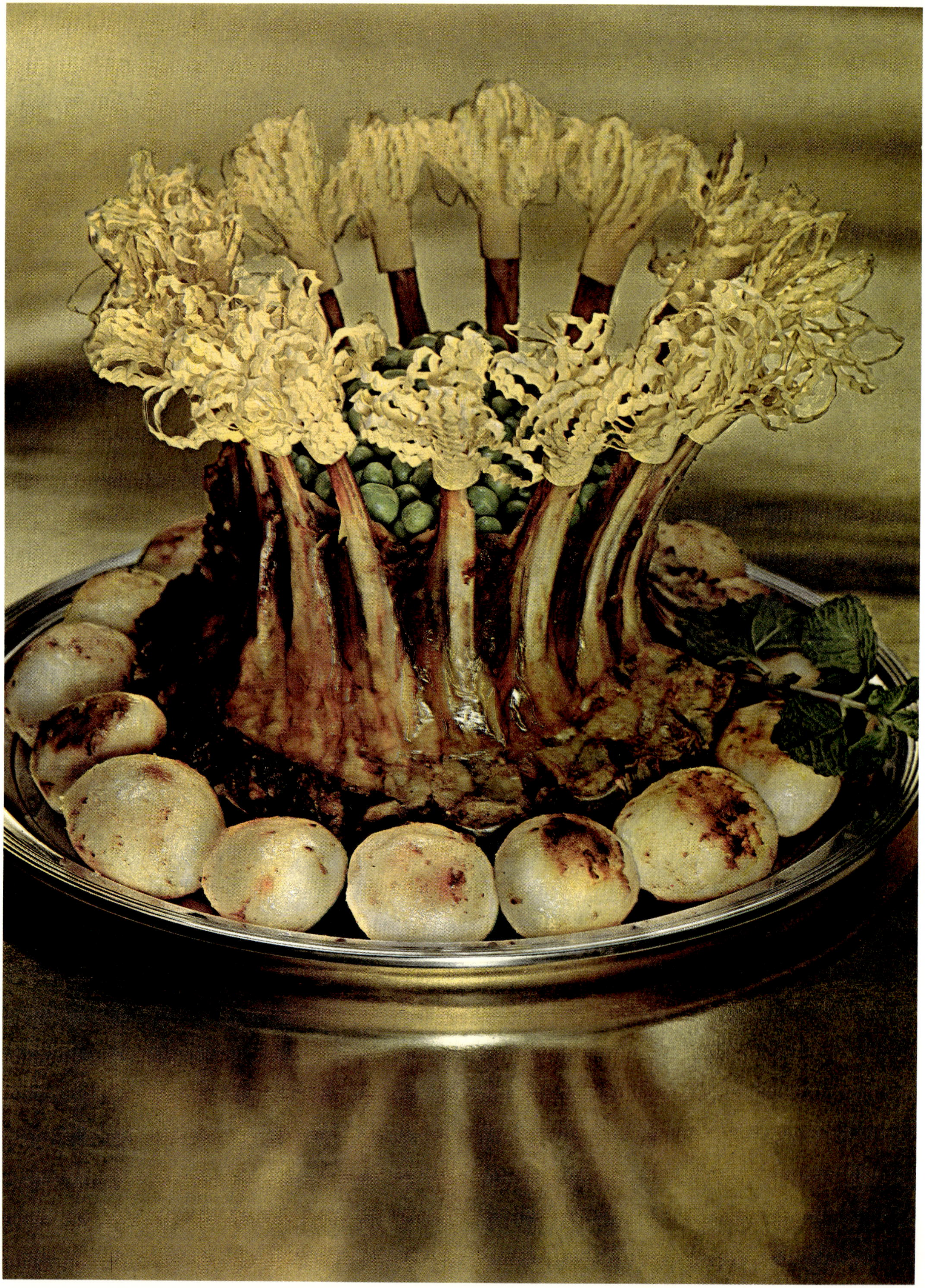

lightly with salt. Continue to roast the lamb (basting the lamb is unnecessary, but baste the potatoes every 15 minutes or so) for about an hour to an hour and 15 minutes, depending upon how well done you prefer your lamb. Ideally, it should be served when it is still somewhat pink, and should register 140° to 150° on a meat thermometer.

When the crown is done, carefully transfer it to a large circular platter, remove the foil and let the lamb rest about 10 minutes to make carving easier. Meanwhile, combine the peas with the melted butter and season them with as much salt as is necessary. Fill the hollow of the crown with as many of the peas as it will hold and serve any remaining peas separately. Put a paper frill on the end of each chop bone and surround the crown with the roasted potatoes. Garnish with mint and serve at once.

To carve the lamb, insert a large fork in the side of the crown to steady it and with a large, sharp knife cut down through each rib to detach the chops. Two rib chops per person is a customary portion.

Boiled Artichokes

Trim the bases of the artichokes flush and flat. Bend and snap off the small bottom leaves and any bruised outer leaves. Lay each artichoke on its side, grip it firmly, and slice about 1 inch off the top. With scissors, trim ¼ inch off the points of the rest of the leaves. Rub all the cut edges with lemon to prevent discoloring. To remove the chokes before cooking, spread the top leaves apart and pull out the inner core of thistlelike yellow leaves. With a long-handled spoon, scrape out the hairy choke inside. Squeeze in a little lemon juice and press the artichoke back into shape.

In a large enameled kettle or soup pot, bring 6 quarts of water and 3 tablespoons of salt to a bubbling boil. Drop in the artichokes and return the water to a boil. Reduce the heat and boil briskly uncovered, turning the artichokes occasionally. It will take about 15 minutes to cook artichokes without their chokes, about 30 minutes with the chokes still in. They are done when their bases are tender when pierced with the tip of a sharp knife. Remove them from the kettle with tongs and drain them upside down in a colander. Serve the artichokes hot with melted butter, hollandaise or béarnaise sauce *(below and overleaf)*.

To serve 6

6 twelve- to fourteen-ounce artichokes
1 lemon, cut
6 quarts water
3 tablespoons salt

Sauce Hollandaise

In a small, heavy pan over low heat, melt 12 tablespoons of butter without letting it brown. Set the butter aside and keep it warm. Off the heat, in a 1½- to 2-quart enameled or stainless steel saucepan, beat the egg yolks vigorously with a wire whisk for 1 minute or until they become thick; the bottom of the pan should show through when the whisk is drawn across it. Beat in the lemon juice. Then place the pan over very low heat and stir in the 1 tablespoon of chilled butter with the whisk. Stir constantly, lift-

To make about 1½ cups

12 tablespoons butter (1½ quarter-pound sticks)
3 egg yolks
1 tablespoon lemon juice
1 tablespoon chilled butter
1 tablespoon heavy cream
Salt
White pepper

Lamb is an Easter tradition in many countries, and a crown roast of lamb, gaily decorated with paper frills, is a dish fit for a king. Whole new potatoes and sprigs of mint embellish this regal dish, whose hollow is filled with fresh peas. The size of the roast is determined by the number of guests—two chops each.

To make about 1½ to 2 cups

¼ cup tarragon wine vinegar
¼ cup dry white wine
1 tablespoon finely chopped shallots or scallions
2 tablespoons finely cut fresh tarragon or 2 teaspoons dried tarragon and 1 tablespoon finely chopped fresh parsley
1½ cups *sauce hollandaise* (recipe above) made without lemon juice
Salt
White pepper

To serve 4

2 hard-cooked eggs, coarsely chopped
1 tablespoon finely chopped fresh parsley
½ teaspoon plus 3 tablespoons salt
⅛ teaspoon white pepper
12 tablespoons unsalted butter (1½ quarter-pound sticks), melted and cooled
2½ to 3 pounds fresh asparagus

To serve 4 to 6

1 firm 7- to 8-inch head Boston lettuce
3 cups fresh shelled green peas (about 3 pounds)
12 peeled white onions, about ¾ inch in diameter
6 parsley sprigs, tied together
6 tablespoons butter, cut into ½-inch pieces
½ cup water
½ teaspoon salt
½ teaspoon sugar
2 tablespoons soft butter

ing the pan off the stove occasionally to prevent it from overheating, until the butter has been absorbed and the mixture thickens enough to coat the wires of the whisk lightly. Remove the pan from the heat and beat in the cream. Still off the heat, pour in the warm, melted butter by droplets, stirring constantly with the whisk. The sauce will thicken into a heavy cream. Taste the hollandaise and season with salt and white pepper.

Sauce Béarnaise

In a small saucepan, briskly boil the vinegar, wine, shallots and 1 tablespoon fresh or 2 teaspoons dried tarragon until reduced to 2 tablespoons. Strain the liquid through a fine sieve into a small mixing bowl, pressing down hard on the herbs with a spoon before discarding them. Then whisk the strained liquid into the *sauce hollandaise* along with 1 tablespoon of fresh tarragon or parsley. Taste and season with salt and pepper.

Asparagus with Egg Sauce

In a small mixing bowl, stir the chopped eggs, parsley, ½ teaspoon of salt and the pepper together with a fork until they are well combined. Then, stirring constantly, pour in the butter in a thin stream. Cover the bowl tightly with foil or plastic wrap and set the sauce aside.

Lay the asparagus spears side by side on a board and trim their bases with a sharp knife. Ideally, all spears should be the same length. With a small, sharp knife—not a vegetable parer—peel each spear, starting at the base. At the base end the peeling may be as thick as ¹⁄₁₆ inch, but it should gradually become paper thin as the knife cuts and slides toward the tip. Be careful not to cut off the tips. When all the spears are peeled, wash them under cold running water.

In an 7- to 8-quart enameled or stainless-steel casserole, bring 6 quarts of water and 3 tablespoons of salt to a vigorous boil over high heat. Drop in the asparagus and boil uncovered and undisturbed for 8 to 10 minutes, or until the ends are tender but still slightly resistant when pierced with a small, sharp knife. Do not overcook.

With tongs, transfer the asparagus spears to a large heated platter and serve at once, accompanied by the egg sauce in a separate bowl.

Fresh Green Peas à la Française

Remove the wilted outer leaves of the lettuce and trim the stem. Rinse the lettuce in cold water, spreading the leaves apart gently, to remove all traces of sand. Cut the lettuce into 4 or 6 wedges, and bind each wedge with soft string to keep it in shape while cooking.

In a heavy 3-quart saucepan, bring the peas, lettuce wedges, onions, parsley, 6 tablespoons butter, water, salt and sugar to a boil over moderate heat, toss lightly to mix flavors, then cover the pan tightly and cook for 30 minutes, stirring occasionally, until the peas and onions are tender and the liquid nearly cooked away. If the liquid hasn't evaporated, cook the peas uncovered, shaking the pan constantly, for a minute or two until it does.

Remove the parsley and cut the strings off the lettuce. Gently stir in 2 tablespoons of soft butter; taste and season. Transfer to a heated vegetable dish and serve.

Scalloped Potatoes Dauphinoises

Preheat the oven to 425°. Rub the bottom and sides of a flameproof baking-and-serving dish, 10 to 12 inches across and 2 inches deep, with the bruised garlic, and grease it lightly with butter. Dry the potato slices with a paper towel, then spread half of the slices in the bottom of the dish. Sprinkle them with half the cheese, butter bits, salt and pepper. Spread the rest of the slices in the dish and sprinkle the remaining cheese, butter, salt and pepper on top. Pour the milk into the side of the dish. Bring to a simmer over low heat and then bake in the upper third of the oven for 20 minutes, or until the potatoes are almost tender when pierced with the tip of a sharp knife. At this point remove any residual liquid with a bulb baster and bake for another 5 minutes, or until the potatoes are tender, the milk absorbed, and the top nicely browned. Serve at once.

To serve 6

1½ cups grated, imported Swiss cheese
6 tablespoons butter, cut in ¼-inch bits
1 teaspoon salt
⅛ teaspoon coarsely ground black pepper
1¼ cups milk
1 garlic clove, peeled and bruised with the flat of a knife
2½ pounds firm boiling potatoes, old or new, peeled and cut into ⅛-inch slices (about 8 cups)

Baked Bourbon-glazed Ham

Preheat the oven to 325°. Place the ham fat side up on a rack set in a shallow roasting pan large enough to hold the ham comfortably. Bake in the middle of the oven, without basting, for two hours, or until the meat can be easily pierced with a fork. For greater cooking certainty, insert a meat thermometer in the fleshiest part of the ham before baking it. It should register between 130° and 140° when the ham is done.

When the ham is cool enough to handle comfortably, cut away the rind with a large, sharp knife. Then score the ham by cutting deeply through the fat until you reach the meat, making the incisions ½ inch apart lengthwise and crosswise. Return the ham to the rack in the pan and raise the oven heat to 450°. With a pastry brush, paint the ham on all sides with ½ cup of the whiskey. Then combine the sugar and mustard and ¼ cup of whiskey, and pat the mixture firmly into the scored fat. Stud the fat at the intersections or in the center of each diamond with a whole clove, and arrange the orange sections as decoratively as you can on the top of the ham with toothpicks or small skewers to secure them. Baste lightly with the drippings on the bottom of the pan and bake the ham undisturbed in the hot oven for 15 to 20 minutes, or until the sugar has melted and formed a brilliant glaze.

To serve 12 to 14

A 12- to 14-pound smoked ham, processed, precooked variety
¾ cup bourbon whiskey
2 cups dark brown sugar
1 tablespoon dry mustard
¾ cup whole cloves
2 navel oranges, peeled and sectioned

Overleaf: A spectacular Easter ham is garnished with oranges and parsley and glazed with brown sugar, mustard and bourbon. This 14-pound ham represents a triumph of American technology. In the old days hams were soaked and boiled for days, but this precooked, cured ham needed to be baked for only two hours.

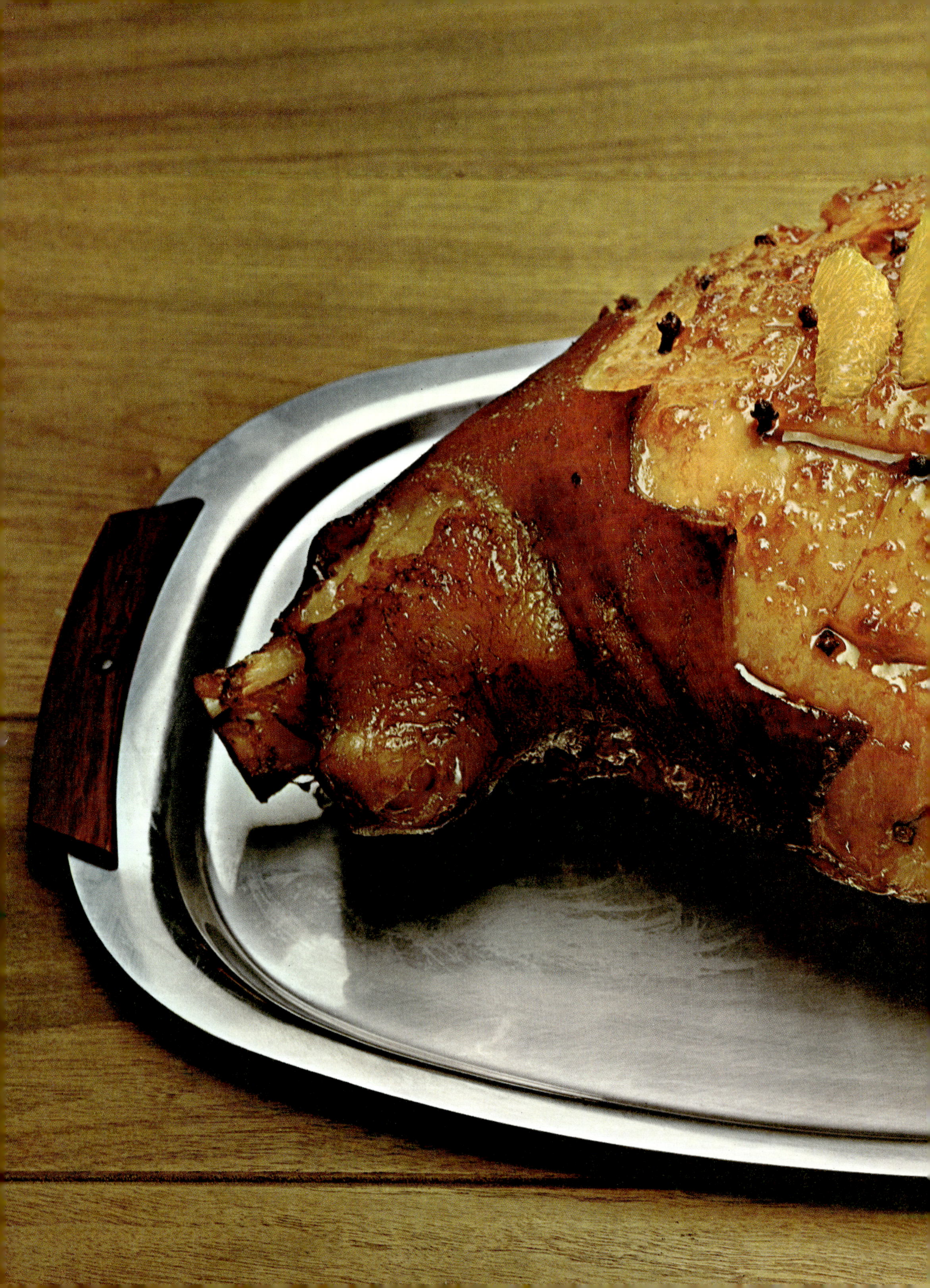

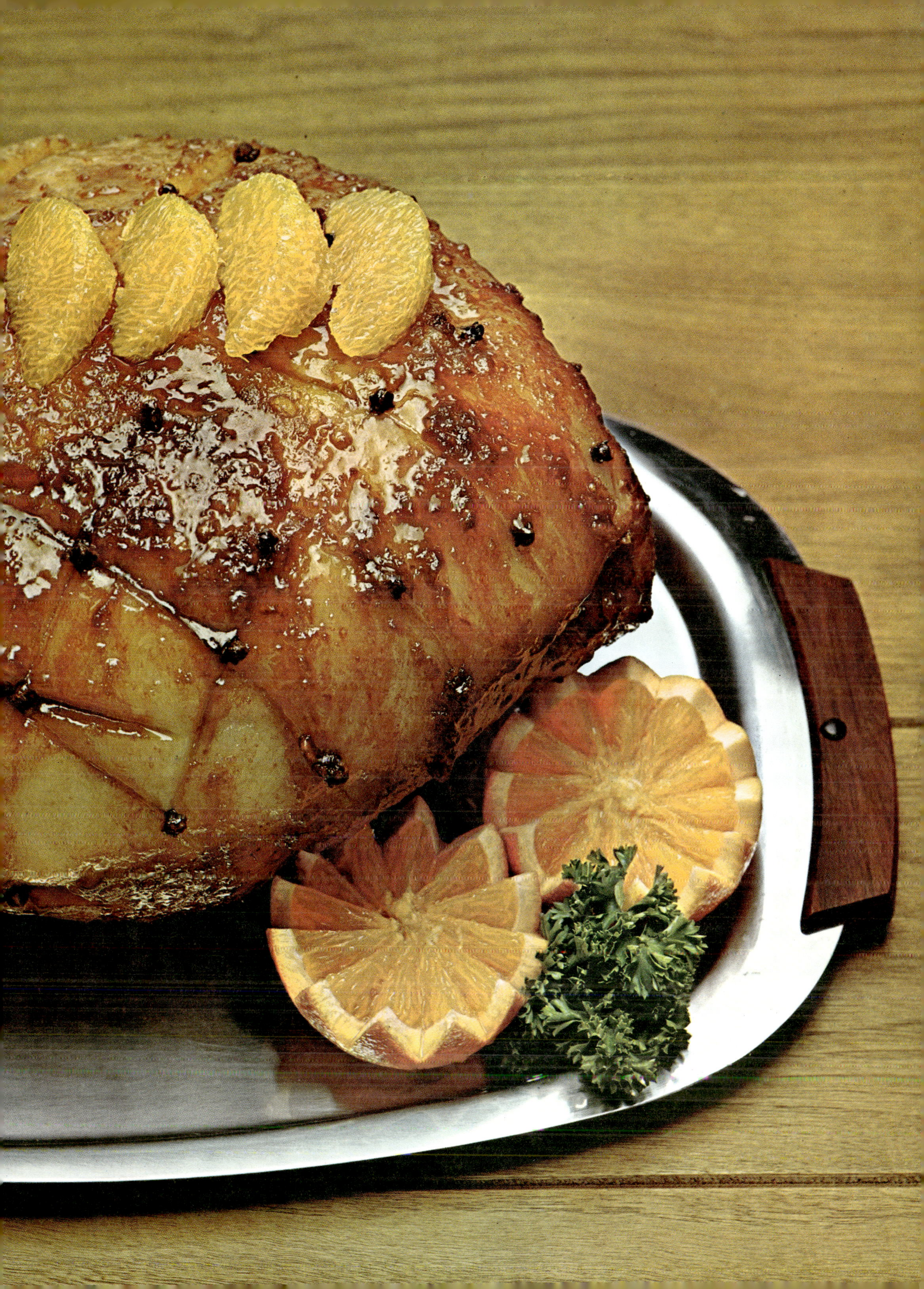

Tsoureki—Greek Easter Bread

To make one 6-inch round loaf

2 packages active dry yeast
½ teaspoon plus ¼ cup sugar
¼ cup lukewarm milk (110° to 115°)
2 to 2½ cups all-purpose flour
1 teaspoon salt
2 eggs
8 tablespoons (1 quarter-pound stick) unsalted butter, cut into small bits, plus 1 tablespoon butter, softened
1 teaspoon finely grated lemon peel
1 hard-cooked egg in the shell, dyed red with vegetable food coloring
1 egg yolk, lightly beaten

In a small, shallow bowl, sprinkle the yeast and the ½ teaspoon of sugar over the lukewarm milk. Let it stand for 2 or 3 minutes, then stir to dissolve the yeast completely. Set the bowl in a warm, draft-free place (such as an unlighted oven) for 8 to 10 minutes, or until the mixture doubles in volume.

Combine 1½ cups of flour, the remaining ¼ cup of sugar, and the salt in a deep mixing bowl. Make a well in the center, and add the yeast and the 2 eggs. Gently stir the center ingredients together with a large spoon, then gradually incorporate the flour and continue beating until all the ingredients are well combined. Beat in the 8 tablespoons of butter and lemon peel, add up to 1 cup more flour, beating it in a few tablespoons at a time and using as much as necessary to form a dough that can be gathered into a soft and still somewhat sticky ball. (When the dough becomes difficult to stir easily, work in the flour with your fingers.)

Place the dough on a lightly floured surface, and knead it by pressing it down, pushing it forward several times with the heel of your hand, and folding it back on itself. Repeat for about 10 minutes, or until the dough is smooth and elastic. Sprinkle the dough with a little extra flour from time to time to prevent it from sticking to the board.

Shape the dough into a ball and place it in a large, lightly buttered bowl. Dust the top with a little flour, drape with a kitchen towel and set aside in a warm, draft-free place for about 1 hour until the dough doubles in bulk.

With a pastry brush, coat a baking sheet with the tablespoon of softened butter. Punch the dough down with a single blow of your fist, then transfer it to a lightly floured surface. To shape the dough into a snail-like loaf, roll it into a thick rope about 2 inches in diameter and 24 inches long. Starting at one end, loop the rope into a circle about 6 inches in diameter, and then into ever-smaller concentric circles. Carefully transfer the loaf to the baking sheet and let it rise in a warm place for about 30 minutes.

Preheat the oven to 350°. Press the dyed egg gently into the center and brush the top of the loaf with the beaten egg yolk. Bake in the middle of the oven for about 45 minutes, or until golden brown and crusty. Cool completely on a cake rack before serving.

Cozonac—Rumanian Easter Bread

To make two 14-inch loaves

DOUGH
1 cup lukewarm milk (110° to 115°)
½ teaspoon plus ¼ cup sugar
1 package active dry yeast
3½ to 4 cups all-purpose flour
1 teaspoon salt
3 eggs
1 tablespoon softened butter

In a small shallow bowl, sprinkle ¼ cup of the lukewarm milk with ½ teaspoon of the sugar and the yeast. Let the mixture stand for 2 or 3 minutes, then stir to dissolve the yeast. Set the bowl in a warm, draft-free place, such as an unlighted oven, for 5 to 8 minutes, or until the yeast mixture has doubled in volume.

In a deep mixing bowl, combine 3½ cups of flour, ¼ cup of sugar and the salt. Make a well in the center and pour in the yeast mixture and the remaining ¾ cup of milk. Drop in the eggs, gently stir together with a large spoon, then beat until the ingredients are well combined.

Transfer the dough to a lightly floured board and knead, pressing it down with the heels of your hands, pushing it forward, and folding it back on itself. Add up to ½ cup more flour by the tablespoonful if necessary to make a medium-firm dough. Continue to knead for about 10 minutes, until the dough is smooth and elastic.

Coat the bottom and sides of a large mixing bowl with the softened butter and drop in the dough. Drape loosely with a kitchen towel and set aside in the warm, draft-free place for about 1 hour, or until the dough doubles in bulk. Punch it down with a blow of your fist and set aside in the warm, draft-free place to rise again.

FILLING: In a 1- to 1½-quart saucepan, combine 1 cup of sugar and 1 cup of water. Bring to a boil over moderate heat, stirring constantly until the sugar is dissolved. Raise the heat and boil, uncovered and undisturbed, for 10 minutes. Remove from the heat and stir in the walnuts, raisins, lemon rind and cinnamon. Set aside to cool to room temperature.

To assemble and bake: Preheat the oven to 400°. Punch the dough down with a blow of your fist and cut the dough in half. Roll out each half to a 12-by-14-inch rectangle about ¼ inch thick. Spread each rectangle with half of the filling and, with the wide side of each rectangle toward you, roll them up jelly-roll fashion. Transfer the loaves to one large or two medium-sized baking sheets and tuck under the ends of the dough. Drape the loaves loosely with kitchen towels and set aside in the draft-free place for about 30 minutes, or until they have doubled in volume. Brush the loaves with the egg-and-milk mixture and bake in the center of the oven for 15 minutes. Lower the oven temperature to 375° and bake for another 15 or 20 minutes, or until the loaves are golden brown. Transfer to wire racks to cool slightly before serving.

FILLING
1 cup sugar
1 cup water
3 cups ground walnuts
2 cups chopped white seedless raisins
1 teaspoon grated lemon rind
1 teaspoon cinnamon

1 egg combined with 2 tablespoons milk

Babka—Polish Easter Cake

Pour the lukewarm milk into a small bowl and sprinkle it with the yeast and ½ teaspoon of the sugar. Let the mixture stand for 2 or 3 minutes, then stir to dissolve the yeast completely. Set the bowl aside in a warm, draft-free place (such as an unlighted oven) for about 10 minutes, or until the mixture almost doubles in volume.

Place 6 cups of the flour, the remaining sugar and the salt in a deep mixing bowl and make a well in the center. Pour in the yeast mixture and the egg yolks and, with a large spoon, gradually stir the flour into the liquid ingredients. Continue to stir until well mixed, then beat in ¾ pound of butter a few tablespoonfuls at a time. The dough should be firm enough to be gathered into a medium-soft ball. If necessary, stir in up to ½ cup more flour, adding it by the tablespoon.

Transfer the dough to an electric mixer equipped with a kneading hook and knead for about 20 minutes, or until the dough is very smooth, glossy and elastic. Or knead the dough by hand—pushing it down with the heels of your hands, pressing it forward and folding it back on itself —for about 40 minutes.

Shape the dough into a ball, place it in a lightly buttered bowl and dust the top with flour. Drape a towel over the bowl and set it aside in the draft-free place for about 1 hour, or until the dough doubles in volume. With a pastry brush, spread the 2 tablespoons of softened butter

To make 1 large cake

CAKE
1¼ cups lukewarm milk (110° to 115°)
2 packages active dry yeast
6 tablespoons sugar
6 to 6½ cups all-purpose flour
½ teaspoon salt
10 egg yolks
¾ pound plus 2 tablespoons unsalted butter, softened
1 cup white seedless raisins
2 tablespoons finely grated orange peel
1 tablespoon finely grated lemon peel

WHITE ICING
2 cups confectioners' sugar
¼ cup cold water
2 teaspoons strained fresh lemon juice

Candlelit *kulich,* surrounded by dyed eggs, are brought to a 17th Century Orthodox church in Moscow to be blessed by the priest.

over the bottom and sides of a Turk head mold or, less traditionally, a 2-quart *Gugelhupf* pan. Sprinkle the butter with the remaining ¼ cup of flour and tip the pan from side to side to spread it evenly. Invert the pan and rap it sharply to remove the excess flour.

Punch the dough down with a single blow of your fist and into it knead the raisins, orange peel and lemon peel. Pat the dough evenly over the bottom of the buttered and floured mold, drape with a towel, and set aside in the draft-free place again for 1 hour, or until the dough has doubled in volume and risen almost to the top of the mold.

Preheat the oven to 375°. Bake the cake in the middle of the oven for about 40 minutes, or until it is golden brown. Turn the cake out onto a cake rack and let it cool briefly at room temperature while you prepare the icing.

In a small bowl, combine the confectioners' sugar, water and lemon juice, and beat vigorously together with a spoon until they are smooth. Pour the icing slowly over the top of the warm cake, allowing it to run down the sides. Let the *babka* cool to room temperature before serving.

Kulich—Russian Easter Cake

Pour the milk into a small bowl and sprinkle in the yeast and granulated sugar. Let the yeast and sugar rest for 2 or 3 minutes, then mix well. Set in a warm, draft-free place (such as an unlighted oven) for about 10 minutes, or until the mixture almost doubles in volume.

Soak the raisins in the rum for at least 10 minutes. With a slotted spoon, transfer the raisins to paper towels to drain. Dissolve the saffron in the rum and set aside.

Combine the confectioners' sugar, 4½ cups of the flour and the salt and sift them into a large mixing bowl. Make a well in the center, pour in the yeast-and-milk mixture, the vanilla, egg yolks and the reserved rum and saffron. With a wooden spoon, gradually incorporate the dry ingredients into the liquid ones. Stir until the mixture is smooth, then beat in the butter bits. Beat until the dough can be gathered into a medium-soft ball.

Place the ball on a lightly floured surface and knead, pushing the dough down with the heels of your hands, pressing it forward and folding it back on itself. Add up to 1½ cups more flour, ¼ cup at a time, until the dough is no longer sticky. Continue to knead for about 10 minutes, or until the dough is smooth, shiny and elastic.

With a pastry brush, spread 1 tablespoon of the softened butter over the inside of a large bowl. Set the dough in the bowl, dust the top lightly with flour and drape the bowl with a kitchen towel. Put it in the draft-free place for about 1 hour, or until the dough doubles in volume.

Combine the almonds, candied fruits and reserved raisins. Sprinkle them with 1 tablespoon of flour and toss them about to coat them evenly. With a single blow of your fist, punch the dough down in the bowl. Add the fruit mixture and knead vigorously until it is more or less evenly distributed throughout the dough.

Coat the bottom and sides of an empty can about 6 inches in diameter and 7 inches high (such as a 3-pound coffee can) with 2 tablespoons of the softened butter. Spread 1 tablespoon of the butter over a sheet of heavy brown paper about 22 inches long and at least 10 inches wide, and line the can with it, unbuttered side against the metal. Cut out a circle of brown paper slightly smaller than the diameter of the can, coat one side with the remaining butter and place it in the bottom of the can, buttered side up. With scissors, slit the paper liner that extends above the can down to the rim at 2-inch intervals. Fold the resulting strips down and tie them snugly in place with cord.

Place the dough in the can, drape it with a towel and set it in the draft-free place for about 30 minutes, or until it rises almost to the top of the can. Preheat the oven to 400° and bake the cake on the lowest shelf for 15 minutes. Reduce the temperature to 350° and bake for one hour longer. The cake will mushroom over the top of the can to form a cap. Remove from the oven and cool in the can for about 5 minutes.

To unmold the cake, turn the can on its side and remove the bottom with a can opener. Insert a long knife into the bottom of the can between the paper and the metal and work the blade around the edge to loosen the cake. Gently set the tin upright and, with the knife, carefully loosen the "mushroom cap" from the sides of the can, taking care not to break the cap. Untie the cord. Pushing from the bottom of the can, gradually slide the cake out

To serve 10 to 12

1 cup lukewarm milk (110° to 115°)
3 packages active dry yeast
½ teaspoon granulated sugar
½ cup sultana raisins
½ teaspoon powdered saffron
¼ cup rum
2 cups confectioners' sugar
5 to 6 cups all-purpose flour
2 teaspoons salt
1 teaspoon vanilla extract
10 egg yolks, lightly beaten
½ pound unsalted butter, cut into small bits and softened
4½ tablespoons butter, softened
½ cup slivered or coarsely chopped toasted almonds
½ cup mixed candied fruits and rinds

Joined in a forest of candles, a towering iced *kulich* (*below*), and a monumental *paskha* recall the significance and grace of a Russian Easter.

ХВ

and place it upright on a wire cake rack to cool, then peel off the paper.

ICING: With a wooden spoon, mix together the sugar, water and lemon juice and pour it over the top of the warm cake, allowing it to run down the cake in thin streams.

The Russians prepare *kulich* for serving by first slicing off the mushroom-shaped cap and placing it in the center of a large serving platter. The cake is cut in half lengthwise and finally cut crosswise into 1½- to 2-inch-thick slices. The slices are then arranged around the top of the cake. A traditional accompaniment is *paskha (below)*.

Paskha—Russian Easter Cheesecake

To serve 12 to 16

3 pounds large-curd pot cheese
½ pound unsalted butter, softened
½ cup chopped candied fruits and rinds
1 teaspoon vanilla extract
1 cup heavy cream
4 egg yolks
1 cup sugar
½ cup finely chopped blanched almonds

GARNISH
¼ to ½ cup candied fruits and rinds

Drain the pot cheese of all its moisture by setting it in a colander, covering it with cheesecloth or a kitchen towel, and weighting it down with a heavy pot or a small, heavy board. Let the cheese drain for 2 or 3 hours. Meanwhile, combine the candied fruits and the vanilla extract in a small mixing bowl, stir together thoroughly and let the mixture rest for 1 hour. With the back of a wooden spoon, rub the cheese through a fine sieve set over a large bowl. Beat the softened butter thoroughly into the cheese, and set aside.

Over high heat, heat the cream in a small saucepan until small bubbles form around the edge of the pan. Set aside. In a mixing bowl beat the eggs and sugar together with a whisk or a rotary or electric beater until they thicken enough to run sluggishly off the beater when it is lifted out of the bowl. Still beating, slowly add the hot cream in a thin stream, then return the mixture to the pan. Stirring constantly, cook over low heat until the mixture thickens to a custardlike consistency. Do not allow it to boil or it may curdle. Off the heat stir in the candied fruits and set the pan in a large bowl filled with ice cubes covered with 2 inches of water. Stir the custard constantly with a metal spoon until it is completely cooled, then mix it gently but thoroughly into the cheese mixture and stir in the chopped almonds.

Although the Russians use a special *paskha* form in which to shape this Easter dessert a 2-quart clay flower pot with an opening in the bottom is a good substitute. Set the pot in a shallow soup plate and line it with a double thickness of damp cheesecloth, cut long enough so that it hangs at least 2 inches over and around the top of the pot. Pour in the batter and fold the ends of the cheesecloth lightly over the top. Set a weight directly on top of the cheesecloth—perhaps a pan filled with 2 or 3 heavy cans of food—and chill in the refrigerator for at least 8 hours, or overnight, until the dessert is firm.

To unmold, unwrap the cheesecloth from the top, invert a flat serving plate on top of the pot and, grasping the two firmly together, turn them over. The *paskha* will slide out easily. Gently peel off the cheesecloth and decorate the top and sides of the cake with candied fruits. The Cyrillic letters XB, which were used to decorate the *paskha* on the preceding pages, stand for *Christos voskres* (Christ is risen).

The *paskha* may be served alone, or spread in a thick layer on slices of *kulich*. Once unmolded, the *paskha* can be safely kept refrigerated for a week.

The Passover Seder

Passover commemorates the flight of the Israelites from Egypt to the Promised Land of Canaan. They made their escape so abruptly that they were unable to leaven or bake bread, and had to make a simple flour and water dough, which produced the crisp flat matzo, the central ingredient of the Passover Seder, or feast.

Gefilte Fish

Place the fish heads, bones and tails in a sieve or colander and wash them under cold running water. Then transfer them to a heavy 8- to 10-quart pot and scatter the onion slices, 2 tablespoons of the coarse salt (or 2 teaspoons of regular salt) and 2 teaspoons of the white pepper over them. Pour in just enough cold water to cover the fish trimmings and onions and bring to a boil over high heat. Reduce the heat to low and simmer, partially covered, for 40 minutes.

Meanwhile, put the filleted pike, whitefish and carp and the quartered onions through the fine blade of a meat grinder twice. Combine the ground fish and onions in a deep mixing bowl.

To make the gefilte fish mixture by hand, chop the fish and onions fine and, with a pestle or the back of a large wooden spoon, mash them into a fairly smooth paste.

Beat the fish and onions with a spoon until the mixture is well combined, then beat in the matzo meal, egg, the remaining 2 tablespoons of coarse salt (or 2 teaspoons of regular salt) and the remaining teaspoon of white pepper. Beat in the ¼ cup of cold water a tablespoon at a time.

Divide the fish mixture into 12 equal parts and shape each into an oval cake about 4 inches long, 2 inches wide and 1 inch thick. Press an oval carrot slice flat on the top of each fish cake.

When the trimmings and onions have cooked their allotted time, scatter the carrot rounds into the pot. Arrange the fish cakes in one layer on top of the carrots; if they do not all fit comfortably, reserve some and cook the fish in two batches. Bring the liquid in the pot to a boil over high heat, reduce the heat to low, cover tightly and steam the fish cakes for 30 minutes, or until they are firm when prodded gently with a finger.

With a slotted spoon, arrange the fish cakes attractively on a large platter. Strain the remaining contents of the pot through a fine sieve set over a large shallow bowl. Stir the grated carrot into the strained stock.

Refrigerate the poached gefilte fish and strained cooking stock separately for at least 3 hours, until they are both thoroughly chilled and the stock is a firm jelly.

Just before serving, chop the jelly fine and mound it on the platter around the fish cakes. Serve with bottled white horseradish or beet horseradish sauce *(below)* as a first course or a light luncheon dish.

To make about 12 oval cakes

3 pounds fish trimmings: the heads, bones and tails of the pike, whitefish and carp *(below)*
5 large onions (2½ pounds), 2 cut into ⅛-inch-thick slices and 3 quartered
4 tablespoons coarse (kosher) salt, or substitute 4 teaspoons regular salt
1 tablespoon white pepper
1 pound each of skinned filleted pike, whitefish and carp
2 tablespoons matzo meal
1 egg, lightly beaten
¼ cup cold water
8 medium-sized carrots, scraped: 1 cut on the diagonal into about 12 ¼-inch-thick ovals, 6 cut crosswise into ½-inch-thick rounds and 1 finely grated

Fresh Horseradish Sauce with Beets

With a small sharp knife cut the tops off the beets, leaving about 1 inch of stem on each. Scrub the beets under cold running water, then place

To make about 1⅓ cups

3 medium-sized beets (1½ pounds)
¼ pound fresh horseradish root
4 tablespoons red wine vinegar
2 teaspoons coarse (kosher) salt, or substitute 1½ teaspoons regular salt
1 teaspoon sugar

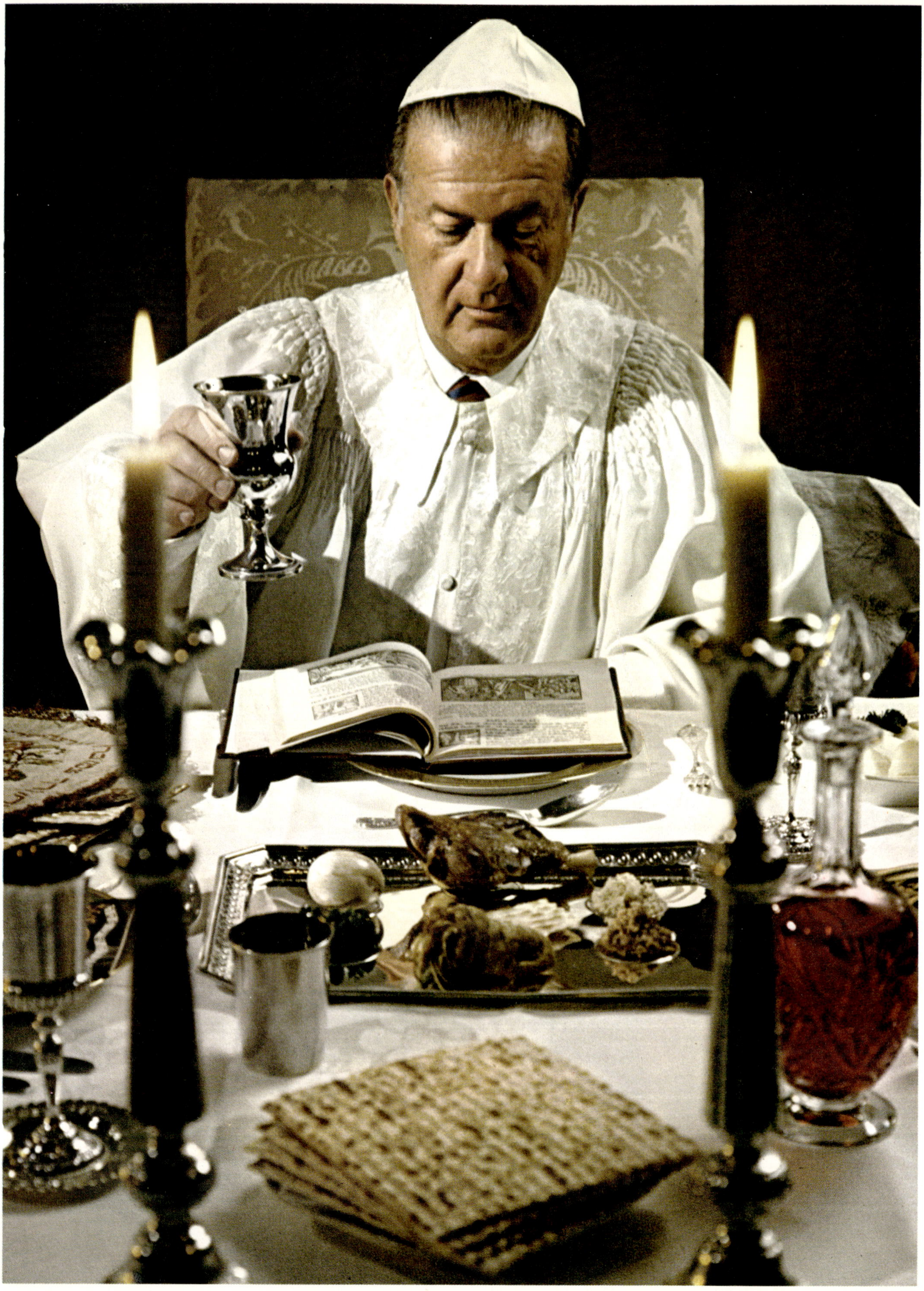

them in a 2- to 3-quart saucepan and add enough cold water to cover them by 2 inches. Bring the water to a boil over high heat, reduce the heat to low, cover the pan tightly and simmer until the beets show no resistance when pierced with the point of a small sharp knife. This may take anywhere from 30 minutes for young beets to as long as 2 hours for older ones. The beets should be kept constantly covered with water; add additional boiling water if necessary.

Drain the beets in a colander and, when they are cool enough to handle, slip off the outer skins and, with a small sharp knife, trim the tops and tails. With the fine side of a four-sided stand-up hand grater, grate the beets into a deep bowl.

With a small sharp knife, trim off the stem and tail end of the horseradish root, then scrape it with the knife or a vegetable peeler with a rotating blade. Grate the horseradish as fine as possible.

Stir the grated horseradish into the beets, then add the red wine vinegar, coarse or regular salt and sugar. Taste for seasoning. Cover tightly and let the sauce stand at room temperature to develop flavor for at least 2 hours before serving.

Tightly covered, it can be kept in the refrigerator for several weeks. Beet horseradish sauce is traditionally served with gefilte fish, and can also accompany boiled beef.

Chicken Soup with Matzo Balls

Place the pieces of fowl and the neck, giblets and feet in a heavy 8- to 10-quart pot and pour the cold water over it. The water should cover the pieces completely; if necessary, add more water. Bring to a boil over high heat, meanwhile skimming off the foam and scum as they rise to the surface. When the soup is clear, add the onions, carrots, celery, parsnip, parsley, dill and 1 tablespoon of coarse salt. Return the soup to a boil, reduce the heat to low and simmer, partially covered, for 2½ to 3 hours, or until the fowl shows no resistance when a piece is pierced with the point of a small sharp knife.

Meanwhile, make the matzo balls in the following fashion: With a whisk or a rotary or electric beater, beat the egg yolks until they are well blended. Whisk in the chicken stock, 2 teaspoons of regular salt, a few grindings of black pepper and the chicken fat. Whisking constantly, add the matzo meal, ¼ cup at a time. In a large bowl, beat the egg whites with a clean whisk or a rotary or electric beater until they are stiff enough to form firm, unwavering peaks on the beater when it is lifted from the bowl. With a wooden spoon or rubber spatula, lightly stir the whites into the matzo-meal mixture until they are well incorporated; do not overstir. Refrigerate the mixture for at least 30 minutes, or until it is stiff enough so that a spoon will stand unsupported in the bowl.

In a 6- to 8-quart pot, bring about 4 quarts of water and 2 tablespoons of coarse salt (or 2 teaspoons of regular salt) to a boil over high heat.

To serve 6

CHICKEN SOUP
A 5- to 5½-pound stewing fowl, cut into 6 or 8 pieces, plus the neck, giblets and feet
3½ quarts cold water
2 medium-sized onions, peeled
2 medium-sized carrots, scraped and each cut crosswise into 3 pieces
1 celery stalk, including the green leaves, cut crosswise into 2 pieces
½ medium-sized parsnip
8 parsley sprigs
3 dill sprigs, or substitute 1 teaspoon dried dill weed
1 tablespoon coarse (kosher) salt, or substitute 1 teaspoon regular salt

MATZO BALLS
6 egg yolks
8 tablespoons chicken stock, fresh or canned
2 teaspoons regular salt
Freshly ground black pepper
8 tablespoons chicken fat, melted and cooled
1½ cups matzo meal
6 egg whites
2 tablespoons coarse (kosher) salt, or substitute 2 teaspoons regular salt

As he reads aloud from the Haggadah, a sacred narrative that recounts the Old Testament story of the exodus of the Jews from Egypt, the head of a family blesses a goblet of wine at the beginning of the Seder, or Passover feast. Each food before him symbolizes an element of the Biblical story.

For each matzo ball, pinch off about a tablespoon of the dough and roll it between your hands. Drop the balls into the boiling water and stir gently once or twice so that they do not stick to one another or the bottom of the pot. Cook covered and undisturbed for 40 minutes. With a slotted spoon, transfer the matzo balls to a bowl of cold water to prevent them from drying out. Set them aside.

When the soup has cooked its allotted time, remove the fowl and vegetables with tongs or a slotted spoon. Discard the vegetables, gizzard, neck and feet, and either reserve the pieces of fowl for later use or serve them, skinned, boned and sliced, with the soup.

Strain the soup through a fine sieve and return it to the pot. With a large spoon, skim as much fat as possible from the surface. Taste the soup for seasoning. Drain the matzo balls, add them to the soup and bring it to a simmer over moderate heat. Reduce the heat to low and cook gently, uncovered, for 15 minutes to heat the matzo balls through.

To serve the soup, place three matzo balls in each of six large soup plates and ladle the soup over them.

Baked Matzo, Chicken and Dill Casserole

To serve 4

6 eggs
½ cup finely chopped onions
½ cup finely cut fresh dill, or substitute 2 tablespoons dried dill weed
¼ cup finely chopped parsley, preferably flat-leaf parsley
2 teaspoons salt
Freshly ground black pepper
3 cups cooked chicken meat cut into strips about ¼ inch wide, ¼ inch thick and 1½ inches long
½ cup vegetable oil
3 plain square matzos
2 cups chicken stock, fresh or canned

Preheat the oven to 400°. In a deep mixing bowl, beat the eggs with a whisk or a rotary or electric beater until frothy, stir in the onions, dill, parsley, salt and a few grindings of pepper, then add the chicken. Turn the pieces gently about with a spoon until they are thoroughly coated.

Heat the oil in a small saucepan until a light haze forms above it, then pour a teaspoon of it into an 8-inch-square shallow baking dish, tilting the dish to spread it evenly. Set the remaining oil aside off the heat.

Dip a matzo into the chicken stock until it is well moistened. Lay it in the bottom of the baking dish, spread half of the chicken and egg mixture evenly over it, moisten a second matzo in the chicken stock and place it over the chicken. Spread the remaining chicken-and-egg mixture on top and cover with the third moistened matzo. Pour about half the remaining oil evenly over the last matzo and bake in the middle of the oven for 15 minutes. Then sprinkle with the rest of the oil and continue baking for 15 minutes longer, or until the top is browned. Serve at once.

NOTE: If you do not have cooked chicken meat on hand, prepare it by poaching 3 pounds of chicken, a sliced onion, 2 celery tops, a bay leaf and a teaspoon of salt in 2 cups of water. Bring to a boil, cover and simmer over low heat for 1 hour. Remove the chicken and when cool bone and skin it. Strain the broth. You should have about 3 cups of meat and 2 cups of broth.

Potato Pancakes

To make about 12 pancakes (to serve 4 to 6)

2 large baking potatoes, peeled
1 small onion, peeled
½ teaspoon salt
Freshly ground black pepper
1 tablespoon matzo meal
1 egg, lightly beaten
4 tablespoons vegetable oil
1 cup applesauce (optional)

Set a large sieve over a mixing bowl and grate the potatoes on the finest side of a stand-up grater directly into the sieve. Using the same side of the grater, grate the onion over the potatoes and, with the back of a large spoon, press as much liquid as possible from the mixture. Discard the liquid and transfer the grated potatoes and onions to a large bowl. Add the salt, several grindings of pepper, the matzo meal and the egg and, with a wooden spoon, beat vigorously until the ingredients are well combined.

Gefilte fish are poached fish ovals garnished with carrots and chopped fish jelly, and complemented by beet horseradish sauce.

Preheat the oven to its lowest setting. Line a large shallow baking dish with paper towels and place it in the oven.

Heat the vegetable oil in a heavy 10- to 12-inch skillet over high heat until a drop of water flicked into it splutters and evaporates instantly. For each pancake, drop 1 to 2 tablespoons of the batter into the skillet and flatten it into a 2- to 2½-inch cake. Fry five or six pancakes at a time for about 2 minutes on each side, or until they are golden brown and crisp around the edges. As they brown, transfer the *latkes* to the towel-lined dish and keep them warm in the oven while you fry the rest.

To serve, arrange the pancakes on a heated platter and present the applesauce, if you use it, in a small bowl. Potato *latkes* may be served as an accompaniment to roast meat or poultry, or as a light luncheon dish.

Almond Macaroons

To make about 4 dozen

2 teaspoons vegetable oil
3 teaspoons matzo meal
3 egg whites
⅛ teaspoon salt
1 cup sugar
2 cups ground blanched almonds

Preheat the oven to 300°. With a pastry brush, coat a baking sheet with the vegetable oil. Sprinkle it evenly with 1 teaspoon of the matzo meal, and set it aside.

In a large mixing bowl, beat the egg whites and salt with a wire whisk or a rotary or electric beater until they form stiff, unwavering peaks on the beater when it is lifted from the bowl. With a rubber spatula, gradually fold the sugar, the remaining matzo meal and almonds into the whites, using an over-under cutting motion rather than a stirring motion.

Drop the cookie batter by the teaspoonful onto the prepared baking sheet, leaving 1 inch between the cookies. Bake in the upper third of the oven for 20 minutes, then transfer the cookies to cake racks to cool.

Derby Day Partying

The Kentucky Derby, on the first Saturday in May, sparks a whirl of parties. Highlight of the entertaining is the race-day breakfast, when all over Louisville guests are served a rich variety of Southern specialties, beginning, of course, with the classic mint julep.

Eggs Derby

To serve 6

1 pair veal sweetbreads (about ½ pound)
Distilled white vinegar
3 cups water
1 cup coarsely diced celery
¼ cup finely chopped onions
2½ teaspoons salt
Freshly ground black pepper
6 tablespoons plus 1 cup heavy cream
1 tablespoon butter, softened, plus 4 tablespoons butter
6 hard-cooked eggs
3 ounces cooked ham, preferably country ham, finely ground or very finely chopped (about ⅓ cup)
1 teaspoon dry mustard
¼ teaspoon ground white pepper
½ pound firm fresh mushrooms, trimmed, wiped with a dampened cloth and cut into ½-inch pieces including the stems
4 tablespoons flour
3 tablespoons pale dry sherry
¼ cup freshly grated imported Parmesan cheese combined with ¼ cup freshly grated sharp natural Cheddar cheese
½ cup slivered blanched almonds

Soak the sweetbreads for 2 hours in enough cold water to cover them by at least 1 inch, changing the water every 30 minutes or so; then soak them for another hour in acidulated cold water, using 1 tablespoon of white vinegar for each quart of water. Gently pull off as much of the outside membrane as possible without tearing the sweetbreads, and cut the two lobes from the tube between them with a small sharp knife; discard the tube.

Place the sweetbreads in a small enameled saucepan and add 3 cups of water, the celery, onions, 1 teaspoon of salt and a few grindings of black pepper. Bring to a boil over high heat, then reduce the heat to its lowest point and simmer uncovered for 15 to 20 minutes. Remove the sweetbreads with a slotted spoon, cut them into ¼-inch bits and set them aside in a small bowl. Strain the cooking liquid through a fine sieve set over a bowl and reserve 1 cup.

Meanwhile, preheat the oven to 350°. With a pastry brush, spread the tablespoon of softened butter evenly over the bottom and sides of an 8- or 9-inch baking-serving dish about 2 to 3 inches deep.

Peel the hard-cooked eggs and cut them lengthwise in half. Set the egg whites aside. Drop the yolks into a small bowl and, with the back of a fork, mash them to a smooth purée. Stir in the ground ham, mustard, ½ teaspoon of salt, ⅛ teaspoon of the white pepper and the 6 tablespoons of cream. Taste for seasoning. Spoon the egg-yolk mixture into the egg-white halves, dividing it evenly and mounding the stuffing slightly. Arrange the eggs in one layer in the baking dish and set aside.

In a heavy 10- to 12-inch skillet, melt the 4 tablespoons of butter over moderate heat. When the foam begins to subside, add the mushrooms and, stirring frequently, cook for 8 to 10 minutes, or until the liquid that accumulates in the pan has evaporated completely. Do not let the mushrooms brown. Stir in the flour and, when it is completely absorbed, pour in the remaining cup of cream and the reserved cup of sweetbread cooking liquid. Stirring the mixture constantly with a whisk, bring to a boil, reduce the heat to low, and simmer for 3 or 4 minutes to remove any taste of raw flour. Then stir in the sweetbreads, sherry, the remaining teaspoon of salt and ⅛ teaspoon of white pepper. Taste for seasoning.

Ladle the sweetbreads-and-mushroom mixture over the stuffed eggs and sprinkle with the cheese and almonds. Bake in the upper third of the oven for 20 to 25 minutes, or until the sauce bubbles and the cheese is delicately browned. Serve at once directly from the baking dish.

Served from a buffet at one elegant Derby Day breakfast spread are bibb lettuce and tomato salad, batty cakes, Jerusalem artichoke pickles, hot rolls, Kentucky ham, bacon, fried apples and scrambled eggs.

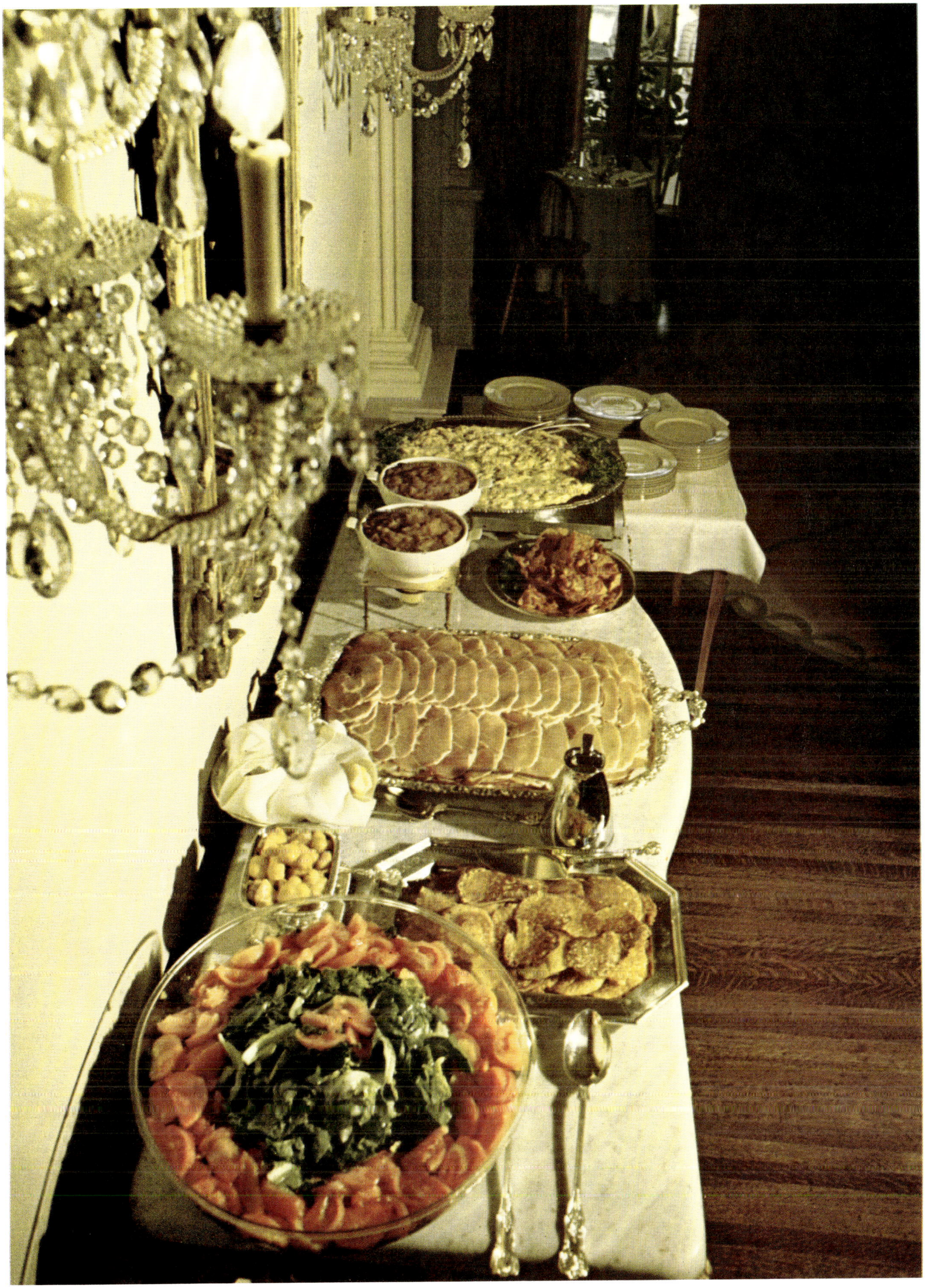

To serve 4

6 slices lean bacon
1 tablespoon butter
1 cup fresh corn kernels, cut from 3 medium-sized ears of corn, or substitute 1 cup canned or defrosted frozen corn kernels, thoroughly drained
½ cup finely chopped green pepper
¼ cup finely chopped pimiento
1½ teaspoons salt
⅛ teaspoon freshly ground black pepper
6 eggs

To serve 6

4 tablespoons butter
2 tablespoons vegetable oil
1½ cups finely chopped onions
¼ cup finely chopped green pepper
½ pound firm fresh mushrooms, trimmed, wiped with a dampened cloth and cut lengthwise, including the stems, into ⅛-inch-thick slices
¼ cup flour
2 cups fresh turkey stock, or fresh or canned chicken stock
4 cups finely diced roasted turkey
¼ cup finely chopped fresh parsley
1 tablespoon Worcestershire sauce
1 teaspoon salt
½ cup heavy cream, if necessary

To make about 2 dozen

¾ cup white cornmeal, preferably water-ground
½ teaspoon double-acting baking powder
½ teaspoon baking soda
½ teaspoon salt
1 cup buttermilk
1 egg, lightly beaten
½ cup bacon fat, or substitute ¼ pound butter, softened

Kentucky Scramble

In a heavy 10- to 12-inch ungreased skillet, fry the bacon over moderate heat. Turn the slices with tongs until they are crisp and brown, then transfer them to paper towels to drain.

Pour off all but 3 tablespoons of the fat remaining in the skillet and in its place add the butter. Drop in the corn and stir over moderate heat for 1 or 2 minutes until the kernels glisten. Then add the green pepper, pimiento, salt and black pepper and cook uncovered, stirring frequently, for 5 minutes, or until the vegetables are soft but not brown.

Break the eggs into a bowl, beat them lightly with a table fork, and pour them into the skillet. Stirring with the flat of the fork or a rubber spatula, cook over low heat until the eggs begin to form soft, creamy curds. Mound the eggs on a heated platter, arrange the bacon slices attractively on top and serve at once.

Turkey Hash

In a heavy 12-inch skillet, melt the butter in the oil over moderate heat. When the foam begins to subside, add the onions and green pepper and, stirring frequently, cook for about 5 minutes, until they are soft but not brown. Add the mushrooms and, stirring occasionally, cook for 8 to 10 minutes, or until almost all the liquid that accumulates in the pan has evaporated. Do not let the mushrooms brown.

Mix in the flour and, when it is completely absorbed, pour in the stock. Stir with a whisk until the sauce comes to a boil, thickens lightly and is smooth. Reduce the heat to low, add the turkey, parsley, Worcestershire and salt and, stirring frequently with a spoon, simmer for 3 or 4 minutes to heat the hash through. If the hash is too dry for your taste, stir in up to ½ cup heavy cream by the tablespoonful.

Transfer the hash to a heated platter and serve it at once, accompanied, if you like, by batty cakes *(below)*.

Lacy-edged Batty Cakes

If you are using regular-ground cornmeal, combine it with the baking powder, soda and salt, and sift them together into a bowl. If you are using water-ground cornmeal, pour it into a bowl and stir in the baking powder, soda and salt. Pour in the buttermilk and beat vigorously with a spoon until it is completely absorbed. Then add the egg and continue to beat until the batter is smooth.

Heat a heavy griddle over high heat until a drop of water flicked onto it steams for a second and evaporates. With a pastry brush, grease the griddle lightly with the bacon fat or butter.

Pour about 1 tablespoon of batter onto the griddle for each batty cake. Fry 4 at a time for 2 to 3 minutes, until the cakes begin to bubble and the bottoms brown. Then turn them over with a spatula and brown the other side. Stack the finished cakes on a heated plate and drape foil over them to keep them warm while you fry the rest. Stir the batter before baking each batch of cakes and brush more bacon fat or butter on the griddle.

Kentucky Burgoo

Combine the beef shank, beef bones, lamb, chicken, chili, salt, a liberal grinding of black pepper and the water in a heavy 6- to 8-quart casserole. Bring to a boil over high heat, meanwhile skimming off the foam and scum as they rise to the surface.

Reduce the heat to low and simmer partially covered for 30 to 40 minutes, or until the chicken is tender. Remove the chicken pieces with tongs or a slotted spoon, and place them on a plate.

Cover the casserole partially again and simmer for about 1½ hours longer, or until the beef and lamb are tender and show no resistance when pierced deeply with the point of a small skewer or sharp knife. Add the beef and lamb to the plate with the chicken. Remove the beef bones and chili and discard them.

Drop the potatoes, onions, corn, carrots, tomatoes, beans, green pepper, okra and garlic into the stock remaining in the casserole. Stirring from time to time, bring to a boil over high heat. Reduce the heat to low and simmer uncovered for 1½ hours. Check the pot from time to time and add up to 2 cups more water, if the stew seems too thick.

With a small knife, remove the skin and bones from the chicken and discard them. Cut the chicken meat, beef shank and lamb into 1-inch pieces and return them to the casserole. Stirring frequently, simmer the burgoo until the meat is heated through. Then stir in the parsley and taste for seasoning.

To serve 6 to 8

2 pounds boneless beef shank
1½ pounds beef bones
½ pound lean boneless lamb
A 2- to 2½-pound chicken, cut into 6 or 8 pieces
A 1-inch piece red chili, seeded (*caution: see note, page 118*)
1 tablespoon salt
Freshly ground black pepper
3 quarts water
2 medium-sized potatoes, peeled and diced (2 cups)
2 cups finely chopped onions
2 cups fresh or frozen corn kernels
3 or 4 medium-sized carrots, scraped and cut crosswise into ¼-inch-thick slices (about 2 cups)
6 medium-sized ripe tomatoes, cored and coarsely chopped
¼ pound butter beans or wax beans, washed, trimmed and cut crosswise into halves
1 seeded green pepper, cut into ½-inch pieces
½ pound fresh or frozen okra, trimmed and cut into 1-inch dice
1 teaspoon finely chopped garlic
1 cup finely chopped fresh parsley

Tomato Aspic

Soften the gelatin in the cold beef stock for about 5 minutes. In a heavy 2- to 3 quart saucepan, melt the butter over moderate heat. When the foam subsides, add the onions and cook, stirring, for 4 or 5 minutes until they are transparent but not brown. Stir in the tomato paste, the canned tomatoes and the softened gelatin, and mix together until the ingredients are thoroughly combined.

Then add the salt, the sugar, Worcestershire sauce and the tarragon, and bring to a boil, stirring constantly. Reduce the heat to its lowest point and simmer the mixture with the pan partially covered for about 30 minutes. Rub the mixture through a fine sieve or food mill into a mixing bowl.

With a pastry brush or paper towel, lightly coat the inside of a 1-quart mold with the vegetable oil. Pour in the tomato mixture, let it cool slightly and then refrigerate for 2 to 3 hours, or until the aspic is firm. To unmold, run a knife around the inside surfaces of the mold and place a serving plate upside down on top of the mold. Grasping the plate and the mold together

To serve 4 to 6

2 envelopes unflavored gelatin
½ cup cold beef stock, fresh or canned
2 tablespoons butter
¼ cup finely chopped onions
3 tablespoons tomato paste
4½ cups canned tomatoes with juice (2 one-pound, 3-ounce cans)
¾ teaspoon salt
¾ teaspoon sugar
½ teaspoon Worcestershire sauce
1 teaspoon finely chopped fresh tarragon or ½ teaspoon dried tarragon
1 teaspoon vegetable oil
1 cup mayonnaise combined with 2 tablespoons finely cut chives, or 1 cup sour cream combined with 1 tablespoon red caviar

firmly, invert the two. Rap the plate firmly on a table, and the aspic should slide out onto the plate. Serve the tomato aspic as a salad course with mayonnaise mixed with finely cut chives, or with sour cream mixed with red caviar.

Kentucky Minted Carrots

To serve 4

1 pound (about 8 to 10) medium-sized carrots, trimmed, washed, scraped and cut diagonally into ¼-inch lengths
1 cup water
1 teaspoon salt
3 tablespoons unsalted butter, cut into bits
Freshly ground black pepper
2 tablespoons coarsely cut fresh mint leaves

Place the carrots in a 1-quart saucepan and add the water and salt. Cover the pan tightly and bring to a boil over high heat, then reduce the heat to moderate and cook the carrots for about 15 minutes, or until the water is almost completely evaporated and the carrots are tender but still slightly resistant to the bite. Stir in the butter and several grindings of pepper, then remove the pan from the heat. Toss the carrots lightly with the mint, taste for seasoning and serve at once, in a heated vegetable dish.

Served ice cold in a silver mug, the mint julep symbolizes Southern hospitality. In Louisville, where it is an indispensable part of Kentucky Derby festivities, the julep is always made of bourbon, sweetened with a syrup of crushed mint and sugar.

Plantation String Beans

Fry the bacon dice in a 10- to 12-inch enameled or stainless-steel skillet, turning them frequently with a wooden spoon until they are brown and crisp and have rendered all their fat. With a slotted spoon, transfer the dice to paper towels to drain.

Drop the scallions into the fat and, stirring occasionally, cook over moderate heat for 3 to 4 minutes, until they are soft but not brown. Now add the beans, stirring them about until they glisten with the fat. Add the tablespoon of water and cover the pan tightly. Cook over low heat for 5 minutes, then uncover the pan and continue to cook until the beans are tender but still slightly resistant to the bite. Sprinkle with the salt and pepper, stir in the vinegar, and remove from the heat. Serve from a heated dish, garnished with the bacon bits and, if you like, with the cut mint leaves.

To serve 4

4 slices lean bacon, cut into ½-inch dice
½ cup thinly sliced scallion rounds
1 pound green beans, washed and trimmed
1 tablespoon cold water
1 teaspoon salt
¼ teaspoon freshly ground black pepper
1½ teaspoons red wine vinegar
2 tablespoons finely cut fresh mint leaves (optional)

Mint Julep

Place the mint leaves, sugar and water in an 8-ounce highball glass or, more traditionally, a silver mint julep mug. With a bar muddler, crush the mint, then stir until the sugar dissolves. Pack the glass tightly almost to the top with shaved or crushed ice and pour in the bourbon. With a long-handled bar spoon, use a chopping motion to mix the ice and whiskey together. Dry the outside of the glass or mug and chill the julep in the refrigerator for at least 1 hour or in the freezer for about 30 minutes, until the outside of the glass or mug is covered with frost.

To serve, remove the mint julep from the refrigerator with paper napkins or towels, taking care not to wipe off the frost. Garnish the drink by planting the sprig of mint in the ice. Insert a straw and serve at once.

To make 1 drink

6 small fresh mint leaves plus 1 sprig fresh mint
1½ teaspoons confectioners' or superfine sugar
1 tablespoon cold water
Shaved or finely crushed ice
4 ounces Kentucky bourbon

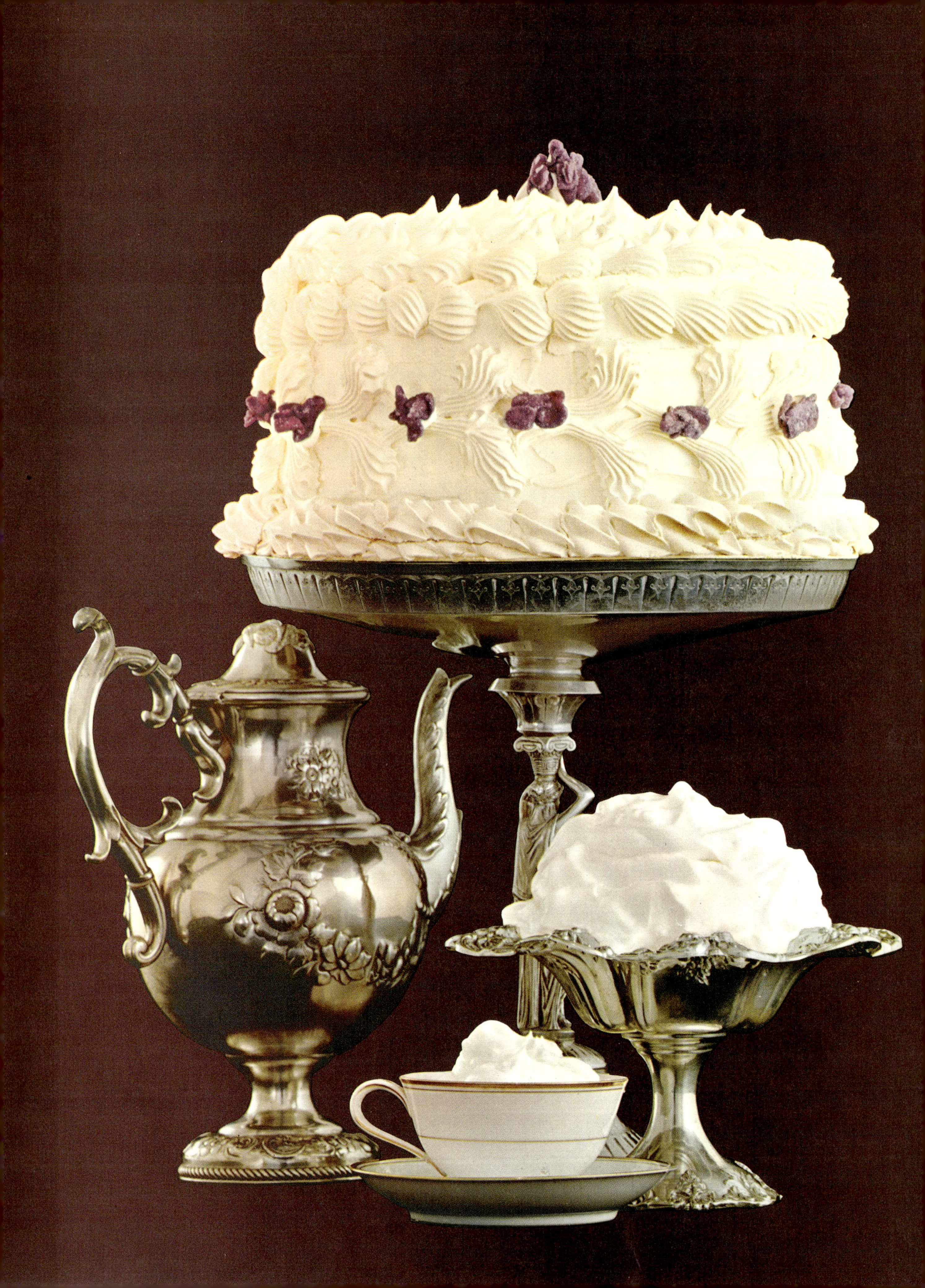

Weddings
Anniversaries
Birthdays

Family Celebrations

Not all holidays have their dates printed on calendars. Every family has its own gala days to celebrate privately or with groups of friends. The event may be as special as a wedding or a silver anniversary; as a contribution to the occasion, a family member who loves to cook might prepare a festive meal centered around a triumph of haute cuisine like a mousse of fresh sole, crab and shrimp or *coulibiac*, a glorious combination of tender salmon and other ingredients in a golden-brown brioche crust.

A family dinner to celebrate a birthday could feature a classic entrée, such as chicken Kiev, ready to release jets of butter at the touch of a fork, lobster flavored with fresh herbs and cognac, topped with a gossamer cheese soufflé or an authentic beef Stroganoff—created by a French chef for a Russian nobleman. And instead of a traditional candle-decked cake, the crowning touch to a birthday dinner could be an extravagantly flamboyant dessert—such as the unexpected delight of flambéed bananas and ice cream or the startling combination of hot and cold ingredients in a baked Alaska.

This Viennese confection, called Spanish Wind cake, is made of airy meringue and fluffy whipped cream. As decorated here with candied violets, it would make a most romantic wedding cake.

Salmon brioche loaf for a bride or a birthday

Festive mousse of crab and sole

Sparkling ginger-ale salad mold

Elegant cold vegetables for summer entertaining

Fresh-fruit-and-wine party punches

Chicken Kiev for a grand-occasion dinner

Steaks fit for a duke—or Father's Day

Lobster soufflé the gourmet way

Seven dramatic desserts and cakes

Family Celebration Recipes

Special Luncheon Parties

Coulibiac—Salmon Brioche Loaf

SALMON: Preheat the oven to 350°. Spread 2 tablespoons of softened butter on the bottom and sides of a 7½-by-12-by-2-inch glass baking dish. Scatter the shallots over the bottom of the dish and season them with ½ teaspoon of the salt and ¼ teaspoon of the black pepper. Arrange the salmon in two parallel rows the length of the dish, overlapping the slices at the middle of the dish. Spread the mushroom slices over the salmon, and sprinkle them with ¼ cup of dill, 1 teaspoon of salt and ½ teaspoon of black pepper. Pour the wine over the fish. Cover tightly with foil and bake in the middle of the oven for 20 minutes, or until the salmon flakes easily when prodded with a fork.

With a bulb baster or spoon, transfer as much of the cooking liquid as possible to a heavy 10- to 12-inch skillet. Let the salmon rest for about 15 minutes, then draw up any additional liquid that accumulates around it and add it to the skillet. Bring the liquid to a boil over high heat and cook briskly until it is reduced to about ½ cup. Reduce the heat to moderate and, stirring constantly with a wire whisk, slowly pour in the *sauce veloutée* and continue to cook for 4 to 5 minutes. Beat the 5 egg yolks lightly with a fork and whisk them into the sauce. Bring to a simmer, stirring all the while with the whisk, and remove the skillet from the heat. Stir in the lemon juice, ½ teaspoon of salt and the red pepper. Taste for seasoning and pour the sauce over the salmon, spreading it (smoothly) with a spatula. As the sauce runs into the dish, spoon it back over the salmon until it is collected on the fish. Cool to room temperature; then cover and refrigerate until the fish is firm to the touch, preferably overnight.

CRÊPES: To make the batter with a blender, combine 1¼ cups of flour, 4 eggs, 1 cup of milk, 1¼ cups of cold water, 3 tablespoons of melted butter and ½ teaspoon of salt in the blender jar. Blend at high speed for a few seconds. Turn off the machine, scrape down the sides of the jar with a rubber spatula and blend again for 40 seconds. Pour the batter into a bowl and stir in 3 tablespoons of parsley and 3 of dill.

To make crêpe batter by hand, stir the flour and eggs together in a mixing bowl and gradually stir in the milk, water and salt. Beat with a whisk or a rotary or electric beater until smooth, then rub through a fine sieve into another bowl and stir in the melted butter, parsley and dill. Cover and refrigerate the batter for at least two hours before using it.

Heat a 6-inch crêpe pan over high heat until a drop of water flicked into it splutters and evaporates instantly. With a hair-bristled (not nylon) pastry brush, grease the bottom and sides of the pan with a little of the clarified butter. Stir the batter lightly. Using a small ladle, pour about 2 tablespoons of the batter into the pan and tip the pan so that the batter

To serve 8

SALMON
2 tablespoons unsalted butter softened
3 tablespoons finely chopped shallots
2 teaspoons salt
¼ teaspoon plus ½ teaspoon freshly ground black pepper
2 pounds center-cut salmon fillets, boned carefully with tweezers, then skinned and cut diagonally into ¼-inch-thick slices
½ pound fresh mushrooms, wiped clean, trimmed and cut lengthwise through cap and stem into ⅛-inch-thick slices (about 2 cups)
¼ cup finely cut fresh dill leaves
1 cup dry white wine
1 cup *sauce veloutée (page 177)* made with *fumet de poisson*
5 egg yolks
2 tablespoons strained fresh lemon juice
⅛ teaspoon ground hot red pepper (cayenne)

CRÊPES (to yield 20)
1¼ cups all-purpose flour
4 eggs
1 cup milk
1¼ cups cold water
3 tablespoons unsalted butter, melted and cooled, plus 6 tablespoons melted clarified butter *(pages 177-178)*
½ teaspoon salt
3 tablespoons finely chopped fresh parsley
3 tablespoons finely cut fresh dill leaves

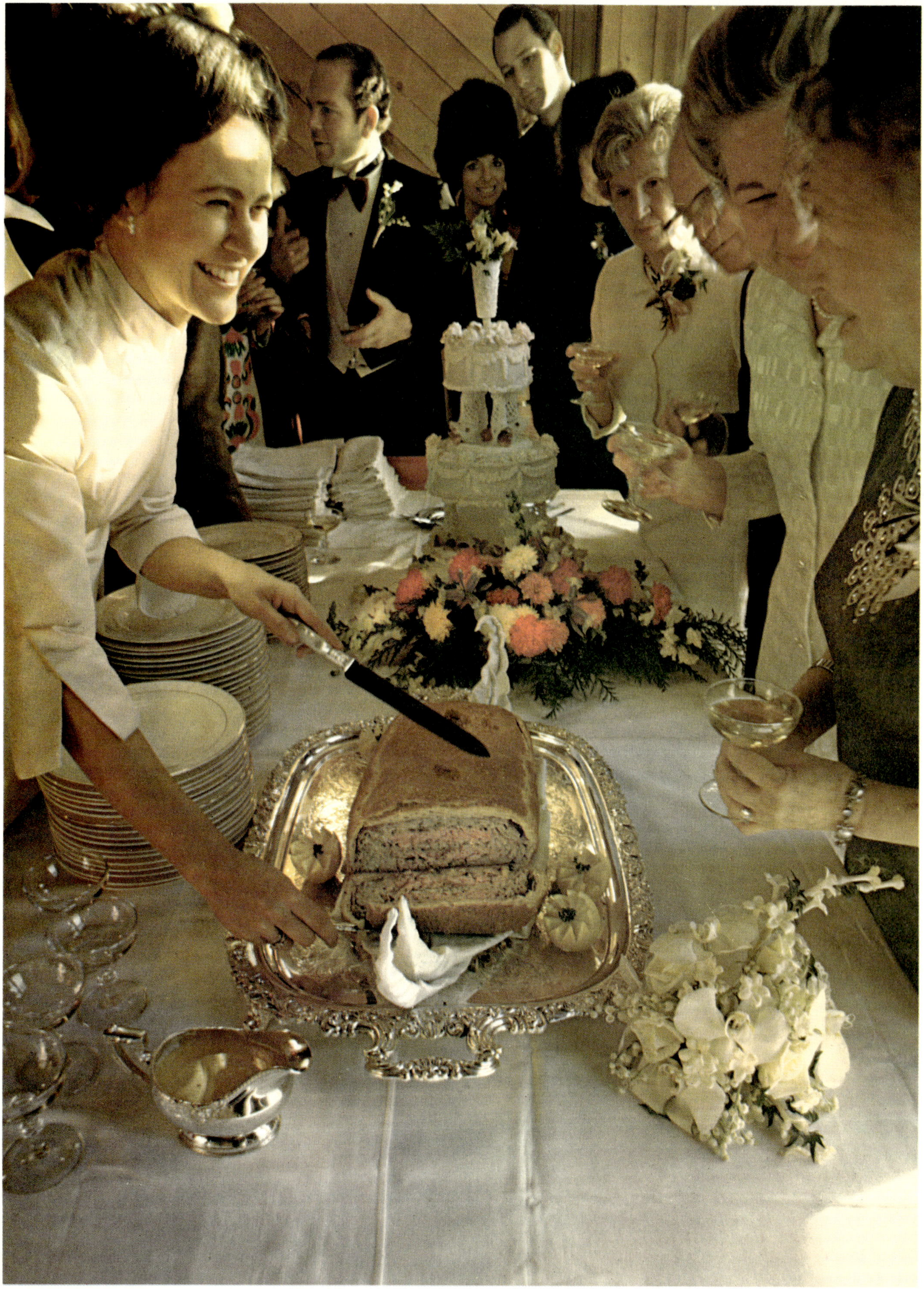

quickly covers the bottom; the batter will cling to the pan and begin to firm up almost immediately. At once tilt the pan over the bowl and pour off any excess batter; the finished crêpe should be paper-thin.

Cook the crêpe for a minute or so until the underside turns golden. Turn it over with a spatula and cook the other side for a minute. Slide the crêpe onto a plate. Brush clarified butter on the pan again and make the remaining crêpes similarly, stacking them on the plate. The crêpes may be made a day ahead of time, cooled to room temperature, covered with plastic wrap and refrigerated. (In this case, they should be brought back to room temperature before they are separated and used.) Or they may be made several hours ahead and kept at room temperature.

EGG-AND-RICE MIXTURE: In a small saucepan or skillet, sprinkle the tapioca over ½ cup of cold water and set aside to soften for 5 minutes. Then, stirring frequently, bring to a boil over high heat. Reduce the heat to low and simmer uncovered for 6 to 8 minutes, until the mixture is very thick. Pour the tapioca into a fine sieve and let it drain for at least 10 minutes. See the note at the end of the recipe.

Meanwhile, in a heavy 1- to 1½-quart saucepan, melt 1 tablespoon of butter over moderate heat. When the foam begins to subside, add the onions and stir for about 2 minutes until they are soft but not brown. Stirring constantly, add the rice in a slow stream and continue to cook until the grains glisten. Do not let the rice brown. Pour in the chicken stock and, still stirring, bring to a boil. Reduce the heat to low, cover tightly, and simmer for 20 minutes, or until the grains are soft and have absorbed all the liquid. Remove the pan from the heat.

In a mixing bowl, combine the sieved hard-cooked eggs, 3 tablespoons of parsley, 1 teaspoon of salt and ¼ teaspoon of black pepper. Add the tapioca and rice and toss gently but thoroughly together.

BRIOCHE: Pour the lukewarm milk into a small, shallow bowl and sprinkle it with the yeast and sugar. Let the mixture stand for 2 or 3 minutes, then stir well. Set in a warm, draft-free place (such as a turned-off oven) for about 5 minutes, or until the mixture almost doubles in volume.

Place 3½ cups of the flour and the 2 teaspoons of salt in a large deep mixing bowl, and make a well in the center. Add the yeast mixture, 12 egg yolks and ½ cup of softened butter to the well and, with a wooden spoon, gradually incorporate the flour into the center ingredients. Stir vigorously until the dough is smooth and can be gathered into a ball.

Place the dough on a lightly floured surface, and knead by pushing it down with the heels of your hands, pressing it forward and folding it back on itself. Repeat for 10 to 15 minutes. A little at a time incorporate only enough flour to keep the dough from becoming shiny on the surface. It should be smooth and elastic. (You may need as much as 1 cup, depending on the brand of flour you use.)

When blisters form on the surface of the dough, shape it into a ball and place it in a buttered bowl. Drape with a kitchen towel and set in the warm place for about 1 hour, or until the dough doubles in bulk.

EGG-AND-RICE MIXTURE
1 tablespoon minute tapioca
½ cup cold water
1 tablespoon unsalted butter
1 teaspoon finely chopped onions
½ cup uncooked long-grain white rice (not the converted variety)
1½ cups canned chicken stock, chilled, then degreased
3 hard-cooked eggs, rubbed through a fine sieve with the back of a spoon
3 tablespoons finely chopped fresh parsley
1 teaspoon salt
¼ teaspoon freshly ground black pepper

BRIOCHE
¾ cup lukewarm milk (110° to 115°)
3 packages active dry yeast
½ teaspoon sugar
3½ to 4½ cups all-purpose flour
2 teaspoons salt
12 egg yolks plus 2 lightly beaten egg yolks
½ cup unsalted butter, softened and cut into ¼-inch bits
2 tablespoons soft fresh crumbs made from homemade-type white bread, trimmed of crusts and pulverized in a blender or finely shredded with a fork
6 tablespoons softened butter plus 1½ cups warm melted butter

Coulibiac is grand enough for a bride's luncheon table. The dish originated in Russia and later became a tour de force of French cuisine, combining fresh salmon, crêpes, eggs and rice, and brioche dough. It can be made in stages, over two days, and then assembled and baked on the festive day.

Punch the dough down with a blow of your fist. Then knead it for a minute, shape it into a ball and return it to the bowl to rise and to double its bulk once more. Use at once or cover and refrigerate overnight.

FINAL ASSEMBLY: Preheat the oven to 400°. With a pastry brush spread 1 tablespoon of the softened butter evenly over a large baking sheet.

Punch the dough down and, on a lightly floured surface, roll it out into a rectangle 19 inches long, 15 inches wide and ¼ inch thick.

Lay 6 of the crêpes in two parallel rows the length of the rectangle, overlapping the crêpes slightly in the center to leave a 2-inch-wide band of uncovered dough all around the rectangle. Sprinkle the crêpes evenly with about ⅓ of the egg-and-rice mixture.

Cut the salmon in half lengthwise and, with the aid of a large wide metal spatula, gently lift one half from the baking dish and turn it mushroom-coated side down over the center of the crêpes. Arrange 6 more crêpes on top as before, sprinkle them with half of the remaining egg-and-rice mixture, and place the remaining half of the salmon on top with the mushroom-coated side up. Scatter the remaining egg-and-rice mixture over the salmon and cover it with 6 more crêpes.

Lightly brush the edge of one of the exposed long sides of the brioche rectangle with the beaten egg yolk. Lift the opposite side over the filling, then fold the egg-coated side on top of it and press gently to seal the sides together along the top. Trim both ends of the *coulibiac* to extend no more than 3 inches beyond the filling. Brush the tops of the ends with beaten egg yolk and tuck the ends snugly over the top of the filled cylinder.

Carefully turn the loaf upside down on its seam and place it on the buttered baking sheet. With a small, round cookie cutter or sharp knife, make two holes 1 inch in diameter, centered about 3 inches from each end of the loaf. Gather the scraps of brioche dough into a ball and roll out ¼ inch thick. Cut two ½-inch-wide and 4-inch-long strips out of the dough, moisten the bottom of each with egg yolk and fit the strips like collars around the openings, pressing gently to secure them. Score the loaf lightly with a knife in an attractive pattern or, if you prefer, with cookie cutters or a small knife cut the remaining dough into decorative leaf and flower shapes. Moistening the bottom of each of the decorative pieces with beaten egg yolk, arrange them attractively on top of the loaf. Brush the surface with the remaining egg yolk and sprinkle it with the 2 tablespoons of bread crumbs.

Cut a strip of aluminum foil about 5 feet long, fold it lengthwise in half and grease one side lightly with 5 tablespoons of softened butter. Wrap the foil around the loaf like a collar and tie it in place with 2 or 3 turns of kitchen string. Place small cylindrical funnels made from a double thickness of heavy foil into each pastry opening. Set the loaf aside in a warm, draft-free place for 30 minutes. Preheat the oven to 400°.

Bake the *coulibiac* in the middle of the oven for 15 minutes. Lower the heat to 375° and continue baking for 30 minutes. Cut off the string and remove the collar of foil and bake for 15 minutes longer, or until the loaf is a rich golden brown. Slide it onto a heated platter and let it rest at room temperature for 15 to 20 minutes before serving. Just before slicing the *coulibiac* pour ¼ cup melted butter into each of the openings in the top of the loaf, and remove the foil funnels. Serve the remaining cup of melted butter separately as a sauce.

NOTE: The tapioca used to thicken the egg-and-rice mixture above is a substitute for the traditional fresh *vesiga,* or sturgeon marrow. If *vesiga* is available, replace the tapioca with 3 ounces of it. Wash the *vesiga* in cold water, then simmer it for 1½ hours in enough lightly salted water to cover it completely. Chop the *vesiga* fine.

Sauce Veloutée for the Coulibiac

To make about 2 cups

2 cups *fumet de poisson (below)*
4 tablespoons unsalted butter, preferably clarified butter *(below)*
6 tablespoons flour

Bring the stock to a simmer over moderate heat. Meanwhile, in a heavy 1½- to 2-quart saucepan, melt the butter over low heat. Remove the pan from the heat and stir in the flour with a wire whisk. Then return to low heat and, stirring constantly, cook for about 2 minutes, or until the roux foams. The roux should be a very pale yellow color.

Pour in the heated stock and beat vigorously with a whisk until the roux and liquid are thoroughly blended. Scrape the sides of the pan to ensure that all of the roux is incorporated into the sauce. Increase the heat to moderate and, still stirring, cook until the sauce comes to a boil and thickens enough to coat the wires of the whisk heavily.

Reduce the heat to the lowest possible point and simmer the sauce gently for 15 minutes, whisking it every few minutes to prevent the bottom from scorching. Then strain the sauce through a fine sieve set over a bowl. If you do not plan to use the sauce immediately, cool it to room temperature, stirring occasionally. Tightly covered, the velouté may safely be kept in the refrigerator for 10 days, or in the freezer up to three months.

Fumet de Poisson

To make about 2 quarts

3 pounds fish trimmings: the heads, tails and bones of any firm white fish, preferably flounder, whiting or halibut
2 quarts cold water
1 cup coarsely chopped onions
¾ cup coarsely chopped celery with the leaves
⅓ cup coarsely chopped leek tops, thoroughly washed
1 medium-sized bay leaf
2 fresh thyme sprigs or ½ teaspoon crumbled dried thyme
1 teaspoon salt
5 whole black peppercorns

Wash the fish trimmings in a deep bowl set under cold running water. Drain, then mash the pieces of fish with the back of a large spoon.

Place the mashed fish in a 6- to 8-quart enameled or stainless-steel saucepan or casserole, and pour in the water. Bring slowly to a simmer over moderate heat and cook uncovered for 5 minutes, skimming off the foam and scum as they rise to the surface. Add the onions, celery tops, leek tops, bay leaf, thyme, salt and peppercorns, and reduce the heat to low. Partially cover the pan and simmer for 30 minutes, skimming the surface of the stock every 10 minutes or so.

Remove the pan from the heat and, with a slotted spoon, lift out and discard the fish and vegetables. Strain the stock into a deep bowl through a fine sieve lined with a double thickness of dampened cheesecloth. The stock will keep refrigerated for 2 or 3 days or it can be cooled to room temperature, covered tightly and frozen.

Clarified Butter

To make 10 or 12 tablespoons

½ pound unsalted butter, cut into ¼-inch bits

In a small, heavy saucepan, heat the butter over low heat, turning it about to melt it slowly and completely without letting it brown. Remove the pan from the heat and let the butter rest for a minute or so. Then skim off the foam and discard it. Tipping the pan slightly, spoon the clear butter into a bowl. Discard the milky solids that will settle at the bottom of the pan. If you are not using the butter immediately, refrigerate it in a tightly covered container. Clarified butter can safely be kept for a month.

Ginger-Ale Salad

To serve 6 to 8

1 tablespoon vegetable oil
1 small Temple or navel orange
½ cup cold water
1 envelope unflavored gelatin
¼ cup sugar
1½ cups ginger ale
2 tablespoons strained fresh lemon juice
2 medium-sized firm ripe peaches, peeled, halved, pitted and cut lengthwise into ⅓-inch-thick slices
½ cup fresh ripe strawberries, washed, hulled and cut lengthwise into ⅓-inch-thick slices
½ cup table grapes, washed, halved and seeded if necessary
1 tablespoon very finely chopped crystallized ginger

With a pastry brush, spread the vegetable oil evenly inside a 1-quart decorative mold. Invert the mold on paper towels to drain off the excess oil.

Remove the peel and all of the white membrane of the orange with a small sharp knife, using short sawing motions. Section the orange by cutting along both sides of each membrane division to the core. As each section is freed, carefully lift it out and set it aside on paper towels to drain.

Pour the water into a heatproof measuring cup and sprinkle the gelatin over it. When the gelatin has softened for 2 or 3 minutes, set the cup in a small skillet of simmering water and stir over low heat until the gelatin dissolves completely. Add the sugar and stir until it dissolves.

Pour the gelatin mixture into a deep bowl and stir in the ginger ale and lemon juice. Then set the bowl into a larger bowl half filled with crushed ice or ice cubes and cold water. With a metal spoon, stir the mixture until it thickens enough to flow sluggishly off the spoon. Stir in the orange sections, peaches, strawberries, grapes and the crystallized ginger.

Pour the mixture into the oiled mold, cover with foil or plastic wrap, and refrigerate for at least 4 hours, or until it is firm to the touch.

To unmold the salad, run a thin knife around the sides of the mold and dip the bottom briefly into hot water. Place an inverted serving plate on top of the mold and, grasping plate and mold together firmly, turn them over. Rap the plate on a table and the ginger-ale salad should slide out easily. Refrigerate until ready to serve. Ginger-ale salad may be served with strawberry-and-sour-cream dressing.

Strawberry-and-Sour-Cream Dressing

To make about 2 cups

A 10-ounce package frozen sliced sweetened strawberries, thoroughly defrosted, and their syrup
1½ cups sour cream
A pinch of salt
Confectioners' sugar (optional)

Place the strawberries and their syrup in a bowl and crush the berries slightly with the back of a large spoon. Add the sour cream and salt, and stir until the ingredients are thoroughly blended. Taste for sweetness and add up to 1 tablespoon of confectioners' sugar if desired. Cover with foil or plastic wrap and refrigerate the dressing for at least 1 hour before serving. Strawberry-and-sour-cream dressing may accompany any fruit salad.

Lime-Gelatin Salad

With a small sharp knife, peel the cucumber and slice it lengthwise in half. Scoop out the seeds by running the tip of a teaspoon down the center of each half. Then cut the cucumber into ¼-inch dice. Place the dice in a fine sieve set over a bowl, add the salt and toss the cucumber about with a spoon to coat the dice evenly. Set aside to drain for at least 30 minutes, then pat the cucumber dice dry with paper towels.

Meanwhile, with a pastry brush, spread the vegetable oil evenly inside a 6-cup ring mold or eight individual 6-ounce molds. Invert the mold or molds on paper towels to allow the excess oil to drain off.

Place the powdered gelatin in a heatproof bowl, pour in the boiling water and mix well. Put the cream cheese in a large bowl, and with an electric mixer, beat it until it is light and fluffy. Beating the mixture constantly, pour in the gelatin in a slow thin stream and, when it is thoroughly incorporated, add the lime juice, Worcestershire sauce and Tabasco.

Set the bowl in a larger bowl half filled with crushed ice or ice cubes and cold water. Stir with a metal spoon until the gelatin mixture thickens enough to flow sluggishly off the spoon. Stir in the cucumber dice, the celery, onions and dill.

Pour the gelatin mixture into the oiled mold or molds, cover with plastic wrap and refrigerate for 4 hours, or until it is firm to the touch.

To unmold the salad, run a thin knife around the sides of the mold and dip the bottom briefly into hot water. Place an inverted serving plate on top of the mold and, grasping plate and mold together firmly, turn them over. Rap the plate on a table and the gelatin salad should slide out easily. Refrigerate until ready to serve.

To serve 6 to 8

1 medium-sized firm ripe cucumber
1 teaspoon salt
1 tablespoon vegetable oil
2 packages lime-flavored gelatin
1 quart boiling water
2 eight-ounce packages cream cheese, cut into ½-inch bits and softened
2 tablespoons strained fresh lime juice
2 teaspoons Worcestershire sauce
¼ teaspoon Tabasco sauce
1 cup finely chopped celery
¼ cup finely chopped onions
¼ cup finely cut fresh dill

Lime-gelatin molds, cucumber "leaves," watercress and fresh strawberries give a party flare to a ring of ginger-ale salad.

To serve 6

Six 10- to 12-ounce artichokes
6 quarts water
3 tablespoons salt

GREEN GODDESS DRESSING

3 cups mayonnaise, freshly made, or a good, unsweetened commercial variety
1 tablespoon tarragon wine vinegar
1 teaspoon lemon juice
1 tablespoon finely chopped anchovies (6 to 8 flat anchovies canned in olive oil)
1 tablespoon chopped fresh tarragon or 1 teaspoon dried crumbled tarragon
¼ cup finely chopped scallions, including part of the green stems
¼ teaspoon finely chopped garlic
¼ cup finely chopped fresh parsley
⅛ teaspoon cayenne

2 pounds shelled, cooked and chilled tiny shrimp
6 rolled, caper-stuffed anchovies (optional)
Lemon slices

Artichokes Stuffed with Shrimp and Green Goddess Dressing

Trim the bases of the artichokes flush and flat so that they will stand upright without wobbling. Bend and snap off the small bottom leaves and any bruised outer leaves. Lay each artichoke on its side, grip it firmly and, with a large, sharp knife, slice about 1 inch off the top.

With scissors trim ¼ inch off the points of the rest of the leaves. Rub all the cut edges with lemon to prevent their discoloring. In an 8-quart enameled or stainless-steel pot (do not use aluminum; it will turn the artichokes gray), bring about 6 quarts of water and 3 tablespoons of salt to a boil. Drop in the artichokes and boil them briskly, uncovered, for about 30 minutes, turning occasionally. They are done when their bases show no resistance when pierced with the tip of a small, sharp knife. Drain them upside down in a colander. When they are cool enough to handle, spread their leaves apart gently, grasp the inner core of yellow, thistlelike leaves firmly and ease it out. Then, with a long-handled spoon, thoroughly scrape out and discard the fuzzy choke.

GREEN GODDESS DRESSING: In a small mixing bowl, beat into the 3 cups of mayonnaise the vinegar, lemon juice, anchovies, tarragon, scallions, garlic, parsley and cayenne. Taste for seasoning and add a little salt if you think it needs it.

In a large mixing bowl combine the shrimp and 1½ cups of the dressing, stirring them gently until the shrimp are well coated. Fill each artichoke cavity with the mixture, mounding it slightly on the top. Arrange the anchovy, if you are using it, in the center of each shrimp mound and chill the stuffed artichokes until ready to serve.

To serve, place the artichokes on chilled plates and surround them with the lemon slices. Pass the remaining Green Goddess dressing separately.

To serve 6 to 8

1½ pounds shoulder of veal cut into 2-inch pieces
1½ pounds fresh pig's knuckles, cracked with a cleaver
1 large onion (about 1 pound), unpeeled
1 large carrot, scraped
2 quarts cold water
6 whole black peppercorns
3 bay leaves
1 tablespoon salt
1 teaspoon finely chopped garlic

Veal in Aspic

In a heavy 4- to 6-quart casserole, combine the veal, pig's knuckles, onion, carrot, and water and bring to a boil over high heat, meanwhile skimming the foam and scum from the surface as they rise to the top. Then add the whole peppercorns and bay leaves, reduce the heat to low, and simmer partially covered for about 3 hours, or until the veal is tender enough to be easily pierced with a fork.

With a slotted spatula, transfer the veal, pig's knuckle and carrot to a plate. Strain the stock through a fine sieve set over a bowl and let it rest about 10 minutes. Then skim off and discard the surface fat. Pour the stock into a small pan and boil briskly, uncovered, until only 4 cups of it remain.

When the veal and pig's knuckle are cool enough to handle, trim off the fat with a small knife and cut the meat away from the bones. Discard the bones and cut the meat into ¼-inch-wide shreds. Slice the carrot into ⅛-inch-thick slices.

Arrange the carrot slices in concentric circles in the bottom of a 2-quart charlotte or similar mold at least 3 inches deep. A teaspoon at a time, sprinkle the carrots evenly with the stock, and continue adding the stock by teaspoons until the carrots are half submerged but not floating. Carefully place the mold in the refrigerator without dislodging the design and chill for at least 1 hour, or until the stock has jelled.

By this time the remaining stock should be cool. Stir in the meat, salt and garlic and taste for seasoning. Then pour the entire mixture into the chilled mold. Refrigerate for at least 4 hours, or until the stock is firm.

To unmold, run a knife around the outside edges of the jellied veal. Dip the bottom of the mold briefly in hot water, then invert a flat serving dish on top. Holding mold and plate firmly together, turn them over. The jellied veal should slide out easily.

Sole-and-Crab Mousse with Shrimp Sauce

First prepare the fish stock in the following manner: Combine the fish trimmings and water in a 3- to 4-quart enameled or stainless-steel saucepan and bring to a boil over high heat, meanwhile skimming off the foam and scum as they rise to the surface. Add the chopped onion, bay leaf, salt and peppercorns, and reduce the heat to low. Simmer partially covered for 30 minutes, then strain the stock through a fine sieve set over a bowl, pressing down hard on the trimmings with the back of a spoon to extract all their juices before discarding the bones. Return the strained stock to the pan.

Meanwhile, shell the shrimp. Devein them by making a shallow incision down their backs with a small sharp knife and lifting out the black or white intestinal vein with the point of the knife.

Bring the fish stock to a simmer over moderate heat, drop in the shrimp and cook uncovered for 3 to 5 minutes, or until the shrimp are pink and firm. Do not overcook the shrimp. With a slotted spoon, transfer the shrimp to a plate. Reserve four whole shrimp to garnish the mousse, chop the rest into small dice and refrigerate them until needed. Bring the remaining fish stock to a boil and cook briskly, uncovered, until it is reduced to about 1 cup. Strain the stock through a fine sieve lined with a double thickness of cheesecloth and set over a bowl. Cool to room temperature, then refrigerate until you are ready to make the shrimp sauce.

To make the mousse, preheat the oven to 350°. With a pastry brush spread the vegetable oil over the bottom and sides of a heavy 6-cup fish mold or other decorative 6-cup mold. Invert the mold on paper towels to drain off the excess oil.

Place about one third of the sole and 2 tablespoons of light cream in the jar of an electric blender and blend at high speed for 30 seconds. Turn off the machine, scrape down the sides of the jar with a rubber spatula and blend again until the sole is a smooth purée. Transfer the puréed sole to a deep bowl and repeat two more times, adding 2 tablespoons of light cream to each batch.

Combine the crabmeat and the remaining 10 tablespoons of light cream in the blender, and purée it in similar fashion. With the spatula, scrape

To serve 6

FISH STOCK
1 pound fish trimmings: the heads, tails and bones of any firm white-fleshed fish
1 quart water
1 medium-sized onion, peeled and coarsely chopped
1 medium-sized bay leaf, crumbled
1 teaspoon salt
6 whole black peppercorns
½ pound raw shrimp

MOUSSE
1 tablespoon vegetable oil
1 pound sole fillets, skinned and cut into 1-inch pieces
1 cup light cream
8 ounces frozen Alaskan king crabmeat, thoroughly defrosted and drained, then cut into 1-inch pieces
4 egg yolks
1 tablespoon finely grated onion
1 tablespoon strained fresh lemon juice
¼ teaspoon ground nutmeg, preferably freshly grated
¼ teaspoon ground white pepper
2 egg whites
½ cup heavy cream, chilled

Overleaf: A California creation, sole-and-crab mousse covered with shrimp sauce and garnished with whole shrimp is elegant enough to be served at a wedding feast or an after-the-rehearsal supper party.

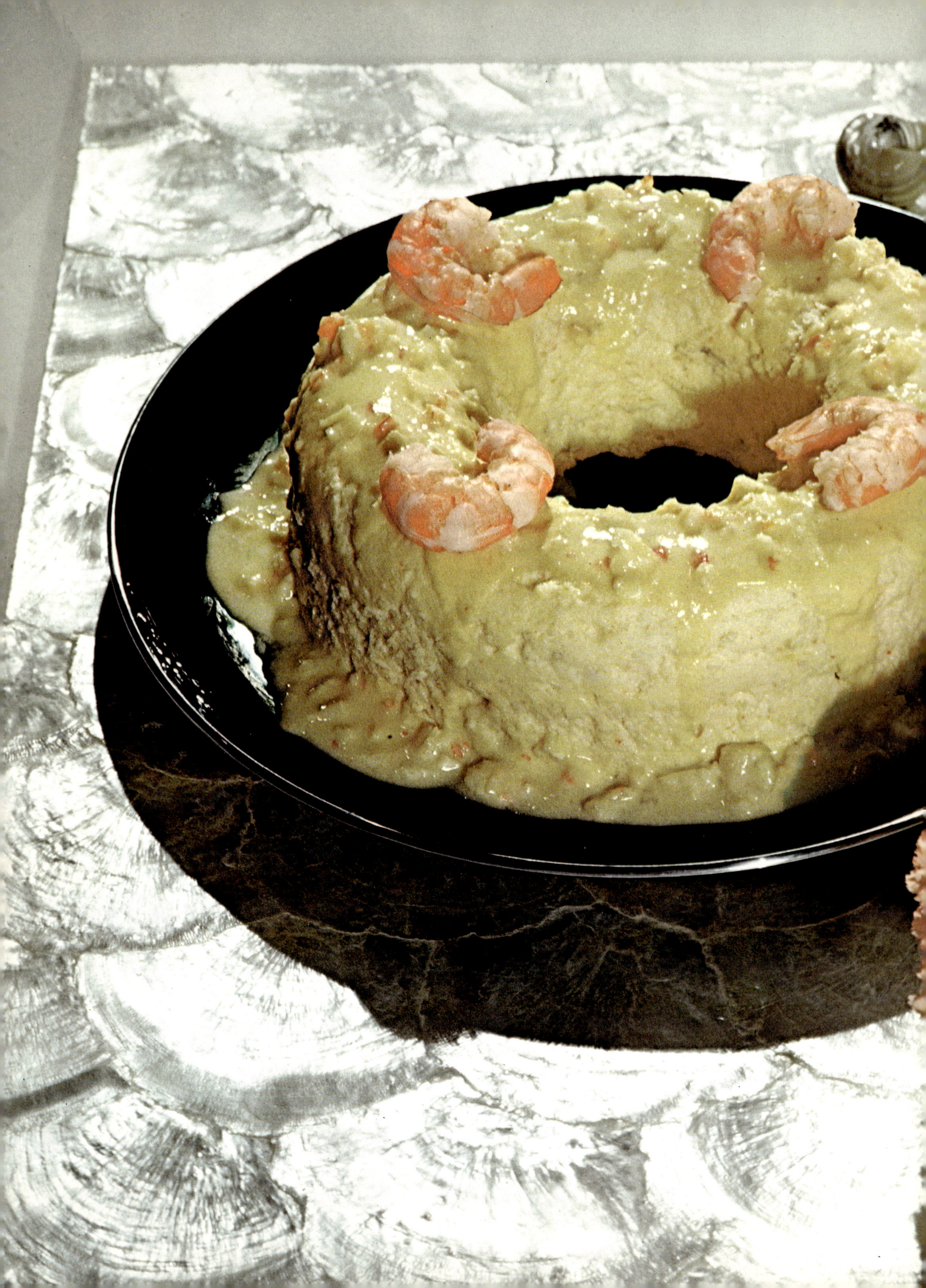

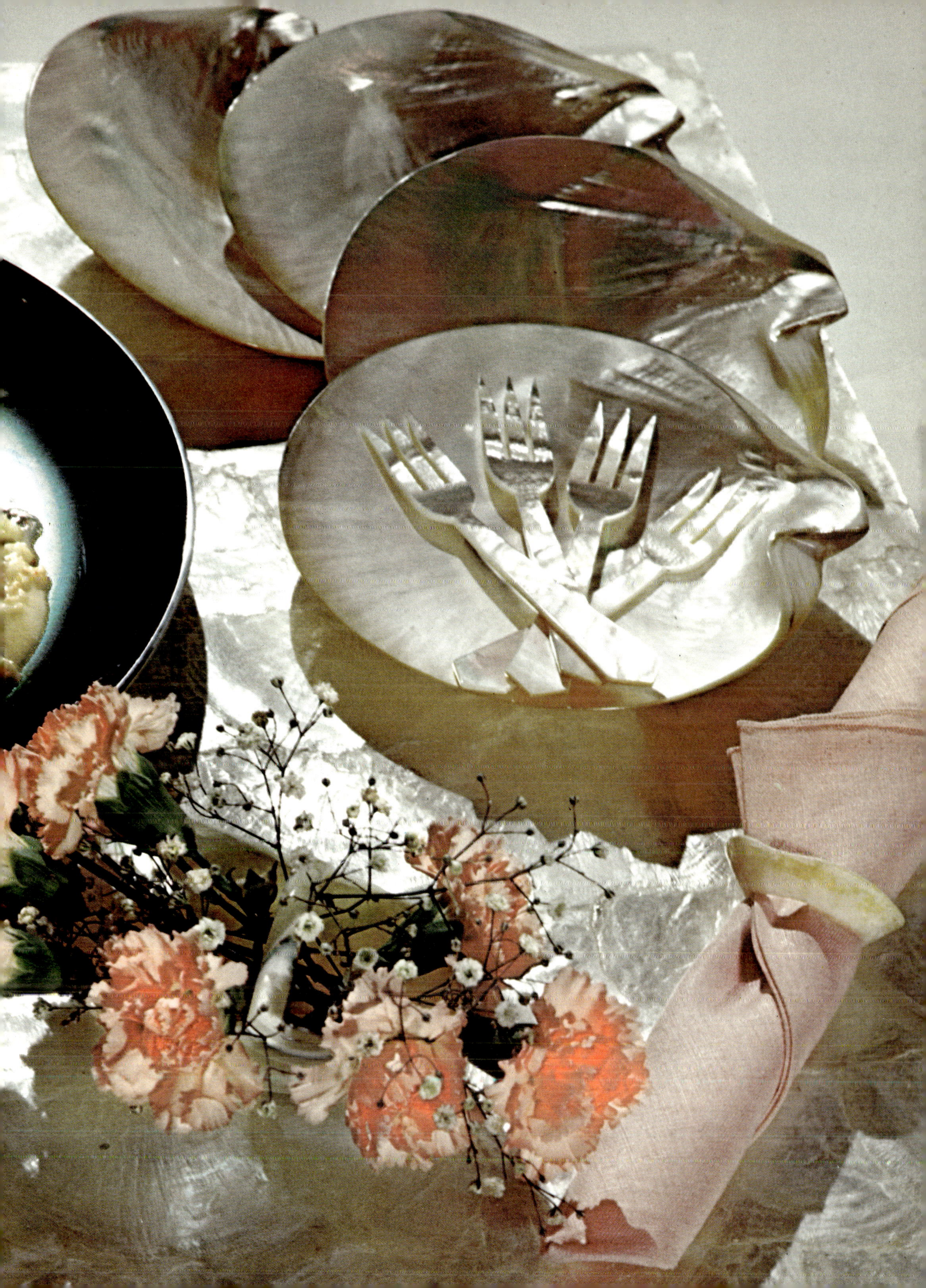

the crab purée over the sole purée. Add the 4 egg yolks and beat vigorously with a wooden spoon until the mixture is smooth. Stir in the grated onion, lemon juice, nutmeg and white pepper.

Beat the egg whites with a wire whisk or a rotary or electric beater until they are stiff enough to stand in unwavering peaks on the beater when it is lifted out of the bowl. In a chilled bowl, whip the heavy cream with the same beater until it stands in firm peaks.

With a rubber spatula, scoop the cream over the sole-and-crab mixture and fold them together gently but thoroughly. Add the egg whites and continue to fold until all the ingredients are well blended.

Spoon the mixture into the oiled mold and place it in a roasting pan set on the middle shelf of the oven. Pour enough boiling water into the pan to come halfway up the sides of the mold. Bake the mousse for 35 to 40 minutes, or until a knife inserted in the center comes out clean.

Meanwhile, complete the shrimp sauce. In a small saucepan, bring the reserved cup of fish stock to a simmer over low heat. Stirring constantly with a wire whisk, add the cornstarch mixture, and cook until the stock clears and thickens. Remove the pan from the heat.

In a heavy 1- to 1½-quart enameled saucepan, beat the 2 egg yolks with a wire whisk or a rotary or electric beater for a minute or so. Stirring constantly, add the ½ cup of light cream and then gradually pour in the hot fish stock in a slow, thin stream. Still stirring, cook the sauce over low heat for 2 or 3 minutes, but do not let it come near a boil or the egg yolks will curdle. Stir in the sherry and the reserved chopped shrimp, and taste for seasoning.

To unmold and serve the finished mousse, run a thin knife around the edges of the mold to loosen the sides. Place an inverted platter on top of the mold and, grasping platter and mold together firmly, turn them over. The mousse should slide out easily. Pour the sauce over the mousse, arrange the four reserved whole shrimp on top and serve at once.

SHRIMP SAUCE
2 teaspoons cornstarch mixed with 2 teaspoons water
2 egg yolks
½ cup light cream
2 tablespoons dry sherry

To serve 6

3 bunches celery, about 2 inches in diameter
1½ cups chicken stock, fresh or canned
An herb bouquet of 4 sprigs parsley, 1 bay leaf and celery leaves tied together
Salt
Freshly ground black pepper
3 tablespoons white-wine vinegar
½ cup olive oil
12 flat anchovy fillets
12 strips pimiento
6 slices tomato (optional)
6 slices hard-cooked eggs (optional)
1½ teaspoons finely chopped fresh parsley

Celery Victor

Remove the outer stalks of the celery, leaving a heart about 1 inch wide and 6 inches long. Cut each celery heart in half lengthwise. Cut away all but the small leaves and trim the root ends (do not cut too deep; the celery halves should hold together). Use the cut-away leaves for the herb bouquet. With a sharp knife, scrape the outer stalks if they seem coarse.

Arrange the celery halves side by side in a 10- or 12-inch skillet, preferably enameled or stainless steel, and pour in the stock, using more stock or water if the celery is not completely covered. Add the herb bouquet, with as much salt and pepper as suits your taste, and bring to a boil. Reduce the heat to its lowest point, cover tightly and simmer the celery for about 15 minutes, or until it shows no resistance when pierced with the tip of a sharp knife. With tongs or a slotted spoon, transfer the celery halves to a deep platter that will hold them in a single layer.

With a whisk, beat the vinegar and the oil together and pour over the celery while it is still warm. Refrigerate for at least an hour before serving. To serve, arrange the celery halves on individual chilled plates and crisscross 2 anchovy fillets and 2 strips of pimiento over each serving. Or instead, if you prefer, garnish the celery with a slice of tomato and a slice of hard-cooked egg. In either case, moisten the celery with a spoonful or so of the vinegar-olive oil sauce and sprinkle with chopped parsley.

Cold Marinated Vegetables, Greek Style

First make the marinade. Stir the ingredients together in a 3- to 4-quart enameled or stainless-steel saucepan, bring to a boil, partially cover the pan and simmer slowly for 45 minutes. Using a fine sieve, strain the marinade into a large bowl, pressing down hard on the ingredients with the back of a spoon to squeeze out their juices before discarding them. Return the marinade to the saucepan and taste it. To be effective, the marinade should be somewhat overseasoned. This makes about 5 cups.

Bring the marinade to a boil and add the onions; cover and cook over moderate heat for 20 to 30 minutes or until the onions are just tender when pierced with the tip of a sharp knife. With a slotted spoon, remove the onions to a large glass or stainless-steel baking dish.

Add the slices of zucchini and yellow squash to the simmering marinade and cook slowly uncovered for 10 to 15 minutes or until they are barely done, then put them in the baking dish with the onions. Finally, add the green-pepper strips and string beans to the marinade and cook them slowly uncovered for 8 to 10 minutes, or until they are just tender. The vegetables must not be overcooked because they will soften as they cool and marinate. Lift the green peppers and string beans out of the pan and add them to the other vegetables. Taste and season the marinade and pour it over the vegetables, making sure that they are all at least partly covered with the hot liquid.

Place the baking dish in the refrigerator to cool the vegetables. Then cover the dish tightly with aluminum foil or plastic wrap and let the vegetables marinate in the refrigerator for at least 4 hours—or overnight if possible—before serving them. To serve, lift the vegetables out of the marinade with a slotted spoon and arrange them attractively on a serving platter. Moisten the vegetables with a little marinade and garnish them with lemon slices.

NOTE: Any other firm vegetable may be added to or substituted for those in the recipe, such as mushrooms, celery hearts, leeks, cucumbers, red peppers and artichoke hearts.

To serve 8 to 10

MARINADE
3 cups chicken stock, fresh or canned
1 cup dry white wine
1 cup olive oil
½ cup lemon juice
6 parsley sprigs
2 large garlic cloves, cut up
½ teaspoon dried thyme
10 peppercorns
1 teaspoon salt

VEGETABLES
24 white onions, 1 inch in diameter, peeled
1 pound small zucchini, unpeeled, sliced 1 inch thick
1 pound small yellow squash, unpeeled, sliced 1 inch thick
3 medium green peppers, seeded and cut lengthwise into ½-inch strips
½ pound whole green string beans, trimmed
2 lemons, cut into ¼-inch slices

Chinese Water-Chestnut-and-Watercress Salad

PREPARE AHEAD: 1. With a small knife, trim and discard the tough ends of the watercress stems. Wash the watercress under cold running water, drop it into a pot of boiling water, then drain and pat the leaves dry with paper towels. With a cleaver or large knife, chop the watercress fine.

2. Wash the water chestnuts, drain and cut them into ⅛-inch slices. Then chop them fine.

To serve 4

2 bunches watercress
8 peeled fresh water chestnuts or drained canned water chestnuts
1 teaspoon soy sauce
2 teaspoons sesame-seed oil
½ teaspoon salt
1 teaspoon sugar

A sparkling drink for a festive family luncheon, a wedding or an anniversary, champagne or Rhine wine cup is served in chilled wine glasses.

TO ASSEMBLE: Combine in a large bowl the soy sauce, sesame-seed oil, salt and sugar, and mix thoroughly. Add the watercress and water chestnuts, and toss them well with a large spoon so that they are well coated with the mixture. Chill and serve.

Russian Cucumber-and-Sour-Cream Salad

In a mixing bowl, combine the cucumber slices, salt and vinegar and toss them about with a large spoon until the cucumber is well moistened. Marinate at room temperature for 30 minutes, then drain the cucumbers through a sieve and pat them thoroughly dry with paper towels. Place them in a large mixing bowl.

Separate the yolks from the whites of the hard-cooked eggs. Cut the whites into strips 1/8 inch wide and 1 to 2 inches long and stir the egg whites into the cucumber.

With the back of a large spoon, rub the egg yolks through a fine sieve set over a small bowl. Slowly beat in the mustard, sour cream, white wine vinegar, sugar and white pepper. When the dressing is smooth, pour it over the cucumbers and toss together gently but thoroughly. Taste for seasoning.

To serve, arrange the lettuce leaves on a large flat serving plate or on small individual plates and mound the salad on top of them. Sprinkle with dill and refrigerate until ready to serve.

To serve 4 to 6

4 medium cucumbers, peeled, halved, seeded, and cut crosswise into ½-inch-thick slices
1 tablespoon coarse salt, or substitute 2 tablespoons table salt
½ teaspoon white distilled vinegar

DRESSING

3 hard-cooked eggs
1 teaspoon prepared mustard, preferably Dijon or Düsseldorf
⅓ cup sour cream
2 teaspoons white wine vinegar
¼ teaspoon sugar
⅛ teaspoon white pepper

4 to 6 large lettuce leaves, well washed and dried
1 tablespoon finely cut fresh dill leaves

Champagne or Rhine Wine Cup

Place the fruits of your choice in a pitcher first, then add the cherries and the brandy, Benedictine and maraschino liqueur. Place the pitcher in the refrigerator (or freezer) for at least 1 hour (½ hour if you use the freezer). Remove the pitcher and fill with ice cubes. A solid block of ice that fits the pitcher is even better; it will be more attractive, and it will not dilute the drink by melting too quickly.

Just before serving, pour in the champagne or Rhine wine and the sparkling water. Stir briefly with a glass stirring rod or a bar spoon and serve in chilled wine glasses or punch cups.

To serve 4

Approximately 1 cup of fruits of the season: peeled orange and/or grapefruit sections, lemon slices, hulled strawberries, peach slices, cucumber peel
4 maraschino cherries
4 ounces brandy
4 ounces Benedictine
4 ounces maraschino liqueur
12 to 16 ice cubes or a block of ice
1 bottle cold champagne or cold Rhine wine
6 ounces cold Perrier water or club soda

Sauternes Cup

Place the fruits of your choice in a pitcher first, then add the brandy, Cointreau and Grand Marnier. Place the pitcher in the refrigerator (or freezer) for at least 1 hour (½ hour if you use the freezer). Remove the pitcher and fill it with ice cubes. A solid block of ice that fits the pitcher is even better, since it will not melt as quickly and dilute the drink. Pour the Sauternes and sparkling water into the pitcher, stir briefly, and serve the Sauternes cup in chilled wine glasses or punch cups.

To serve 4

Approximately 1 cup of fruits of the season: peeled orange and/or grapefruit sections, lemon slices, hulled strawberries, peach slices, cucumber peel
4 ounces brandy
4 ounces Cointreau
4 ounces Grand Marnier
12 to 16 ice cubes or a block of ice
1 bottle imported Sauternes
6 ounces cold Perrier water or club soda

Special Occasion Entrées

Rolled Stuffed Fish Fillets

To serve 4 to 6

8 fillets of white firm-fleshed fish, such as pike, perch or sole
6 tablespoons unsalted butter, plus 1 tablespoon butter, softened, and 1 tablespoon butter, cut into ¼-inch bits
4 to 6 slices white bread, trimmed and cut into ¼-inch dice (2½ cups)
3 tablespoons finely cut chives
¼ teaspoon thyme
½ teaspoon tarragon
½ teaspoon salt
¼ teaspoon white pepper

SAUCE
½ cup sour cream
1 tablespoon flour
1 teaspoon strained fresh lemon juice
½ teaspoon salt
1 tablespoon tomato purée

Wash the fish fillets under cold running water and pat them thoroughly dry with paper towels. Place the fillets side by side on a flat surface and trim them evenly to 8- or 9-inch lengths. Gather all the fish you have trimmed from the fillets and chop it fine.

In a 10- to 12-inch skillet, melt 2 tablespoons of the butter over moderate heat. Stir in the chopped fish and, stirring it constantly, cook over moderate heat for 4 or 5 minutes, until the flesh becomes opaque. Transfer to a bowl and set aside.

Add 4 tablespoons of butter to the skillet and drop in the bread cubes. Toss them constantly with a wooden spoon until they are a light gold, then add them to the bowl of fish. Sprinkle the fish and bread cubes with the chives, thyme, tarragon, ½ teaspoon of salt and the pepper, and toss together lightly but thoroughly.

Preheat the oven to 400°. With a pastry brush, lightly coat the bottom and sides of a 9-by-12-inch flameproof baking dish with the tablespoon of softened butter. Place 2 tablespoons of the herbed stuffing on the narrow end of each fillet and gently roll up the fillets. Arrange them seam side down in the baking dish, and dot with the tablespoon of butter bits. Bake in the center of the oven for 12 to 15 minutes, or until the fish feels firm when prodded gently with a finger. With a spatula, transfer the fish rolls to a heated platter and keep them warm in the turned-off oven while you make the sauce.

In a small bowl, combine the ½ cup of sour cream with the 1 tablespoon of flour. Place the flameproof baking dish over moderate heat and, with a wire whisk, gradually beat in the sour-cream-and-flour mixture, the lemon juice and ½ teaspoon of salt. Stir in the tomato purée and taste for seasoning.

Spoon the sauce over the fish rolls. Or, if you prefer, present the sauce separately in a heated sauceboat.

Boeuf à la Mode—Two Ways, Hot and Cold

To serve 10 to 12

THE BEEF
1 tablespoon salt
1 teaspoon coarsely ground black pepper
A 5-pound boneless beef chuck or bottom round roast at least 5 inches in diameter, trimmed and tied

THE MARINADE
3 cups red Burgundy or other dry red wine
1 cup thinly sliced onions
¾ cup thinly sliced carrots
1 teaspoon finely chopped garlic
2 bay leaves, crumbled
2 tablespoons finely chopped fresh parsley
1 teaspoon dried thyme, crumbled

MARINATING THE BEEF: Press 1 tablespoon of salt and 1 teaspoon of pepper into the surface of the beef. In a large glass, porcelain or stainless-steel bowl, mix the marinade ingredients. Add the beef and turn it in the marinade until it is well moistened on all sides. Let it marinate for at least 6 hours at room temperature or 12 to 24 hours in the refrigerator, turning it over every few hours.

THE ONIONS AND CARROTS À BRUN: Preheat the oven to 350°. In a heavy 10- to 12-inch skillet, sauté the diced pork fat over moderate heat, stirring constantly, until crisp and brown. Remove the diced pork fat and reserve it. In the fat left in the skillet, brown the whole onions and the carrots lightly over moderately high heat, shaking the pan occasionally to roll them around and color them as evenly as possible. Transfer them to a

Easy, decorative and delicate, fish rolls, with a pink sour-cream sauce, are perfect entrées for a meal to mark a special occasion.

shallow baking dish large enough to hold them in one layer, and sprinkle them with about 3 tablespoons of pork fat. (Set the skillet aside, without removing the remaining fat.) Bake the onions and carrots uncovered on the middle shelf of the oven, turning and basting them once or twice, for 30 minutes, or until they are barely tender. Remove from the oven, pour out the cooking fat and set the vegetables aside.

BRAISING THE BEEF: While the vegetables bake or when they are done, remove the beef from the marinade and dry it thoroughly with paper towels. Strain the marinade into a small bowl, and drain the vegetables on paper towels. Heat the pork fat remaining in the skillet to the smoking point and brown the beef over moderate heat until it is richly colored on all sides. While the beef is browning, melt 4 tablespoons of butter in a heavy, 6-quart flameproof casserole or Dutch oven. Add the marinated vegetables and cook over low heat, turning frequently, until most of their moisture has boiled away and they are lightly colored. When the beef is browned, use a bulb baster to draw off all but a thin film of fat from the skillet.

The next step is to flame the beef. Experts simply flame the beef with Cognac directly in the pan. But a more reliable way is to warm the Cognac

THE ONIONS AND CARROTS À BRUN
½ pound fresh pork fat, diced
20 to 24 white onions, about 1 inch in diameter, peeled
6 to 8 carrots, peeled and cut into 1½-inch cylinders or olive shapes

THE BRAISING STOCK
4 tablespoons butter
⅓ cup Cognac
2 calf's feet and/or 1 large veal knuckle, sawed into pieces
2 medium tomatoes, peeled, seeded and coarsely chopped
Bouquet garni made of 6 parsley sprigs, 1 bay leaf and the white part of 1 leek, tied together
3 cups beef stock, fresh or canned
Salt
Freshly ground black pepper
½ cup finely chopped fresh parsley

first in a small saucepan over low heat, ignite it with a match, and pour it flaming over the beef a little at a time, shaking the skillet gently until the flame dies. Transfer the beef to the casserole and surround it with the pieces of calf's feet and / or veal knuckle, the chopped tomatoes, the diced pork fat and the *bouquet garni*.

Pour the strained marinade and 3 cups of beef stock into the skillet, and bring them to a boil over high heat, stirring and scraping in any browned bits that cling to the pan. Boil briskly for 1 or 2 minutes, then pour it into the casserole. The liquid should come about halfway up the side of the meat; add more beef stock if needed. Bring the casserole to a boil on top of the stove, then cover tightly and place on the middle shelf of the oven. Regulate oven heat so the beef simmers slowly, and turn and baste the meat 2 or 3 times during the cooking. After 2½ to 3 hours the meat should be tender when pierced with the tip of a sharp knife.

To serve the beef and the vegetables hot, transfer the beef from the casserole to a plate. Remove and discard the bones and *bouquet garni* and strain the rest of the contents of the casserole through a large, fine sieve into a 3- to 4-quart saucepan, pressing down hard on the vegetables before discarding them. Let the strained braising liquid, or sauce, settle for a few minutes, then skim as much fat as possible from the surface. Boil the sauce briskly over high heat until it has been reduced to half its original quantity (about 3 to 4 cups). Taste and season with salt and pepper. Return the meat and sauce to the casserole and add the baked onions and carrots. Simmer slowly on top of the stove to heat the beef and vegetables thoroughly. Transfer the beef to a carving board to remove the strings. Then arrange the roast on a large heated platter, surrounded with the onions and carrots. Spoon some of the sauce over it, and serve the rest separately in a warm sauceboat.

BOEUF À LA MODE EN GELÉE (cold pot roast of beef in aspic): To prepare the cold version of *boeuf à la mode*, let the beef cool for an hour in the braising liquid, turning it once or twice. Transfer the beef to a platter, let it cool to room temperature, then wrap and refrigerate it. Strain the braising liquid; cool, cover and refrigerate it. Cool, cover and refrigerate the baked onions and carrots.

When the braising liquid is thoroughly chilled, carefully remove and discard all of the fat that has solidified on the surface. In a 2- or 3-quart saucepan, melt the braising liquid over low heat and then measure it. Add enough beef stock to make 5 cups in all, and return it to the pan. Soften the gelatin in an additional 1 cup of cold fresh stock, and add it. Beat the egg whites to a froth with a wire whisk, and stir them into the stock, together with the lemon juice, thyme, bay leaf, peppercorns and salt. Bring to a boil over moderate heat, stirring constantly. When the aspic begins to froth and rise, remove the pan from the heat. Let it rest off the heat for 5 minutes, then strain it into a deep bowl through a fine sieve lined with a dampened kitchen towel. Allow the aspic to drain without disturbing it at any point. When it has drained completely through, add the Madeira, and taste and season the aspic with more salt if needed. Pour a thin layer of aspic—about ⅛ inch thick—into the bottom of a large serving platter, and refrigerate it until the aspic is set. Then carve the

THE ASPIC FOR BOEUF À LA MODE EN GELÉE

2 to 4 cups beef stock, fresh or canned
3 envelopes unflavored gelatin
3 egg whites
½ teaspoon lemon juice
½ teaspoon dried thyme, crumbled
½ bay leaf
10 peppercorns
1 teaspoon salt
½ cup dry Madeira

cold beef into ¼-inch slices and arrange the meat, onions and carrots attractively on the platter. Heat about ¾ cup of the aspic in a small pan just until it melts, then set it in a bowl filled with crushed ice or ice cubes immersed in water. Stir the aspic gently with a metal spoon until it thickens almost to the point of setting. Working quickly, spread a thin glaze of aspic over the sliced beef and vegetables. Chill until the aspic sets. Repeat this process two more times to make three coatings of aspic—melting and chilling the aspic for each layer. Refrigerate the platter until the glaze is firm. Meanwhile, melt the remaining aspic and pour it into a large flat roasting pan to make a sheet or film no more than ¼ inch deep; chill it.

When all the aspic is very firm, remove the roasting pan from the refrigerator, and score the sheet of aspic into diamonds with the tip of a sharp knife by cutting crossing diagonal lines about 1 to 1½ inches apart. Arrange the diamonds decoratively around the aspic-covered beef. Chop any scraps into fine dice, and garnish the platter with it as fancifully as you like. You can even put the chopped aspic into a pastry bag with a plain tip and press the aspic out in scrolls on the beef.

Chicken Kiev

To skin the chicken breasts, insert your thumb under the skin and strip it off. To bone the breasts, slip the point of a knife under the base of the rib bones, press the flat of the knife up against the bone, and gently pull the bone toward you, scraping away the flesh adhering to the ribs. Cut off the wing tip.

Place the 8 halved breasts smooth side down on a cutting board. With a small, sharp knife and your fingers, remove the small fillet from each breast. Lay the breasts and fillets, one pair at a time, on a sheet of wax paper. Cover the breast and fillet with a sheet of wax paper and, with the flat side of a cleaver or a metal meat pounder, pound them to a thickness of ⅛ inch. If holes appear in the flesh, overlap the edges of the tear slightly, cover the patch with wax paper, and pound gently until the meat joins together.

Cut the 1½ sticks of butter into 8 equal parts. Shape each piece of butter into a cylinder about ½ inch thick and 3 inches long. Wrap them in wax paper and chill until firm. (Or, cream the butter by mashing it against the side of a bowl with a wooden spoon and beating into it the optional seasoning—lemon juice, chives or tarragon, parsley, salt and pepper—and cut and shape the butter as described above. Chill until firm.)

To assemble the cutlets, gently peel off the wax paper and sprinkle the chicken lightly with salt and freshly ground black pepper. Wrap the chicken breasts and fillets snugly around the butter cylinders.

In a small bowl, beat the eggs just long enough to combine them. Spread flour and the bread crumbs on two separate strips of wax paper and, one at a time, dip the cutlets into the flour. Shake each one gently free of excess flour and, cradling it in your palms, pat the cutlet into a long cylinder tapering slightly at each end. Now dip the cutlet into the eggs, making sure

To serve 4

4 whole fresh chicken breasts, ½ to ¾ pound each, cut in half, with wing bone attached
12 tablespoons chilled unsalted butter (1½ sticks)
2 eggs
Flour
2 cups fine, dry white bread crumbs
Vegetable oil for deep-frying
Salt
Freshly ground black pepper

OPTIONAL SEASONING
1 teaspoon fresh, strained lemon juice
1 teaspoon finely cut fresh chives or tarragon
1 tablespoon finely chopped parsley
2 teaspoons salt
Freshly ground black pepper

Chicken Kiev—boned chicken breast stuffed with butter and fried a golden brown—is a classic and elegant Russian dish, traditionally served with fresh peas and straw potatoes. The servings can be easily multiplied to suit the number of diners.

its entire surface is coated, and roll in the bread crumbs, again making sure it is thoroughly coated. Arrange the cutlets side by side on a platter and refrigerate for 1 or 2 hours before frying.

About 30 minutes before you plan to serve the chicken, preheat the oven to 200°. Line a shallow baking dish with a double thickness of paper towels and place it in the oven. Pour enough oil to rise 3 or 4 inches up the side of a deep-fat fryer or a heavy saucepan into which a frying basket will fit. Set the pan over high heat until the oil registers 360° on a deep-fat thermometer. Fry the cutlets, 4 at a time, in the frying basket for about 5 minutes, or until golden brown, then transfer them with tongs or a slotted spoon to the lined baking dish. Fry the remaining cutlets similarly. The finished cutlets may remain in the low oven for no longer than 10 minutes before serving or they will lose their freshness and their butter may escape.

Straw Potatoes

To serve 4 to 6

4 medium-sized baking potatoes (about 2 pounds)
Vegetable oil for deep-frying
Salt

Peel the potatoes and cut them into straw-shaped strips, about 2½ inches long and ⅛ inch thick. Drop them into a bowl of ice water and set them aside until ready to fry. Drain the potatoes in a colander, spread them out on a double thickness of paper towels and pat them thoroughly dry.

Pour enough oil into a deep fryer to come 3 or 4 inches up the sides of the pan. For the first frying of the potatoes (there will be two in all), heat the oil until it reaches a temperature of 370° on a deep-frying thermometer. Drop the potatoes into the frying basket and immerse the basket in the hot oil, shaking it gently from time to time to prevent the potatoes from sticking together. Fry them for about 15 seconds, or until the potatoes are tender and a pale golden brown. Drain on a double thickness of paper towels, then fry and drain the remaining potatoes similarly. The potatoes may now rest for as long as an hour before refrying and serving.

Immediately before serving, reheat the oil until it reaches a temperature of 385° on a deep-frying thermometer. Drop all the potatoes into the basket and, shaking the basket occasionally, fry for 15 seconds, or until the potatoes are crisp and brown. Drain on paper towels and transfer to a large platter or bowl. Sprinkle lightly with salt, and serve at once.

Shrimp Curry

To serve 4

2 pounds large raw shrimp (12 to 15 per pound)
1½ teaspoons cumin seeds
1½ teaspoons coriander seeds
1½ teaspoons mustard seeds
1½ teaspoons whole black peppercorns
1½ teaspoons turmeric
½ teaspoon crushed hot red pepper
3 tablespoons vegetable oil
1 cup finely chopped onions
1 teaspoon finely chopped garlic
1 tablespoon scraped and finely chopped fresh ginger root
6 medium-sized firm ripe tomatoes, peeled, seeded and finely chopped, or 2 cups chopped drained canned tomatoes
1 cup water
1 teaspoon salt
2 tablespoons strained fresh lime juice

Shell the shrimp. Devein them by making a shallow incision down their backs with a small, sharp knife, and lifting out the black or white intestinal vein with the point of the knife.

Combine the cumin, coriander, mustard, peppercorns, turmeric and red pepper in the jar of an electric blender, and blend at high speed until the spices are completely pulverized. By hand, grind the spices with a mortar and pestle or in a small bowl with the back of a heavy spoon.

In a heavy 12-inch skillet, heat the oil over moderate heat until a light haze forms above it. Drop in the onions, garlic and ginger and, stirring frequently, cook for about 5 minutes, until the onions are soft and transparent but not brown. Watch carefully for any sign of burning and regulate the heat accordingly. Add the pulverized spices and stir for 2 or 3 minutes, then add the tomatoes, water and salt, and bring to a boil over high heat. Stirring constantly, cook briskly until most of the liquid in the pan has evaporated and the mixture is thick enough to hold its shape almost solidly in the spoon.

Add the shrimp and turn them about with the spoon to coat them well. Reduce the heat to the lowest possible point, cover tightly and simmer for about 5 minutes or until the shrimp are firm and pink. Remove the pan from the heat, stir in the lime juice, and taste for seasoning. Spoon the curry attractively onto a heated platter, and serve at once with rice.

Lobster Soufflé with Lobster Sauce

Place the truffle rounds in a small, shallow bowl and pour 3 tablespoons of the cognac over them. Set aside at room temperature.

With a cleaver or large, heavy knife, chop off the tail section of each lobster at the point where it joins the body and twist off the large claws. Slice each tail crosswise into 4 or 5 pieces, and make a gash on the flat side of each of the large claws.

Split the body shells in half lengthwise and remove and discard the gelatinous sac (stomach) in the head and the long intestinal vein attached to it. Scoop out the greenish-brown tomalley (or liver) and the black caviarlike coral (or eggs) if any. Place the tomalley and coral in a small bowl, add ¼ cup of the wine, any juice left from cutting up the lobster and 6 tablespoons of flour and mix well. Set aside.

In a heavy 12-inch sauté pan, heat the ½ cup of clarified butter over high heat for 10 seconds. Add the pieces of lobster and turn them about with a slotted spoon until they are evenly coated on all sides and the shells have begun to turn red. Add the remaining 1½ cups of wine, 2 tablespoons of cognac, the *fumet de poisson,* onions, carrots, tomato, tomato paste, celery, garlic, parsley, bay leaf, tarragon, thyme, salt and a liberal grinding of pepper. Stirring constantly, bring to a boil. Reduce the heat to low, cover the pan tightly and simmer for 15 minutes. With tongs or a slotted spoon, transfer the pieces of lobster to a large platter to cool.

Stirring constantly with a whisk, add the reserved tomalley-and-flour mixture to the mixture remaining in the pan. Still whisking, bring to a boil over high heat, then set the pan aside off the heat.

Shell the tail pieces and the lobster claws with a pick or small knife, and cut all the meat into small pieces. Set the meat aside. Remove the small lobster legs and chop them and the body shells coarsely.

Add all the chopped shells to the sauté pan and, stirring constantly, bring to a boil over high heat. Reduce the heat to low and, stirring occasionally, simmer uncovered for about 10 minutes, or until the sauce thickens. Strain the entire contents of the pan through a fine sieve lined with a double thickness of dampened cheesecloth and set over a deep bowl. Press down hard on all the vegetables and lobster shells with the back of a spoon to extract their juices before discarding them. There should be about 1¾ to 2 cups of lobster sauce.

Ladle ¾ cup of the sauce into a heavy 1- to 1½-quart enameled-iron or tin-lined copper saucepan and stir in ¾ cup of the heavy cream with a

To serve 4 to 6

6 black truffle rounds from a thinly peeled truffle, sliced ⅛ inch thick
6 tablespoons cognac
Two 1½- to 2-pound live lobsters
1¾ cups dry white wine
6 tablespoons flour
½ cup clarified butter *(pages 177-178),* plus 5 tablespoons unsalted butter, cut into ¼-inch bits and chilled
1 cup *fumet de poisson (page 177)*
⅔ cup finely chopped onions
⅓ cup finely chopped scraped carrots
1 large firm ripe tomato, washed, stemmed and coarsely chopped
3 tablespoons canned tomato paste
2 tablespoons finely chopped celery
1 teaspoon coarsely chopped garlic
⅓ cup fresh parsley leaves
1 medium-sized bay leaf
1 teaspoon finely cut fresh tarragon, or substitute ½ teaspoon crumbled dried tarragon
¼ teaspoon finely cut fresh thyme, or substitute ⅛ teaspoon crumbled dried thyme
1 tablespoon salt
Freshly ground black pepper
1¼ cups heavy cream

wire whisk. Whisking constantly, pour in the remaining tablespoon of cognac and cook over moderate heat for 2 or 3 minutes. Remove the pan from the heat, dot the surface of the sauce with about 1 tablespoon of butter bits and set aside.

Ladle the remaining lobster sauce into a 3- to 4-quart enameled or stainless-steel saucepan and stir in ½ cup of heavy cream. Taste for seasoning. Then add the reserved lobster meat and turn the pieces about with a spoon until they are evenly coated. Set aside.

SOUFFLÉ: Preheat the oven to 400°. With a pastry brush, spread the tablespoon of softened butter evenly over the bottom and sides of a 2-quart *gratin* or baking dish about 2½ inches deep.

In a heavy 2- to 3-quart saucepan, warm the *sauce béchamel* over low heat for a minute or so. Whisk in the egg yolks, one at a time. Remove the pan from the heat and set aside.

With a large balloon whisk, beat the egg whites in an unlined copper bowl (glass or ceramic will do) until they are stiff enough to form unwavering peaks on the beater when it is lifted from the bowl. Stir 2 heaping tablespoons of the whites into the waiting sauce, then stir in the grated cheese. Scoop the remaining egg whites over the sauce and, using an over-under cutting motion rather than a stirring one, fold them together gently but thoroughly.

Pour the lobster and its sauce into the buttered dish, spreading the lobster meat out evenly. Spoon the soufflé mixture over the top and gently spread and smooth it to the edges of the dish with a spatula. With the dull side of a large knife, quickly and carefully make crisscrossing diagonal lines about 2 inches apart and ¼ inch deep over the surface of the soufflé. Bake in the middle of the oven for about 25 minutes, or until the soufflé has risen an inch or more above the edge of the dish and the top of the soufflé is golden brown.

Meanwhile, warm the reserved lobster sauce over low heat and swirl in the remaining 4 tablespoons of butter bits. Taste for seasoning.

Just before serving, pat the truffle rounds dry with paper towels and gently place them in a ring around the center of the soufflé. Serve at once, accompanied by the sauce presented separately in a sauceboat.

SOUFFLÉ
1 tablespoon butter, softened
1 cup *sauce béchamel (below)*
3 egg yolks
5 egg whites
¼ cup freshly grated imported Gruyère cheese

To make about 2 cups

2 cups milk
1 tablespoon finely chopped onions
⅛ teaspoon ground nutmeg, preferably freshly grated
1 sprig fresh thyme or ⅛ teaspoon crumbled dried thyme
⅛ teaspoon ground white pepper
4 tablespoons unsalted butter, preferably clarified butter *(pages 177-178)*
6 tablespoons flour

Sauce Béchamel

Combine the milk, onions, nutmeg, thyme and pepper in a small saucepan and bring to a boil over moderate heat. Immediately remove the pan from the heat, cover tightly and set aside for about 10 minutes.

In a heavy 1- to 2-quart enameled-iron or copper saucepan, melt the butter over low heat. Remove the pan from the heat and stir in the flour with a wire whisk to make a smooth roux. Then return to low heat and, stirring constantly, cook for about 2 minutes, or until the roux foams.

Pour in the milk mixture and beat vigorously with a whisk until the roux and liquid are thoroughly blended. Scrape the sides of the pan to ensure that all of the roux is incorporated into the sauce. Increase the heat to moderate and, still stirring constantly, cook until the béchamel sauce comes to a boil and thickens enough to coat the wires of the whisk heavily.

Reduce the heat to the lowest possible point and, stirring occasionally, simmer the sauce gently for about 15 minutes to remove any taste of raw flour. Then strain the sauce through a fine sieve set over a bowl, pressing down gently on the onions with the back of a spoon to extract all their moisture before throwing them away. If you do not plan to use the sauce immediately, cool it to room temperature, stirring occasionally. Tightly covered, the béchamel may safely be kept in the refrigerator for 10 days, or in the freezer up to three months.

Sautéed Lamb Chops

Pat the lamb chops completely dry with paper towels and season them evenly on both sides with salt and a few grindings of pepper.

In a heavy 12-inch skillet, heat the clarified butter over high heat until a drop of water flicked into it splutters and evaporates instantly. Add the lamb chops and sauté them for 3 to 4 minutes on each side, or until they are cooked to the state of doneness you prefer. Ideally they should be medium rare. Arrange the chops attractively on a heated platter and serve at once accompanied, if you like, by *pommes soufflées (below)*.

To serve 4

8 rib lamb chops, 4 to 5 ounces each, cut 1 inch thick and French style
Salt
Freshly ground black pepper
¼ cup clarified butter (*pages 177-178*)

Pommes Soufflées

Peel and shape the potatoes into smooth ovals about 2 inches in diameter at the widest part, dropping them into cold water as you proceed. With an adjustable-bladed *mandoline* or other slicer, cut the potatoes into ⅜-inch-thick rounds. Wrap the slices in a damp towel to prevent discoloring.

Pour vegetable oil into two large, heavy saucepans at least 8 inches deep, filling them both to a depth of 3 inches. Heat the oil in one pan until it reaches a temperature of 325° on a deep frying thermometer, and the oil in the second pan until it reaches 375°.

A handful at a time, pat the slices completely dry with paper towels and drop them one by one into the 325° oil. Sliding the pan gently back and forth on the burner so that the potatoes cook evenly, deep-fry them for 6 minutes. Transfer the slices to the 375° oil with a skimmer. They should puff up almost immediately. As they puff, place them on a linen towel to drain. (Set the potatoes which have not puffed aside separately to serve as plain *pommes frites;* there may be a few in each batch.) Proceed in similar fashion with the remaining slices. At this point, the potatoes can wait for several hours before final cooking.

Just before serving, heat one pan of oil to 385°. Drop in the potatoes a few at a time and deep-fry for 1 minute or until they puff up again and are golden. Remove them from the oil with a skimmer, drain briefly on paper towels, salt to taste and serve.

To serve 6

3 pounds firm baking potatoes, all of the same size
Vegetable oil or shortening for deep frying
Salt

Named for a family of Hungarian princes, steaks Eszterházy, garnished with braised aromatic vegetables, are ideal for a Father's Day dinner.

Beef Stroganoff

In a small bowl combine the mustard, 1½ teaspoons of the sugar, a pinch of the salt and enough hot water (perhaps a tablespoon) to form a thick paste. Let the mustard rest at room temperature for about 15 minutes.

Heat 2 tablespoons of the oil in a heavy 10- to 12-inch skillet over high heat until a light haze forms above it. Drop in the onions and mushrooms, cover the pan, and reduce the heat to low. Stirring from time to time, simmer 20 to 30 minutes, or until the vegetables are soft. Drain them in a sieve, discard the liquid and return the mixture to the skillet.

With a large, sharp knife cut the fillet across the grain into ¼-inch-wide rounds. Lay each round on a board and slice it with the grain into ¼-inch-wide strips. Heat 2 tablespoons of oil in another heavy 10- to 12-inch skillet over high heat until very hot but not smoking. Drop in half the meat and, tossing the strips constantly with a large spoon, fry for 2 minutes or so until the meat is lightly browned. With a slotted spoon transfer the meat to the vegetables in the other skillet and fry the remaining meat similarly, adding additional oil if necessary. When all the meat has been combined with the vegetables, stir in the remaining salt, pepper and the mustard paste. Stir in the sour cream, a tablespoon at a time, then add the remaining ½ teaspoon of sugar and reduce the heat to low. Cover the pan and simmer 2 or 3 minutes, or until the sauce is heated through. Taste for seasoning.

To serve 4 to 6

1 tablespoon powdered mustard
1 tablespoon sugar
2 teaspoons salt
4 to 5 tablespoons vegetable oil
4 cups thinly sliced onions separated into rings
1 pound fresh mushrooms, thinly sliced lengthwise
2 pounds fillet of beef, trimmed of all fat
1 teaspoon freshly ground black pepper
1 pint sour cream

Steaks Eszterházy

Salt and pepper the steaks, then dip them in flour and shake them to remove the excess. Heat the lard in a 12-inch skillet until a light haze forms over it, then brown the steaks over high heat for about 3 minutes on each side. Remove them to a platter and reduce the heat to medium.

Add the onions, garlic and carrots and cook for about 8 minutes, stirring frequently, until the vegetables are lightly colored.

Off the heat, stir in the 3 tablespoons of flour, continuing to stir until all the flour is absorbed. Return the skillet to the heat, add the stock and bring it to a boil, stirring constantly with a whisk until the sauce is smooth and thick. Add the allspice, bay leaves, peppercorns, thyme, lemon peel, bacon, parsley and vinegar. Return the meat to the skillet and bring the stock to a boil again. Reduce the heat to low, partially cover the pan and simmer for 50 minutes to an hour, or until the steaks show no resistance when pierced with the tip of a small sharp knife.

Drop the parsnip and carrot strips into a saucepan of boiling, lightly salted water. Boil uncovered for 2 or 3 minutes, or until the vegetables are slightly tender, then drain in a colander or sieve. Arrange the steaks on a platter and keep them warm in a 200° oven while you prepare the sauce.

Strain the contents of the frying pan, pressing hard on the vegetables before discarding them. Skim off the surface fat from the sauce. Whisk the cream and lemon juice into the sauce and add the carrot, parsnip and gherkin strips. Simmer 2 or 3 minutes. Taste for seasoning. Pour the vegetables and the sauce over the steaks and serve at once.

To serve 6

Salt
Freshly ground black pepper
2 pounds top round steak ½ inch thick, cut into 6 equal portions
Flour
3 tablespoons lard
1½ cups finely chopped onions
½ teaspoon finely chopped garlic
½ cup finely chopped carrots
3 tablespoons flour
3 cups beef stock, fresh or canned
3 whole allspice or ⅛ teaspoon ground allspice
3 medium-size bay leaves
4 peppercorns
⅛ teaspoon thyme
⅛-inch-wide strip lemon peel
4 slices lean bacon, coarsely chopped (⅓ cup)
2 tablespoons finely chopped parsley
¼ cup white wine vinegar
¾ cup heavy cream
1 teaspoon fresh lemon juice

THE GARNISH

2 parsnips, scraped and cut into 3-by-½-inch julienne strips
1 medium-sized carrot, cut into 3-by-½-inch julienne strips
4 sour gherkin pickles, cut into 3-by-½-inch julienne strips

Dramatic Desserts

Rum Layer Cake with Praline Topping

To serve 10

THE CAKE

1 tablespoon butter, softened
2 tablespoons flour
¼ pound plus 4 tablespoons unsalted butter (1½ sticks), softened
1 cup sugar
1 cup all-purpose flour
1½ teaspoons finely grated lemon peel
6 eggs, at room temperature
¾ cup cornstarch
1 tablespoon double-acting baking powder
¾ cup rum

FILLING

10 egg yolks, at room temperature
1 pound unsalted butter (4 sticks), softened
1⅓ cups sugar
⅛ teaspoon cream of tartar
⅔ cup water
½ cup rum

TOPPING

1 tablespoon butter
1 cup sugar
½ cup cold water
1 cup blanched almonds

Preheat the oven to 325°. With a pastry brush or paper towel, coat the bottom, sides and tube of a 9-inch tube cake pan with 1 tablespoon of soft butter. Sprinkle the butter with 2 tablespoons of flour, tip the pan from side to side to spread the flour evenly, then invert it and rap the bottom sharply to remove the excess flour.

In a large bowl, cream ¼ pound plus 4 tablespoons of butter, 1 cup of sugar, 1 tablespoon of the flour and the lemon peel together by mashing and beating them against the sides of the bowl with a large spoon. Then beat in the eggs, one at a time, and continue to beat until smooth. Combine the remaining flour, cornstarch and baking powder, and sift them into the butter a little at a time, beating well after each addition.

Pour the batter into the cake pan and bake in the middle of the oven for 40 minutes, or until a cake tester inserted in the center comes out clean. Let the cake cool in the pan for 10 minutes. Then run a knife around the inside edges of the pan, place a wire cake rack on top and, grasping rack and pan firmly together, turn them over. The cake should slide easily out of the pan. When the cake has cooled completely, slice it crosswise with a large, sharp knife into three equal layers. (It is easiest to cut if baked a day in advance.) Spread the layers on a long strip of foil or wax paper and sprinkle each layer with ¼ cup of rum.

To make the butter-cream filling, beat the 10 egg yolks in a large bowl with a whisk or a rotary or electric beater until they are thick and lemon colored. Set the beaten yolks aside. Cream the pound of soft butter by mashing and beating it against the sides of a bowl with a large spoon until it is light and fluffy. Set it aside.

Bring 1⅓ cups of sugar, ⅛ teaspoon cream of tartar and ⅔ cup of water to a boil over moderate heat in a small saucepan, stirring only until the sugar dissolves. Increase the heat to high and boil the syrup briskly without stirring until it reaches a temperature of 236° on a candy thermometer, or until a drop spooned into cold water immediately forms a soft ball.

Pour the syrup in a thin stream into the reserved egg yolks, beating constantly with a whisk or a rotary or electric beater. Continue beating for 4 or 5 minutes longer, or until the mixture is thick and smooth. Gradually add ½ cup of rum, and continue to beat until the mixture has cooled to room temperature and is thick. Now beat in the reserved butter, a tablespoon or so at a time, and when it is completely absorbed, cover the bowl with wax paper or plastic wrap and refrigerate the butter cream for at least 30 minutes, or until it can be spread easily.

Meanwhile prepare the praline topping in the following fashion: With a pastry brush or paper towel, coat a baking sheet with 1 tablespoon of butter and set it aside. In a small saucepan, bring 1 cup of sugar and ½ cup of water to a boil over moderate heat, stirring until the sugar dissolves. Increase the heat to high and boil briskly, undisturbed, until the syrup reaches a temperature of 236° on a candy thermometer, or a drop of syrup spooned into cold water immediately forms a soft ball. Stir in the nuts and cook until the syrup reaches a temperature of 310° on a candy thermometer, or until the syrup caramelizes and turns a rich golden brown.

Pour the syrup evenly onto the baking sheet. When it is cool and firm, break the praline into small pieces and pulverize it in a blender for a few seconds or crush it with a mortar and pestle. Spread it out on wax paper.

To assemble the cake, place the bottom layer in the center of a large cake plate and, with a spatula, spread it with about ½ inch of butter cream. Set the second layer on top and spread it with another ½-inch layer of butter cream. Finally set the top layer of cake in place and mask the top and sides with the remaining butter cream (if you like, reserve some butter cream to decorate the cake). Gently press the crushed praline over the sides of the cake and sprinkle the remainder over the top. Any extra butter cream may be piped on top of the cake through a pastry tube fitted with a decorative tip.

Birthday Cake with Maple-Sugar Icing

Preheat the oven to 350°. With a pastry brush, spread the 4 tablespoons of softened butter over the bottom and sides of four 9-inch layer-cake pans. Add the 4 tablespoons of unsifted flour and tip the pans from side to side to distribute it evenly. Invert the pans and rap the bottoms sharply to remove the excess flour. Combine the 3 cups of sifted flour, the cornstarch, baking powder and salt, and sift them together into a bowl.

In a deep bowl, cream the remaining ½ pound of softened butter and the sugar by beating and mashing them against the sides of the bowl with the back of a large spoon until the mixture is light and fluffy. Add about 1 cup of the flour mixture and, when it is well incorporated, beat in about ⅓ cup of the milk. Repeat two more times, alternating 1 cup of the flour mixture with ⅓ cup of milk and beating well after each addition. Beat in 2 teaspoons of vanilla.

With a wire whisk or a rotary or electric beater, beat 12 egg whites in a separate bowl until they are stiff enough to stand in unwavering peaks on the beater when it is lifted from the bowl. With a rubber spatula, scoop the egg whites over the batter and fold them together gently.

Pour the batter into the prepared pans, dividing it equally among them and smoothing the tops with the spatula. Bake in the middle of the oven for about 25 minutes, or until a toothpick or cake tester inserted in the centers comes out clean. Let the cakes cool in the pans for 4 or 5 minutes, then turn them out on wire racks to cool completely.

To prepare the icing, beat 2 egg whites with a wire whisk or a rotary or electric beater until they are stiff enough to form unwavering peaks on the beater when it is lifted out of the bowl. Set aside. Combine the maple (or brown) sugar and water in a heavy 2- to 3-quart saucepan. Bring to a boil over high heat, stirring until the sugar dissolves. Then cook briskly, uncovered and undisturbed, until the syrup reaches a temperature of 238° on a candy thermometer or until a drop spooned into ice water immediately forms a soft but compact ball. Remove the pan from the heat.

Beating the egg whites constantly, slowly pour in the hot syrup and con-

To make one 9-inch 4-layer cake

CAKE
4 tablespoons plus ½ pound butter, softened
4 tablespoons unsifted flour plus 3 cups flour, sifted before measuring
½ cup cornstarch
1 tablespoon double-acting baking powder
1 teaspoon salt
2 cups sugar
1 cup milk
2 teaspoons vanilla extract
12 egg whites

ICING
2 egg whites
1½ cups maple sugar, or substitute 1½ cups dark brown sugar
⅓ cup water
1 teaspoon vanilla extract

FILLING

1½ cups peach preserves, or substitute 1½ cups strawberry or raspberry jam

To serve 4

1 pint vanilla ice cream
8 tablespoons butter, cut into ½-inch bits
½ cup brown sugar
4 firm ripe bananas, peeled and cut lengthwise into halves
½ teaspoon ground cinnamon
½ cup banana liqueur
1 cup rum

To serve 6 to 8

2 tablespoons soft butter
4 egg whites
Pinch of salt
¼ cup sugar
4 egg yolks
½ teaspoon vanilla
½ cup flour
1 cup orange marmalade or apricot preserves
1 to 2 tablespoons orange juice (optional)
1 quart vanilla ice cream, slightly softened

THE MERINGUE

8 egg whites at room temperature
Pinch of salt
¾ cup superfine sugar

tinue to beat until the icing mixture is smooth and thick. Beat in 1 teaspoon of vanilla.

To assemble the cake, place one layer on an inverted 9-inch cake pan and, with a metal spatula, spread ½ cup of the fruit preserves or jam over it. Repeat two more times, spreading each cake layer with about ½ cup of the preserves. Carefully set the fourth layer in place and spread the top and sides of the cake with the icing. With a large spatula, transfer the cake to a serving plate.

Bananas Flambé

Prepare and assemble the banana dessert at the dinner table when you are ready to serve it. Light an alcohol burner or table-top stove and set a 12-inch copper flambé or crêpe-suzette pan over the flame. Arrange all the ingredients conveniently beside the pan. Place a scoop of ice cream on each of four chilled individual dessert plates and set them to one side.

Combine the butter and brown sugar in the *flambé* pan and stir until the mixture becomes a smooth syrup. Add the bananas and baste them with the syrup for 3 or 4 minutes, then sprinkle in the cinnamon.

Carefully pour in the banana liqueur and rum, and let the liquors warm for a few seconds. They may burst into flame spontaneously. If not, ignite them with a match. Slide the pan back and forth until the flames die, basting the bananas all the while. Place two banana halves around each scoop of ice cream, spoon the sauce over the top and serve at once.

Baked Alaska

Brush a tablespoon of soft butter over the bottom and sides of an 11-by-16-inch jelly-roll pan. Line the pan with a 22-inch strip of wax paper and let the extra paper extend over the ends of the pan. Brush the remaining butter over the paper and scatter a small handful of flour over it. Tip the pan from side to side to spread the flour evenly. Then turn the pan over and rap it sharply to dislodge the excess flour.

Preheat the oven to 400°. In a mixing bowl, beat the egg whites and salt until they form soft, wavering peaks. Add the sugar, two tablespoons at a time, and beat until the whites cling to the beater solidly when it is lifted out of the bowl. In another small bowl, beat the egg yolks for about a minute, then add the vanilla. Mix a large tablespoon of the whites into the yolks, then pour the mixture over the remaining egg whites. Fold together, adding the ½ cup flour, two tablespoons at a time.

Pour the batter into the jelly-roll pan and spread it out evenly. Bake in the middle of the oven for about 12 minutes, or until the cake draws slightly away from the sides of the pan, and a small knife inserted in its center comes out dry and clean. Turn the cake out on a sheet of wax paper, then gently peel off the top layer of paper. Let the cake cool and cut it in half crosswise. Spread one layer with the cup of marmalade or apricot preserves (if it is too thick to spread, thin it by beating into it 1 or 2 tablespoons of orange juice) and place the second layer on top. Mold the

Bananas flambé is a spectacular dessert but one that is easily assembled. The bananas are peeled, halved and cooked in a brown-sugar syrup. They are then flamed with banana liqueur and rum, and served over vanilla ice cream.

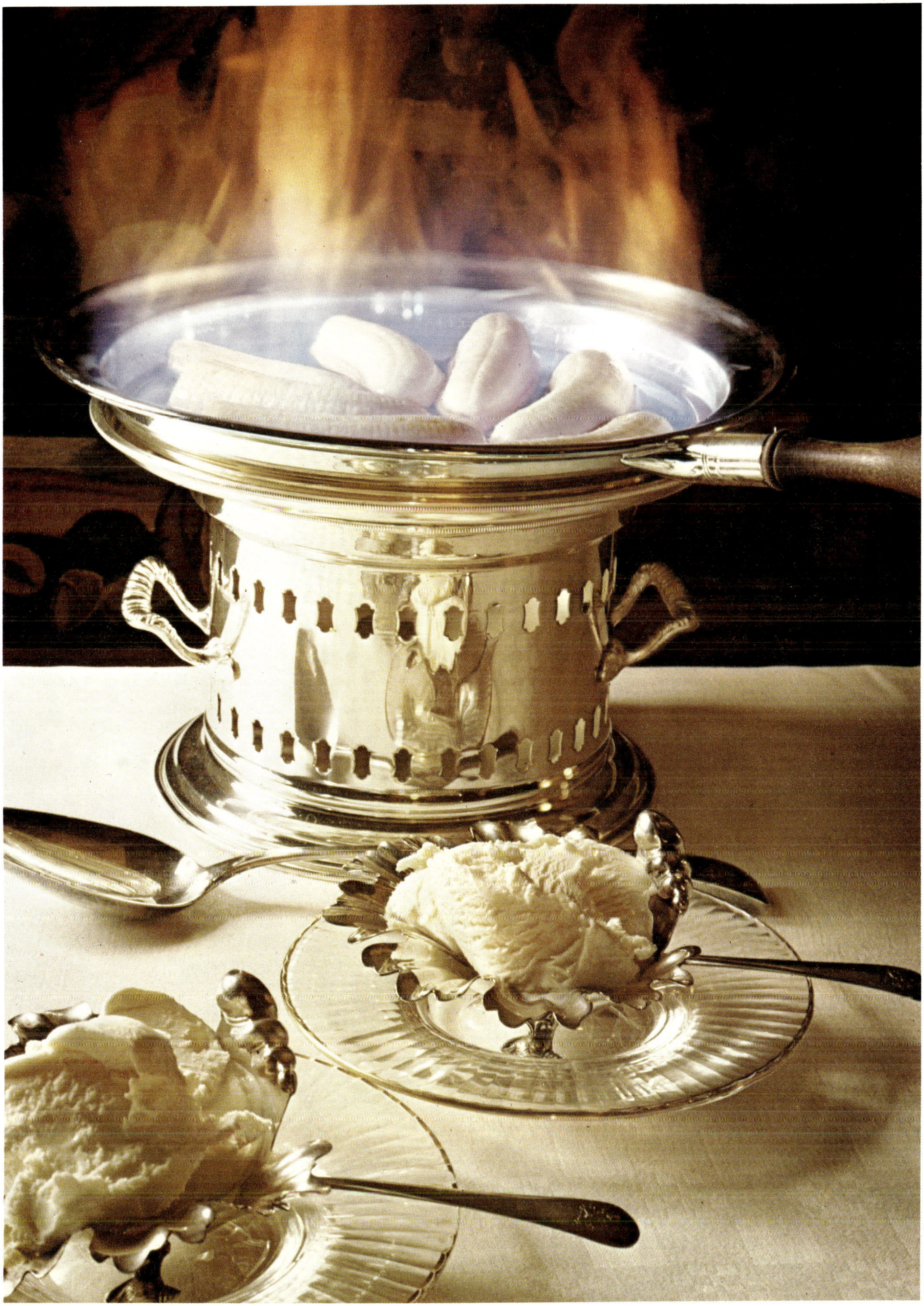

softened ice cream on a sheet of aluminum foil into a brick the length and width of the cake. Wrap in the foil and freeze until solid.

About 10 minutes before serving, make the meringue. First, preheat the broiler to its highest point. Then, beat the egg whites and salt until they form soft peaks. Still beating, slowly pour in the sugar, and continue to beat for about 5 minutes, or until the egg whites are stiff and glossy. Remove the ice cream from the freezer and place it on top of the cake on a flat, ovenproof baking dish. Mask the cake and ice cream on all sides with the meringue, shaping the top as decoratively as you like. Slide the cake under the broiler for 2 to 3 minutes, and watch it carefully; it burns easily. The meringue should turn a pale, golden brown in 2 to 3 minutes. Serve at once before the ice cream begins to melt.

Bavarois Clermont

To serve 10 to 12

BAVAROIS
Vegetable oil
2 envelopes unflavored gelatin
⅓ cup water
3 cups milk
1 vanilla bean
5 egg yolks
1½ cups sugar
3 cups heavy cream, chilled
1 cup finely chopped *marrons glacés* (glacéed chestnuts, not the chestnuts packed in syrup)

BAVAROIS (BAVARIAN CREAM): Brush the inside of a 2½-quart decorative mold with oil and remove the excess with a paper towel. Sprinkle the gelatin into ⅓ cup of water in a heatproof cup. When the gelatin has softened for 2 or 3 minutes, set the cup in a skillet of simmering water and stir over low heat until the gelatin dissolves. Remove from the heat but leave the cup of gelatin in the water to keep warm. In a heavy 3-quart enameled-iron or copper saucepan, bring 3 cups of milk and the vanilla bean to a boil over moderate heat. Cover and set aside.

With a wire whisk or a rotary or electric beater, beat the 5 egg yolks and 1½ cups of sugar together in a deep bowl for 3 or 4 minutes, or until the yolks fall in a slowly dissolving ribbon when the beater is lifted from the bowl. Remove the vanilla bean from the milk and reserve it. Whisking constantly, pour the milk into the egg yolks in a slow thin stream. When thoroughly blended, return the mixture to the saucepan. Stir over low heat until the custard thickens enough to coat a spoon evenly or reaches 180° on a candy thermometer. Do not let it come to a boil or the custard will curdle. Add the gelatin and stir until it is completely absorbed. Strain the custard through a fine sieve into a stainless-steel bowl.

With a wire whisk or a rotary or electric beater, whip the cream in a chilled bowl until it forms almost firm peaks. Then set the bowl of custard into a larger bowl filled with crushed ice or ice cubes and water and stir until the custard is just cool. Do not let it chill enough to become the least bit lumpy.

Remove the bowl of custard from the ice and scoop the whipped cream over it. With a rubber spatula, fold the two quickly but gently and thoroughly together, using an over-under cutting motion rather than a stirring motion, until no trace of white remains. Fold in the chestnuts, then pour the mixture into the oiled mold and smooth the top with the spatula. Cover with foil or plastic wrap and refrigerate for at least 6 hours, or preferably overnight until the Bavarian cream is firm.

CRÈME ANGLAISE
2 cups milk
1 vanilla bean (re-use the bean above)
4 egg yolks
½ cup sugar

CRÈME ANGLAISE (ENGLISH CUSTARD): Combine 2 cups of milk and the reserved vanilla bean in a 3-quart enameled saucepan. Bring to a boil and immediately remove the milk from the heat. Cover and set aside.

Beat the 4 egg yolks and ½ cup of sugar together with a wire whisk or a rotary or electric beater until they are thick enough to form a slowly dissolving ribbon when the beater is lifted. Remove the vanilla bean and pour the hot milk gradually into the yolks, whisking all the while. Return the mixture to the saucepan and stir over low heat until the *crème anglaise* thickens lightly. (Do not let it come near a boil or it will curdle.) Pour the *crème anglaise* into a bowl, and cool to room temperature. Cover tightly and refrigerate until ready to serve.

MARRONS CARAMÉLISÉS (CARAMELIZED CHESTNUTS): In a heavy 2- to 3-quart saucepan, bring 2 cups of sugar, 2 cups of water and the cocoa to a boil over high heat, stirring until the sugar dissolves. Bring the syrup to a boil, then reduce the heat to low and simmer the syrup for 25 to 30 minutes until it reaches 300° on a candy thermometer. As soon as the syrup reaches the proper state, remove the pan from the heat and place it in a pot half-filled with hot water to keep the caramel fluid and warm.

To make each caramelized chestnut, impale one chestnut half on a thin long skewer. Holding the skewer vertically, submerge the chestnut in the hot syrup and twirl it around until it is heavily coated with caramel. Lift the chestnut and, holding the skewer horizontally over wax paper, let the excess caramel drip off. The caramel will form a thin iciclelike thread as it drips. With scissors, keep this thread to a length of about 6 inches, cutting it repeatedly until the caramel stops dripping and becomes firm.

Place the chestnut on a sheet of buttered aluminum foil and carefully pull out the skewer. Repeat the entire procedure with all of the remaining chestnut halves. Set the caramelized nuts aside.

FINAL ASSEMBLY: To unmold the *bavarois,* run a thin knife or spatula carefully around the inside rim of the mold and briefly dip the bottom of the mold into hot water. Wipe the mold dry, place a chilled serving plate upside down over the top and, grasping the mold and plate securely together, quickly invert them. The *bavarois* should slide out easily.

Spoon the chilled *crème anglaise* around the base of the *bavarois* and arrange the caramelized chestnuts in a ring surrounding it. If you like you may decorate the *bavarois* or outline the details of its form by piping melted semisweet chocolate onto it with a pastry tube fitted with a very small plain pastry tip. A few spoons of chopped *marrons glacés* may be stirred into the *crème anglaise.* Place the remaining whole glacéed chestnut decoratively on the top of the *bavarois* and serve.

MARRONS CARAMÉLISÉS

2 cups sugar

2 cups water

2 tablespoons unsweetened imported cocoa

7 whole *marrons glacés* (glacéed chestnuts), 6 cut in half and rounded with a knife and one reserved

Mousse au Chocolat

Brush the inside of a 1-quart charlotte (cylindrical) or ring mold with a film of vegetable oil. Invert the mold on paper towels to drain.

In a heatproof mixing bowl, beat the egg yolks and sugar with a whisk, rotary or electric beater for 2 or 3 minutes, or until they are pale yellow and thick enough to form a ribbon when the whisk is lifted from the bowl. Beat in the Cognac.

Set the mixing bowl over a pan of barely simmering (not boiling) water, and continue beating for 3 or 4 minutes, or until the mixture is foamy and hot. Then set the bowl over a pan of iced water and beat for 3 or 4 min-

To serve 6 to 8

4 egg yolks

¼ cup superfine sugar

2 tablespoons Cognac

6 ounces semisweet chocolate, cut in small chunks

3 tablespoons strong coffee

8 tablespoons soft unsalted butter (1 quarter-pound stick), cut in ½-inch pieces

4 egg whites

½ cup heavy cream, whipped

The *bavarois Clermont,* a molded vanilla-flavored Bavarian cream with glacéed chestnuts, is a dessert for the most festive of occasions —an engagement party, a wedding, an anniversary. The chestnuts that decorate the dish are dipped in hot caramel, then held up in the air while a thin strand of caramel descends from them and hardens like an icicle. The hardened caramel becomes the "spokes" that radiate out from this dessert.

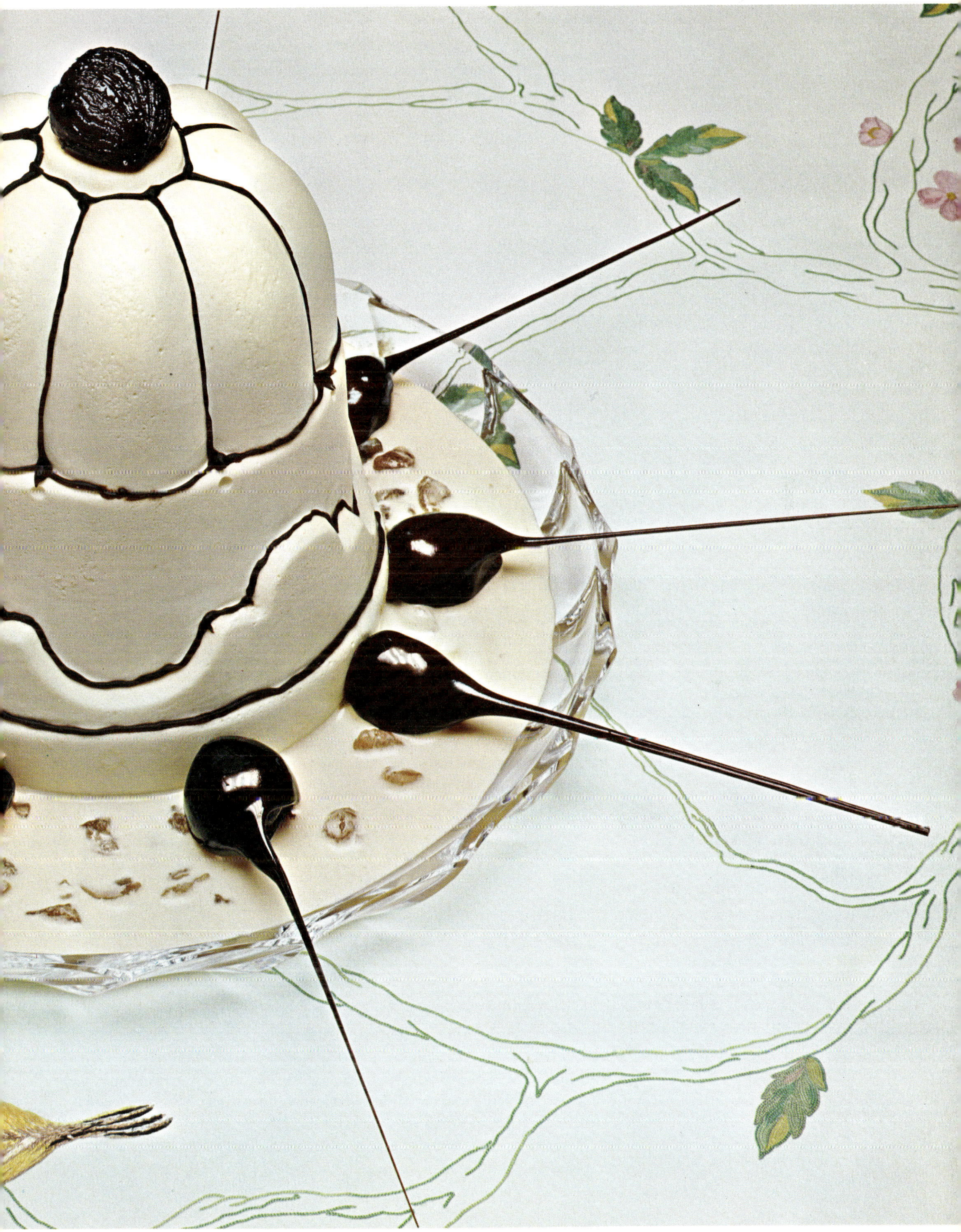

utes longer, or until the mixture is cool again and as thick and creamy as mayonnaise.

In a heavy 1- to 1½-quart saucepan set over low heat, or in the top of a double boiler over simmering water, melt the chocolate with the coffee, stirring constantly. When all the chocolate has dissolved, beat in the butter, one piece at a time, to make a smooth cream. Then beat the chocolate mixture into the egg yolks and sugar. In a separate bowl, with a clean whisk or beater, beat the egg whites until they are stiff enough to form stiff peaks on the wires of the whisk. Stir about one fourth of the egg whites into the chocolate mixture to lighten it, then very gently fold in the remaining egg whites. Spoon the mousse into the oiled mold or dessert cups, and refrigerate for at least 4 hours or until it has set.

To unmold and serve the *mousse au chocolat*, run a long, sharp knife around the sides of the mold and dip the bottom of it in hot water for a few seconds. Then wipe the outside of the mold dry, place a chilled serving plate upside down over the mold and, grasping both sides firmly, quickly turn the plate and mold over. Rap the plate on a table and the mousse should slide easily out of the mold. If the mousse doesn't unmold at once, repeat the whole process.

With a wire whisk, rotary or electric beater, whip the chilled cream in a large chilled bowl until it is firm enough to hold its shape softly. Garnish the mousse with the whipped cream.

Spanish Wind Torte

To make 1 eight-inch *Torte*

THE SHELL
8 egg whites
½ teaspoon cream of tartar
2½ cups superfine sugar

THE DECORATION (optional)
4 egg whites
¼ teaspoon cream of tartar
1¼ cups superfine sugar
6 candied violets

THE FILLING
1½ pints heavy cream
2 tablespoons sugar
¼ cup Cognac
3 cups strawberries, raspberries or blueberries, washed and hulled

THE SHELL: Preheat the oven to 200°. With a pastry brush or paper towel, lightly butter two 11-by-17-inch baking sheets, sprinkle them with flour, tip them from side to side to spread the flour evenly, then invert them and strike them on the edge of a table to knock out the excess. Invert an 8-inch plate or layer-cake pan on the floured surface of one baking sheet and tap it with your hand, making a ring to serve as a guide in making the layers of the shell. Repeat the process on the first sheet and outline 2 similar rings on the other sheet, making 4 guide rings in all, none of them touching one another.

With a wire whisk, or rotary or electric beater, beat the 8 egg whites with the cream of tartar until they begin to foam, then gradually beat in 2¼ cups of the sugar, continuing to beat for at least 5 minutes, or until the whites form stiff, unwavering peaks when the beater is lifted from the bowl. With a rubber spatula, gently fold in the remaining ¼ cup of sugar. Fit a No. 8 plain-tipped pastry tube onto a large pastry bag and fill the bag with the meringue. Pipe a ½- to ¾-inch-thick circle of the meringue just inside one of the marks on the baking sheets and continue it in a closed spiral that ends in the center of the ring (this will be the bottom of the *Torte*). Carefully smooth the top of the spiral with a spatula. Then make plain rings of meringue about ¾ inch thick just inside the 3 other circles on the baking sheets. Bake them in the middle of the oven for 45 minutes, then gently slide them off on racks to cool.

To make a top (optional) for the *Torte*, make another spiral layer like the first one and bake for 45 minutes. (The top is used to make a more spectacular Spanish Wind cake like the one in the photograph on page 170.)

Construct the shell by piping about a teaspoon of the meringue onto each of 5 or 6 equidistant spots around the edge of the bottom circle to serve as a cement, then fit one of the rings over this. Continue the process with the 2 other rings, one on the other. When the shell is completed, set it on a baking sheet and let it dry out in the 200° oven for about 20 minutes or longer if necessary. Let the shell cool.

THE DECORATION (OPTIONAL): Use a flat spatula to apply the rest of the meringue in the pastry bag to the outside of the shell to make it smooth, then return it to the oven to dry for another 20 minutes. Meanwhile prepare more meringue, if you plan to use it, following the directions for the first batch. Fit a No. 6 star tube onto the pastry bag, put the meringue into the bag and make swirls and rosettes on the outside of the shell and on the circle to be used as a top (optional). Return both circles to the oven again to dry for about 20 minutes. If you wish to decorate the shell with candied violets, pipe small dabs of meringue around the center of the shell, and one dab in the center of the top spiral circle, and secure the violets on them.

THE FILLING: Whip the chilled cream until it begins to thicken, then gradually beat in the sugar. Continue to beat until the cream is firm enough to hold its shape softly, then beat in the Cognac, and last, fold in the berries with a rubber spatula.

Gently spoon the filling into the shell. If you have prepared the top spiral, lay it gently on top.

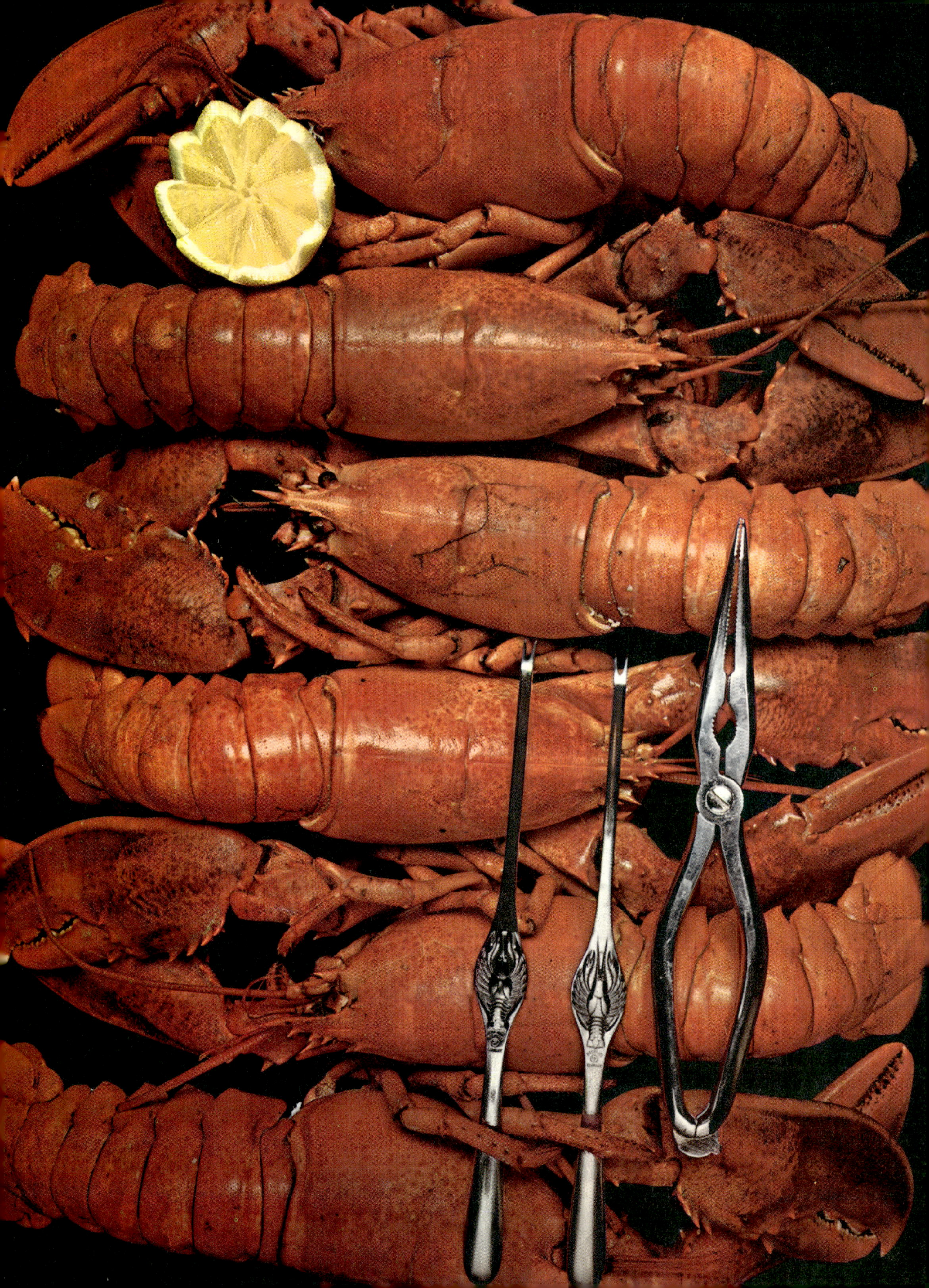

The Fourth of July

Maybe it's the fresh air, maybe it's the surroundings, but in the summer food seems to taste better outdoors, and the Fourth of July is a traditional occasion for a picnic or a cookout. The meal may be a leisurely family dinner grilled on the patio, a backyard picnic or a full-scale Independence Day celebration centered around a Texas-style barbecue or a Yankee clambake.

Barbecues are always associated with tender, flavorsome meats, but the kinds of spicy marinades and sauces that characterize roasting ribs and kabobs adapt as well to seafood dishes like barbecued shrimp or stuffed fresh salmon. Boiling and steaming also coax out the delicate flavor of shellfish in such dishes as clams and lobster served with liberal quantities of melted butter, or the peppery Southern steamed crab, traditionally accompanied by glasses of icy beer. Crisp summer produce makes salads as simple as a side dish of coleslaw or as ornate as a platter of eight different vegetables molded in aspic. And to turn a picnic into a patriotic feast, there are recipes here for such favorite desserts as strawberry shortcake, blueberry pie and homemade vanilla ice cream, all as American as the Stars and Stripes.

Lobsters, red as a firecracker after boiling, are delicious, hot or cold, with no more seasoning than a squeeze of lemon juice. They are the main attraction of classic New England clambakes.

Three ways with barbecued spareribs

Perfect charcoal-broiled steak

Southwest chili con carne

Kentucky fried chicken

New England boiled lobster

Four hot-weather soups

A dozen salad ideas

Fourth of July blueberry pie

Old-fashioned vanilla ice cream

Cooling summer drinks

Fourth of July Recipes

Cookouts and Picnics

Barbecued Spareribs with Red Sauce

First prepare the red sauce in the following manner: In a heavy 10- to 12-inch skillet, heat the vegetable oil over moderate heat. Add the onions and garlic and, stirring frequently, cook for about 5 minutes, or until they are soft and translucent but not brown. Stir in the tomatoes and their liquid, the tomato purée, chilies, mustard, sugar, vinegar and salt, and bring to a boil over high heat. Cook briskly, uncovered, until the sauce is thick enough to hold its shape almost solidly in the spoon. Remove the pan from the heat and taste the red sauce for seasoning. Set it aside.

To barbecue the ribs, light a 2-inch-thick layer of charcoal briquettes in a charcoal grill equipped with a rotating spit. Let the coals burn until white ash appears on the surface.

Thread the spareribs on the spit, running the spit through the meat over and under alternate pairs of ribs. Then secure them at both ends with the sliding prongs. Fit the spit into place about 6 inches above the surface of the coals and barbecue the ribs for 45 minutes, or until they are lightly and evenly browned. Watch carefully for any sign of burning and regulate the height of the spit accordingly.

With a pastry brush, spread the red sauce evenly on both sides of the spareribs. Basting the ribs every 5 minutes or so, continue to barbecue them for about 30 minutes longer, or until they are richly colored and glazed with sauce.

To serve, remove the spit from the grill, unscrew the prongs and slide the spareribs off the spit onto a heated platter. Before serving, insert skewers into each section of ribs if you like.

To serve 4 to 6

½ cup vegetable oil
3 cups coarsely chopped onions
1 tablespoon finely chopped garlic
A 1-pound can tomatoes, drained and coarsely chopped with the liquid reserved
1 cup canned tomato purée
¼ cup coarsely chopped fresh hot red chilies including the seeds (*caution: see note, page 118*)
2 tablespoons dry mustard
2 tablespoons sugar
1 tablespoon distilled white vinegar
1½ teaspoons salt
4 pounds spareribs, in 4 pieces, trimmed of excess fat

Barbecued Spareribs with Sweet or Spicy Sauce

Preheat the oven to 400°. While it is heating, prepare the barbecue basting sauce: combine the onions, catsup or peach preserves, brown sugar, vinegar, Worcestershire, mustard and Tabasco in a 1- to 1½-quart enameled or stainless-steel saucepan. Stirring constantly with a wooden spoon, bring the sauce to a boil over high heat. Reduce the heat to low and simmer for 4 or 5 minutes until the onions are soft.

Arrange the spareribs, flesh side up, side by side on a rack set in a large shallow roasting pan and sprinkle them with the salt and a few grindings of pepper. With a pastry brush, spread about ½ cup of the basting sauce evenly over the ribs and lay the lemon slices on top. Bake uncovered in the middle of the oven for about 1½ hours, brushing the ribs 3 or 4 more times with the remaining sauce. The ribs are done if the meat

To serve 4 to 6

1 cup finely chopped onions
1 cup tomato catsup or
  1 cup peach preserves
  (depending on whether you prefer a very spicy or slightly sweet sauce)
¼ cup dark brown sugar
¼ cup distilled white vinegar
¼ cup Worcestershire sauce
1 teaspoon dry mustard
¼ teaspoon Tabasco
4 pounds spareribs, in 2 or 3 pieces, trimmed of excess fat
2 teaspoons salt
Freshly ground black pepper
2 lemons, cut crosswise into ¼-inch-thick slices

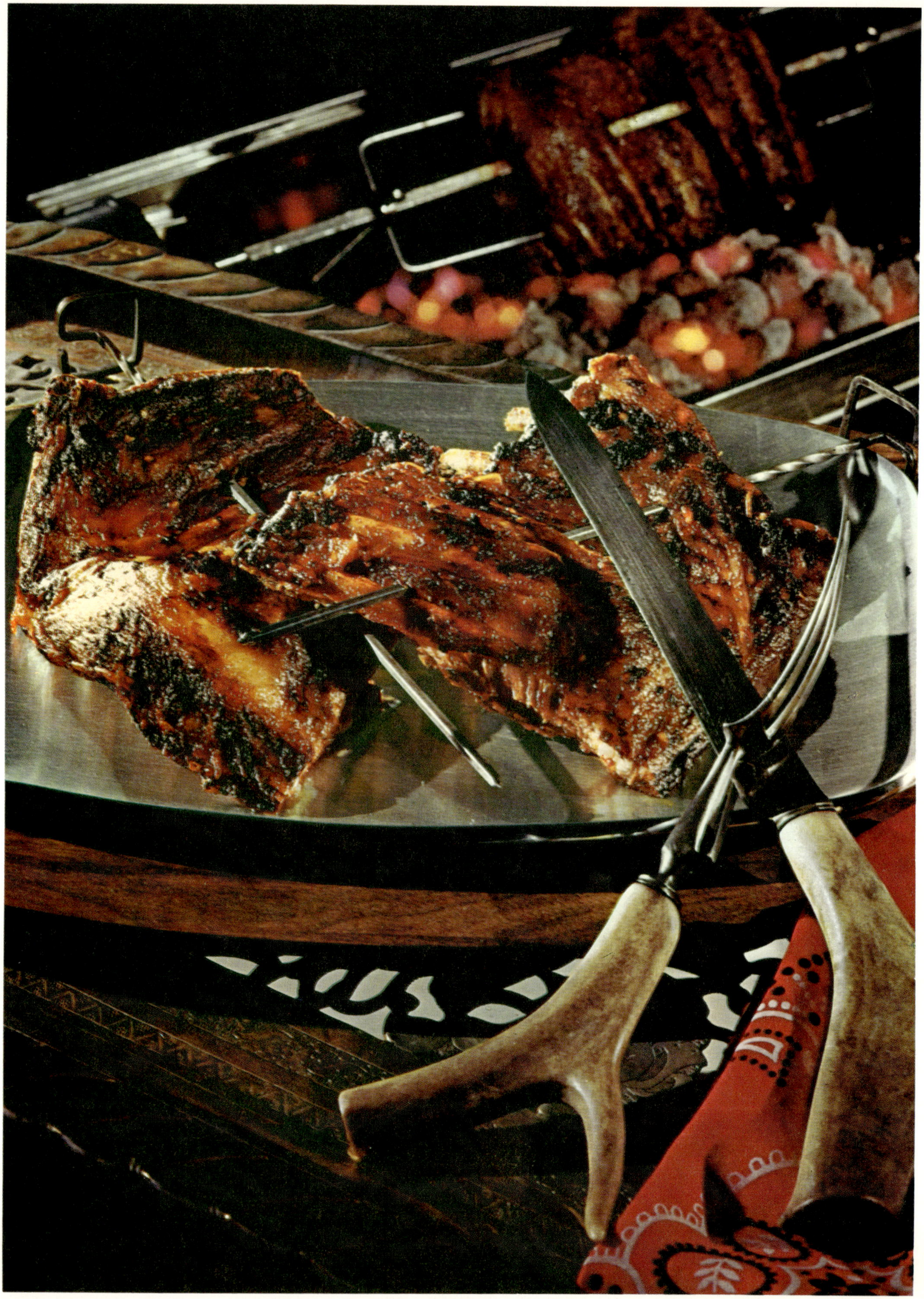

shows no resistance when pierced deeply with the point of a small skewer or knife. Arrange the spareribs on a heated platter and serve at once.

Maple Barbecue Spareribs

Preheat the broiler to its highest point. Pat the spareribs completely dry with paper towels and brush them on all sides with the mustard. Arrange the ribs fat side up in one layer on the rack of the broiler pan and broil 3 or 4 inches from the heat for 5 minutes. With tongs, turn the ribs meat side up and broil them for 5 minutes longer. Remove the rack, with the ribs on it, from the pan. Discard all of the fat that has accumulated and pour the water into the broiler pan. Return the ribs and rack to the pan.

Preheat the oven to 350°. In a bowl, combine the tomato purée, ¼ cup maple syrup, vinegar, onions, Worcestershire sauce, salt, Tabasco and pepper. Mix well, then taste the sauce and add up to ¼ cup more maple syrup if desired.

With a pastry brush, spread about ¼ cup of the sauce over the ribs and place them in the middle of the oven. Turning the ribs and basting them with the sauce every 15 minutes, bake for about 1 hour, or until the ribs are brown and crisp. Serve at once on a heated platter.

Barbecued Stuffed Salmon

First prepare the marinade in the following manner: Combine the wine, lemon juice, ½ cup of the oil, the onion, garlic, parsley sprigs, ginger, thyme, Tabasco, salt and pepper in a small enameled saucepan and, stirring occasionally, bring to a boil over high heat. Pour the marinade into an enameled casserole or roasting pan large enough to hold the salmon comfortably, and set it aside to cool to room temperature.

Wash the salmon inside and out under cold running water and pat it dry with paper towels. With a sharp knife, score both sides of the fish by making four or five evenly spaced diagonal slits about 4 inches long and ¼ inch deep. Place the salmon in the cooled marinade and turn it over to moisten it evenly.

Cover the pan tightly with foil or plastic wrap and marinate at room temperature for about 3 hours, or in the refrigerator for about 6 hours, turning the fish occasionally.

Light a layer of briquettes in a charcoal broiler and let them burn until a white ash appears on the surface, or preheat the broiler of your stove to its highest setting.

Transfer the salmon to paper towels and pat it completely dry with more paper towels. Strain the marinade through a fine sieve set over a bowl. To prepare the stuffing, combine the rice, scallions, chopped parsley and lemon strips in a small bowl. Pour in ¼ cup of the strained marinade and mix well. Set the remaining marinade aside.

Loosely fill the salmon with the stuffing, then close the opening with small skewers and kitchen cord. With a pastry brush, spread the remain-

To serve 4

2½ to 3 pounds lean spareribs, trimmed of all excess fat and cut into 2-rib serving pieces
¼ cup prepared mustard
1 cup cold water
½ cup tomato purée
¼ to ½ cup pure maple syrup
¼ cup cider vinegar
¼ cup finely grated onions
¼ cup Worcestershire sauce
½ teaspoon Tabasco sauce
2 teaspoons salt
½ teaspoon freshly ground black pepper

To serve 6 to 8

1½ cups dry white wine
½ cup strained fresh lemon juice
½ cup plus 1 tablespoon vegetable oil
1 medium-sized onion, peeled and thinly sliced
3 medium-sized garlic cloves, crushed with the side of a cleaver or a large heavy knife
3 sprigs fresh parsley
1 teaspoon ground ginger
½ teaspoon crumbled dried thyme
¼ teaspoon Tabasco sauce
1 teaspoon salt
¼ teaspoon freshly ground black pepper
A 5- to 5½-pound coho or other salmon, cleaned and with head and tail removed
1 cup freshly cooked rice, made from ½ cup long-grain white rice, not the converted variety
¼ cup finely chopped scallions, including 2 inches of the green tops
¼ cup finely chopped fresh parsley
The peel of ½ lemon, cut into matchlike strips
1 lemon, cut crosswise into ¼-inch-thick rounds

Charcoal-barbecued spareribs are grilled on a rotating spit and basted with a chili-seasoned Texas-style red sauce for a special tang and a toothsome crunch.

ing tablespoon of oil over the hot grill or the broiler rack. Place the salmon on top and brush it with a few spoonfuls of the reserved marinade. Broil 3 or 4 inches from the heat, basting the salmon frequently with the remaining marinade. The salmon should be broiled for about 15 minutes on each side, or until it is evenly and delicately browned and feels firm when prodded gently with a finger.

Serve the salmon at once from a heated platter, with the lemon slices arranged attractively in a row along the top of the fish. Garnish it further, if you like, with red and green pepper strips and onion rings.

Barbecued Shrimp

To serve 4 to 6

2 pounds fresh shrimp, 16 or 18 to the pound

MARINADE
1 cup olive oil
2 tablespoons red-wine vinegar
1 tablespoon tomato paste
1 tablespoon oregano
1 teaspoon minced garlic
3 tablespoons finely chopped fresh parsley
1 teaspoon salt
Freshly ground black pepper

Shell each shrimp carefully by breaking off the shell just above the point where it joins the tail, but don't remove the tail. With a small knife, make a shallow incision down the back of the shrimp and lift out the intestinal vein. Wash the shrimp thoroughly in cold water and pat them dry with paper towels. In a large mixing bowl combine the olive oil, vinegar, tomato paste, oregano, garlic, parsley, salt and a few grindings of black pepper. Drop in the shrimp, mix and turn them about in the marinade until they are well coated. Marinate at room temperature for about 2 hours, stirring gently every ½ hour or so.

Preheat the broiler to its highest point. Pour the shrimp and all its marinade into a shallow, ovenproof baking dish and spread the shrimp out in one layer. Slide the baking dish onto the broiler rack set about 3 inches from the heat. Broil for about 5 minutes, basting the shrimp with the marinade at the end of 3 minutes. Then turn them over with tongs and broil for 3 to 5 minutes longer, or until the shrimp are lightly browned and the flesh firm to the touch. Be careful not to overcook. Serve the barbecued shrimp either directly from the baking dish or in a large serving platter with a well deep enough to hold the sauce. The shrimp are customarily eaten by holding one by the tail and dipping it into the sauce. Hot French or Italian bread for dunking is almost a must with this.

Stuffed Baked Potatoes with Cheese

To serve 6

3 tablespoons butter, softened, plus 4 tablespoons butter, cut into ¼-inch bits and softened
6 eight-ounce baking potatoes, each about 4 inches long, thoroughly scrubbed and patted dry with paper towels
3¾ cups (about 1 pound) freshly grated sharp Cheddar cheese
½ cup sour cream
1 teaspoon salt
½ teaspoon ground white pepper

Preheat the oven to 350°. With a pastry brush, spread 2 tablespoons of the softened butter evenly over the skins of the potatoes. Bake the potatoes on a rack set in the middle of the oven for about 45 minutes. The potatoes are fully baked if they feel soft when squeezed gently between your thumb and forefinger.

Cut a ¼-inch-thick lengthwise slice from each baked potato. With a spoon, scoop the potato pulp into a bowl, leaving a boatlike shell about ¼ inch thick. Set the potato shells aside.

Mash the pulp to a smooth purée with the back of a fork, or force the pulp through a ricer or food mill into a deep bowl. Add 3 cups of the grated cheese and mix well. Then beat in the sour cream and, when it is completely incorporated, add the 4 tablespoons of butter bits, the salt and the pepper. Taste for seasoning.

Cushioned on bales of hay, guests at a Texas ranch celebrate with an informal early-evening barbecue supper party.

Spoon the potato mixture into a large pastry bag fitted with a No. 5B decorative tip and pipe it into the reserved potato shells. Or spoon the mixture directly into the potato shells, dividing it equally among them and mounding it slightly in the center of each one. Brush a jelly-roll pan evenly with the remaining tablespoon of softened butter and arrange the stuffed potato shells side by side in the pan.

If you wish to serve the potatoes at once, preheat the broiler to its highest setting. Sprinkle the remaining ¾ cup of grated cheese evenly over the potatoes, then slide them under the broiler for a minute or two to melt the topping.

If you prefer, the stuffed potatoes may be arranged on the buttered pan, draped with wax paper and kept at room temperature for 2 or 3 hours before serving.

In that event, preheat the oven to 400°, sprinkle the ¾ cup of grated cheese over the potatoes, and bake the potatoes in the middle of the oven for 15 to 20 minutes, or until they are heated through and the tops are golden brown and crusty. Serve them at once.

Charcoal-broiled T-Bone or Porterhouse Steak

To serve 4 to 6

A 3½- to 4-pound T-bone or porterhouse steak, cut 2 inches thick
Salt
Freshly ground black pepper

Light a 1- to 2-inch-thick layer of briquettes in a charcoal grill and let the coals burn until white ash appears on the surface.

Broil the steak about 4 inches from the heat until it is done to suit your taste, turning it once with heavy tongs or with a kitchen fork inserted into the outer rim of fat. Broil it about 7 to 8 minutes on each side for rare steak, 9 to 10 minutes for medium, and 11 to 12 minutes on each side for well done.

Transfer the steak to a heated platter, season it lightly with salt and a few grindings of pepper, and serve at once.

Grilled Swordfish

To serve 4

8 tablespoons (1 quarter-pound stick) butter, cut into ½-inch bits
1 tablespoon strained fresh lemon juice
1 teaspoon finely cut fresh tarragon leaves or ½ teaspoon crumbled dried tarragon
A 2-pound swordfish steak cut about 1½ inches thick
1 teaspoon salt
Freshly ground black pepper
1 tablespoon vegetable oil
2 lemons, each cut lengthwise into 4 or 8 wedges

Light a layer of briquettes in a charcoal broiler and let them burn until a white ash appears on the surface, or preheat the broiler of your range to its highest setting.

Meanwhile, in a small saucepan or skillet set over low heat melt the butter without letting it brown. Remove the pan from the heat and stir in the lemon juice and tarragon. Sprinkle both sides of the swordfish steak with the salt and a few grindings of pepper.

With a pastry brush, spread the tablespoon of oil over the hot grill of the broiler and place the swordfish steak on it. Brush the top of the steak with about 2 tablespoons of the melted butter mixture. Broil the steak about 3 to 4 inches from the heat, basting it frequently with the remaining butter. The steak should be broiled for about 8 minutes on each side, or until it is evenly and delicately browned and feels firm when prodded gently with a finger.

Serve the swordfish at once from a heated platter, with the lemon wedges arranged attractively in a ring around it.

Three-Bean Salad

To serve 6 to 8

1 cup red kidney beans, freshly cooked or canned
1 cup white kidney beans, freshly cooked or canned
1 cup chick peas, freshly cooked or canned
¾ cup finely chopped onion or scallions
½ teaspoon finely chopped garlic
2 tablespoons finely chopped parsley
1 small green pepper, seeded and coarsely chopped (optional)
1 teaspoon salt
Freshly ground black pepper
3 tablespoons wine vinegar
½ cup olive oil

If you plan to use canned cooked beans and chick peas, drain them of all their canning liquid, wash them thoroughly under cold running water, drain again and pat dry with paper towels. If you plan to cook the beans yourself, follow the initial soaking directions for beans in the recipe for baked beans on page 224, and then cook them until tender. One half cup of dry uncooked beans yields approximately 1¼ cups cooked.

In a large bowl, combine the chick peas, red kidney beans and white kidney beans, the chopped onion or scallions, garlic, parsley and the chopped green pepper if you plan to use it.

Add the salt, a few grindings of pepper and the wine vinegar. Toss gently with a large spoon. Pour in the olive oil and toss again. This salad will be greatly improved if it is allowed to rest for at least an hour before serving it.

Favorite cookout fare for the Fourth of July (or any other time) is charcoal-broiled steak. This two-inch T-bone is accompanied here by stuffed baked potatoes with a topping of melted Cheddar cheese.

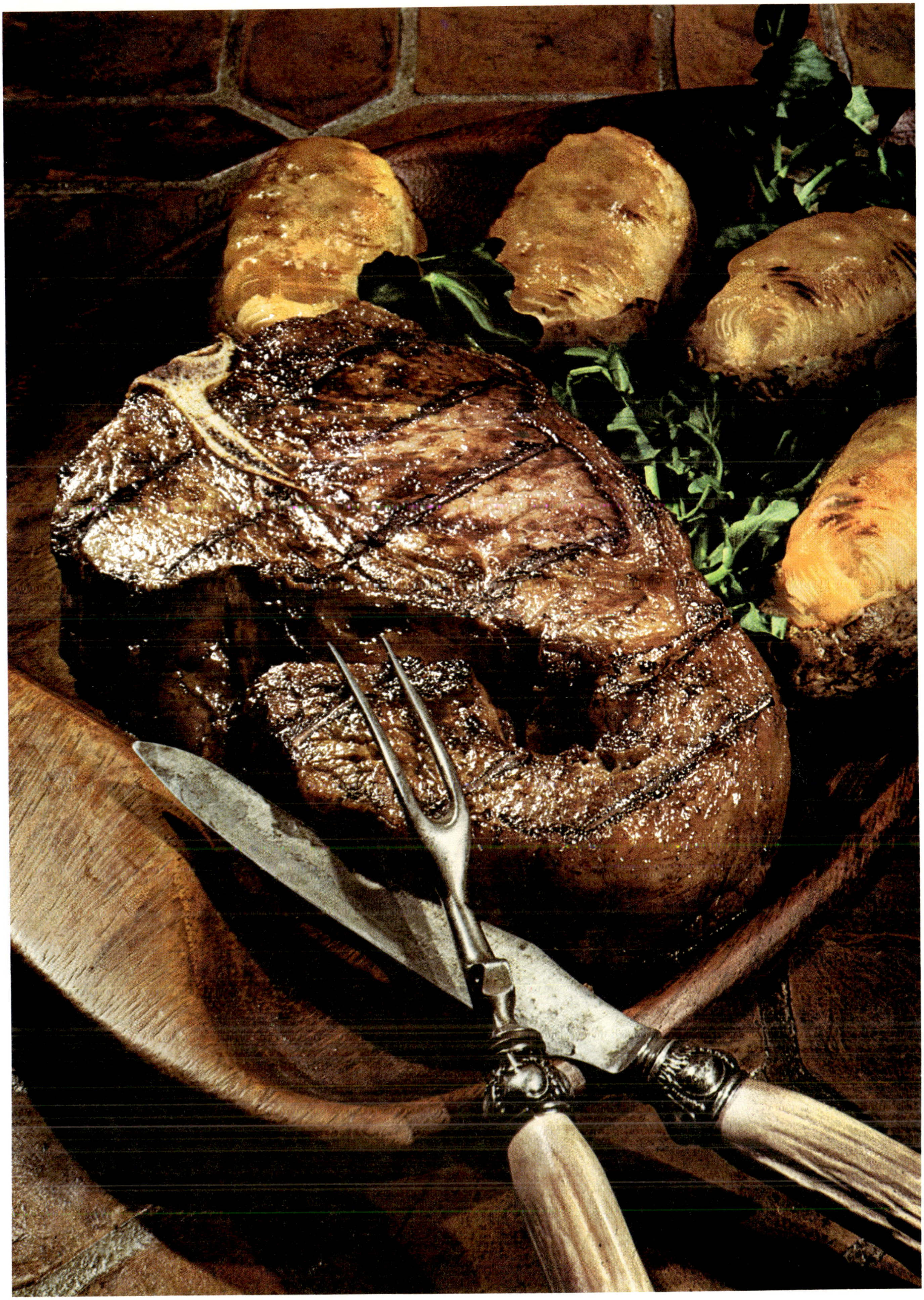

Chili con Carne

To serve 6 to 8

3 pounds top round, cut into ½-inch cubes
6 tablespoons vegetable oil
2 cups coarsely chopped onion
2 tablespoons finely chopped garlic
4 tablespoons chili powder
1 teaspoon oregano
1 teaspoon ground cumin
1 teaspoon red-pepper flakes
1 six-ounce can tomato paste
4 cups beef stock, fresh or canned
1 teaspoon salt
Freshly ground black pepper
1½ cups freshly cooked red kidney beans or drained canned kidney beans (optional)

Pat the meat dry with paper towels. Then, in a 12-inch heavy skillet, heat 4 tablespoons of the oil until a light haze forms above it. Add the meat and cook over high heat for 2 to 3 minutes, stirring, until the meat is lightly browned. With a slotted spoon transfer it to a 4-quart heavy flameproof casserole. Add the remaining 2 tablespoons of oil to the skillet and in it cook the onion and garlic for 4 to 5 minutes, stirring frequently.

Remove the skillet from the heat, add the 4 tablespoons chili powder, or to taste, oregano, cumin and pepper flakes, and stir until the onions are well coated with the mixture. Then add the tomato paste, pour in the beef stock and with a large spoon mix the ingredients together thoroughly before adding them to the meat in the casserole. Add the salt and a few grindings of black pepper. Bring to a boil, stirring once or twice, then half cover the pot, turn the heat to low and simmer for 1 to 1½ hours, or until the meat is tender.

If you plan to use the beans, add them to the casserole 15 minutes or so before the meat is done or, if you prefer, serve the chili with the three-bean salad. In either case, before serving the chili, skim it of as much of the surface fat as you can. If the chili is refrigerated overnight, the fat will rise to the surface and can be easily skimmed off before reheating.

NOTE: Chili con carne is often made with coarsely ground chuck in place of the cubed round steak. Follow the above recipe, but be sure to break up the ground chuck with a fork as you brown it.

Ratatouille

To serve 6 to 8

3 pounds firm ripe tomatoes
1½ to 2 pounds eggplant, peeled and sliced ¾ inch thick
1½ pounds zucchini, unpeeled, sliced ½ inch thick
¼ to ½ cup olive oil
¾ pound green peppers, seeded and cut in 1-inch squares (about 2 cups)
2½ cups thinly sliced onions
½ cup finely chopped fresh parsley
1 tablespoon finely cut fresh basil or 2 teaspoons dried basil, crumbled
2 teaspoons finely chopped garlic cloves
Salt
Freshly ground black pepper

Peel the tomatoes, cut them into quarters, and cut away the pulp and seeds, leaving only the shells. Cut the shells into ½-inch-wide strips and drain on paper towels. Lightly salt the eggplant and zucchini slices, spread them in one layer between paper towels, and weight them with a large, heavy platter. After 20 to 30 minutes, dry the eggplant and zucchini thoroughly with fresh paper towels.

In a heavy 10- to 12-inch skillet, bring ¼ cup of olive oil almost to the smoking point over moderately high heat, and brown the eggplant slices for a minute or two on each side, working quickly to prevent them from soaking up too much oil. Don't worry if they don't brown evenly. Remove them to paper towels to drain. In the same skillet, lightly brown the zucchini, peppers and onions one after another, adding more oil whenever necessary. Drain the zucchini and peppers on paper towels, but remove the onions to a plate. With a fork, stir the parsley, basil and garlic together in a small bowl.

Pour 1 tablespoon of the oil remaining in the skillet into a heavy 4- to 5-quart enameled casserole. Spread one third of the eggplant slices on the bottom, sprinkle with 1 teaspoon of the herb and garlic mixture, and season with salt and pepper. Arrange successive layers of half the zucchini, half the peppers, half the onions and half the tomatoes—sprinkling herbs and salt and pepper on each layer. Repeat. Finish with a layer of the remaining eggplant. Sprinkle with the remaining parsley mixture, salt and pepper, and pour in the oil left in the skillet.

Over moderately high heat, bring the casserole to a boil, cover and reduce the heat to a simmer. Every 7 or 8 minutes, use a bulb baster to draw up the liquid that will accumulate in the casserole. Transfer the liquid to a small saucepan. In 20 to 30 minutes, when the vegetables are tender but still somewhat firm, remove the casserole from the heat. Briskly boil the liquid in the saucepan for a few minutes to reduce it to about 2 tablespoons of glaze, and pour it into the casserole. Serve the *ratatouille* directly from the casserole, either hot or cold.

Lamb Shish Kabob

Drop the onion rings into a deep bowl and sprinkle them with the olive oil, lemon juice, salt and pepper. Add the lamb and turn the pieces about with a spoon to coat them well. Marinate at room temperature for at least 2 hours, or in the refrigerator for 4 hours, turning the lamb occasionally.

Light a layer of coals in a charcoal broiler and let them burn until a white ash appears on the surface, or preheat a stove broiler to its highest point.

Remove the lamb from the marinade and string the cubes tightly on 3 or 4 long skewers, pressing them firmly together. Thread the tomato slices and green pepper quarters alternately on a separate skewer. If you are broiling the lamb in a stove, suspend the skewers side by side across the length of a roasting pan deep enough to allow a 1-inch space below the meat.

Brush the meat evenly on all sides with the cream. Broil 4 inches from the heat, turning the skewers occasionally, until the vegetables brown richly and the lamb is done to your taste. For pink lamb, allow about 10 minutes; for well-done lamb, which is more typical of Middle Eastern cooking, allow about 15 minutes. Watch the vegetables carefully; they will take less time to cook than the lamb and should be removed when done.

Slide the lamb off the skewers onto heated individual plates. Serve with pilaf and the broiled tomato and green pepper.

To serve 4

1 large onion, peeled and cut into ⅛-inch-thick slices and separated into rings
2 tablespoons olive oil
4 tablespoons fresh lemon juice
2 tablespoons salt
½ teaspoon freshly ground black pepper
2 pounds lean boneless lamb, preferably from the leg, trimmed of excess fat and cut into 2-inch cubes
1 large, firm, ripe tomato, cut crosswise into four slices
1 large green pepper, cut into quarters, seeded and deribbed
2 tablespoons heavy cream

Swordfish Shish Kabob

In a deep bowl combine the onions, 2 tablespoons of lemon juice, 2 teaspoons of oil, the salt and pepper. Add the fish, tossing it about with a spoon to coat it well. Marinate at room temperature for 2 hours, or in the refrigerator for 4 hours, turning the fish occasionally. Place the bay leaves in a bowl, pour in 2 cups of boiling water and let them soak for 1 hour.

Light a layer of coals in a charcoal broiler and let them burn until a white ash appears on the surface, or preheat a stove broiler to its highest point.

Drain the bay leaves and remove the fish from the marinade. String the cubes of fish and the bay leaves alternately on 3 or 4 skewers, pressing them firmly together. Combine the remaining 2 tablespoons of lemon juice and 2 teaspoons of oil and brush the mixture evenly over the fish. If you are broiling the fish in a stove, suspend the skewers side by side across the length of a roasting pan deep enough to allow a 1-inch space below the fish. Broil 3 inches from the heat, turning the skewers occasionally, for 8 to 10 minutes,

To serve 4

1 small onion, cut into ¼-inch-thick slices and separated into rings
4 tablespoons fresh lemon juice
4 teaspoons olive oil
2 teaspoons salt
½ teaspoon freshly ground black pepper
1½ pounds swordfish sliced 1 inch thick, skinned, boned and cut into 1-inch cubes
20 large bay leaves

For many citizens of the Southwest, pure joy on the Fourth of July is a pot of chili, a three-bean salad and some beer.

The region's great humorist, Oklahoma-born Will Rogers, once claimed that he judged a town by the quality of its chili.

or until the fish is golden brown and feels firm when pressed lightly with a finger. Slide the fish off the skewers onto heated individual plates, and serve with pilaf.

Pilaf

To serve 4 to 6

2 tablespoons butter plus 4 tablespoons melted butter
1 cup uncooked long- or medium-grain white rice
2 cups chicken stock, fresh or canned
½ teaspoon salt
Freshly ground black pepper

In a heavy 2- to 3-quart saucepan, melt the 2 tablespoons of butter over moderate heat. When the foam begins to subside, add the rice and stir for 2 or 3 minutes until all the grains are evenly coated. Do not let the rice brown. Pour in the stock, add the salt and a few grindings of pepper, and bring to a boil, stirring constantly. Cover the pan and reduce the heat to its lowest point. Simmer for 20 minutes, or until all the liquid has been absorbed and the rice is tender but still slightly resistant to the bite.

Pour in the 4 tablespoons of melted butter and toss the rice with a fork until the grains glisten. Drape a towel over the rice and let it stand at room temperature for about 20 minutes before serving.

Potato Salad

To make 2 quarts

3 pounds new potatoes, unpeeled
1 teaspoon salt
2 tablespoons white-wine vinegar
¾ cup finely chopped celery
¾ cup finely chopped onion
1½ cups finely chopped green pepper
2 tablespoons finely chopped fresh parsley

MAYONNAISE
3 egg yolks, at room temperature
1 teaspoon lemon juice
1 tablespoon white-wine vinegar
¼ teaspoon dry mustard
1 teaspoon salt
¼ teaspoon white pepper
2 cups vegetable oil

3 hard-cooked eggs, sliced
2 tablespoons finely chopped fresh parsley

Place the potatoes in boiling salted water to cover, and cook until they are tender but do not fall apart when gently pierced with a knife. Drain them in a colander and when they are cool enough to handle, peel and cut them into ½- to ¾-inch cubes. Place the potatoes in a large bowl and gently stir in the salt, vinegar, celery, onion, green pepper and parsley.

To make the mayonnaise, beat the egg yolks with a whisk or rotary or electric beater for 2 to 3 minutes until they thicken and cling to the beater. Add the lemon juice, vinegar, mustard, salt and pepper. Beat in the oil ½ teaspoon at a time until ¼ cup is used, making sure each spoonful is absorbed. Still beating, slowly add the rest of the oil. Gently fold the mayonnaise into the potatoes. Taste for seasoning. Garnish with egg slices and chopped parsley.

Boston Baked Beans

To serve 6 to 8

4 cups dried pea or Great Northern beans
2 teaspoons salt
2 medium-sized whole onions, peeled
4 cloves
½ cup molasses
1 cup brown sugar
2 teaspoons dry mustard
1 teaspoon black pepper
2 cups water
½ pound salt pork, scored

Put the beans in a large saucepan and pour in enough cold water to cover them by at least 2 inches. Bring to a boil over high heat, cook briskly for 2 minutes, then remove the pan from the heat and let the beans soak for about 1 hour. Bring them to a boil again, add 1 teaspoon of the salt, half cover the pan and simmer the beans as slowly as possible for about 30 minutes, or until they are partially done. Drain the beans and discard the bean water.

Preheat the oven to 250°. To bake the beans, choose a traditional 4-quart bean pot or a heavy casserole with a tight-fitting cover. Place 2 onions, each stuck with 2 cloves, in the bottom of the bean pot or casserole and cover with the beans. In a small mixing bowl, combine the molasses, ¾ cup of the brown sugar, mustard, and 1 teaspoon each of salt and black pepper. Slowly stirring with a large spoon, pour in the 2 cups of water.

Kabobs of lamb, swordfish and vegetables have been charcoal-broiled on skewers, a Middle Eastern cooking style that has moved to American backyards.

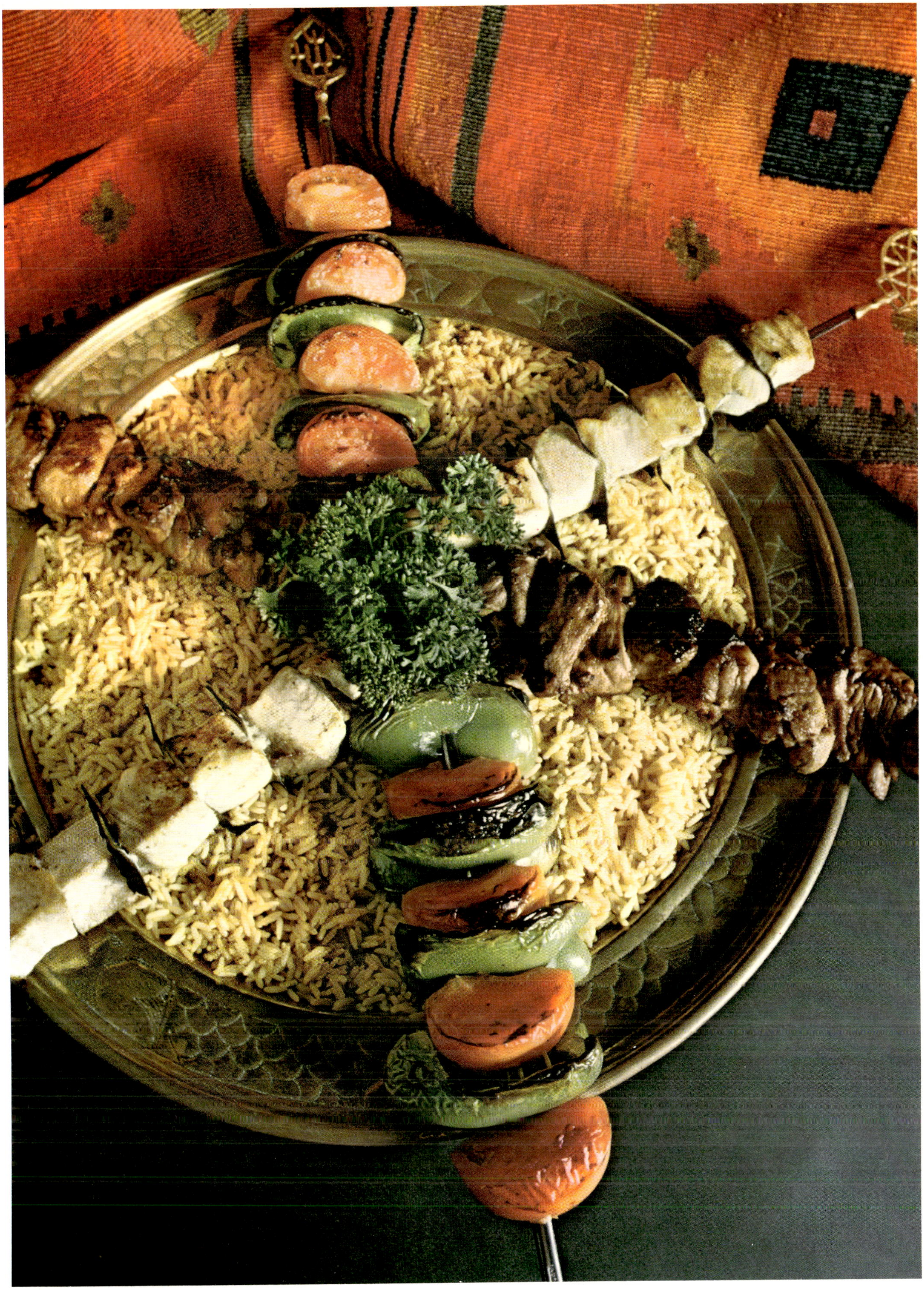

Pour this mixture over the beans and push the salt pork slightly beneath the surface. Cover tightly and bake in the center of the oven for 4½ to 5 hours. Then remove the cover and sprinkle with the remaining ¼ cup of brown sugar. Bake the beans uncovered for another ½ hour and serve.

Kentucky Fried Chicken

To serve 4

2 to 4 pounds lard
A 2½- to 3-pound chicken, cut into 8 serving pieces
2 teaspoons salt
Freshly ground black pepper
1 egg, lightly beaten and combined with ½ cup milk
1 cup flour

Preheat the oven to its lowest setting. Then line a large shallow baking dish with paper towels and place it in the center of the oven.

Melt 2 pounds of the lard over high heat in a deep fryer or large heavy saucepan. When melted, the fat should be 1½ to 2 inches deep; add more lard if necessary. Heat the lard to a temperature of 375° on a deep-frying thermometer, or until it is very hot but not smoking.

Pat the pieces of chicken completely dry with paper towels and season them on all sides with the salt and a few grindings of pepper. Immerse the chicken pieces one at a time in the egg-and-milk mixture, then dip them in the flour and turn to coat them lightly but evenly.

Fry the chicken thighs and drumsticks, starting them skin side down and turning them frequently with tongs, for about 12 minutes, or until they color richly and evenly. As they brown, transfer them to the paper-lined dish and keep them warm in the oven. Then fry the wings and breast, separately if necessary to avoid overcrowding the pan. The white meat will be fully cooked in 7 or 8 minutes.

Corn Sticks

To make fourteen 5½-inch sticks

1½ cups cornmeal, preferably white water-ground
½ cup all-purpose flour
1 tablespoon double-acting baking powder
1 teaspoon salt
2 eggs
1½ cups buttermilk
1 tablespoon butter, melted

Preheat the oven to 350°. Combine the cornmeal, flour, baking powder and salt and sift them into a deep bowl. In a separate bowl, beat the eggs lightly with a wire whisk or fork, then add the buttermilk and mix well. Pour the liquid ingredients over the dry ones and, with a wooden spoon, stir them together until the batter is smooth; do not overbeat.

Brush the inside surfaces of the molds in a corn-stick pan with the melted butter. Spoon the batter into the molds, dividing it evenly among them. Bake in the middle of the oven for 25 to 30 minutes, or until the corn sticks are golden brown.

Turn the corn sticks out of the pan, arrange them attractively on a heated platter and serve at once.

NOTE: Corn-stick pans, in aluminum or cast iron, are available at hardware, houseware and kitchen-supply stores.

Kentucky fried chicken and crisp corn sticks, two of the South's most distinctive dishes, are finger foods that make them picnic favorites.

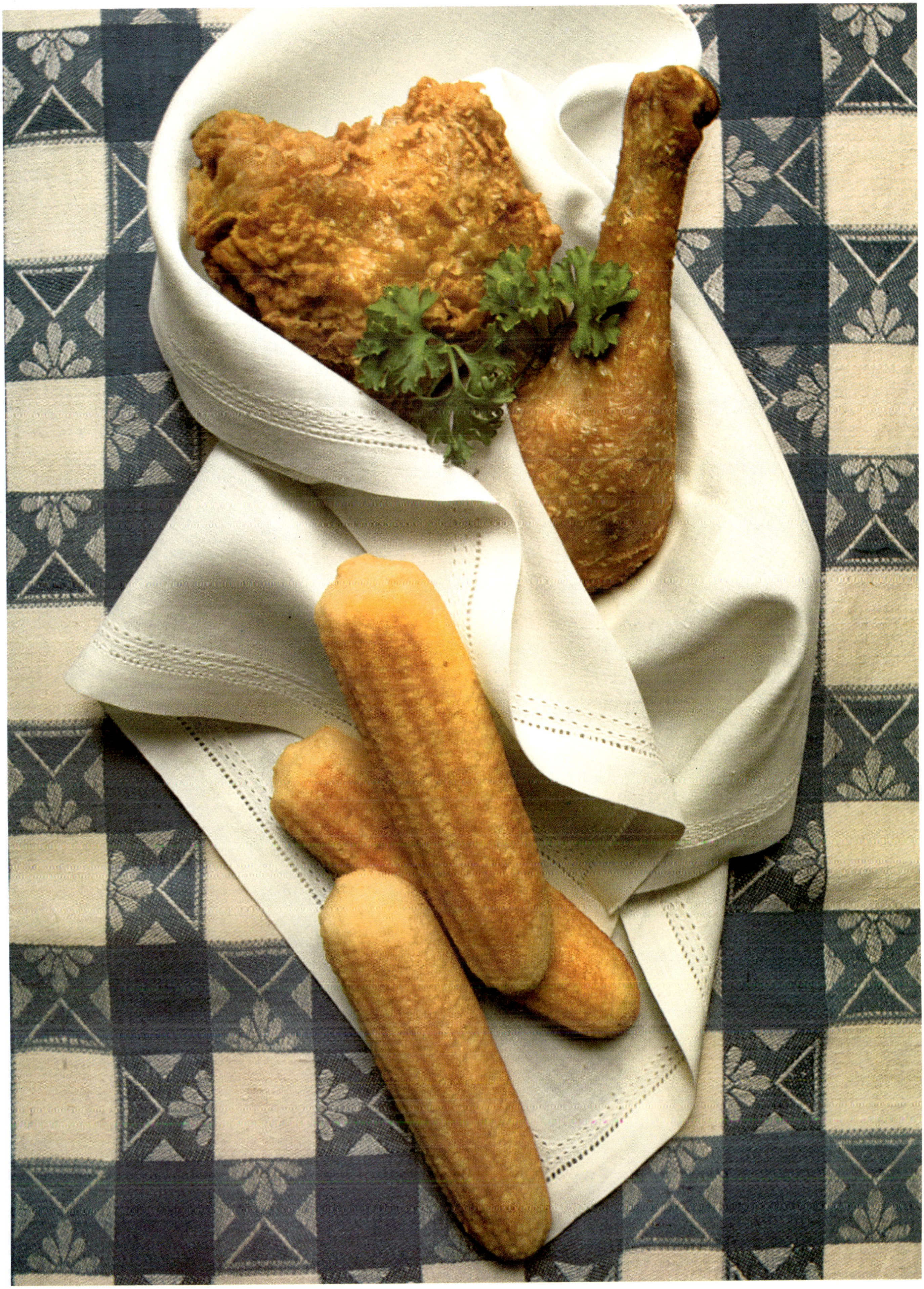

To serve 2 to 4

Two 1- to 3-pound live lobsters
½ pound butter, melted

Boiled Lobster

Pour enough water into a 12- to 14-quart pot to fill it halfway and bring the water to a boil over high heat. Plunge the lobsters head first into the pot. They should be entirely submerged; if not add more boiling water.

Cover the pot tightly, return the water to a boil, then reduce the heat to moderate. Regulate the heat as needed to prevent the water from boiling over, but keep the liquid at a boil throughout the cooking. Do not overcook the lobsters. Allow about 12 minutes cooking time for 1-pound lobsters; 15 to 18 minutes for 1½ pounds; 20 to 22 minutes for 2 pounds; and 30 to 35 minutes for 3-pound lobsters. (The shell may turn red before the water even returns to a boil, therefore color is not a reliable test for doneness.) A better test is to remove one of the lobsters from the pot and grasp the end of one of the small legs at either side of the body. Jerk the lobster sharply. If the leg pulls away from the body, the lobster is done. If the leg remains attached to the body, boil the lobster for 2 or 3 minutes longer.

With tongs or a slotted spoon, transfer the lobsters to a heated platter or individual plates and serve at once. Pour the melted butter into small bowls and present it separately with the lobsters.

To serve 4 as a first course

4 dozen large mussels in their shells
4 tablespoons butter cut into small bits, plus ½ pound butter, melted
½ cup finely chopped onions
1½ cups dry white wine
1 cup water
2 tablespoons finely chopped fresh parsley
⅛ teaspoon crumbled dried thyme

Steamed Mussels in White Wine

Scrub the mussels thoroughly under cold running water with a stiff brush or soapless steel-mesh scouring pad. With a small, sharp knife scrape or pull the black hairlike tufts off the shells and discard them.

In a 6- to 8-quart enameled or stainless-steel casserole, melt the butter bits over moderate heat. When the foam begins to subside, add the onions and, stirring frequently, cook for about 5 minutes until they are soft and translucent but not brown. Stir in the wine, water, parsley and thyme. Drop in the mussels and bring to a boil over high heat. Cover tightly, reduce the heat to low and let the mussels steam for about 10 minutes, turning the mussels about once or twice with a slotted spoon. When the mussels have steamed the allotted time, all the shells should have opened; discard any that remain shut.

With a slotted spoon, transfer the mussels to a large, heated platter or individual serving plates. Strain the broth into a bowl, using a fine sieve lined with a double thickness of dampened cheesecloth. Pour the broth into 4 heated soup cups and serve the melted butter separately in individual bowls on the side.

To eat a steamed mussel, remove it from the shell with a small fork, dip it into the broth to moisten the mussel and remove any traces of sand, and then immerse it in the melted butter.

To serve 4

8 dozen steamer or small soft-shell or long-neck clams
4 tablespoons butter, cut into ½-inch bits, plus ½ pound butter, melted
½ cup finely chopped onions
2 tablespoons finely chopped fresh parsley
3 cups water

Steamed Clams

Wash the clams thoroughly under cold running water, discarding any with broken shells as well as those whose necks do not retract when prodded gently with a finger.

In an 8- to 10-quart steamer or casserole, melt the 4 tablespoons of butter bits over moderate heat. When the foam begins to subside, add the onions and, stirring frequently, cook for about 5 minutes. When the onions are soft and translucent, stir in the parsley and 3 cups of water and bring to a boil over high heat. Add the clams, cover tightly, and steam for 5 to 8 minutes, turning them about in the pot once or twice with a slotted spoon. All the shells should open; discard any clams that remain shut.

With tongs or a slotted spoon, transfer the clams to a deep heated platter or serving bowl. Strain the broth remaining in the steamer through a sieve lined with a double thickness of damp cheesecloth and set over a bowl. Pour the broth into 4 heated soup cups and serve the melted butter separately in individual bowls.

To eat a steamed clam, remove it from the shell with a small fork or your fingers, dip it into the broth to moisten the clam and remove any trace of sand, and then immerse it in the melted butter.

NOTE: Though steamers taste best when fresh, they can be safely kept in the refrigerator for 2 or 3 days. Place them in a bowl or pan and store them uncovered so that the clams can breathe. Do not wash them until you are ready to steam them.

Steamed Crabs

Mix the salt and seafood seasoning together in a bowl and set aside.

Set a rack in the bottom of a 10- to 12-quart enameled or stainless-steel pot 10 to 12 inches in diameter. Pour in the vinegar and water. Then place 6 or 7 crabs on the rack and sprinkle them evenly with 2 or 3 tablespoonfuls of the salt-seasoning mixture. Add another layer of 6 or 7 crabs, sprinkle them with several tablespoons of seasoning, and repeat 4 or 5 times, seasoning each layer of crabs as before.

Bring to a boil over high heat, cover tightly, reduce the heat to low, and steam the crabs for 20 minutes. Transfer the crabs to large heated platters with tongs and serve at once. Because these steamed crabs are so highly spiced, they are eaten without any accompaniment except, traditionally, tall glasses of cold beer.

Seafood Seasoning

Combine all the ingredients in a deep bowl and stir until they are thoroughly mixed. Transfer the seafood seasoning to a jar, cover tightly, and store at room temperature until ready to use.

Cioppino—California Fisherman's Stew

To prepare the fish stock, combine the fish trimmings and water in a 4- to 5-quart enameled or stainless-steel pot and bring to a boil over high heat, skimming off the foam and scum that rise to the surface. Add the coarsely chopped onion and the bay leaf, peppercorns and 1 teaspoon of salt, reduce the heat to low, and simmer partially covered for 20 minutes.

To serve 8 to 12

⅔ cup coarse (kosher) salt
⅔ cup seafood seasoning (*below*)
2 cups cider vinegar
2 cups water
3 dozen live blue crabs, each about 4 inches across

To make about 3 cups

3 cups coarse (kosher) salt
6 tablespoons coarsely ground black pepper
1 tablespoon ground hot red pepper (cayenne)
3 tablespoons dry mustard
1 tablespoon mustard seeds
1 tablespoon celery seeds
1 tablespoon ground ginger
2 teaspoons paprika

To serve 8

FISH STOCK

2 pounds fish trimmings: the heads, tails and bones of any firm white-fleshed fish
6 cups water
1 large onion, peeled and coarsely chopped
1 medium-sized bay leaf, crumbled
6 whole black peppercorns
1 teaspoon salt

On the shores of Lake Pontchartrain, a New Orleans family picnics on boiled crawfish, crab, soft drinks, beer and watermelon.

Strain the contents of the pot through a fine sieve into a bowl, pressing down hard on the fish trimmings with the back of a spoon to extract all their juices. Measure and reserve 4 cups of the fish stock.

Wash the pot, add the oil and heat it over moderate heat until a light haze forms above it. Add the cup of coarsely chopped onions and the garlic, and, stirring frequently, cook for about 5 minutes, until the onions are soft and translucent but not brown. Stir in the reserved stock, the tomato purée, wine and parsley, and bring to a boil over high heat. Reduce the heat and simmer partially covered for 15 minutes.

Meanwhile, prepare the crabs. Holding a crab tightly in one hand, lift off the top shell and discard it. Pull out the spongy gray lungs, or "dead man's fingers," from each side and scrape out the intestines in the center. Place the crab on its back and, with the point of a small sharp knife, pry off the pointed flap or apron. Cut away the head just behind the eyes. With a cleaver or heavy knife, cut the crab into quarters. Shell, clean and quarter the second crab in the same manner and set both aside on a plate.

Under cold running water, scrub the mussels and clams thoroughly with a stiff brush or soapless steel-mesh scouring pad, and remove the black ropelike tufts from the mussels. Season the cod on both sides with ½ teaspoon of salt. Set the mussels and clams and the cod aside on wax paper or plates.

To assemble the cioppino, arrange the pieces of crab in the bottom of a 6- to 8-quart enameled casserole. Lay the mussels and clams on top and pour in the tomato mixture. Bring to a boil over high heat, reduce the heat to low, cover tightly and cook for 10 minutes. Add the pieces of cod, cover the casserole again and continue to cook for 8 to 10 minutes longer. The cioppino is done when the mussel and clam shells have opened and the cod flakes easily when prodded gently with a fork. Discard any mussels or clams that remain closed.

Serve at once, directly from the casserole, or spoon the cod and shellfish into a large heated tureen and pour the broth over them.

Molded Salmon with Cucumber Sauce

Place the salmon in an enameled or stainless-steel casserole just large enough to hold it and pour in enough cold water to cover the fish completely. Add the distilled white vinegar, bay leaf, thyme, 2 tablespoons of the salt and the 6 peppercorns, and bring to a boil over high heat. Reduce the heat to low and simmer partially covered for about 25 minutes, or until the salmon flakes easily when prodded gently with a fork.

With a slotted spatula, transfer the fish to a plate; discard the cooking liquid and seasonings. Remove the skin and discard it, then break the salmon into large flakes with a fork, discarding any bones you find. Cover the fish with foil or plastic wrap and set aside.

FISH STEW
¼ cup olive or vegetable oil
1 cup coarsely chopped onions
1 tablespoon finely chopped garlic
3 medium-sized firm ripe tomatoes, washed, coarsely chopped and puréed in a food mill, or substitute 1 cup canned puréed tomatoes
1 cup dry white wine
2 tablespoons finely chopped fresh parsley
Two 1½-pound precooked Dungeness crabs, thoroughly defrosted if frozen, or 3 pounds other available precooked crabs in shells
3 dozen large mussels in their shells
2 dozen small hard-shell clams in their shells
2 pounds fresh cod steaks, cut into 8 equal portions
½ teaspoon salt

To serve 4

MOLDED SALMON
1 pound fresh salmon
¼ cup distilled white vinegar
1 medium-sized bay leaf
¼ teaspoon crumbled dried thyme
2 tablespoons plus 1 teaspoon salt
6 whole black peppercorns
1 tablespoon vegetable oil
¼ cup plus 1 tablespoon cold water
2 teaspoons unflavored gelatin
¼ cup wine vinegar
1½ teaspoons dry mustard
1 teaspoon sugar
2 egg yolks
2 tablespoons unsalted butter, cut into ¼-inch bits
¾ cup milk

Overleaf: Cioppino, a highly seasoned seafood stew, is at its best when made with a mixture of finned- and shellfish. The version shown here includes crabs, mussels, clams and cod steaks. White wine adds flavor to the broth, but cioppino is normally served with a red wine. A San Francisco version of fisherman's stew, it can be made from a summer haul of seafood anywhere.

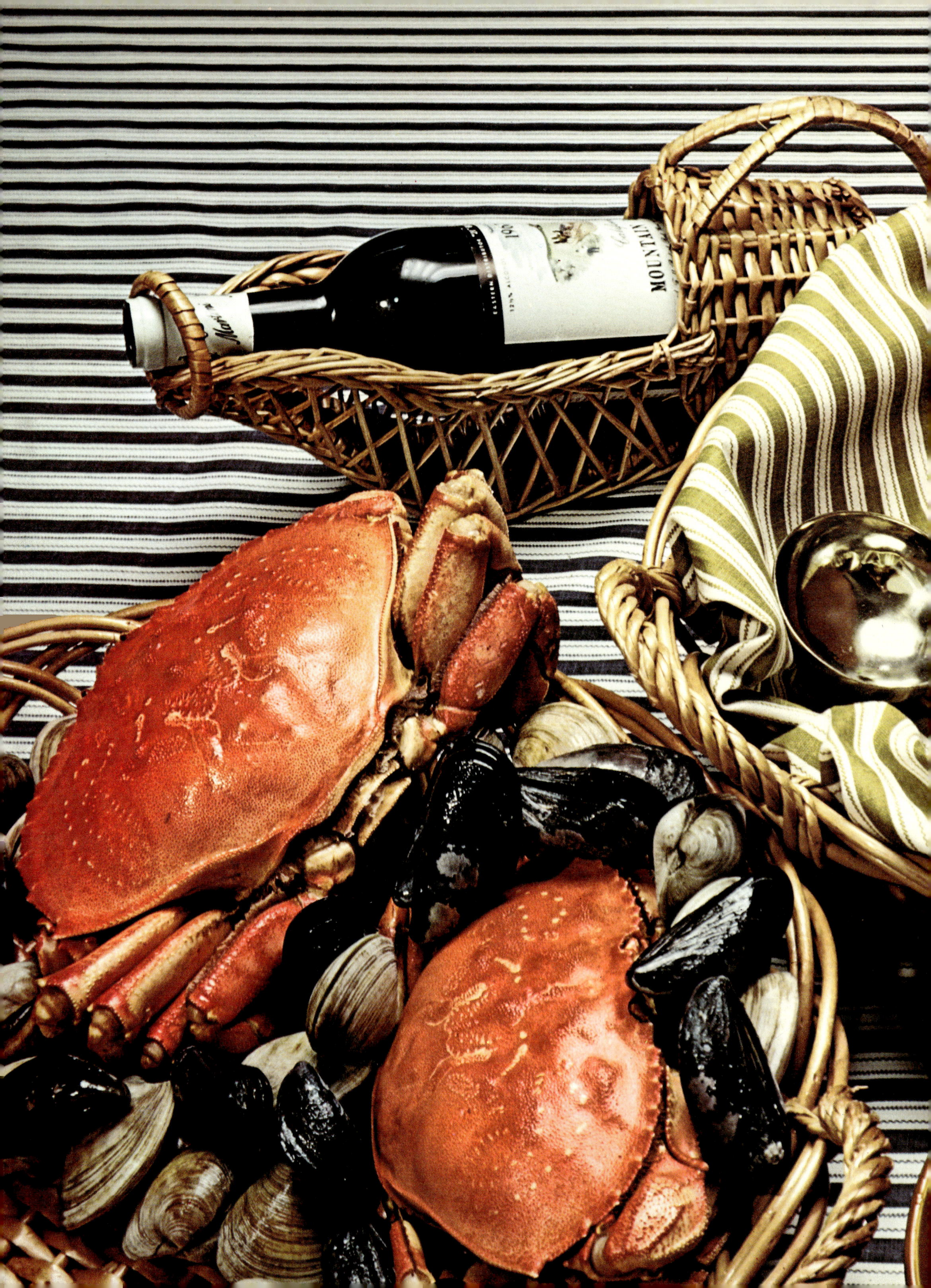
MOUNTAIN

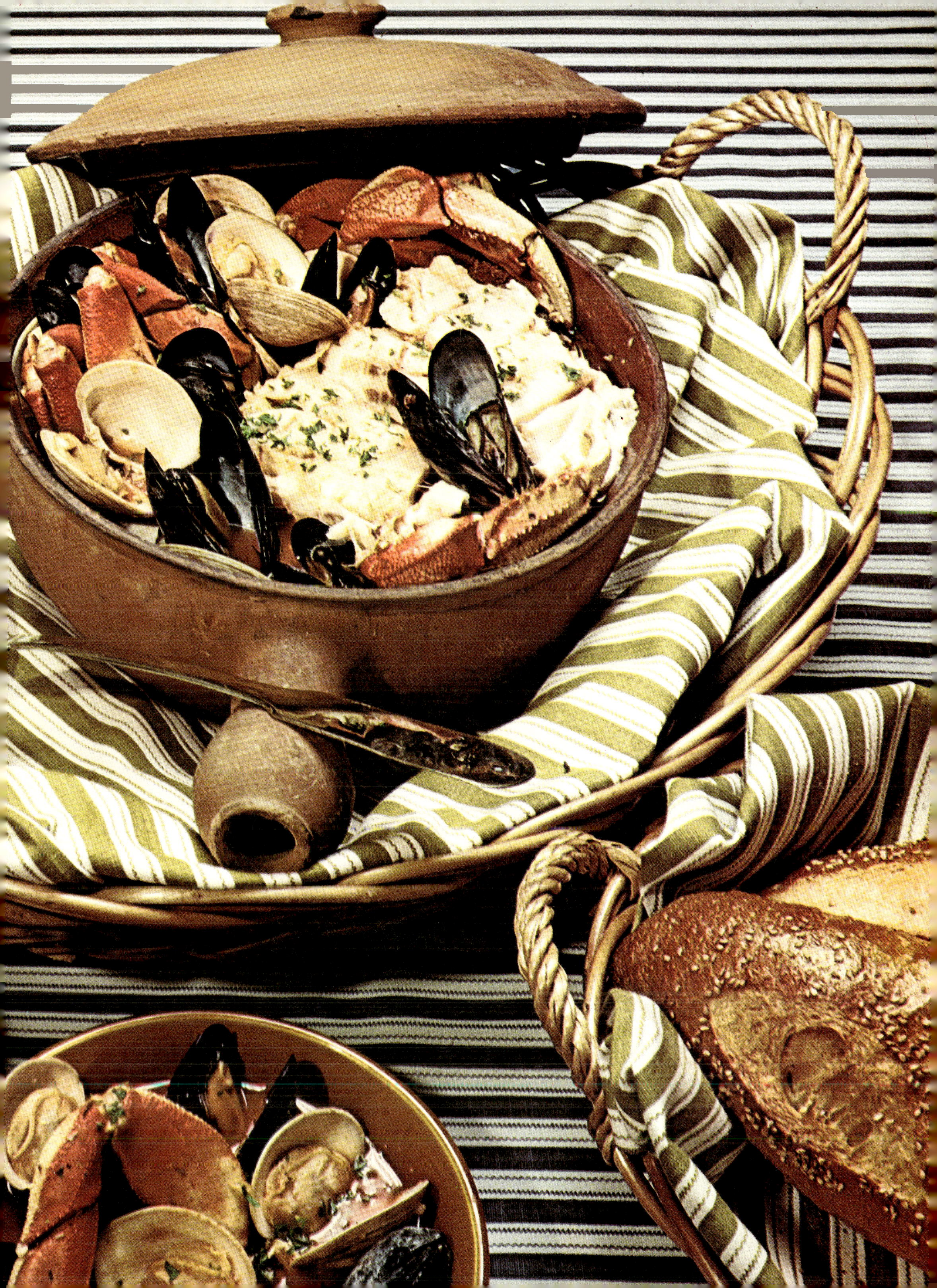

CUCUMBER SAUCE
1 large firm cucumber
½ cup heavy cream, chilled
1 tablespoon wine vinegar
⅛ teaspoon ground hot red pepper (cayenne)
1 teaspoon salt
1 tablespoon finely cut fresh dill leaves, or substitute 1 teaspoon dried dill weed

With a pastry brush, spread the vegetable oil evenly over the bottom and sides of four 6-ounce individual molds. Invert the molds over paper towels to drain.

Pour ¼ cup of the cold water into a small bowl, sprinkle in the gelatin and let it soften for a few minutes. Meanwhile, combine the wine vinegar, the dry mustard, the sugar and the remaining teaspoon of salt in a 1-quart enameled or stainless-steel saucepan. Stir until the dry ingredients are completely dissolved, then boil briskly to reduce the mixture to about 3 tablespoons. Remove the pan from the heat and stir in the remaining tablespoon of cold water.

Stirring the vinegar mixture constantly with a wire whisk, add the egg yolks one at a time. Still whisking, cook over the lowest possible heat for 1 minute, or until it thickens lightly. Do not let the mixture get too hot or it will curdle. Immediately remove the pan from the heat and whisk in the butter bits.

In a separate small saucepan, heat the milk over moderate heat until bubbles begin to appear around the edges. Add the gelatin to the milk and stir until it dissolves completely. Stirring the vinegar mixture with the whisk, pour in the milk and gelatin in a slow, thin stream, then stir in the flaked salmon. Taste for seasoning. Pour the mixture into the oiled molds, spreading it and smoothing the top with a spatula. Refrigerate for at least 4 hours, or until the molded salmon is very firm.

Just before serving, prepare the cucumber sauce in the following fashion: With a small, sharp knife, peel the cucumber and slice it lengthwise in half. Scoop out the seeds by running the tip of a teaspoon down the center of each half. Chop the cucumber fine and squeeze it handful by handful to remove the excess liquid. Spread the cucumber on a paper towel to drain completely.

In a chilled bowl, beat the cream with a wire whisk or a rotary or electric beater until it is stiff enough to stand in firm peaks on the beater when it is lifted from the bowl. Beat in the wine vinegar, red pepper and 1 teaspoon of salt. Add the cucumber and dill, and fold them into the cream mixture gently but thoroughly.

To unmold and serve the salmon, dip the bottom of the molds briefly into hot water and run a thin knife around the edges. Place an inverted serving plate over each mold and, grasping plate and mold together firmly, turn them over. Rap the plate on a table and the salmon should slide out easily. Serve the cucumber sauce separately in a bowl or sauceboat.

Cold Soups and Garden Salads

Cold Avocado and Tomato Soup

In a deep bowl, beat the puréed tomatoes, sour cream, milk, lemon juice, tomato paste and oil together with a whisk or spoon until they are well blended. Stir in the parsley, salt and pepper, and taste for seasoning. Cover tightly with foil or plastic wrap and refrigerate the soup for at least 2 hours, until thoroughly chilled.

With a small, sharp knife, peel the cucumber and slice it lengthwise in half. Scoop out the seeds by running the tip of a teaspoon down the center of each half. Cut the cucumber into ¼-inch dice and set it aside in a small serving bowl.

Just before serving, beat the puréed avocado into the soup and taste for seasoning. Ladle the soup into a chilled tureen or individual bowls and serve at once accompanied by the chopped cucumbers.

To serve 4

6 medium-sized firm ripe tomatoes, coarsely chopped and puréed (about 3 cups of purée)
⅔ cup sour cream
½ cup milk
3 tablespoons strained fresh lemon juice
2 tablespoons tomato paste
1 tablespoon olive oil
3 tablespoons finely chopped fresh parsley
1½ teaspoons salt
¼ teaspoon freshly ground black pepper
1 small cucumber
1 small ripe avocado, seeded, peeled and puréed

Cold Lentil Soup

In a heavy 3- to 4-quart saucepan, melt the butter over moderate heat. When the foam begins to subside, add the onions and garlic and, stirring frequently, cook for about 5 minutes, until they are soft and translucent but not brown. Stir in the chicken stock, lentils, puréed tomato, basil and a few grindings of pepper, and bring to a boil over high heat. Reduce the heat to low and simmer partially covered for 1 hour.

Rub the soup through a fine sieve into a bowl with the back of a spoon, or put it through the finest blade of a food mill. Cool to room temperature, cover with foil or plastic wrap, and refrigerate the soup for at least 2 hours, or until it is thoroughly chilled.

To serve, ladle the soup into a chilled tureen or individual soup plates. Mound the chopped hard-cooked eggs, radishes and scallions (if used) attractively in separate bowls and present them with the soup.

To serve 8 to 10

2 tablespoons butter
1 cup finely chopped onions
1 teaspoon finely chopped garlic
2 quarts chicken stock
2 cups (1 pound) dried lentils
1 medium-sized firm ripe tomato, chopped and puréed, or ½ cup canned tomato purée
½ teaspoon crumbled dried basil
Freshly ground black pepper
2 hard-cooked eggs, finely chopped
½ cup finely sliced radishes
½ cup finely chopped scallions (optional)

Cold Split Pea Soup with Mint

Wash the split peas thoroughly under cold running water and continue to wash until the draining water runs clear. Pick over the peas and discard any discolored ones. In a heavy 4- to 5-quart saucepan or soup kettle, bring the chicken stock to a boil and drop in the peas slowly so that the stock does not stop boiling. Add the onions, celery, cloves, bay leaf and mint. Reduce the heat and simmer with the pan partially covered for 1½ hours or until the peas can be easily mashed with a spoon.

Purée the soup through a food mill or fine sieve into a large bowl, and then rub it through the sieve back into the saucepan or into another bowl. Add the salt and pepper, and chill the soup in the refrigerator. (If you wish to serve the soup immediately, place the soup in a bowl and

To serve 6 to 8

2 cups dry green split peas
2 quarts chicken stock
1 cup coarsely chopped onion
1 stalk celery, coarsely chopped
⅛ teaspoon ground cloves
1 bay leaf
1 cup coarsely chopped fresh mint
1 teaspoon salt
Pinch white pepper
½ to 1 cup chilled heavy cream
Sprigs of fresh mint

To serve 6 to 8

SOUP

2 medium-sized cucumbers, peeled and coarsely chopped
5 medium-sized tomatoes, peeled and coarsely chopped
1 large onion, coarsely chopped
1 medium-sized green pepper, deribbed, seeded and coarsely chopped
2 teaspoons finely chopped garlic
4 cups coarsely crumbled French or Italian bread, trimmed of crusts
4 cups cold water
¼ cup red wine vinegar
4 teaspoons salt
4 tablespoons olive oil
1 tablespoon tomato paste

set the bowl in a larger container filled with crushed ice or ice cubes. With a metal spoon, stir the soup until it is ice cold.) Before serving, stir in ½ to 1 cup of chilled heavy cream, thinning the soup as desired, and taste for seasoning. Garnish with sprigs of fresh mint.

Gazpacho

In a deep bowl, combine the coarsely chopped cucumbers, tomatoes, onion and green pepper, garlic and crumbled bread, and mix together thoroughly. Then stir in the water, vinegar and salt. Ladle the mixture, about 2 cups at a time, into the jar of a blender and blend at high speed for 1 minute, or until reduced to a smooth purée. Pour the purée into a bowl and with a whisk beat in the olive oil and tomato paste.

(To make the soup by hand, purée the vegetable and bread mixture in a food mill or, with the back of a large spoon, rub it through a sieve set over a bowl. Discard any pulp left in the mill or sieve. Beat the olive oil and tomato paste into the purée.)

Cover the bowl tightly with foil or plastic wrap and refrigerate for at least

Encased in an ice-filled container, chilled, mint-flavored split pea soup is unusual and refreshing for a summer buffet or picnic.

2 hours, or until thoroughly chilled. Just before serving, whisk or stir the soup lightly to recombine it. Then ladle it into a large chilled tureen or individual soup plates.

Accompany the *gazpacho* with the bread cubes and the vegetable garnishes presented in separate serving bowls to be added to the soup at the discretion of each diner.

NOTE: If you prefer crisp croutons for the garnish, fry the bread cubes. In a 6- to 8-inch skillet, heat ¼ cup of olive oil over moderate heat until a light haze forms above it. Drop in the bread cubes and, turning them frequently, cook them until they are crisp and golden brown on all sides. Drain on paper towels and cool.

GARNISH

1 cup ¼-inch bread cubes, trimmed of crusts
½ cup finely chopped onions
½ cup peeled and finely chopped cucumbers
½ cup finely chopped green peppers

Coleslaw with Boiled Dressing

In a 2- to 3-quart saucepan, combine the vinegar, water, sugar, flour, mustard and salt and beat vigorously with a wire whisk until the mixture is smooth. Place over moderate heat and, whisking constantly, add the cream and butter and cook until the butter melts and the sauce comes to a simmer. Stir 2 or 3 tablespoonfuls of the simmering liquid into the beaten eggs and, when they are well incorporated, pour the mixture into the sauce, whisking it constantly. Reduce the heat to low and continue to whisk until the sauce thickens heavily. With a rubber spatula, scrape the contents of the saucepan into a deep bowl and cool to room temperature.

Wash the head of cabbage under cold running water, remove the tough outer leaves, and cut the cabbage into quarters. To shred the cabbage, cut out the core and slice the quarters crosswise into ⅛-inch-wide strips.

Add the shredded cabbage and the carrots to the sauce, toss together gently but thoroughly and taste for seasoning. Cover with foil or plastic wrap and refrigerate for 2 or 3 hours before serving.

To serve 8 to 10

½ cup cider vinegar
⅓ cup water
2 tablespoons sugar
2 tablespoons flour
2 teaspoons dry mustard
2 teaspoons salt
½ cup heavy cream
2 tablespoons butter
4 eggs, lightly beaten
2 pounds firm white cabbage
1 cup grated scraped carrots

Celery Slaw

With a small sharp knife, remove the leaves from the celery. Separate the celery into individual ribs, trim the roots ends with the knife and scrape off the heavy outside strings and any brown blemished areas. Wash the ribs thoroughly under cold running water and pat them dry with paper towels. Then, holding the knife at a diagonal, cut the ribs crosswise into ⅛-inch-thick slices, and drop them into a large bowl. Set aside.

Combine the vinegar, sugar, paprika, salt and a few grindings of pepper in a small deep bowl and beat with a wire whisk until the sugar dissolves. Whisking the mixture constantly, pour in the vegetable oil in a very slow, thin stream. When the sauce thickens and is smooth, beat in the sour cream with the whisk. Taste for seasoning.

Pour the sauce over the celery, add the onion rings and toss together gently but thoroughly. Cover with foil or plastic wrap and marinate in the refrigerator for about 3 hours.

Just before serving, taste for seasoning again and gently stir in the pimiento strips.

To serve 4 to 6

1 medium-sized bunch of celery (about 1 pound)
¼ cup wine vinegar
1 tablespoon sugar
¼ teaspoon paprika
2 teaspoons salt
Freshly ground black pepper
⅔ cup vegetable oil
½ cup sour cream
1 medium-sized onion, peeled, cut crosswise into ⅛-inch-thick slices and separated into rings
1 pimiento, cut into strips about 1 inch long and ⅛ inch wide

Cold Marinated Zucchini

To serve 4 to 6 as a first course

1 large firm ripe zucchini (about 1 pound)
1 large firm ripe yellow straightneck squash (about 1 pound)
5 cups chicken stock, fresh or canned
2 celery tops, 8 fresh parsley sprigs and 1 medium-sized bay leaf, tied together with string
¼ cup distilled white vinegar
¼ teaspoon salt
⅛ teaspoon ground white pepper
⅔ cup olive oil
1 canned pimiento, drained and cut lengthwise into ⅛-inch-wide strips
8 flat anchovy fillets, drained
Sprigs of watercress for garnish

Using a vegetable brush, scrub the zucchini and straightneck squash thoroughly under cold running water and pat them dry with paper towels. With a sharp knife, remove the stems and cut both squash in half crosswise. Then slice each half lengthwise into eight thin strips.

In a heavy 3- to 4-quart saucepan, bring the chicken stock and the tied celery leaves, parsley sprigs and bay leaf to a boil over high heat. Add the squash, cover the pan partially, and reduce the heat to moderate. Cook for about 5 minutes, or until a slice of squash shows only slight resistance when pierced with the point of a small sharp knife. Pick out and discard the tied herbs and drain the squash in a sieve or colander. (If you like, you may drain the stock into a bowl and reserve it for another use.)

Meanwhile, combine the vinegar, salt and pepper in a deep bowl and stir with a wire whisk until the salt dissolves. Whisking constantly, pour in the olive oil in a slow, thin stream and beat until the marinade mixture is thick and smooth. Taste for seasoning. Add the squash and turn the pieces about gently with a spoon to coat them evenly. Then cover the bowl tightly with foil or plastic wrap and marinate the squash in the refrigerator for about 12 hours or overnight.

To serve, transfer the squash to a chilled platter with a slotted spoon. Moisten the squash with a few spoonfuls of the marinade and arrange the pimiento strips and anchovies attractively on top. Garnish the platter with watercress and serve at once.

Summertime Vegetable Aspic

To serve 4 to 6

9 medium-sized firm ripe tomatoes (about 3 pounds), washed, cored and coarsely chopped
2 medium-sized onions, peeled and coarsely chopped
½ cup coarsely chopped celery leaves
2 fresh parsley sprigs
1 small bay leaf
½ cup cold water
4 teaspoons unflavored gelatin
1 tablespoon strained fresh lemon juice
2 teaspoons salt
Freshly ground black pepper
1 cup finely shredded cabbage
½ cup coarsely chopped celery
⅓ cup finely chopped green pepper
1 medium-sized carrot, scraped and cut crosswise into ⅛-inch-thick slices
2 tablespoons finely chopped fresh parsley
1 tablespoon finely chopped pimiento

Combine the tomatoes, onions, celery leaves, parsley sprigs, bay leaf and ¼ cup of cold water in a 3- to 4-quart enameled or stainless-steel saucepan and bring to a boil over high heat, stirring from time to time. Reduce the heat to low and simmer partially covered for 30 minutes, or until the vegetables are very soft. Strain the contents of the pan through a fine sieve set over a bowl, pressing down on the vegetables and herbs with the back of a spoon to extract their juices before discarding them.

Meanwhile, pour the remaining ¼ cup of cold water into a small heatproof bowl and sprinkle the gelatin over it. When the gelatin has softened for 2 or 3 minutes, set the bowl in a skillet of simmering water and cook over low heat, stirring constantly, until the gelatin dissolves completely.

Stir the dissolved gelatin into the vegetable juices, add the lemon juice, salt and a few grindings of black pepper, and taste for seasoning. Refrigerate until the mixture begins to thicken and is syrupy. Then stir in the cabbage, celery, green pepper, carrot, parsley and pimiento.

Rinse a 3-cup mold under cold running water and invert it to drain. Pour the vegetable aspic mixture into the mold, cover with foil or plastic wrap and refrigerate for at least 4 hours, or until firm to the touch.

To unmold and serve the aspic, run a thin-bladed knife around the edges of the mold to loosen the sides and dip the bottom briefly in hot water. Place an inverted serving plate over the mold and, grasping plate and mold together firmly, turn them over. Rap the plate sharply on a table and the vegetable aspic should slide out easily.

Tender young spinach, usually thought of as a cooked vegetable, is combined with celery and cucumbers in this crisp, refreshing salad.

Spinach Salad

Wash the spinach under cold running water, drain and pat thoroughly dry with paper towels. Strip the leaves from the stems and discard the stems along with any tough or discolored leaves. Peel the cucumber and slice it in half lengthwise. Run the tip of a teaspoon down the center to scrape out the seeds. Cut the halves into strips ¼ inch wide and then crosswise into ¼-inch dice. To rid the cucumber of excess moisture, in a small bowl mix the diced cucumber with 1 teaspoon of salt. Let it rest for 15 minutes to ½ hour, then drain the liquid that will accumulate and pat the cucumber dice dry with paper towels.

Trim the leaves and stems of the celery; wash the stalks under cold water and dry them thoroughly with paper towels. Cut each stalk in ¼-inch strips and then cut into ¼-inch dice. Toss the spinach, cucumber and celery in a salad bowl, preferably of glass, add the olives and nuts and toss again. Chill until ready to serve.

For the dressing, with a whisk beat the vinegar, salt, pepper and mustard together in a small bowl. Still whisking, gradually pour in the oil and beat until the dressing is smooth and thick. Pour over the salad, toss until all the ingredients are thoroughly coated with the dressing and serve at once on chilled salad plates.

To serve 4 to 6

½ pound uncooked young spinach
1 large cucumber
1 teaspoon salt
4 medium-sized stalks celery
¼ cup coarsely chopped black olives
½ cup pine nuts

DRESSING

2 tablespoons red wine vinegar
½ teaspoon salt
Freshly ground black pepper
½ teaspoon dry mustard
6 tablespoons vegetable oil

Vegetable, Yoghurt and Herb Salad

To serve 4

1 medium-sized cucumber
2 tablespoons finely chopped green pepper
2 tablespoons finely chopped scallions, including 2 inches of the green tops
2 tablespoons finely cut fresh tarragon, or substitute 1 tablespoon dried tarragon
1 tablespoon finely cut fresh dill, or substitute 1 teaspoon dried dill weed
½ teaspoon fresh lemon juice
¼ teaspoon salt
1 cup unflavored yoghurt

With a small, sharp knife peel the cucumber and slice it lengthwise into halves. Scoop out the seeds by running the tip of a teaspoon down the center of each half. Chop the cucumber finely and place it in a deep bowl. Add the green pepper, scallions, tarragon, dill, lemon juice and salt and stir together thoroughly. Then add the yoghurt and turn the vegetables and herbs about with a spoon until they are well coated. Cover tightly with foil or plastic wrap and chill in the refrigerator for about 1 hour before serving.

Caesar Salad

To serve 4 to 6

2 medium-sized heads romaine lettuce
10 to 12 croutons, preferably made from French or Italian-style bread
4 to 8 tablespoons vegetable oil
1 teaspoon finely chopped garlic
2 eggs
⅛ teaspoon salt
⅛ teaspoon freshly ground black pepper
½ cup olive oil
4 tablespoons lemon juice
1 cup freshly grated Parmesan cheese
6 to 8 flat anchovies (optional)

Separate the romaine lettuce and wash the leaves under cold running water. Dry each leaf thoroughly with paper towels. Then wrap the lettuce in a dry kitchen towel and chill while you assemble the other ingredients. Cut a loaf of bread into 1½-inch-thick slices. Trim the crusts and cut each slice into 1½-inch squares. In a heavy skillet, large enough to hold all the croutons in one layer, heat 4 tablespoons of the vegetable oil over high heat until a light haze forms above it. Add the croutons and brown them on all sides, turning them with tongs, and, if necessary, add up to another 4 tablespoons of oil. Remove the pan from the heat, then add the chopped garlic and toss the croutons about in the hot fat. Remove the croutons to paper towels to drain, cool and crisp.

Plunge the eggs into rapidly boiling water for 10 seconds, remove and set aside. Break the chilled romaine into serving-sized pieces and scatter them in the bottom of a large salad bowl, preferably glass or porcelain. Add the salt, pepper and olive oil, and toss the lettuce with two large spoons or, better still, with your hands. Then break the eggs on top of the salad, add the lemon juice and mix again until the lettuce is thoroughly coated with the dressing. Add the cheese and the anchovies, if you are using them, and mix once more. Scatter the croutons over the top and serve at once on chilled salad plates.

Shaker Salad

To serve 4 to 6

½ pound green string beans, trimmed, washed and cut into 1½-inch lengths
3 tablespoons tarragon vinegar
1 tablespoon finely chopped onions
½ teaspoon crumbled dried thyme
½ teaspoon crumbled dried savory
½ teaspoon dry mustard
1 teaspoon salt
Freshly ground black pepper
½ cup olive or vegetable oil or a combination of both
2 firm heads bibb or Boston lettuce, trimmed, washed, separated in leaves and cut into 1-inch pieces (about 3 cups)
2 tablespoons finely chopped scallions, including 1 inch of the green tops

Drop the string beans into enough lightly salted boiling water to cover them by at least 1 inch. Boil briskly, uncovered, for 4 to 5 minutes, or until the beans are tender but still somewhat crisp to the bite. Drain the beans in a sieve or colander and run cold water over them to cool them quickly and set their color. Spread the beans on paper towels to drain and pat them dry with fresh paper towels. Refrigerate until ready to serve.

Just before serving, combine the vinegar, onions, thyme, savory, dry mustard, salt and a few grindings of pepper in a serving bowl and mix well with a wire whisk. Whisking constantly, pour in the oil in a slow stream and stir until the dressing is smooth and thick. Add the beans, lettuce and scallions, and toss together gently but thoroughly. Serve at once.

All-American Desserts

Fresh Blueberry Pie

In a 1- to 1½-quart enameled or stainless-steel saucepan, combine 1 cup of the blueberries, the sugar, water, lemon rind and cornstarch. Bring to a boil over high heat, then reduce the heat and, stirring almost constantly, cook for 5 to 10 minutes, until the sauce is thick and glossy. Remove from the heat and, with a rubber spatula, transfer the mixture to a small bowl to cool to lukewarm.

Spread the remaining 4 cups of blueberries out in a single layer on paper towels and pat them thoroughly dry with additional towels. Then spoon them into the pastry shell and mound the berries slightly in the center. When the sauce has cooled sufficiently, pour it into the shell.

With a whisk or a rotary or electric beater, whip the heavy cream in a cold mixing bowl until the cream begins to thicken. Then beat in the confectioners' sugar and continue to beat until the cream is stiff enough to form firm peaks on the beater when it is lifted from the bowl. Spoon the whipped cream into a pastry bag fitted with a plain or decorative tip and pipe a border around the edge of the pie. Or spoon the cream over the pie and swirl the top attractively with a spatula. Serve the pie at once.

To make one 9-inch pie

2 pints fresh whole blueberries, washed and thoroughly drained (5 cups)
1 cup sugar
1 cup water
1 teaspoon grated lemon rind
3 tablespoons cornstarch
A 9-inch fully baked pastry shell, cooled *(below)*
1 cup heavy cream
2 teaspoons confectioners' sugar

Short-Crust Pastry

PASTRY DOUGH: In a large, chilled bowl, combine the butter bits, lard, flour, sugar and salt. With your fingers rub the flour and fat together until they look like flakes of coarse meal. Do not let the mixture become oily.

Pour 3 tablespoons of ice water over the mixture all at once, toss together lightly, and gather the dough into a ball. If the dough crumbles, add up to 1 tablespoon more ice water by drops until the particles adhere.

Dust the pastry dough with a little flour and wrap it in wax paper. Refrigerate for at least 1 hour before using.

PASTRY FOR AN UNFILLED PIE SHELL: To prepare an unfilled, or "blind," pie shell, spread 1 tablespoon of softened butter over the bottom and sides of a 9-inch pie tin with a pastry brush.

Preheat the oven to 400°. On a lightly floured surface, pat the dough into a rough circle about 1 inch thick. Dust a little flour over and under it and roll it out, from the center to within an inch of the far edge of the pastry. Lift the dough and turn it clockwise about 2 inches; roll out again from the center to within an inch or so of the far edge. Repeat—lifting, turning, rolling—until the circle is about ⅛ inch thick and 13 to 14 inches in diameter. If the dough sticks to the board or table, lift it gently with a metal spatula and sprinkle flour under it.

Drape the dough over the rolling pin, lift it up and unroll it slackly over the buttered pie tin. Gently press the dough into the bottom and sides of the tin, being careful not to stretch it. With a pair of scissors, cut

To make one 9-inch pie shell

6 tablespoons unsalted butter, chilled and cut into ¼-inch bits, plus 1 tablespoon butter, softened
2 tablespoons lard, chilled and cut into ¼-inch bits
1½ cups unsifted all-purpose flour
1 tablespoon sugar
¼ teaspoon salt
3 to 4 tablespoons ice water

off the excess dough from the edges leaving a ½-inch overhang all around the outside rim. Fold the overhang under the outer edges of the dough and crimp it firmly around the rim of the pan with your fingers or the tines of a fork. To prevent the unfilled pastry from buckling as it bakes, spread a sheet of buttered aluminum foil across the tin and press it gently into the pastry shell.

TO MAKE A PARTIALLY BAKED PIE SHELL: Bake on the middle shelf of the oven for 10 minutes, then remove the foil and bake another 2 minutes.

TO MAKE A FULLY BAKED PIE SHELL: Bake the shell on the middle shelf of the oven for 10 minutes, then remove the foil and bake for another 8 minutes, or until the shell begins to brown.

Strawberry Shortcake

To make 6 small shortcakes

4 cups all-purpose flour
6 tablespoons sugar
5 teaspoons baking powder
2 teaspoons salt
12 tablespoons butter (1½ quarter-pound sticks) chilled and cut into bits
1½ cups heavy cream
6 teaspoons melted and cooled butter
2 pints of fresh, ripe strawberries
1½ teaspoons sugar
1 pint heavy cream for topping

Preheat the oven to 450°. Sift the flour, sugar, baking powder and salt together into a large bowl. Add the butter, and, with your fingertips, rub the dry ingredients and butter together until most of the lumps disappear and the mixture resembles coarse meal. Pour in the cream and mix thoroughly until a soft dough is formed. Gather it into a compact ball and place on a lightly floured board. Knead the dough for about a minute by folding it end to end and pressing down and pushing forward several times with the heel of your hand. Roll the dough out into a circle about 1 inch thick. With a 3-inch cookie cutter, cut out 6 circles. Cut the remaining dough into 6 2½-inch circles. (If there isn't enough dough, gather the scraps, knead briefly and roll out again.) Arrange the 3-inch circles on a lightly buttered cookie sheet. Brush each with a teaspoon of melted butter; top with a smaller circle. Bake in the middle of the oven for 12 to 15 minutes until firm to the touch and golden brown.

Meanwhile, chop half the strawberries coarsely, reserving the most attractive ones for the top. Separate the shortcakes. Spread a layer of chopped strawberries on the bottom circles, sprinkle with sugar and gently place the smaller circles on top. Garnish with the whole strawberries. Strawberry shortcake is traditionally served with heavy cream.

Blackberry Cobbler

To serve 4 to 6

1 pint fresh blackberries
1 cup all-purpose flour
2 teaspoons double-acting baking powder
1 cup sugar
2 eggs
¾ cup milk
1 teaspoon vanilla extract
1 teaspoon grated lemon rind
1½ cups heavy cream, chilled
2 tablespoons confectioners' sugar

Preheat the oven to 350°. Wash the blackberries in a colander set under cold running water; discard any stems or blemished fruit. Spread the berries on paper towels and pat them completely dry with additional towels. Then pour the berries into a 2-quart ovenproof mold or soufflé dish and set aside.

Sift the flour and baking powder into a large mixing bowl and drop in the sugar, eggs, milk, vanilla and lemon rind. With a wooden spoon, beat the ingredients briskly until they are thoroughly combined. Pour the batter over the berries and bake in the center of the oven for one hour, or

An old-fashioned strawberry shortcake, one of America's most popular desserts, is topped with heavy cream before being served.

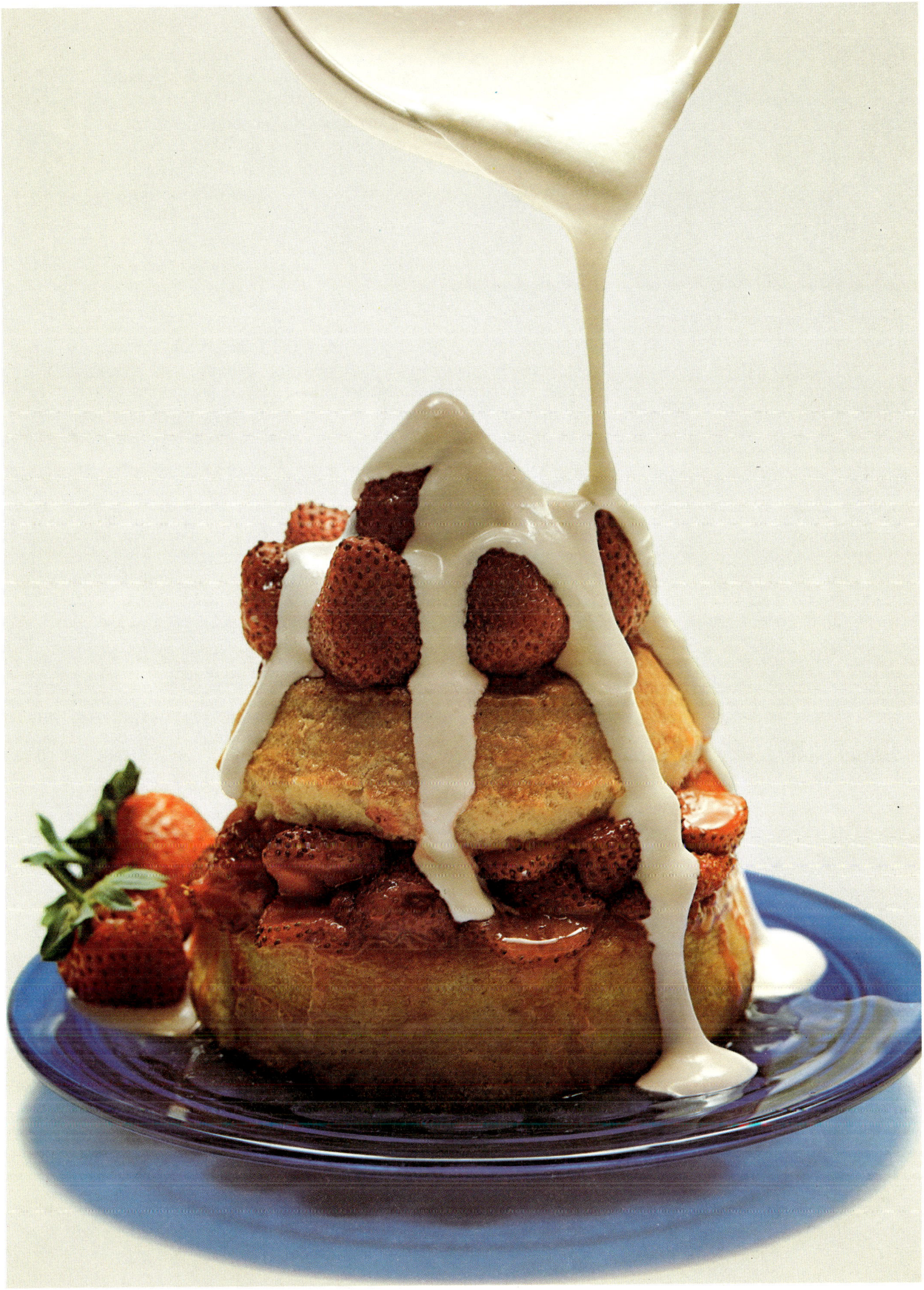

until the top is crusty brown. Remove the cobbler from the oven and let it rest while you whip the cream.

With a whisk or a rotary or electric beater, beat the cream until it foams. Then beat in the confectioners' sugar and continue to beat until the cream forms soft peaks when the beater is lifted out of the bowl. Serve the cobbler hot, accompanied by a bowl of the whipped cream.

Huckleberry Cake

To make one 8-inch cake

1 tablespoon plus ½ pound unsalted butter, softened
2 tablespoons plus 2½ cups all-purpose flour
1¼ cups sugar
4 eggs
2½ teaspoons double-acting baking powder
¼ teaspoon salt
1½ teaspoons vanilla extract
1½ cups huckleberries, or substitute 1½ cups blueberries, washed
1 cup heavy cream, chilled
2 tablespoons confectioners' sugar

Preheat the oven to 375°. With a pastry brush, spread the bottom and sides of an 8-inch springform cake pan with 1 tablespoon of the softened butter. Sprinkle evenly with 2 tablespoons of the flour, then invert and rap against a hard surface to dislodge any excess flour. Set aside.

Cream the ½ pound of softened butter and the sugar together by beating and mashing them against the sides of a bowl with the back of a wooden spoon, or by using an electric mixer set at medium speed. When light and fluffy, beat in the eggs, 1 at a time.

Sift together 2¼ cups of the flour, the baking powder and salt. Beat this into the creamed butter mixture ¼ cup at a time and, when the ingredients are well combined, beat in the vanilla extract. Place the berries in a small mixing bowl and toss with the remaining ¼ cup of flour. With a rubber spatula, gently fold the berries into the batter, being careful not to mash them. Pour into the prepared springform pan and bake in the middle of the oven for about 1 hour, or until a toothpick inserted in the center of the cake comes out clean. Remove the sides of the springform pan and cool the cake for about 15 minutes.

In a chilled mixing bowl, beat the cream with a whisk or a rotary or electric beater until it begins to thicken. Beat in the confectioners' sugar and continue to beat until the cream is thick enough to form firm peaks. Serve at once with the warm huckleberry cake. Transfer the whipped cream to a serving bowl and present it separately.

Blueberry Roll

To serve 6

1 pint (2 cups) fresh ripe blueberries
½ cup plus 2 tablespoons sugar
3 tablespoons butter, softened, plus 6 tablespoons butter, chilled and cut into ¼-inch bits
2 cups flour
2 teaspoons double-acting baking powder
½ teaspoon salt
1 egg
⅓ cup milk

Preheat the oven to 325°. Wash the blueberries in a sieve or colander set under cold running water, discarding any that are blemished. Then spread the berries on paper towels and pat them completely dry. Drop the berries into a bowl, add ½ cup of the sugar and toss gently but thoroughly together.

With a pastry brush, spread 1 tablespoon of the softened butter evenly over the bottom of a 16-by-11-inch jelly-roll pan.

Combine the remaining 2 tablespoons of sugar, the flour, baking powder and salt in a deep bowl. Add the 6 tablespoons of butter bits and, with your fingertips, rub the flour and butter together until they resemble flakes of coarse meal. Add the egg and milk, and beat vigorously with a spoon until the dough is smooth and can be gathered into a compact ball.

On a lightly floured surface, roll the dough out into a rectangle about

16 inches long, 10 inches wide and ¼ inch thick. Spread the surface of the dough with the remaining 2 tablespoons of softened butter and scatter the sugared berries evenly over it. Starting at one long end, roll up the rectangle jelly-roll fashion into a tight cylinder, sealing the ends.

Carefully transfer the blueberry roll to the buttered pan and bake in the middle of the oven for 1 hour, or until it is golden brown. Slide the roll onto a wire rack to cool to room temperature before serving.

Deep-Dish Peach Pie with Cream-Cheese Crust

In a large mixing bowl, cream the butter and cheese by beating them together with a large spoon until smooth and fluffy. Sift the combined flour, sugar and salt into the mixture, add the cream and, with your hands or a large spoon, mix thoroughly until the dough can be gathered into a compact ball. Dust lightly with flour, wrap in wax paper and refrigerate while you prepare the filling.

Preheat the oven to 350°. To peel the peaches easily, drop them into a pan of boiling water. Scoop them out after about 30 seconds, and while they are still warm, remove their skins with a small, sharp knife. Cut the peaches in half, discard the pits and slice thinly.

Combine the peaches, flour, brown sugar, melted butter and vanilla in a large bowl, and with a large spoon mix them together gently but thoroughly. With a rubber spatula, scrape the entire contents of the bowl into an 8-inch-square baking dish about 2½ inches deep. Spread the peaches out evenly. On a lightly floured surface, roll the pastry into a 10- to 11-inch square. Lift it up on the rolling pin and gently drape it over the top of the dish. Crimp the edges of the pastry to secure it around the outside of the dish and brush the pastry evenly with the egg-yolk-water mixture, then sprinkle with the sugar. Cut 2 small slits in the top of the pie to allow steam to escape and bake in the middle of the oven for 35 to 40 minutes, or until the crust is golden brown. Serve directly from the dish.

To serve 6

8 tablespoons butter (1 quarter-pound stick), softened
8 tablespoons cream cheese, softened
1¼ cups all-purpose flour
2 tablespoons sugar
¼ teaspoon salt
2 tablespoons heavy cream
FILLING
1½ pounds fresh peaches (8 to 10 medium-sized peaches)
1 tablespoon flour
2 tablespoons brown sugar
3 tablespoons melted butter
2 teaspoons vanilla
1 egg yolk, lightly beaten with 2 teaspoons cold water
1 teaspoon sugar

Old-fashioned Vanilla Ice Cream

In a heavy 1½- or 2-quart enameled or stainless-steel saucepan, heat 1 cup of the cream, the sugar, salt and the vanilla bean over low heat, stirring until the sugar is dissolved and the mixture is hot but has not come to a boil. Remove from heat and lift out the vanilla bean. Split the bean in half lengthwise and, with the tip of a small knife, scrape the seeds into the cream mixture. When the mixture has cooled somewhat, stir in the remaining 3 cups of cream.

Pack a 2-quart ice-cream freezer with layers of finely crushed or cracked ice and coarse rock salt in the proportions recommended by the freezer manufacturer, adding cold water if the directions call for it. Then pour or ladle the cream mixture into the ice-cream container and cover it. Let it stand for 3 or 4 minutes. Then turn the handle, starting slowly at first, and crank continuously until the handle can barely be moved. Wipe the lid care-

To make about 1½ quarts

4 cups heavy cream
¾ cup sugar
⅛ teaspoon salt
1½-inch piece of vanilla bean

fully, remove it and lift out the dasher. Scrape the ice cream off the dasher into the container and pack down with a spoon. Cover the container securely. Drain off any water in the bucket and repack it with ice and salt. Replace the container and let it stand 2 or 3 hours before serving.

Ginger Peach Ice Cream

To make about 1½ quarts

4 cups heavy cream
¾ cup sugar
⅛ teaspoon salt
1½ teaspoons vanilla extract
6 medium-sized firm ripe peaches
½ cup crystallized ginger, coarsely chopped

In a heavy 2- to 3-quart saucepan, heat 1 cup of the cream, the sugar and salt over low heat, stirring until the sugar is dissolved; do not let the mixture come to a boil. Pour the cream mixture into a deep bowl, stir in the remaining 3 cups of cream and the vanilla, and refrigerate until chilled.

Meanwhile, drop the peaches, 2 or 3 at a time, into enough boiling water to cover them completely and boil briskly for 2 to 3 minutes. With a slotted spoon, transfer the peaches to a sieve or colander and run cold water over them. Peel the peaches with a small sharp knife, halve them and discard the stones, then chop the fruit coarsely. Cover with foil or plastic wrap and refrigerate until ready to use.

Pack a 2-quart ice-cream freezer with layers of finely crushed or cracked ice and coarse rock salt in the proportions recommended by the freezer manufacturer. Add cold water if the manufacturer advises it. Then ladle the chilled cream mixture into the ice-cream can and cover it.

If you have a hand ice-cream maker, fill it with the chilled cream mixture and let it stand for 3 or 4 minutes before beginning to turn the handle. Then, beginning slowly at first, crank continuously for about 5 minutes. Stir in the peaches and ginger and crank for 10 to 15 minutes more. Do not stop turning at any time or the ice cream may be lumpy.

When the handle can barely be moved, the ice cream is ready to serve. If you wish to keep it for an hour or two, remove the lid and dasher. Scrape the ice cream off the dasher and pack it firmly into the container with a spoon. Cover securely, pour off any water in the bucket and repack the ice and salt solidly around it.

If you have an electric ice-cream maker, fill the can with the chilled cream mixture, cover it, turn on the switch and let the mixture churn for about 5 minutes. Stir in the peaches and ginger, cover again and continue to churn for about 10 to 15 minutes more, or until the motor slows or actually stops. Serve the ice cream immediately or follow the procedure above to keep it for an hour or two.

Lacking an ice-cream maker, stir the peaches and ginger into the chilled cream mixture and pour the mixture into three ice-cube trays from which the dividers have been removed. Spread the ice cream evenly and smooth the top with a rubber spatula. Freeze for 3 to 4 hours, stirring every 30 minutes or so and scraping into the ice cream the ice particles that form around the edges of the tray.

Tightly covered, the ice cream may safely be kept in the freezer for several weeks. Before serving, place it in the refrigerator for 20 or 30 minutes to let it soften slightly so that it can be easily served.

Red wine, brandy, fresh fruit and soda make *Sangría* a refreshing summer drink almost as popular in America as in its native Spain.

Sangría

Combine the lemon, orange, apple and ¼ cup sugar in a large pitcher. Pour in the wine and brandy and stir with a long-handled spoon until well mixed. Taste. If you prefer the *sangría* sweeter, add up to ¼ cup more sugar.

Refrigerate for at least 1 hour or until thoroughly chilled. Just before serving, pour in chilled club soda to taste, adding up to 24 ounces of the soda. Stir again, and serve at once in chilled wine glasses. Or the glasses may be filled with ice cubes before adding the *sangría*.

Mai-Tai

Combine the juice of half a lime, the apricot brandy, curaçao, rum and ice cubes in a mixing glass. Place a shaker on top of the mixing glass and, grasping them together firmly with both hands, shake vigorously. Remove the shaker, place a strainer on top of the mixing glass, and pour into a cocktail glass. Garnish with a stick of fresh pineapple.

To serve 4 to 6

½ lemon, cut into ¼-inch slices
½ orange, cut into ¼-inch slices
½ large apple, cut in half lengthwise, cored, and cut into thin wedges
¼ to ½ cup superfine sugar
1 bottle dry red wine, preferably imported Spanish wine
2 ounces (¼ cup) brandy
Club soda, chilled

To make 1 cocktail

Juice of ½ lime
½ ounce apricot brandy
½ ounce curaçao
2 ounces dark Jamaica rum
3 to 4 ice cubes
1 stick fresh pineapple, about ½ inch wide and 2 to 3 inches long

Lined up on a beach are frosty rum drinks for summer *(from left):* peach Daiquiri, Mai-Tai, Daiquiri, planter's punch and Bacardi.

To make 1 cocktail

½ fresh peach, peeled, or substitute
  ½ canned peach or 3 ounces frozen peaches
½ ounce fresh lime juice
1½ teaspoons superfine sugar
1½ ounces light rum
4 to 6 ounces shaved or finely cracked ice

Peach Daiquiri

Combine the peach, lime juice, sugar, rum and ice in the container of an electric blender, and blend at medium speed for 20 seconds. Pour the contents of the container, unstrained, into a large wine glass.

NOTE: If you have substituted a canned or frozen peach that has been packed in syrup, do not add any sugar.

To make 1 cocktail

1 teaspoon grenadine
3 ounces light Bacardi rum
1 ounce fresh lime juice
3 to 4 ice cubes

Bacardi

Combine the grenadine, rum, lime juice and ice cubes in a mixing glass. Place a shaker on top of the mixing glass and, grasping them firmly together with both hands, shake vigorously. Remove the shaker, place a strainer over the mixing glass, and pour into a cocktail glass.

Daiquiri

Combine the lime juice and sugar in a mixing glass and stir with a bar spoon to dissolve the sugar. Now add the Cointreau or Triple Sec, rum and ice. Place a shaker on top of the mixing glass and, grasping them firmly together with both hands, shake vigorously. Remove the shaker, place a strainer on top of the mixing glass, and pour into a cocktail glass.

To make your Daiquiri even foamier, try adding just a dash of egg white to the mixing glass before shaking.

To make 1 cocktail

3/4 ounce fresh lime juice
1 teaspoon superfine sugar
1 teaspoon Cointreau or Triple Sec
3 ounces light rum
3 to 4 ice cubes
Egg white (optional)

Frozen Daiquiri

Combine the lime juice, sugar, Cointreau or Triple Sec, rum and ice in an electric blender, and blend for 20 seconds at medium speed. Pour the contents of the container, unstrained, into a large wine glass, and serve with a short straw.

To make 1 cocktail

2 ounces fresh lime juice
1 teaspoon superfine sugar
1 teaspoon Cointreau or Triple Sec
3 ounces light rum
6 ounces shaved or cracked ice

Planter's Punch

Combine the lime juice and brown sugar in a Tom Collins glass. Stir with a muddler or bar spoon to dissolve the sugar, then add the rum. Fill the glass 3/4 way with shaved ice and stir again. Decorate with the slices of lime and a cherry, and if you wish, the fresh mint. Serve with a straw.

To make 1 tall drink

1½ ounces fresh lime juice
1 teaspoon brown sugar
4 ounces Jamaica rum
1½ to 2 cups finely shaved ice
2 slices lime
1 maraschino cherry
1 sprig fresh mint (optional)

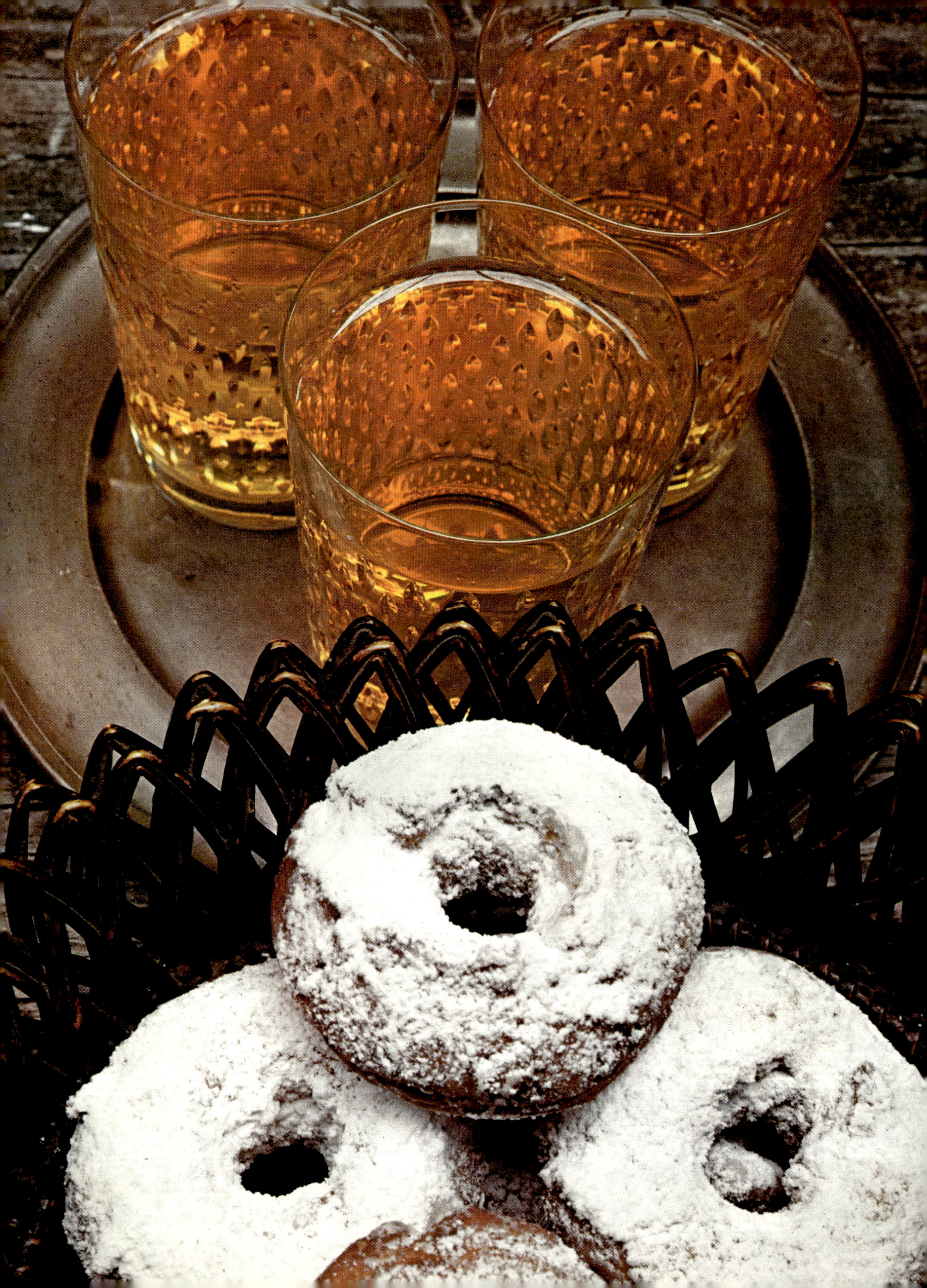

Autumn Beer Fest
Columbus Day
Succoth
Halloween

October Festivals

Autumn is the time of harvest, of warming soups, hearty meals and sweet, sticky delights for young trick-or-treaters. Apart from the 16 cookie and doughnut recipes for Halloween, all the foods on the following pages have a foreign flavor, for this is a month of ethnic festivals—Oktoberfest for Germans, Columbus Day for all Americans, but particularly for those of Italian heritage, and the Jewish harvest festival of Succoth.

German food is robustly satisfying—spareribs stuffed with apples and prunes, roasted smoked pork loin, potato pancakes and dumplings—but it also has a subtle side, revealed in such dishes as bratwurst in a sour-cream sauce or spicy fresh sauerkraut much lighter in texture and more delicate in flavor than its American counterpart. Italian pizza, minestrone and fruit-flavored ices have become all-American favorites, but the instructions for making them are all from the old country, as are the recipes for homemade ravioli and fettuccine. The recipes for a Succoth feast combine the old with the new—a traditional beef-and-sweet-potato stew with prunes along with a modern Israeli innovation, chicken and kumquats.

Apples and doughnuts mean Halloween parties. Here the apples become golden glasses of cider, and the doughnuts, lighter than any store-bought ones, are delicately flavored with nutmeg.

Beer-festival Sauerbraten

Hearty dumplings, delicate Spätzle

German potato salad

Spiced sauerkraut and red cabbage

Pizza and pasta for Columbus Day

Minestrone, Genoa style

Italy's zesty ices and rich ice creams

A harvest of Succoth dishes

Israeli chicken with kumquats

Halloween-party apple fritters

Cookie and doughnut treats

October Recipes

An Autumn Beer Fest

The biggest beer party in the world, the Oktoberfest, has spread from its native Munich to German neighborhoods in New York, Milwaukee, St. Louis and other American cities. It is a good time to hoist a stein over such autumnal fare as *Sauerbraten* and dumplings, sausages and sauerkraut.

Sauerbraten

To serve 6 to 8

½ cup dry red wine
½ cup red wine vinegar
2 cups cold water
1 medium-sized onion, peeled and thinly sliced
5 black peppercorns and 4 whole juniper berries coarsely crushed with a mortar and pestle
2 small bay leaves
1 teaspoon salt
4 pounds boneless beef roast, preferably top or bottom round or rump, trimmed of fat
3 tablespoons lard
½ cup finely chopped onions
½ cup finely chopped carrots
¼ cup finely chopped celery
2 tablespoons flour
½ cup water
½ cup gingersnap crumbs

In a 2- to 3-quart saucepan, combine the wine, vinegar, water, sliced onion, crushed peppercorns and juniper berries, bay leaves and salt. Bring this marinade to a boil over high heat, then remove it from the heat and let it cool to room temperature. Place the beef in a deep crock or a deep stainless-steel or enameled pot just large enough to hold it comfortably and pour the marinade over it. The marinade should come at least halfway up the sides of the meat; if necessary, add more wine. Turn the meat in the marinade to moisten it on all sides. Then cover the pan tightly with foil or plastic wrap and refrigerate for 2 to 3 days, turning the meat over at least twice a day.

Remove the meat from the marinade and pat it completely dry with paper towels. Strain the marinade through a fine sieve set over a bowl and reserve the liquid. Discard the spices and onions.

In a heavy 5-quart flameproof casserole, melt the lard over high heat until it begins to splutter. Add the meat and brown it on all sides, turning it frequently and regulating the heat so that it browns deeply and evenly without burning. This should take about 15 minutes. Transfer the meat to a platter, and pour off and discard all but about 2 tablespoons of the fat from the casserole. Add the chopped onions, carrots and celery to the fat in the casserole and cook them over moderate heat, stirring frequently, for 5 to 8 minutes, or until they are soft and light brown. Sprinkle 2 tablespoons of flour over the vegetables and cook, stirring constantly, for 2 or 3 minutes longer, or until the flour begins to color. Pour in 2 cups of the reserved marinade and ½ cup of water and bring to a boil over high heat. Return the meat to the casserole. Cover tightly and simmer over low heat for 2 hours, or until the meat shows no resistance when pierced with the tip of a sharp knife. Transfer the meat to a heated platter and cover it with aluminum foil to keep it warm while you make the sauce.

Pour the liquid left in the casserole into a large measuring cup and skim the fat from the surface. You will need 2½ cups of liquid for the sauce. If you have more, boil it briskly over high heat until it is reduced to that amount; if you have less, add some of the reserved marinade. Combine the liquid and the ½ cup of gingersnap crumbs in a small saucepan, and cook over moderate heat, stirring frequently, for 10 minutes. The crumbs disintegrate in the sauce and thicken it slightly. Strain the sauce through a fine

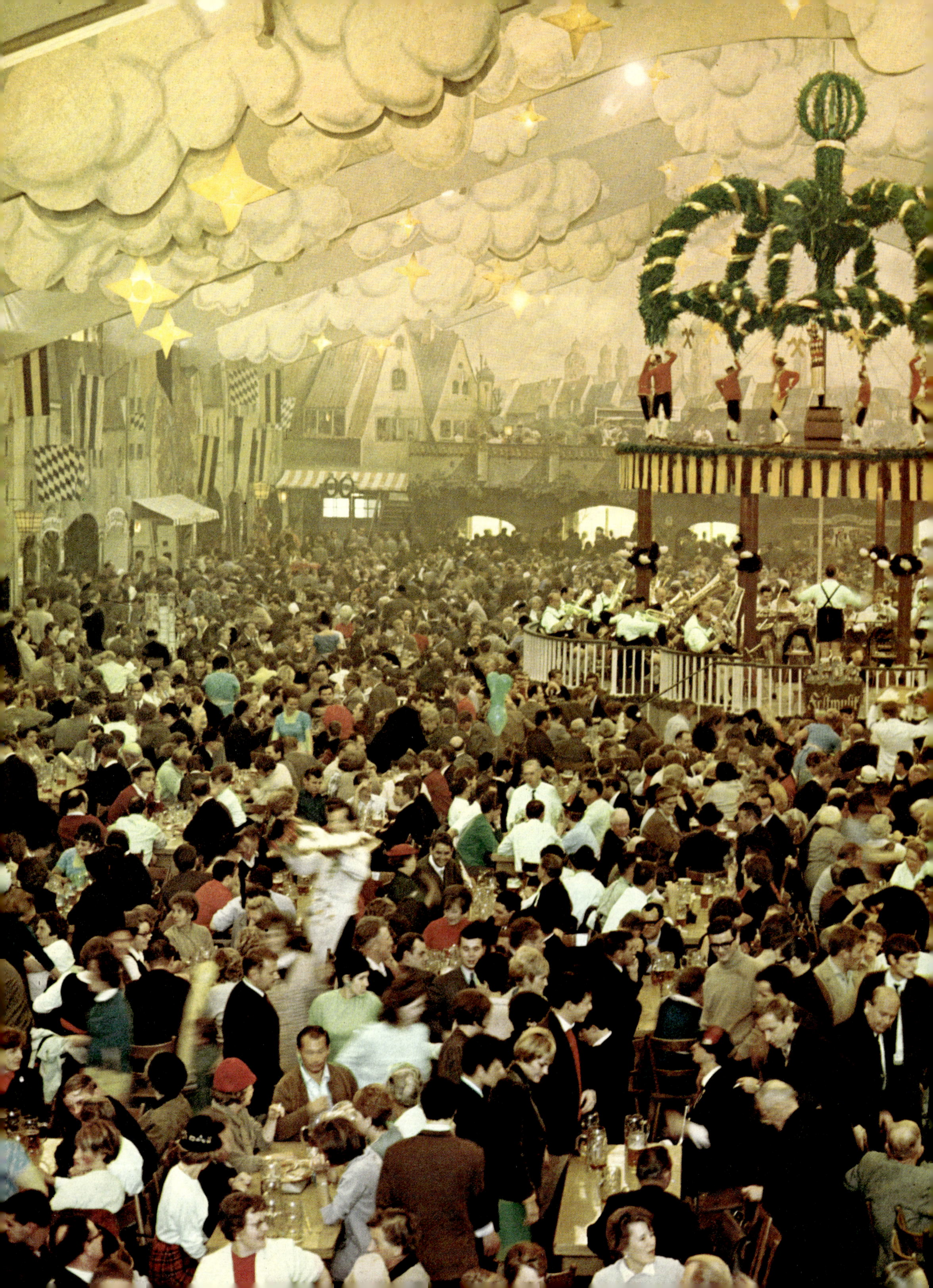

In one of seven huge tents erected by leading breweries to celebrate Munich's Oktoberfest, beer and *Gemütlichkeit* flow furiously as revelers sway arm in arm, singing and stamping their feet to the *oom-pa-pa's* of a Bavarian band. About 10 million visitors drop in on Munich in late September during this 16-day orgy of beer and food; in an average *Fest* they consume four million quarts of beer, a million sausages, almost 400,000 roast chickens, 50 tons of fish and scores of whole oxen roasted on spits.

sieve, pressing down hard with a wooden spoon to force as much of the vegetables and crumbs through as possible. Return the sauce to the pan, taste for seasoning and let it simmer over a low heat until ready to serve.

To serve, carve the meat into ¼-inch-thick slices and arrange the slices attractively in overlapping layers on a heated platter. Moisten the slices with a few tablespoons of the sauce and pass the remaining sauce separately in a sauceboat. Traditionally, *Sauerbraten* is served with dumplings or boiled potatoes and red cabbage *(pages 256 and 260)*.

NOTE: If you prefer, you may cook the *Sauerbraten* in the oven rather than on top of the stove. Bring the casserole to a boil over high heat, cover tightly and cook in a preheated 350° oven for about 2 hours.

German Yeast Dumplings

To make 12 dumplings

- ¼ cup lukewarm water (110° to 115°)
- 1 package active dry yeast
- 1 teaspoon sugar
- 1 egg
- 4 tablespoons butter, melted and cooled, plus 1 teaspoon butter, softened
- ¾ cup lukewarm milk (110° to 115°)
- 1 teaspoon salt
- ¼ teaspoon ground nutmeg
- 3½ cups all-purpose flour

Pour the lukewarm water into a small bowl and sprinkle it with the yeast and sugar. Let it stand for 2 or 3 minutes, then stir to dissolve the yeast and sugar completely. Set in a warm, draft-free place (such as a turned-off oven) for about 5 minutes, or until the mixture almost doubles in volume.

In a large mixing bowl, beat the egg with a large spoon until it is smooth and well mixed. Beat in the 4 tablespoons of melted butter, add the warm milk, salt, nutmeg and yeast solution. Then add the flour, ½ cup at a time, beating well after each addition. Mix with the spoon or your hands until the dough is firm enough to be gathered into a compact ball.

Place the dough on a lightly floured surface and knead it by pushing it down with the heels of your hands, pressing it forward and folding it back on itself. Repeat this procedure for about 10 minutes, lightly flouring the surface from time to time to prevent the dough from sticking. When the dough is smooth and elastic, place it in a bowl coated with 1 teaspoon of soft butter, drape it with a towel and let it rise in a warm draft-free place for about 1 hour, or until it doubles in bulk. Then punch the dough down with a sharp blow of your fist and knead it again for 3 or 4 minutes. Flour your hands lightly, pinch off pieces of the dough and shape them into 12 balls about 1½ inches in diameter.

Spread a damp kitchen towel over a rack set in a large roasting pan and on it arrange the dumplings about 2 inches apart. Add enough water to the pan to come to within 1 inch of the rack. Bring to a boil over high heat, cover tightly, and reduce the heat to moderate. Steam the dumplings undisturbed for 20 minutes, or until they are firm to the touch. Serve as hot as possible on a large, heated platter.

Spätzle

To make about 4 cups

- 3 cups all-purpose flour
- 1 teaspoon salt
- ¼ teaspoon ground nutmeg
- 4 eggs
- 1 cup milk
- 1 cup fine dry bread crumbs (optional)
- ¼ pound (1 stick) butter (optional)

In a large mixing bowl, combine the flour, ½ teaspoon of the salt and the nutmeg. Break up the eggs with a fork and beat them into the flour mixture. Pour in the milk in a thin stream, stirring constantly with a large spoon, and continue to stir until the dough is smooth.

Bring 2 quarts of water and the remaining ½ teaspoon of salt to a boil in a heavy 4- to 5-quart saucepan. Set a large colander, preferably one with large holes, over the saucepan and with a spoon press the dough a few tablespoons at a time through the colander directly into the boiling water. Stir the *Spätzle* gently to prevent them from sticking to each other, then boil briskly for 5 to 8 minutes, or until they are tender. Taste to make sure. Drain the *Spätzle* thoroughly in a sieve or colander. When *Spätzle* are served as a separate dish with roasted meats, such as *Sauerbraten (page 253)*, they are traditionally presented sprinkled with toasted bread crumbs. To toast the crumbs, melt ¼ pound of butter in a heavy 6- to 8-inch skillet over moderate heat. When the foam almost subsides, drop in 1 cup of bread crumbs and cook, stirring constantly, until the crumbs are golden brown.

Steamed Spiced Sauerkraut

Drain the sauerkraut, wash it thoroughly under cold running water, and let it soak in a pot of cold water for 10 to 20 minutes, depending upon its acidity. A handful at a time, squeeze the sauerkraut vigorously until it is completely dry.

In a heavy 3- to 4-quart casserole or saucepan, melt the lard over moderate heat until a light haze forms above it. Add the chopped onions and cook, stirring frequently, for 8 to 10 minutes, or until the onions are light brown. Add the sauerkraut, sugar and 2 cups of water, and mix together thoroughly, separating the strands of sauerkraut with a fork. Bury the bag of spices in the sauerkraut and place the pork or bacon on top of it. Bring to a boil over high heat, then reduce the heat to its lowest point, cover the casserole and cook, undisturbed, for 20 minutes.

Grate the raw potato directly into the casserole, and with a fork stir it into the sauerkraut mixture. Cover the casserole tightly, and cook over low heat for 1½ to 2 hours, or until the sauerkraut has absorbed most of its cooking liquid and the meat is tender when pierced with the tip of a fork. Remove and discard the spices. Taste for seasoning.

To serve, cut the meat into ¼-inch slices. Then transfer the sauerkraut to a large heated platter. Spread the sauerkraut into an even mound and arrange the slices of meat on top.

To serve 4 to 6

2 pounds fresh sauerkraut
1 tablespoon lard
½ cup finely chopped onions
1 tablespoon sugar
2 cups cold water
5 whole juniper berries, 6 whole black peppercorns, 2 small bay leaves, ¼ teaspoon caraway seeds (optional) and 1 whole allspice, wrapped together in cheesecloth
½ pound boneless smoked pork loin or butt, in 1 piece, or substitute ½ pound Canadian-style bacon in 1 piece
1 large raw potato, peeled

Roasted Smoked Pork Loin

Preheat the oven to 350°. In a heavy 8- to 10-inch skillet, melt the lard over moderate heat. Add the onions and carrots and cook over moderate heat, stirring frequently for 8 to 10 minutes, or until the vegetables are soft and light brown. With a rubber spatula, scrape the entire contents of the skillet into a heavy casserole or roasting pan just large enough to hold the pork comfortably. Place the pork loin, fat side up, on top of the vegetables and strew the crushed juniper berries around the pork. Pour in the 4 cups of water and roast uncovered in the middle of the oven, basting occasionally with the cooking juices, for 1½ hours, or until the pork is golden brown. (If you prefer to use a meat thermometer, insert it into the pork loin before placing the loin in the casserole. Be sure the tip of the thermometer does not touch any bone. Roast the pork until the thermometer reaches a temperature of 175°.)

Cut away the strings and carve the pork into ½-inch-thick chops. Ar-

To serve 4 to 6

2 tablespoons lard
1 cup coarsely chopped onions
1 cup coarsely chopped carrots
A 3½ to 4 pound smoked pork loin in one piece, with the backbone (chine) sawed through at ½-inch intervals, but left attached and tied to the loin in 2 or 3 places
4 whole juniper berries, coarsely crushed with a mortar and pestle or wrapped in a towel and crushed with a rolling pin
4 cups cold water
2 teaspoons cornstarch dissolved in 1 tablespoon cold water

range the slices attractively in slightly overlapping layers on a large heated platter. Cover and set aside.

Strain the pan juices through a fine sieve set over a bowl, pressing down hard on the vegetables with the back of the spoon before discarding them. Skim as much fat as possible from the surface, then measure the juices. If there is more than 1½ cups, boil briskly over high heat until the juices are reduced to that amount; if there is less, add water. Bring the pan juices to a boil over moderate heat in a small saucepan. Give the cornstarch mixture a quick stir to recombine it and add it to the pan. Cook, stirring constantly, until the sauce clears and thickens slightly. Moisten the meat slices with a few spoonfuls of the sauce and serve the rest in a heated sauceboat.

Steamed Bratwurst in Sour-Cream Sauce

To serve 4

8 bratwurst sausages, separated
2 tablespoons butter
¼ cup cold water
1 tablespoon flour
½ teaspoon salt
1 cup sour cream

Drop the bratwurst into 2 quarts of boiling water, remove from the heat, and let the sausages soak for 5 minutes. Drain and pat the bratwurst dry with paper towels.

Melt the butter over moderate heat in a heavy 10- to 12-inch skillet, add the bratwurst and cook, turning them frequently with tongs until they are a golden brown on all sides. Add the ¼ cup of water to the skillet, reduce the heat, and simmer, uncovered, for 15 to 20 minutes, turning the bratwurst over after 10 minutes. Replenish the water with a few tablespoons of boiling water if the cooking water boils away. Transfer the sausages to a plate, and cover them with foil.

With a whisk, beat the flour and salt into the sour cream. Then, a few tablespoons at a time, stir the sour-cream mixture into the liquid remaining in the skillet. Cook over low heat, stirring constantly, for 5 to 8 minutes, until the sauce is smooth and slightly thickened. Do not let it boil. Slice the sausages into ¼-inch rounds, drop them into the skillet, baste with the sauce and simmer only long enough to heat the bratwurst through. Transfer the entire contents of the skillet to a large, deep platter and serve immediately.

German Potato Salad with Bacon Bits

To serve 6 to 8

3 pounds medium-sized boiling potatoes (about 9), scrubbed and unpeeled
½ pound bacon, cut into ½-inch dice (about 1½ cups)
½ cup finely chopped onions
¼ cup white wine or cider vinegar
¼ cup water
½ teaspoon salt
¼ teaspoon freshly ground black pepper
1 teaspoon dry mustard
2 tablespoons finely cut fresh chives

Drop the potatoes into enough lightly salted boiling water to cover them completely, and boil briskly, uncovered, until they show only slight resistance when pierced with the point of a sharp knife. Do not overcook. Drain the potatoes in a colander, peel and cut them into ¼-inch-thick slices. Set aside in a large bowl and cover tightly with foil.

In a heavy 8-inch skillet, fry the bacon over moderate heat until brown and crisp. With a slotted spoon, transfer the dice to paper towels to drain. Add the onions to the fat remaining in the pan and stir over moderate heat until they are soft and golden. Add the vinegar, water, salt, pepper and mustard and bring the sauce to a boil. Pour the hot sauce over the potatoes, turning the slices with a rubber spatula to coat them evenly. Stir in the bacon and chives and taste for seasoning. Serve at once.

Spareribs with stuffing of apples and prunes, served with hot German potato salad and beer, are Oktoberfest favorites in Milwaukee.

Stuffed Spareribs

Preheat the oven to 350°. Sprinkle the meaty sides of the spareribs with 2 teaspoons of the salt and a few grindings of pepper. Place one strip of ribs meat side down and spread it evenly with all the prunes and apples. Sprinkle with the brown sugar, the remaining salt and the cinnamon, and cover with the other strip of spareribs, meat side up. Tie the two together, crosswise and lengthwise, securely enclosing the stuffing. Place the ribs on a rack set in a shallow roasting pan and bake in the middle of the oven for 1½ hours, or until the ribs show no resistance when pierced with the tip of a knife. Cut away the strings and serve the spareribs.

To serve 4

2 strips of spareribs, each about 10 inches long, trimmed of excess fat (about 3 to 3½ pounds in all)
3 teaspoons salt
Freshly ground black pepper
1 pound pitted dried prunes, halved (about 2 cups)
4 large firm apples, preferably green cooking apples, peeled, cored and cut into ½-inch-thick slices
¼ cup light-brown sugar
1 tablespoon ground cinnamon

Rouladen—Braised Stuffed Steak Rolls

To serve 6

3 pounds top round steak, sliced ½ inch thick, trimmed of all fat, and pounded ¼ inch thick
6 teaspoons Düsseldorf-style prepared mustard, or substitute 6 teaspoons other hot prepared mustard
¼ cup finely chopped onions
6 slices lean bacon, each about 8 inches long
3 dill pickles, rinsed in cold water and cut lengthwise into halves
3 tablespoons lard
2 cups water
1 cup coarsely chopped celery
¼ cup thinly sliced leeks, white part only
1 tablespoon finely chopped scraped parsnip
3 parsley sprigs
1 teaspoon salt
1 tablespoon butter
2 tablespoons flour

Cut the steak into 6 rectangular pieces about 4 inches wide and 8 inches long. Spread each rectangle with a teaspoon of mustard, sprinkle it with 2 teaspoons of onions, and place a slice of bacon down the center. Lay a strip of pickle across the narrow end of each piece and roll the meat around it, jelly-roll fashion, into a cylinder. Tie the rolls at each end with kitchen cord.

In a heavy 10- to 12-inch skillet melt the lard over moderate heat until it begins to splutter. Add the beef rolls, and brown them on all sides, regulating the heat so they color quickly and evenly without burning. Transfer the rolls to a plate, pour the water into the skillet and bring it to a boil, meanwhile scraping in any brown particles clinging to the bottom and sides of the pan. Add the celery, leeks, parsnip, parsley and salt, and return the beef rolls to the skillet. Cover, reduce the heat to low, and simmer for 1 hour, or until the meat shows no resistance when pierced with a fork. Turn the rolls once or twice during the cooking period. Transfer the rolls to a heated platter, and cover with foil to keep them warm while you make the sauce.

Strain the cooking liquid left in the skillet through a fine sieve, pressing down hard on the vegetables before discarding them. Measure the liquid, return it to the skillet, and boil briskly until it is reduced to 2 cups. Remove from the heat. Melt the butter in a small saucepan over moderate heat and, when the foam subsides, sprinkle in the flour. Lower the heat and cook, stirring constantly, until the flour turns a golden brown. Be careful not to let it burn. Gradually add the reduced cooking liquid, beating vigorously with a whisk until the sauce is smooth and thick. Taste for seasoning and return the sauce and the *Rouladen* to the skillet. Simmer over low heat only long enough to heat the rolls through. Serve the rolls on a heated platter and pour the sauce over them. *Rouladen* are often accompanied by red cabbage (*below*) and dumplings or boiled potatoes.

Red Cabbage with Apples

To serve 4 to 6

A 2- to 2½-pound red cabbage
⅔ cup red wine vinegar
2 tablespoons sugar
2 teaspoons salt
2 tablespoons lard or bacon fat
2 medium-sized cooking apples, peeled, cored and cut into ⅛-inch-thick wedges
½ cup finely chopped onions
1 whole onion, peeled and pierced with 2 whole cloves
1 small bay leaf
1 cup boiling water
3 tablespoons dry red wine
3 tablespoons red currant jelly (optional)

Wash the head of cabbage under cold running water, remove the tough outer leaves, and cut the cabbage into quarters. To shred the cabbage, cut out the core and slice the quarters crosswise into ⅛-inch-wide strips.

Drop the cabbage into a large mixing bowl, sprinkle it with the vinegar, sugar and salt, then toss the shreds about with a spoon to coat them evenly with the mixture. In a heavy 4- to 5-quart casserole, melt the lard or bacon fat over moderate heat. Add the apples and chopped onions and cook, stirring frequently, for 5 minutes, or until the apples are lightly browned. Add the cabbage, the whole onion with cloves, and the bay leaf; stir thoroughly and pour in the boiling water. Bring to a boil over high heat, stirring occasionally, and reduce the heat to its lowest possible point. Cover and simmer for 1½ to 2 hours, or until the cabbage is tender. Check from time to time to make sure that the cabbage is moist. If it seems dry, add a tablespoon of boiling water. When the cabbage is done, there should be almost no liquid left in the casserole. Just before serving remove the onion and bay leaf, and stir in the wine and the currant jelly. Taste for seasoning, then transfer the entire contents of the casserole to a heated platter or bowl and serve.

A rich brown *roulade*—steak roll—accompanied by red cabbage and dumplings makes an autumn meal that will be very satisfying.

Potato Dumplings

To make 15 to 20 dumplings

½ cup plus 2 tablespoons butter
1 cup fine dry white bread crumbs
2 or 3 slices fresh white homemade-type bread, crusts removed
½ cup all-purpose flour
½ cup regular farina, not the quick-cooking type
3½ teaspoons salt
⅛ teaspoon ground nutmeg
⅛ teaspoon white pepper
3½ cups hot or cold riced potatoes, made from 4 or 5 medium-sized baking potatoes (about 1½ pounds), boiled, peeled and forced through a ricer
2 eggs

In a heavy 6- to 8-inch skillet, melt ½ cup of the butter over moderate heat. When the foam begins to subside, drop in the bread crumbs and cook, stirring constantly, until they are light brown. Set the toasted crumbs aside off the heat.

With a small, sharp knife, cut the bread into ½-inch squares (there should be about 1½ cups). Melt the remaining 2 tablespoons of butter in a heavy 8- to 10-inch skillet, add the bread and cook over moderate heat, stirring frequently, until the cubes are light brown on all sides. Add more butter, a tablespoon at a time, if necessary to prevent the bread from burning. Spread the croutons on a double thickness of paper towels to drain.

Combine the flour, farina, 1½ teaspoons of salt, the nutmeg and white pepper in a small bowl. Then, with a large spoon, beat them, a few tablespoons at a time, into the riced potatoes. Lightly beat the two eggs with a fork, and then beat them into the potato mixture. Continue to beat until the dough holds its shape lightly in a spoon. If it seems too thin, stir in a little more flour, a teaspoon at a time until the desired consistency is reached.

Lightly flour your hands and shape each dumpling in the following fashion: Scoop off about 2 tablespoons of dough and form it into a rough ball. Press a hole in the center with a fingertip, drop in 3 or 4 of the reserved croutons, then gather the outer edges of the opening together. Gently roll the dumpling into a ball again.

Bring 4 quarts of water and the remaining 2 teaspoons of salt to a bubbling boil in a deep 6- to 8-quart pot. Drop in all the dumplings, and stir gently once or twice to prevent them from sticking to one another or to the bottom of the pan. Simmer over moderate heat for 12 to 15 minutes, or until the dumplings rise to the surface of the water. Cook 1 minute longer, then remove the dumplings from the pot with a slotted spoon and arrange them on a large heated platter. Serve at once, sprinkled with the reserved toasted bread crumbs.

Potato Pancakes with Applesauce

To make about 8 pancakes

6 medium potatoes (about 2 pounds), preferably baking potatoes
2 eggs
¼ cup finely grated onion
⅓ cup flour
1 teaspoon salt
Bacon fat or lard
Applesauce or imported lingonberry preserves

Peel the potatoes and as you proceed drop them into cold water to prevent their discoloring. In a large mixing bowl, beat the eggs enough to break them up, add the onion and gradually beat in the flour and salt. One at a time, pat the potatoes dry and grate them coarsely into a sieve or colander. Press each potato down firmly into the sieve to squeeze out as much moisture as possible, then immediately stir it into the egg and onion batter.

Preheat the oven to 250°. In a heavy 8- to 10-inch skillet melt 8 tablespoons of bacon fat or lard over high heat until it splutters. Pour in ⅓ cup of the potato mixture and, with a large spatula, flatten it into a pancake about 5 inches in diameter. Fry it over moderate heat for about 2 minutes on each side. When the pancake is golden brown on both sides and crisp around the edges, transfer it to a heated, ovenproof plate and keep it warm in the oven. Continue making similar pancakes with the remaining batter, adding more fat to the pan when necessary to keep it at a depth of ¼ inch. Serve the pancakes as soon as possible with applesauce or lingonberry preserves.

Columbus Day Dishes

For Americans of Italian origin, October 12 has become a day to honor their famous countryman from Genoa, Christopher Columbus. For all Americans it is a time to enjoy the foods later Italian discoverers brought to U.S. shores.

Pizza

Sprinkle the yeast and a pinch of sugar into ¼ cup of lukewarm water. Be sure that the water is lukewarm (110° to 115°—neither hot nor cool to the touch). Let it stand for 2 or 3 minutes, then stir the yeast and sugar into the water until completely dissolved. Set the cup in a warm, draft-free place (a turned-off oven would be best) for 3 to 5 minutes, or until the yeast bubbles up and the mixture almost doubles in volume. If the yeast does not bubble, start over again with fresh yeast.

Into a large bowl, sift the all-purpose flour and salt, or pour in the granulated flour and salt. Make a well in the center of the flour and pour in the yeast mixture, 1 cup of lukewarm water and ¼ cup of the olive oil. Mix the dough with a fork or your fingers. When you can gather it into a rough ball, place the dough on a floured board and knead it for 15 minutes, or until smooth, shiny and elastic. (If you have an electric mixer with a paddle and dough hook, put the ingredients in a bowl and, at medium speed, mix with the paddle until combined. At high speed knead them with the dough hook for 6 to 8 minutes.) Dust the dough lightly with flour, put in a large clean bowl and cover. Set the bowl in a warm, draft-free spot for 1½ hours, or until the dough has doubled in bulk.

Now preheat the oven to 500°. Punch the dough down with your fists and break off about one fourth of it to make the first of the 4 pizzas. Knead the small piece on a floured board or pastry cloth for a minute or so, working in a little flour if the dough seems sticky. With the palm of your hand, flatten the ball into a circle about 1 inch thick. Hold the circle in your hands and stretch the dough by turning the circle and pulling your hands apart gently at the same time. When the circle is about 7 or 8 inches across, spread it out on the floured board again and pat it smooth, pressing together any tears in the dough. Then roll the dough with a rolling pin, from the center to the far edge, turning it clockwise after each roll, until you have a circle of pastry about 10 inches across and about ⅛ inch thick. With your thumbs, crimp or flute the edge of the circle until it forms a little rim. Dust a large baking sheet lightly with corn meal and place the pizza dough on top of it. Knead, stretch and roll the rest of the dough into 3 more pizzas. Pour ½ cup of the tomato sauce on each pie and swirl it around with a pastry brush or the back of a spoon. To make a cheese pizza, sprinkle the sauce with ½ cup of grated *mozzarella* and 2 tablespoons of grated Parmesan. Dribble 2 tablespoons of the olive oil over the pizza and bake it on the lowest shelf or the floor of the oven for 10 minutes, or until the crust is lightly browned and the filling bubbling hot.

ALTERNATIVE GARNISHES: You may top the pizza with almost any sort of seafood, meat or vegetable you like, using or omitting the *mozzarella* or

---

To make 4 ten-inch pizzas

2 packages active dry yeast
Pinch of sugar
1¼ cups lukewarm water
3½ cups all-purpose or granulated flour
1 teaspoon salt
¾ cup olive oil
Corn meal
2 cups tomato and garlic sauce (*page 265*)
1 pound *mozzarella* cheese, coarsely grated or cut in ¼-inch dice
½ cup freshly grated imported Parmesan cheese

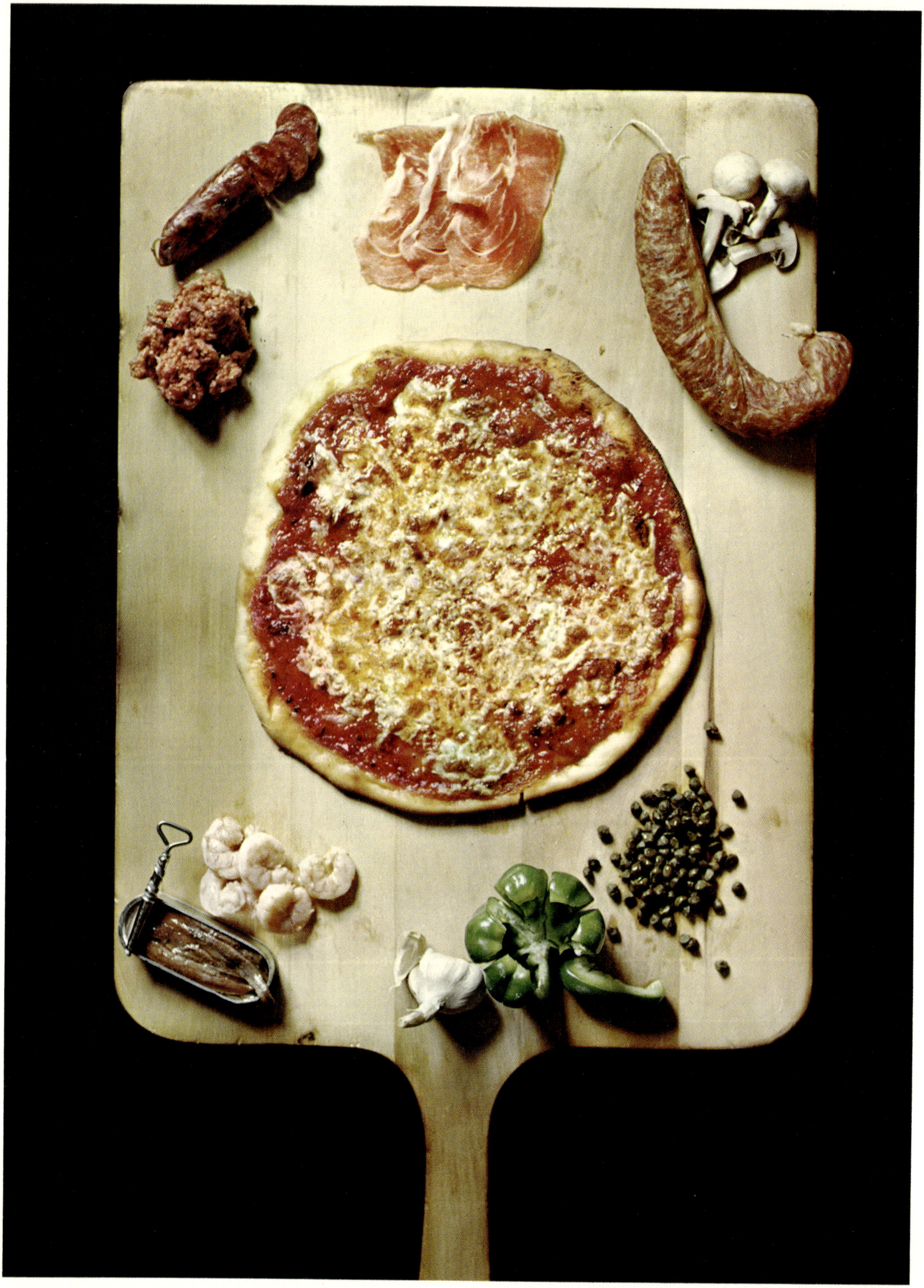

Parmesan. Swirl the pie with ½ cup of tomato sauce first, as for a cheese pizza. Then top with such garnishes as shrimp, anchovies, sausage or *peperoni* slices, prosciutto slivers, tiny meatballs, garlic slices, strips of green pepper, capers, whole or sliced mushrooms. They may be used alone or in suitable combinations. Dribble 2 tablespoons of olive oil over the pizza after garnishing and before baking it.

Salsa Pizzaiola —Tomato-and-Garlic Sauce

In a 3- to 4-quart enameled or stainless-steel saucepan, heat the 3 tablespoons of olive oil and cook the finely chopped onions in it over moderate heat, stirring frequently, for 7 or 8 minutes. When the onions are soft and transparent but are not brown, add the tablespoon of finely chopped garlic and cook for another 1 or 2 minutes, stirring constantly. Then stir in the coarsely chopped tomatoes and their liquid, the tomato paste, oregano, basil, bay leaf, sugar, salt and a few grindings of black pepper. Bring the sauce to a boil, turn the heat very low and simmer uncover, occasionally, for about 1 hour.

When finished, the sauce should be thick and fairly smooth. Remove the bay leaf. Taste and season the sauce with salt and freshly ground black pepper. If you wish a smoother texture, purée the sauce through a food mill, or rub it through a sieve with the back of a large spoon.

To make about 3 cups

3 tablespoons olive oil
1 cup finely chopped onions
1 tablespoon finely chopped garlic
4 cups Italian plum or whole-pack tomatoes, coarsely chopped but not drained
1 six-ounce can tomato paste
1 tablespoon dried oregano, crumbled
1 tablespoon finely cut fresh basil or 1 teaspoon dried basil, crumbled
1 bay leaf
2 teaspoons sugar
1½ teaspoons salt
Freshly ground black pepper

Minestrone, Genoa Style

Bring 1 quart of water to a bubbling boil in a heavy 3- to 4-quart saucepan. Add the ½ cup of beans (either marrow, Great Northern, white kidney or navy) and boil them briskly for 2 minutes. Remove the pan from the heat and let the beans soak undisturbed in the water for 1 hour. Then return the pan to the stove, and over low heat simmer the beans uncovered for 1 to 1½ hours, or until they are barely tender. Drain the beans thoroughly and set them aside in a bowl.

Melt the butter over moderate heat in a heavy 10- to 12-inch skillet. When the foam subsides, add the peas, zucchini, carrots, potatoes and celery. Tossing the vegetables constantly with a wooden spoon, cook for 2 or 3 minutes, or until they are all lightly coated with butter but not browned. Set aside.

Render the salt pork dice by frying them in a 6- to 8-quart soup pot or kettle over moderate heat, stirring frequently. When the pork dice are crisp and brown, lift them out with a slotted spoon and set them aside to drain on paper towels. Stir the onions and leeks (or if leeks are unavailable, substitute another ½ cup of onions) into the fat remaining in the pot and cook, stirring constantly, for 7 or 8 minutes, or until the vegetables are soft and lightly browned. Stir in the coarsely chopped tomatoes, the vegetables from the skillet, the chicken stock, the bay leaf and parsley sprigs, salt and a few grindings of pepper. Bring the soup to a boil over high heat, reduce

To serve 8

½ cup dry white beans
4 tablespoons butter
1 cup fresh green peas (about 1 pound unshelled)
1 cup diced unpeeled but scrubbed zucchini (about ½ pound)
1 cup diced carrots
1 cup diced potatoes
⅓ cup thinly sliced celery
2 ounces salt pork, diced
2 tablespoons finely chopped onions
½ cup finely chopped leeks
2 cups drained canned whole-pack tomatoes, coarsely chopped
2 quarts chicken stock, fresh or canned
1 bay leaf and 2 parsley sprigs, tied together
1 teaspoon salt
Freshly ground black pepper
½ cup plain white raw rice

All of the ingredients surrounding the pie in the picture can be used to garnish a pizza, one of America's favorite Italian foods. Reading clockwise from top, center, they are: prosciutto, mushrooms and salami, capers, green peppers, garlic, shrimp and anchovies, chopped beef, *peperoni*.

GARNISH
1 tablespoon finely cut fresh basil or 1 teaspoon dried basil, crumbled
1 tablespoon finely chopped fresh parsley
½ teaspoon finely chopped garlic
½ cup freshly grated imported Parmesan cheese

the heat and simmer, with the soup pot partially covered, for 25 minutes.

Remove and discard the bay leaf and parsley sprigs, add the rice, white beans and salt pork dice and cook for about 15 to 20 minutes longer, or until the rice is tender. Taste the soup and season it with salt and pepper if needed. Serve, sprinkled with the herb and garlic garnish. Pass a bowl of the grated cheese separately.

To make about 45
1 cup *ricotta*
½ cup farmer cheese, rubbed through a fine sieve
¾ cup freshly grated imported Parmesan cheese
2 teaspoons grated onion
3 egg yolks
1½ teaspoons salt
Pasta dough *(opposite)*

Ravioli

In a large mixing bowl, combine the 1 cup of *ricotta*, the farmer cheese, the ¾ cup of grated Parmesan cheese, grated onion, 3 egg yolks and 1½ teaspoons of salt and carefully stir them together until they are well mixed. Set aside until you have rolled out the dough.

Divide the pasta dough into four pieces and roll out the first one quarter of the dough to make it as thin as possible. Cover the rolled pasta with a damp towel to prevent its drying out, and roll out the second quarter of dough to a similar size and shape.

Using the first sheet of rolled-out pasta as a sort of checkerboard, place a mound of about 1 teaspoon of the cheese-and-egg-yolk mixture every 2 inches across and down the pasta. Dip a pastry brush or your index finger into a bowl of water and make vertical and horizontal lines in a checkerboard pattern on the sheet of pasta, between the mounds of cheese-and-egg-yolk filling. Be sure to use enough water to wet the lines evenly (the water will act as a bond to hold the finished ravioli together). Then carefully spread the second sheet of rolled-out pasta on top of the first one, pressing down firmly along the wetted lines.

With a ravioli cutter, a pastry wheel or a small, sharp knife, cut the pasta into squares along the wetted lines. Separate the mounds of ravioli and set them aside on wax paper. In the same fashion, roll out, fill and cut the 2 other portions of dough.

To cook, drop the ravioli into 6 to 8 quarts of rapidly boiling salted water and stir them gently with a wooden spoon, to keep them from sticking to one another or to the bottom of the pot. Boil the ravioli for about 8 minutes, or until they are tender, then drain them thoroughly in a large sieve or colander. Serve the ravioli with tomato sauce *(page 268)* or add butter and freshly grated imported Parmesan cheese, and gently stir them all together immediately before serving.

MEAT FILLING
3 tablespoons butter
4 tablespoons finely chopped onions
¾ pound finely ground raw veal
1 ten-ounce package frozen chopped spinach, defrosted, thoroughly squeezed and chopped again, or ¾ pound fresh spinach, cooked, squeezed and chopped
½ cup freshly grated imported Parmesan cheese
Pinch of ground nutmeg
3 eggs
Salt

MEAT FILLING FOR RAVIOLI: Melt the 3 tablespoons of butter in a small skillet and cook the onions, stirring frequently for about 7 or 8 minutes, or until they are soft and transparent but not brown. Add the ¾ pound finely ground raw veal and cook, stirring constantly, until the veal loses its red color and any accumulating liquid in the pan cooks completely away. Transfer the entire contents of the skillet to a mixing bowl and stir in the chopped spinach, grated Parmesan cheese and a pinch of nutmeg. In a separate bowl, beat the eggs lightly and add them to the onion, veal and spinach mixture. Taste and season with salt.

Pasta Dough

Pour the flour into a large mixing bowl or in a heap on a pastry board, make a well in the center of the flour and in it put the egg, egg white, oil and salt. Mix together with a fork or your fingers until the dough can be gathered into a rough ball. Moisten any remaining dry bits of flour with drops of water and press them into the ball.

TO MAKE PASTA BY HAND: Knead the dough on a floured board, working in a little extra flour if the dough seems sticky. After about 10 minutes, the dough should be smooth, shiny and elastic. Wrap it in wax paper and let the dough rest for at least 10 minutes before rolling it.

Divide the dough into 2 balls. Place 1 ball on a floured board or pastry cloth and flatten it with your hand into an oblong about 1 inch thick. Dust the top lightly with flour. Using a heavy rolling pin, start at one end of the oblong and roll it out lengthwise away from yourself to within an inch or so of the far edge. Turn the dough crosswise and roll across its width. Repeat, turning and rolling the dough, until it is paper thin. If the dough begins to stick, lift it carefully and sprinkle more flour under it.

To make about ¾ pound

1½ cups unsifted all-purpose flour
1 egg
1 egg white
1 tablespoon olive oil
1 teaspoon salt
A few drops of water

Topped with a masking of tomato sauce and a sprinkling of Parmesan cheese, the completed squares of ravioli—pasta stuffed with a meat mixture—are ready for the table.

Salsa di Pomodori—Tomato Sauce

To make about 1½ cups

2 tablespoons olive oil
½ cup finely chopped onions
2 cups Italian plum or whole-pack tomatoes, coarsely chopped but not drained
3 tablespoons tomato paste
1 tablespoon finely cut fresh basil or 1 teaspoon dried basil
1 teaspoon sugar
½ teaspoon salt
Freshly ground black pepper

Using a 2- to 3-quart enameled or stainless-steel saucepan, heat the olive oil until a light haze forms over it. Add the onions and cook them over moderate heat for 7 to 8 minutes, or until they are soft but not browned. Add the tomatoes, tomato paste, basil, sugar, salt and a few grindings of pepper. Reduce the heat to very low and simmer, with the pan partially covered, for about 40 minutes. Stir occasionally.

Press the sauce through a fine sieve (or a food mill) into a bowl or pan. Taste for seasoning and serve hot.

Pesto—Basil Sauce, Genoa Style

To make about 1½ to 2 cups

2 cups fresh basil leaves, stripped from their stems, coarsely chopped and tightly packed; or substitute 2 cups fresh flat-leaf Italian parsley, coarsely chopped, and 2 tablespoons dried basil leaves
1 teaspoon salt
½ teaspoon freshly ground black pepper
1 to 2 teaspoons finely chopped garlic
2 tablespoons finely chopped pine nuts or walnuts
1 to 1½ cups olive oil
½ cup freshly grated imported *sardo*, *romano* or Parmesan cheese

TO MAKE THE PESTO IN A BLENDER, combine the coarsely chopped fresh basil (or fresh parsley and dried basil), salt, pepper, garlic, pine nuts or walnuts and 1 cup of olive oil in the blender jar. Blend them at high speed until the ingredients are smooth, stopping the blender every 5 or 6 seconds to push the herbs down with a rubber spatula.

The sauce should be thin enough to run off the spatula easily. If it seems too thick, blend in as much as ½ cup more olive oil. Transfer the sauce to a bowl and stir in the grated cheese.

TO MAKE THE PESTO BY HAND, crush the coarsely chopped fresh basil (or fresh parsley and dried basil) with a mortar and pestle or place in a heavy mixing bowl and crush with the back of a large wooden spoon until the herbs are smooth and almost pastelike. Work in the salt and pepper, garlic, and pine nuts or walnuts, and then add the olive oil ½ cup at a time, continuing to crush the herbs. When the sauce is thin enough to run off the pestle or spoon easily, mix in the grated cheese. Serve the *pesto* thoroughly mixed into hot drained pasta that has been tossed first with a few tablespoons of soft butter.

Fettuccine with Butter Sauce

To serve 4

8 tablespoons (1 quarter-pound stick) butter, softened
¼ cup heavy cream
½ cup freshly grated imported Parmesan cheese
6 to 8 quarts water
1 tablespoon salt
1 pound *fettuccine*
Freshly grated imported Parmesan cheese

Cream the ¼ pound of softened butter by beating it vigorously against the sides of a heavy bowl with a wooden spoon until it is light and fluffy. Beat in the cream a little at a time, and then, a few tablespoonfuls at a time, beat in ½ cup of grated cheese. Cover the bowl and set it aside—in the refrigerator, if the sauce is not to be used at once. If you do refrigerate the sauce, be sure to bring to room temperature before tossing it with the *fettuccine*.

Set a large serving bowl or casserole in a 250° oven to heat while you cook the *fettuccine*. Bring the water and salt to a bubbling boil in a large soup pot or kettle. Drop in the *fettuccine* and stir it gently with a wooden fork for a few moments to prevent the strands from sticking to one another or to the bottom of the pot. Boil over high heat, stirring occasionally, for 5 to 8 minutes, or until the pasta is tender. (Test it by tasting; it should be soft but *al dente*—that is, slightly resistant to the bite.) Immediately drain the *fettuccine* into a colander and lift the strands with 2 forks to make sure it is thoroughly drained. Transfer it at once to the hot serving bowl.

Add the creamed butter-and-cheese mixture and toss it with the *fettuccine* until every strand is well coated. Taste and season generously with salt and pepper. Serve the *fettuccine* at once. Pass the extra grated cheese separately.

Fresh from the broiler, spinach *gnocchi* balls are delicate in taste and texture. They are a specialty of Genoa, Columbus' birthplace.

Spinach Gnocchi

In an 8- to 10-inch enameled or stainless-steel skillet, melt 4 tablespoons of butter over moderate heat. Add the chopped fresh or frozen spinach and cook, stirring constantly, for 2 to 3 minutes, or until almost all moisture has boiled away and the spinach begins to stick lightly to the skillet. Add the ¾ cup of *ricotta* and cook, stirring, for 3 or 4 minutes longer.

With a rubber spatula, transfer the contents of the skillet to a mixing bowl and mix in the 2 lightly beaten eggs, 6 tablespoons of flour, ¼ cup of the grated cheese, ½ teaspoon salt, pepper and nutmeg. Refrigerate for 30 minutes to 1 hour, or until the *gnocchi* mixture is quite firm.

Preheat the broiler. Bring the 6 to 8 quarts of water and 1 tablespoon of salt to a simmer over moderate heat in a large soup pot or saucepan. Flour your hands lightly and pick up about 1 tablespoon of the chilled *gnocchi* mixture at a time. Shape the tablespoonfuls into small balls about 1½ inches in diameter. Gently drop the balls into the simmering water and cook them uncovered for 5 to 8 minutes, or until they puff slightly and are somewhat firm to the touch. With a slotted spoon, lift the *gnocchi* out of the water and set them aside on a paper towel to drain.

Pour 2 tablespoons of the melted butter into a shallow 8-by-12-inch flameproof serving dish and swirl the butter around until the bottom of the dish glistens. Arrange the *gnocchi* in the dish in one layer ¼-inch apart, dribble the remaining 2 tablespoons of melted butter over them, and sprinkle with the remaining ½ cup of grated cheese. Set under the broiler, 3 inches from the heat, for 3 minutes, or until the cheese melts.

Serve the *gnocchi* at once, directly from the flameproof dish. Serve additional grated cheese separately, if you wish.

To serve 4 to 6

4 tablespoons butter
2 ten-ounce packages frozen chopped spinach, thoroughly defrosted, squeezed completely dry, and chopped very fine (about 1½ cups), or 1½ pounds fresh spinach, cooked, squeezed and chopped
¾ cup *ricotta* cheese, or substitute whole-curd cottage cheese, rubbed through a sieve
2 eggs, lightly beaten
6 tablespoons flour
¾ cup freshly grated imported Parmesan cheese
½ teaspoon salt
½ teaspoon freshly ground black pepper
Pinch of ground nutmeg
6 to 8 quarts water
1 tablespoon salt
4 tablespoons melted butter

To make about 1½ pints of each flavor

LEMON ICE
2 cups water
1 cup sugar
1 cup lemon juice

ORANGE ICE
2 cups water
¾ cup sugar
1 cup orange juice
Juice of 1 lemon

COFFEE ICE
1 cup water
½ cup sugar
2 cups strong *espresso* coffee

STRAWBERRY ICE
1 cup water
½ cup sugar
2 cups fresh ripe strawberries, puréed through sieve or food mill
2 tablespoons lemon juice

To make 1 to 1½ quarts of each flavor

VANILLA ICE CREAM
2 cups light cream
2-inch piece of vanilla bean or
 1 teaspoon vanilla extract
8 egg yolks
½ cup sugar
1 cup heavy cream

PISTACHIO ICE CREAM
2 cups light cream
8 egg yolks
6 tablespoons sugar
2½ tablespoons ground or crushed shelled pistachio nuts
1 cup heavy cream
7 drops green food coloring
5½ tablespoons chopped shelled pistachio nuts
¼ cup ground blanched almonds

COFFEE ICE CREAM
2 cups light cream
2-inch strip of fresh lemon peel
8 egg yolks
6 tablespoons sugar
2 tablespoons *espresso* coffee
2 cups heavy cream

Granite—Italian Ices

In a 1½- to 2-quart saucepan, bring the water and sugar to a boil over moderate heat, stirring only until the sugar dissolves. Timing from the moment the sugar and water begin to boil, let the mixture cook for exactly 5 minutes. Immediately remove the pan from the heat and let the syrup cool to room temperature.

Depending on which of the flavored ices you want to make, stir in the lemon juice, or the orange and lemon juices, or *espresso* coffee, or the puréed strawberries and lemon juice. Pour the mixture into an ice-cube tray from which the divider has been removed.

Freeze the *granita* for 3 to 4 hours, stirring it every 30 minutes and scraping into it the ice particles that form around the edges of the tray. The finished *granita* should have a fine, snowy texture. For a coarser texture that is actually more to the Italian taste, leave the ice-cube divider in the tray and freeze the *granita* solid. Then remove the cubes and crush them in an ice crusher.

NOTE: If you use frozen strawberries rather than fresh ones, make the syrup with only ¼ cup of sugar.

Gelati—Italian Ice Creams

VANILLA: In a 1½- or 2-quart enameled or stainless-steel saucepan, bring the light cream and the vanilla bean almost to a boil over low heat. (If you are using vanilla extract, do not add it now.) Meanwhile combine the egg yolks and sugar in a bowl. Beat them with a whisk, rotary or electric beater for 3 to 5 minutes, or until they are pale yellow and thick enough to fall from the whisk or beater in a lazy ribbon. Then discard the vanilla bean from the saucepan and pour the hot cream slowly into the beaten egg yolks, beating gently and constantly. Pour the mixture back into the saucepan and cook over moderately low heat, stirring constantly with a wooden spoon, until it thickens to a custard that lightly coats the spoon. Do not allow the mixture to boil or it will curdle. Stir in the heavy cream, and if you are using the vanilla extract instead of the vanilla bean, add it now. Strain the custard through a fine sieve into a mixing bowl and allow it to cool to room temperature.

Now pack a 2-quart ice cream freezer with layers of finely crushed or cracked ice and coarse rock salt in the proportions recommended by the freezer manufacturer. Add cold water if the manufacturer advises it. Then pour or ladle the cooled *gelato* into the ice cream can and cover it. If you have a hand ice cream maker, let it stand for 3 or 4 minutes before turning the handle. It may take 15 minutes or more for the ice cream to freeze, but do not stop turning at any time, or the *gelato* may be lumpy. When the handle can barely be moved, the ice cream should be firm. If you have an electric ice cream maker, turn it on and let it churn for about 15 minutes, or until the motor slows or actually stops.

To harden the *gelato*, scrape the ice cream from the sides down into the bottom of the can and cover it very securely. Drain off any water that is in the bucket and repack it with ice and salt. Let it stand for 2 or 3 hours.

PISTACHIO: Heat the light cream and beat the egg yolks and sugar together. Add the ground pistachio nuts and make the custard as above. Then stir in the heavy cream and vegetable coloring, and strain this mixture. Add the chopped pistachio nuts and ground almonds. Cool and freeze.

COFFEE: Heat the light cream with the lemon peel and beat the egg yolks and sugar together. Discard the peel and make the custard as described above. Add the *espresso* coffee (instant or freshly brewed) and heavy cream; strain, cool and freeze.

CHOCOLATE: Heat the milk, beat the egg yolks and sugar together, and make the custard as described above. Then stir in the heavy cream, melted chocolate and vanilla extract. Strain, cool and freeze.

CHOCOLATE ICE CREAM
2 cups milk
4 egg yolks
10 tablespoons sugar
2 cups heavy cream
4 ounces semisweet chocolate, melted
½ teaspoon vanilla extract

These Italian desserts include chocolate, pistachio, coffee and vanilla ice cream and coffee, lemon, strawberry and orange ice.

Succoth—the Harvest Holiday

During the week-long autumn harvest celebration of Succoth, Orthodox Jewish families feast on the season's bounty in decorated straw huts called *sukkahs*. At this festival of joy, children learn ancient traditions and friends are invited to share meals featuring the family's favorite dishes.

Cold Borscht

To serve 8

3 pounds beets, trimmed, peeled and coarsely grated (4 cups)
1 medium-sized onion, peeled and halved
2½ quarts cold water
2 teaspoons salt
2 tablespoons sugar
½ teaspoon sour (citric) salt, or substitute 3 tablespoons strained fresh lemon juice
4 eggs
1 pint sour cream

Combine the beets, onion, water and 2 teaspoons of salt in a 3- to 4-quart enameled or stainless-steel casserole. Bring to a boil over high heat, then reduce the heat and simmer, partially covered, for 1 hour. Skim the foam from the surface frequently with a slotted spoon.

Stir the sugar and sour salt (or lemon juice plus regular salt) into the soup. In a small bowl, beat the eggs together with a fork or wire whisk. Slowly beat in ½ cup of the simmering soup, then pour the warmed egg mixture slowly into the casserole, stirring constantly. Remove the casserole from the heat, discard the onion and set the soup aside to cool to room temperature. When it is cool, taste for seasoning and refrigerate for at least 2 hours, or until thoroughly chilled. You may either stir the sour cream into the soup directly before serving it or present it in a separate bowl to be added to each serving at the table.

Kreplach—Meat-filled Dumplings

To make 3 dozen

DOUGH
1½ cups all-purpose flour
3 eggs
2 to 3 tablespoons cold water
½ teaspoon salt

FILLING
4 tablespoons rendered chicken fat, or substitute 4 tablespoons vegetable oil
1 cup finely chopped onions
½ pound ground beef
1 egg
¾ teaspoon salt
3 quarts water

DOUGH: Place the flour in a large mixing bowl and make a well in the center. Drop in the 3 eggs, 2 tablespoons of water and ½ teaspoon of salt and, with a large wooden spoon, stir the flour into the liquid ingredients. Continue to stir until the dough can be gathered into a ball; add up to 1 more tablespoon of water by the teaspoonful if necessary.

Place the ball of dough on a lightly floured surface and knead by pressing it down with the heels of your hands, pushing it forward and folding it back on itself. When the dough is smooth and elastic, wrap it in wax paper and set it aside to rest for at least 30 minutes.

FILLING: In a 10- to 12-inch skillet, melt the chicken fat over moderate heat. Stir in the onions and, stirring frequently, cook for 4 to 6 minutes, or until they are soft and translucent. Add the ground beef and, mashing it constantly with a wooden spoon to prevent any lumps, cook until there is no longer any trace of pink in the meat. Stir in the egg and ¾ teaspoon of salt, and remove the pan from the heat. Taste for seasoning, and cool the filling to room temperature.

On a lightly floured surface, roll out the dough to a 12-inch square ⅛ inch thick. With a small sharp knife or pastry wheel, cut the dough into 2-inch squares. Top each of the squares with 1 teaspoon of the filling and, with your finger, brush the exposed edges of dough with cold water.

On the Succoth table of a New York family is a wand of willow and myrtle, next to a citron fruit, both symbolizing the earth's fruitfulness. The hut, decorated with gourds and flowers, commemorates the time the Jews escaped Egypt's bondage and lived in temporary shelters in the desert.

FESTIVAL
OF
JOY

Draw one point of the square diagonally over the filling to meet another point, thus forming a triangle. Press the edges firmly closed.

Bring 3 quarts of water to a boil in a heavy 4- to 6-quart pot and lower the *kreplach* into the water. Bring back to a boil, then reduce the heat and simmer uncovered for 20 minutes.

Serve the boiled *kreplach* in hot chicken soup, or place them under the broiler for 2 to 3 minutes, until they are crisp and brown, and serve them as an accompaniment to meat or as an hors d'oeuvre.

NOTE: After the *kreplach* are shaped and before they are cooked, they may be covered with a damp cloth and refrigerated, or wrapped in aluminum foil and frozen.

Dag Kavush—Pickled Fish

To serve 6 as a first course

3 pounds carp heads, bones and trimmings, or substitute other fish trimmings
3 cups white wine vinegar
2 cups coarsely chopped onions
4 medium-sized bay leaves
3 whole cloves
2 tablespoons salt
12 whole black peppercorns
3 pounds carp fillets, skinned and cut into serving pieces similarly sized, or substitute pike or other firm white fish
½ teaspoon white pepper
2 medium-sized onions, cut into ⅛-inch slices and separated into rings
1 medium-sized carrot, scraped and finely grated

Wash the fish heads, bones and trimmings in a large sieve or colander under cold running water, then place them in 3- to 4-quart pot. Add the vinegar, 3 cups of cold water, the chopped onions, bay leaves, cloves, 1 tablespoon of the salt, and the peppercorns. Bring to a boil over high heat, reduce the heat to low, cover tightly and simmer for 30 minutes. Strain the liquid through a fine sieve set over a bowl and discard the trimmings, onions and seasonings.

Place the fish fillets in a 4- to 5-quart enameled casserole. Sprinkle the fish with the remaining tablespoon of salt and the white pepper and pour in the strained stock. Bring to a boil over high heat, then reduce the heat to low and simmer uncovered for 12 to 15 minutes, or until the fish flakes easily when prodded with a fork.

With a slotted spoon, transfer the fillets to a large deep serving platter. Arrange them in rows, and scatter the sliced onions on top. Sprinkle the fish with the grated carrot. Pour in the stock and refrigerate for at least 3 hours, or until the stock has thickened into a delicate jelly.

Kasha Varnischkes—Noodles with Buckwheat Groats

To serve 6 to 8

KASHA
4 tablespoons rendered chicken fat
1 cup finely chopped onions
1 cup medium-grain *kasha* (buckwheat groats)
1 egg, lightly beaten
1 teaspoon salt
2 cups water

NOODLES
6 to 8 quarts water
2 teaspoons salt
½ pound broad egg noodles
Freshly ground black pepper

KASHA: Melt the chicken fat in a 10- to 12-inch skillet and stir in the onions. Stirring frequently, cook for 6 to 8 minutes, or until the onions are soft and translucent. Off the heat, stir in the *kasha,* the beaten egg and 1 teaspoon of salt. Pour in 2 cups of water, cover the pan tightly, and bring to a boil over high heat. Reduce the heat to low and cook undisturbed for 20 to 25 minutes, or until all of the water has been absorbed and the grains of *kasha* are separate and fluffy.

NOODLES: Bring 6 to 8 quarts of water and 2 teaspoons of salt to a boil in a large kettle or pot. Drop in the noodles and stir them briefly with a wooden spoon or fork. Boil briskly for 15 to 20 minutes, or until they are tender. Drain in a colander and transfer to a large heated bowl.

With wooden spoons, toss the *kasha* and noodles together until they are well combined. Sprinkle with freshly ground black pepper.

Holishkes—Sweet-and-sour Stuffed Cabbage

Drop the cabbage into a large pot of boiling water and let it cook briskly for about 10 minutes. Remove the cabbage (letting the water continue to boil), carefully detach as many of the outer leaves as you can and reserve them. Return the rest of the cabbage to the boiling water and cook for a few minutes longer. Remove and again detach as many more leaves as you can. Repeat this process until you have separated 18 individual leaves; discard the smallest inner leaves.

Bring the 2 cups of water to a boil in a 1-quart saucepan, add the rice and boil briskly, uncovered, for about 12 minutes. Drain the rice in a sieve and set it aside.

In a large mixing bowl, combine the ground chuck, egg, grated onions, carrot, potato, 1 teaspoon of the salt and a few grindings of black pepper. Add the rice and mix together until the ingredients are well combined.

Lay the cabbage leaves side by side and, with a small knife, trim the tough rib end from the base of each leaf. Place 2 heaping tablespoons of meat filling in the center of each leaf and roll up all of the leaves tightly, tucking in the ends as if you were wrapping a package. Line the bottom of a 2- to 2½-quart casserole with the onion slices and arrange the cabbage rolls over them, seam side down, in one or more layers.

In a large bowl, mix the raisins, ⅓ cup of brown sugar, the chopped tomatoes, tomato purée, the remaining ½ teaspoon of salt and ½ teaspoon sour salt or ¼ cup of lemon juice. Bring the sauce to a boil. When the sour salt has thoroughly dissolved, taste the sauce for seasoning; add up to ¼ teaspoon more of sour salt or up to 3 tablespoons more of brown sugar, depending on whether you prefer a more pronounced sweet or sour flavor. Bring the sauce to a boil again, and pour this mixture over the stuffed cabbage rolls. Cover the casserole tightly and simmer for 1 to 1½ hours, or until the cabbage is tender. Serve hot, as either a main or first course.

To make 18 small rolls

A 3-pound head of white cabbage
2 cups water
¼ cup long-grain unconverted rice
1 pound ground chuck
1 egg
2 medium-sized onions, grated (¼ cup)
1 medium-sized carrot, scraped and grated (¼ cup)
1 small potato (about ¼ pound), peeled and grated (⅓ cup)
1½ teaspoons salt
Freshly ground black pepper
1 large onion, sliced
¼ cup seedless white raisins
⅓ to ½ cup light brown sugar
2 cups canned whole tomatoes, drained and chopped
¾ cup tomato purée
½ to ¾ teaspoon sour (citric) salt, or substitute ¼ cup strained fresh lemon juice

Tsimmes—Beef-and-Sweet-Potato Stew

Place the prunes in a small mixing bowl and pour the boiling water over them. Set aside to soak for 30 minutes, then remove the prunes from the water and set them and the soaking water aside separately.

Preheat the oven to 350°. Melt the chicken fat in a heavy 10- to 12-inch skillet and, when it is very hot, add the meat chunks. Tossing the chunks about constantly, brown them on all sides, then transfer them to a 2½- to 3-quart casserole. Stir the onions into the fat remaining in the skillet and cook for 5 to 8 minutes, or until they are soft and translucent. Scrape the onions into the casserole with the meat.

Pour the prune liquid into the skillet and bring to a boil over high heat, meanwhile scraping in any browned bits that may be clinging to the skillet. Pour the contents of the skillet into the casserole and add the prunes, salt, sweet potatoes, honey, cloves and cinnamon. Cover the casserole tightly and place it in the center of the oven for 1½ hours, until

To serve 6

1½ pounds pitted prunes
3 cups boiling water
2 tablespoons rendered chicken fat
3 pounds chuck, cut into 1½-inch chunks
1½ cups finely chopped onions
1 tablespoon salt
5 medium-sized sweet potatoes (about 2½ pounds), peeled and cut into 1½-inch chunks
½ cup honey
2 whole cloves
½ teaspoon cinnamon

the meat is tender and the potatoes offer no resistance when pierced with the tip of a sharp knife. Taste for seasoning and serve the *tsimmes* hot, directly from the casserole or from a deep heated platter.

Beef Tongue in Sweet-and-Sour Sauce

To serve 4 to 6

A 5-pound fresh beef tongue
4 tablespoons vegetable oil
2 cups finely chopped onions
10 gingersnaps, pulverized in a blender or wrapped in a kitchen towel and crushed with a rolling pin (½ cup)
2 tablespoons slivered blanched almonds
7 tablespoons cider vinegar
¼ cup seedless raisins
2 teaspoons salt
5 tablespoons brown sugar
½ lemon, thinly sliced

Place the tongue in a large pot or casserole and pour in enough cold water to cover it by at least 2 inches. Bring to a boil over high heat, then partially cover the pot and simmer for 3 to 3½ hours, or until the tongue is tender and offers no resistance when pierced with a fork.

Remove the tongue from the water and transfer it to a cutting board. Do not discard the water. When the tongue is just cool enough to handle, skin it with a small sharp knife, cutting away the fat, bones and gristle at its base. Cut the tongue crosswise into ½-inch-thick slices. Strain the tongue broth through a fine sieve and set 4 cups aside.

In a heavy 10- to 12-inch enameled or stainless-steel skillet, heat the oil until a light haze forms above it. Stir in the onions and cook, stirring frequently, for 5 to 8 minutes, or until they are soft and lightly colored. Now stir in the gingersnaps, the reserved 4 cups of tongue broth, and the almonds, vinegar, raisins, salt and brown sugar, and bring to a boil. Place the tongue slices in the sauce and turn them about to coat them thoroughly. Top with the slices of lemon, cover the skillet, and simmer the tongue for 15 to 20 minutes, or until it is heated through and the sauce is thick and smooth. Taste for seasoning, then transfer to a deep heated platter and serve at once.

Israeli Chicken with Kumquats

To serve 4

A 2½- to 3-pound chicken, cut into 6 to 8 serving pieces
Salt
1 cup fresh orange juice
2 tablespoons fresh lemon juice
¼ cup honey
2 tablespoons drained, rinsed, seeded and finely chopped canned or bottled hot chili peppers
10 preserved kumquats
Lemon or orange slices

Preheat the oven to 375°. Pat the pieces of chicken completely dry with paper towels, sprinkle liberally with salt, and arrange them side by side in a baking dish large enough to hold them in one layer. Mix the orange juice, lemon juice and honey together and pour it over the chicken, turning the pieces about in the mixture until they are well moistened.

Rearrange the chicken pieces skin side down in the baking dish and scatter the chopped peppers over them. Bake uncovered and undisturbed in the middle of the oven for 15 minutes. Turn the pieces over, add the kumquats and baste thoroughly with the pan liquid. Basting occasionally, bake the chicken 30 minutes longer, or until the leg or thigh shows no resistance when pierced with a fork.

To serve, arrange the chicken and kumquats attractively on a heated platter, pour the pan juices over them and garnish with lemon or orange slices.

Chicken glazed with honey, lemon and orange juice and baked with kumquats is a newly created Israeli dish. The melange of fruits makes it a festive platter to serve family and guests at a Succoth meal.

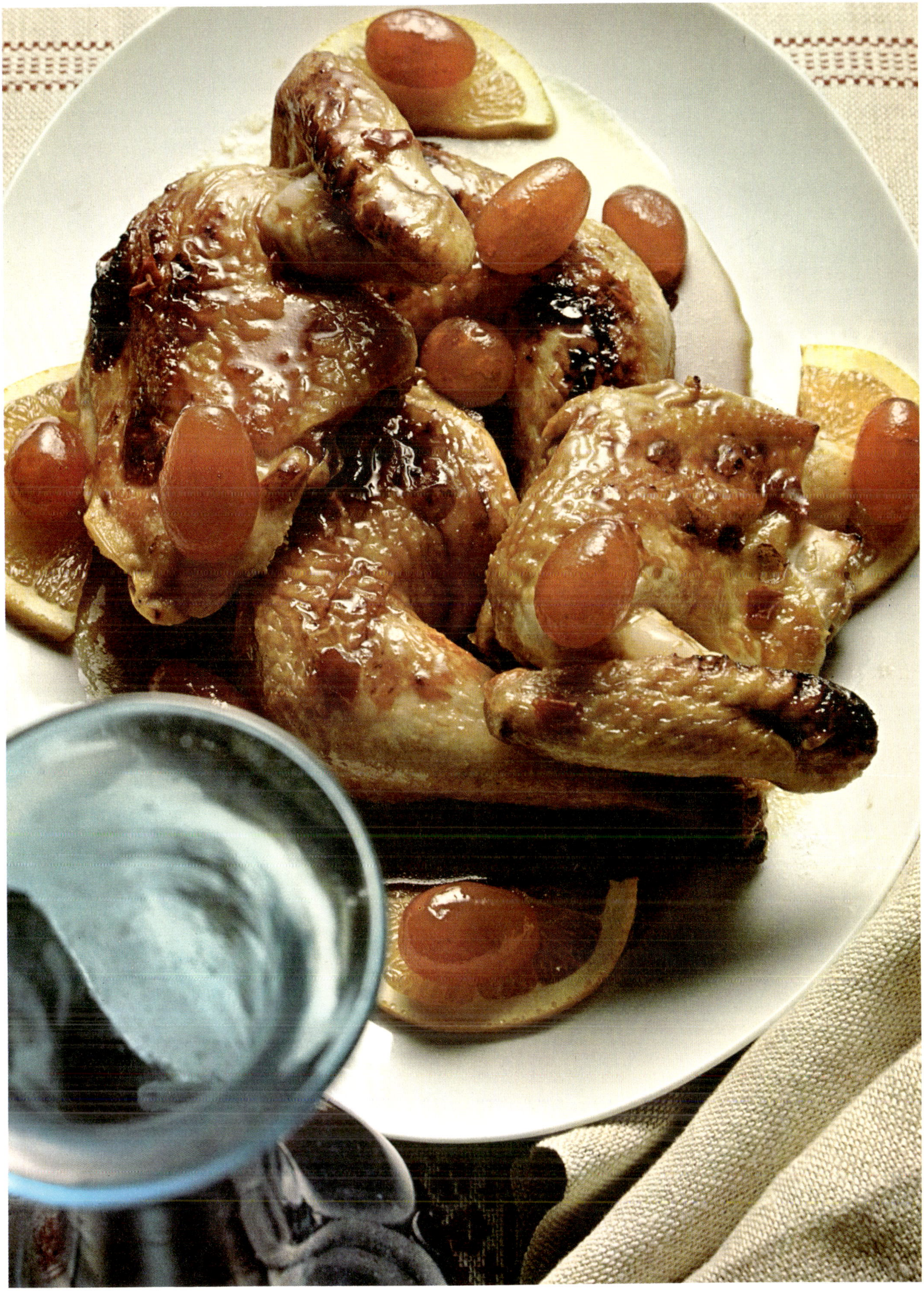

Sugar Doughnuts

To make about 1½ dozen doughnuts and 2 to 3 dozen doughnut balls

4 to 5 cups unsifted flour
4 teaspoons double-acting baking powder
¼ teaspoon ground nutmeg
½ teaspoon salt
¾ cup milk
4 tablespoons butter, melted and cooled
1 teaspoon vanilla
3 eggs
1 cup granulated sugar
Vegetable oil for deep frying
2 cups confectioners' sugar, sifted

Combine 4 cups of the flour, the baking powder, nutmeg and salt, and sift them onto a plate or a sheet of wax paper. Pour the milk, cooled melted butter and vanilla into a measuring cup and mix well. Set aside.

In a deep bowl, beat the eggs and the granulated sugar with a wire whisk or a rotary or electric beater for 4 or 5 minutes, until the mixture falls in a slowly dissolving ribbon from the beater when it is lifted from the bowl. Add about 1 cup of the flour mixture and stir with a wooden spoon. When the flour is well incorporated, beat in about ¼ cup of the milk-and-butter mixture. Repeat three more times, alternating 1 cup of the flour with ¼ cup of the milk, and beating well after each addition. Add up to 1 cup more flour by the tablespoonful and continue to stir with the spoon, or knead with your hands, until the dough can be gathered into a compact ball. Cover the bowl with wax paper and refrigerate for at least 30 minutes.

Line two large baking sheets with wax paper. Cut off about one quarter of the dough and place it on a lightly floured surface. Flour a rolling pin and roll the dough out about ⅓ inch thick. If the dough sticks, dust a little flour over and under it.

With a 2¾-inch doughnut cutter, cut out as many doughnuts as you can. Using a wide metal spatula, transfer the doughnuts and their centers to the paper-lined pans. Refrigerate until ready to fry. Break off another quarter of the dough, roll it out, cut out more doughnuts and refrigerate as before. Repeat until all the dough has been used, but do not reroll the scraps or the doughnuts made from them may be tough. Instead use a 1-inch cutter to form balls out of the scraps.

Pour vegetable oil into a deep fryer or large heavy saucepan to a depth of 3 inches and heat the oil until it reaches a temperature of 375° on a deep-frying thermometer. Meanwhile place ½ cup of the confectioners' sugar in a paper bag and set it aside.

Deep-fry the doughnuts and balls 4 or 5 at a time, turning them about with a slotted spoon for 3 minutes, or until they are puffed and brown. Drain the doughnuts briefly on paper towels, then drop 2 at a time into the paper bag and shake to coat them with sugar. (Add sugar to the bag as needed.) Place the doughnuts on wire racks to cool while you fry and sugar the rest.

Toll-House Cookies

To make 24 cookies

8 tablespoons (1 quarter-pound stick) softened butter
6 tablespoons granulated sugar
6 tablespoons dark brown sugar
½ teaspoon salt
½ teaspoon vanilla
¼ teaspoon cold water
1 egg
½ teaspoon baking soda
1 cup all-purpose flour
1 six-ounce package semisweet chocolate bits
¾ cup coarsely chopped pecans
1 tablespoon soft butter

Preheat the oven to 375°. In a large mixing bowl, combine the butter, white and brown sugar, salt, vanilla and water, and beat them together with a large spoon until the mixture is light and fluffy. Beat in the egg and baking soda and when they are well combined add the flour, beating it in ¼ cup at a time. Then, gently but thoroughly fold in the chocolate bits and nuts.

With a pastry brush coat a cookie sheet evenly with the tablespoon of soft butter. Drop the cookie batter onto the sheet a tablespoon at a time, leaving about 1½ inches between the cookies. Gently pat down the tops of each cookie with a spatula, but don't flatten them entirely. Bake in the middle of the oven for about 12 minutes, or until the cookies are firm to the touch and lightly brown. Cool on a cake rack.

Chocolate Brownies

Preheat the oven to 350°. Melt the chocolate in a small heavy saucepan over low heat, stirring constantly, but do not let it come to a boil. Set it aside to cool slightly. Meanwhile, in a mixing bowl cream the butter and sugar together by beating them with a large spoon until the mixture is light and fluffy. Beat in the eggs, one at a time, and then the cooled chocolate. Sift the flour, baking powder and salt together into the mixture, and beat for 10 or 15 seconds, or until the ingredients are well combined. Stir in the vanilla and walnuts. Lightly butter an 8-inch-square baking pan. Pour in the batter and bake the brownies in the center of the oven for 30 to 35 minutes, or until a small knife inserted in the center comes out clean. Cool for about 10 minutes, then cut into 2-inch squares.

To make 16 brownies

2 squares unsweetened chocolate
½ cup butter
1 cup sugar
2 eggs
½ cup all-purpose flour
½ teaspoon baking powder
½ teaspoon salt
1 teaspoon vanilla
1 cup coarsely chopped walnuts

Butterscotch Brownies

Preheat the oven to 350°. Line an 8-inch-square baking pan with lightly buttered wax paper. Over low heat, melt the 4 tablespoons of butter in a small saucepan and add the brown sugar. Stir constantly until the sugar dissolves, then pour the mixture into a medium-sized mixing bowl. Cool until tepid. Beat in the egg and vanilla, and when they are thoroughly incorporated beat in the flour, baking powder and salt, first sifted together. Gently fold in the chopped walnuts and pour the batter into the baking pan. Bake in the center of the oven for about 25 minutes until the cake is firm to the touch and a small knife inserted in the center comes out clean. Let the cake cool for about 10 minutes, then cut it into 2-inch squares.

To make 16 brownies

4 tablespoons butter
1 cup dark brown sugar
1 egg
1 teaspoon vanilla
½ cup all-purpose flour
1 teaspoon baking powder
½ teaspoon salt
½ cup coarsely chopped walnuts

Pecan-stuffed Date Cookies

Preheat the oven to 350°. With a pastry brush, spread 1 tablespoon of the softened butter evenly over each of two large baking sheets. Gently pry each date open along the slit in its side, insert a pecan half and press the edges of the date securely together. Set aside.

Combine the flour, baking powder, soda and salt, and sift them together into a bowl. In a deep mixing bowl, cream the remaining 4 tablespoons of softened butter with the brown sugar by beating and mashing them against the sides of the bowl with the back of a large spoon until the mixture is light and fluffy. Beat in the eggs, one at a time. Add 1 cup of the flour mixture and, when it is thoroughly incorporated, beat in ¼

To make 45 cookies

COOKIES
6 tablespoons butter, softened
45 pitted dates (about 12 ounces)
45 shelled pecan halves (about 4 ounces)
2 cups unsifted flour
½ teaspoon double-acting baking powder
½ teaspoon baking soda
½ teaspoon salt
¾ cup light brown sugar
2 eggs
⅓ cup sour cream
1 teaspoon vanilla extract

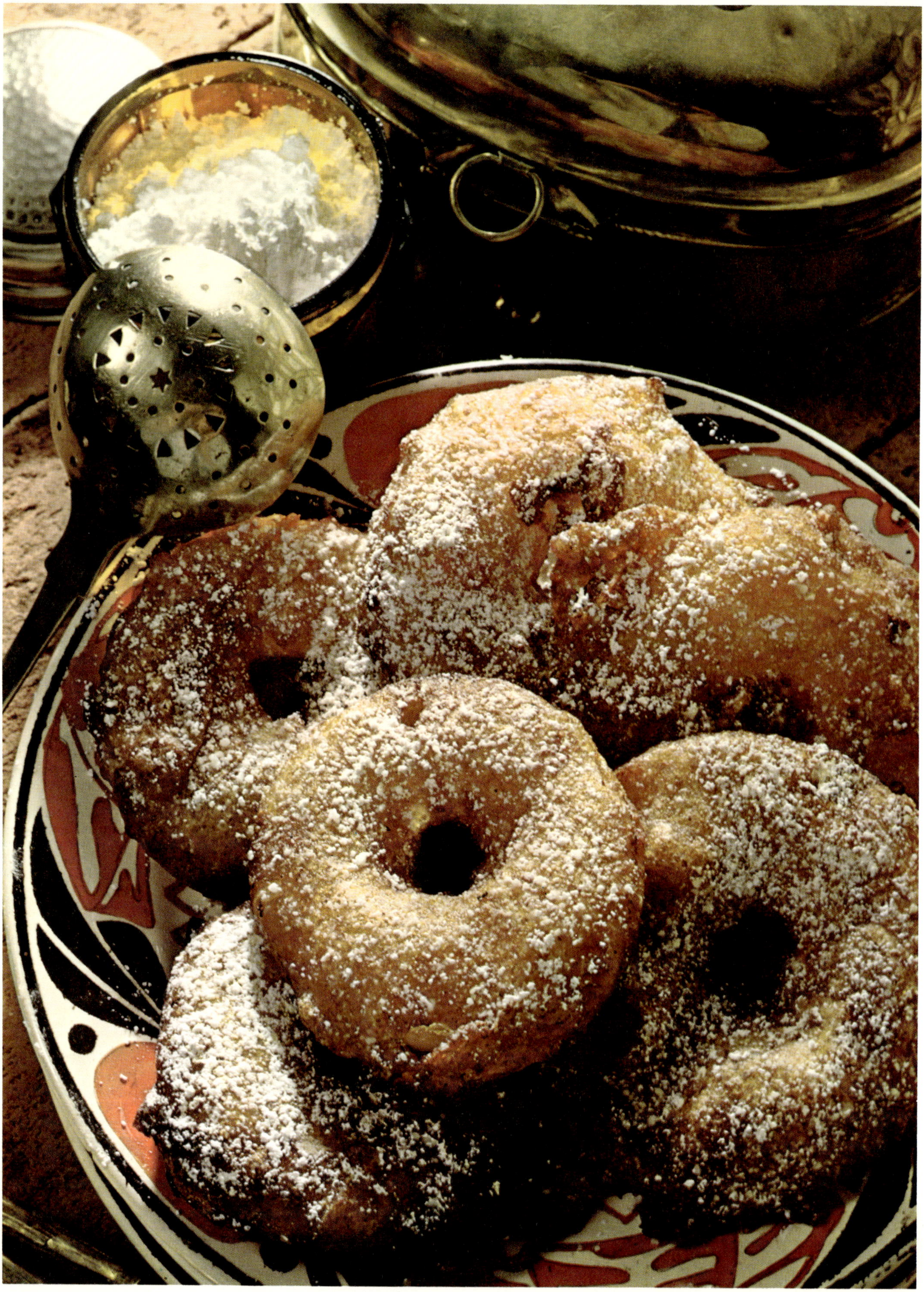

cup of the sour cream. Repeat, alternating 1 cup of the flour with ¼ cup of sour cream and beating the batter well after each addition. Stir in 1 teaspoon of vanilla extract.

With kitchen tongs or your fingers, pick up one pecan-stuffed date at a time and swirl it in the batter to coat the entire surface evenly. As they are coated, arrange the dates about 1 inch apart on the buttered baking sheets. Bake in the middle of the oven for about 10 minutes, until the coating is delicately browned. Then transfer the cookies to wire racks to cool to room temperature.

When the cookies are cool, prepare the icing in the following fashion: Melt the 8 tablespoons of butter bits over low heat in a small heavy skillet, stirring so that the bits melt evenly without burning. Pour the melted butter into a mixing bowl and, when it has cooled, sift in the confectioners' sugar. Mix well, then stir in 1 tablespoon of vanilla extract and 3 tablespoons of milk. If the icing is too stiff to spread easily, add up to 1 tablespoon more milk by the teaspoonful.

With a small metal spatula, spread the icing evenly over the entire outside surface of each of the stuffed-date cookies and arrange them side by side on wax paper to dry. In a tightly covered jar or tin, the cookies may safely be kept for about 2 weeks.

ICING
8 tablespoons butter, cut into ½-inch bits
3 cups confectioners' sugar
1 tablespoon vanilla extract
3 to 4 tablespoons milk

Apple Fritters

Sift the flour into a deep mixing bowl and make a well in the center. Slowly pour in the beer and, stirring gently, gradually incorporate the flour. Continue to stir until the mixture is smooth, but do not beat or overmix. Set the batter aside to rest at room temperature for 3 hours before using.

Fifteen minutes or so before you plan to make the fritters, peel and core the apples and cut them crosswise into ⅓-inch-thick rounds. Lay the rounds side by side on a strip of wax paper. Then combine the sugar and cinnamon in a small bowl and sprinkle the mixture evenly over both sides of each apple round.

Preheat the oven to its lowest setting. Line a large shallow baking dish or jelly-roll pan with a double thickness of paper towels and set it in the middle of the oven. Pour vegetable oil into a deep fryer or large heavy saucepan to a depth of about 3 inches and heat the oil until it reaches a temperature of 375° on a deep-frying thermometer.

One at a time, pick up an apple slice with tongs or a slotted spoon, immerse it in the batter and, when it is well coated on all sides, drop it into the hot oil. Deep-fry 3 or 4 fritters at a time for about 4 minutes, turning them occasionally, until they are delicately and evenly browned. As they brown, transfer the fritters to the paper-lined pan and keep them warm in the oven while you coat and deep-fry the remaining apples.

Arrange the fritters on a heated platter and sprinkle them lightly with confectioners' sugar just before serving.

To make about 24 fritters

BATTER
2 cups sifted all-purpose flour
1 pint (2 cups) beer, at room temperature

APPLES
5 medium-sized tart cooking apples
1 cup sugar
1 tablespoon ground cinnamon
Vegetable oil for deep frying
Confectioners' sugar

After a Halloween apple-dunking party, apples, flour and beer can be transformed into delicate fritters, dusted with sugar.

To make about 3 dozen 2-by-1-inch cookies

BOTTOM LAYER

9 tablespoons butter, softened
½ cup dark brown sugar
1 cup flour, sifted before measuring

TOP LAYER

2 eggs
1 teaspoon vanilla extract
1 cup dark brown sugar
2 tablespoons flour
½ teaspoon double-acting baking powder
A 3½-ounce can moist shredded coconut
1 cup finely chopped walnuts
Confectioners' sugar

Tom Thumb Cookies

Preheat the oven to 325°. With a pastry brush, spread 1 tablespoon of the butter over the bottom and sides of a shallow 13-by-9-inch baking dish and set it aside.

In a deep bowl, cream the remaining 8 tablespoons of butter with ½ cup of dark brown sugar by beating and mashing them against the sides of the bowl with the back of a large spoon until the mixture is light and fluffy. Beat in 1 cup of sifted flour, a few tablespoonfuls at a time.

With a rubber spatula, scrape the mixture into the buttered baking dish and spread it evenly over the bottom of the dish with the spatula or your fingers. Bake in the middle of the oven for 15 minutes.

Meanwhile, in a deep bowl, beat the eggs and vanilla with a wire whisk or a rotary or electric beater until they begin to froth. Add 1 cup of dark brown sugar and continue beating for 4 or 5 minutes longer, or until the mixture is thick enough to fall in a slowly dissolving ribbon when the beater is lifted from the bowl. Combine the 2 tablespoons of flour and the baking powder, sift them together over the egg mixture, and mix well. Add the coconut and walnuts and fold them gently into the batter with a rubber spatula.

When the cake has baked its allotted time, remove the dish from the oven and let it cool for a minute or so. Then, pour the coconut batter on top, spreading it evenly and smoothing it with the spatula. Bake for about 20 minutes, or until the topping is golden brown.

Cool to room temperature, then sprinkle the top lightly with confectioners' sugar and cut the cake into 2-by-1-inch cookies.

To make about 20 four-inch-round cookies

4 cups flour
2 teaspoons ground ginger
½ teaspoon ground cloves
½ teaspoon ground nutmeg, preferably freshly grated
¼ teaspoon ground allspice
1½ teaspoons salt
1 cup dark molasses
1 teaspoon baking soda
12 tablespoons butter, softened
1 cup sugar
2 tablespoons rum combined with 6 tablespoons water, or substitute ½ cup water

Joe Froggers—Rum-and-Molasses Cookies

Combine 3½ cups of the flour, the ginger, cloves, nutmeg, allspice and salt and sift them into a large bowl. Stir the molasses and soda together in a small bowl until the mixture stops foaming.

In another bowl, cream 8 tablespoons of softened butter with the sugar, beating and mashing them against the sides of the bowl with the back of a spoon until they are light and fluffy. Beat in the molasses mixture and when it is well incorporated, add the rum and water or the water alone. Stir in the flour-and-spice mixture, about 1 cup at a time, beating well after each addition, and continue to beat until the dough is smooth. Cover with wax paper or plastic wrap and refrigerate the dough for at least 8 hours, or overnight.

Preheat the oven to 375°. With a pastry brush, spread 2 tablespoons of the softened butter evenly over two large baking sheets.

Sprinkle a board with the remaining ½ cup of flour, and on it roll the dough out into a rough circle about ¼ to ⅓ inch thick. With a cookie cutter or the rim of a glass, cut the dough into 3-inch rounds. Gather the scraps together, roll them out as before and cut out as many more rounds as you can. Place about half of the rounds 2 inches apart on the baking sheets.

Bake the cookies in the middle of the oven for 10 to 15 minutes, or until they are crisp around the edges and the tops feel firm when prodded gently with a finger. With a wide metal spatula, transfer them to wire racks. Let the baking sheets cool completely, spread them with the remaining 2 tablespoons of softened butter and bake the remaining cookies in the preheated oven. In a tightly covered jar or box, the Joe Froggers can safely be kept for 2 or 3 weeks.

Licorice Cookies

Combine the flour and salt, sift them into a bowl and set aside. In a deep bowl, cream the lard and the sugar together by beating and mashing them against the sides of the bowl with the back of a large spoon until the mixture is light and fluffy. Beat in the egg and egg yolk, then add the anise seed and anise extract. Beat in the flour mixture about ½ cup at a time. If the dough becomes too stiff to stir easily, incorporate the remaining flour mixture with your hands. Pat and shape the dough into two cylinders, each about 1½ inches in diameter. Wrap them in wax paper and refrigerate them for at least 1 hour.

Preheat the oven to 350°. With a pastry brush, spread 2 tablespoons of the softened butter evenly over two large baking sheets.

Slice one cylinder of dough crosswise into ¼-inch-thick rounds. For each cookie, roll a slice between your palms until it forms a rope about 4 inches long and ¼ inch in diameter. Drape the rope into a loop on a buttered baking sheet and cross the ends so that the loop looks like a handwritten letter "l." Arrange the cookies 1 inch apart to allow room for them to spread slightly. Bake in the middle of the oven for 10 to 12 minutes, or until the cookies are delicately browned. With a wide metal spatula, transfer them to wire racks.

Let the baking sheets cool completely and spread them with the remaining 2 tablespoons of softened butter. Then cut, shape and bake the remaining cookies in the same fashion. In a tightly covered jar or box, the cookies can safely be kept for 2 to 3 weeks.

To make about 60 cookies

2½ cups unsifted flour
½ teaspoon salt
1 cup lard
¾ cup sugar
1 whole egg plus 1 egg yolk
1 tablespoon anise seed
½ teaspoon anise extract
4 tablespoons butter, softened

Walnut Cookies with Chocolate Filling

DOUGH: In a large mixing bowl, cream 12 tablespoons of butter by beating against the sides of the bowl with a large spoon. Beat in the egg yolk and ½ teaspoon of vanilla extract, then beat in the ⅔ cup of sugar, the walnuts, salt and flour, ¼ cup at a time. Beat well after each addition, and continue to beat until the dough can be gathered into a ball. Wrap the dough in wax paper and refrigerate for 30 minutes.

Preheat the oven to 400°. On a lightly floured surface, roll out the dough to a rough circle about ¼ inch thick and, with a cookie cutter or small sharp knife, cut out as many 1½-inch circles as you can. Gather the scraps together, reroll them, and cut out additional circles of dough. Place the circles on a baking sheet and bake in the center of the oven for 15 minutes, until they are a light gold. Transfer to wire racks to cool.

FILLING: Combine the butter bits and chopped chocolate in a heavy 8- to

To make about 4 dozen

DOUGH
12 tablespoons (1½ quarter-pound sticks) unsalted butter, softened
1 egg yolk
½ teaspoon vanilla extract
⅔ cup confectioners' sugar
1 cup ground walnuts
⅛ teaspoon salt
1½ cups all-purpose flour

FILLING
8 tablespoons (1 quarter-pound stick) unsalted butter, cut into bits
3 ounces unsweetened chocolate, coarsely chopped
2 eggs, well beaten
½ cup confectioners' sugar
½ teaspoon vanilla extract

When the trick-or-treat set ring the doorbell, a good supply of chewy oatmeal cookies is excellent insurance against any mischief.

10-inch skillet and melt over low heat, stirring constantly and adjusting the heat if necessary to prevent the butter and chocolate from burning. Remove from the heat, then beat in the eggs, ½ cup of confectioners' sugar and the ½ teaspoon of vanilla extract.

Spread half of the cookies with the chocolate filling, and top with the remaining cookies. Decorate the top of the cookie sandwiches with any remaining chocolate.

Oatmeal Cookies

To make 24 cookies

1 cup all-purpose flour
½ teaspoon baking powder
½ teaspoon salt
8 tablespoons (1 quarter-pound stick) unsalted butter, softened
¾ cup dark brown sugar
¼ cup granulated sugar
1 egg
1 teaspoon vanilla
1 tablespoon milk
1¼ cups uncooked oatmeal

Preheat the oven to 350° and lightly butter two 11-by-17-inch baking sheets. Sift the flour, baking powder and salt together into a mixing bowl. Cream the butter, the brown sugar and the granulated sugar together by mashing them against the side of another mixing bowl with a wooden spoon. Stir in the egg, the vanilla extract and the milk, continuing to stir until the mixture is smooth. Beat in the flour mixture, a little at a time, then add the oatmeal, stirring until the mixture is well blended. Drop the batter by the tablespoonful onto the baking sheets, leaving space between for the cookies to expand. Bake for 12 minutes, or until the cookies are lightly browned on top.

Lemon Bars

First prepare the base in the following manner: Preheat the oven to 350°. With a pastry brush, spread 1 tablespoon of the softened butter evenly over the bottom of an 8-inch square cake pan. Set it aside.

In a deep bowl, cream the remaining 8 tablespoons of butter and ¼ cup of the confectioners' sugar together by beating and mashing them against the sides of the bowl with the back of a large spoon until the mixture is light and fluffy. Beat in 1 cup of the flour ½ cup at a time. Place the mixture in the buttered pan and, with your fingers, pat it smooth. Bake in the middle of the oven for 15 minutes, or until the cookie base is delicately colored and firm to the touch.

Meanwhile, combine the granulated sugar, the remaining 2 tablespoons of flour and the baking powder, and sift them into a bowl. Add the eggs and beat vigorously with a spoon until the mixture is smooth. Stir in 2 tablespoons of the lemon juice and the 2 teaspoons of lemon peel.

When the cookie base has baked its allotted time, pour the egg batter over it and smooth the top with the back of the spoon. Continue baking for about 25 minutes longer, or until the top is golden brown and firm. Remove the pan from the oven and let cool to room temperature.

To prepare the icing: Combine the remaining cup of confectioners' sugar and 2 tablespoons of lemon juice in a bowl and mix well. If the icing is stiff, stir in up to 1 tablespoon more lemon juice by the teaspoonful until the icing becomes creamy enough to spread. With a rubber spatula, scoop the icing onto the cooled lemon-bar cake and spread it evenly over the top.

Set the lemon-bar cake aside for about 15 minutes, until the icing hardens, then cut the cake into 2-by-1-inch bars. Drape foil or wax paper over the pan and let the lemon bars rest at room temperature for about a day before serving them. The three layers—cookie base, lemon topping and icing—will blend with one another and give the lemon bars the chewy, somewhat sticky consistency of gumdrops.

To make about 32 two-by-one-inch bars

9 tablespoons butter, softened
1¼ cups confectioners' sugar
1 cup plus 2 tablespoons unsifted flour
1 cup granulated sugar
½ teaspoon double-acting baking powder
2 eggs
4 to 5 tablespoons strained fresh lemon juice
2 teaspoons finely grated fresh lemon peel

Moravian Sand Tarts

Combine the flour, baking powder and salt, and sift them together onto a plate or a sheet of wax paper.

In a deep bowl, cream ½ pound of the softened butter with 2 cups of the sugar, beating and mashing the mixture against the sides of the bowl with the back of a spoon until it is light and fluffy. Beat in the eggs, one at a time and, when they are well incorporated, stir in the flour mixture by the cupful. Add the vanilla and continue to beat until the dough is smooth. Cover with wax paper or plastic wrap and refrigerate the dough for at least 8 hours, or overnight.

Preheat the oven to 350°. With a pastry brush, spread 1 tablespoon

To make about 8 dozen medium-sized cookies

3½ cups flour, sifted before measuring
2 teaspoons double-acting baking powder
1 teaspoon salt
½ pound plus 4 tablespoons butter, softened
2⅓ cups sugar
3 eggs
1 teaspoon vanilla extract
2 teaspoons ground cinnamon
1 cup very finely chopped walnuts
½ cup milk

of the remaining softened butter evenly over two large baking sheets. Mix the remaining ⅓ cup of sugar, the cinnamon and nuts together and set them aside.

Cut off about one quarter of the dough and shape it into a ball. (Return the rest to the refrigerator.) On a lightly floured surface, roll the ball of dough out into a rough circle about ⅛ inch thick. Cut the dough into any shapes you like, using a star, heart or other decorative cookie cutter. Gather the scraps together into a ball and roll out as before. Then cut as many more cookies as you can. Brush the tops of the cookies lightly with milk and sprinkle them with a little of the sugar-and-nut mixture.

With a wide metal spatula, arrange the sand tarts about 1 inch apart on the baking sheets. Bake in the middle of the oven for 8 to 10 minutes, or until the cookies are crisp around the edges and the tops feel firm when prodded gently with a finger. With the spatula, transfer the sand tarts to wire racks to cool.

Let the baking sheets cool completely, then repeat the entire procedure three more times—using 1 tablespoon of the softened butter to grease the pans for each batch of cookies and rolling and baking one quarter of the dough at a time. In a tightly covered jar or box, the Moravian sand tarts can safely be kept for 2 or 3 weeks.

Wine-and-Spice Cookies

To make about 30 two-inch cookies

5 tablespoons butter, softened
2 to 2¼ cups all-purpose flour
1 teaspoon baking soda
1 teaspoon ground cinnamon
½ teaspoon ground ginger
¼ teaspoon ground cloves
¼ teaspoon salt
1¼ cups dark-brown sugar
1 egg, lightly beaten
¼ cup port, Madeira or sweet sherry
½ cup blanched almonds, finely chopped or pulverized in a blender or with a nut grinder, plus 15 whole blanched almonds, split lengthwise into halves
1 egg white combined with 2 teaspoons of water and beaten to a froth

Preheat the oven to 350°. With a pastry brush, spread 1 tablespoon of the softened butter evenly on two large baking sheets. Sift the flour, baking soda, cinnamon, ginger, cloves and salt together onto a strip of wax paper and set aside.

In a deep bowl, cream the remaining 4 tablespoons of butter and the dark-brown sugar together, mashing and beating them against the sides of the bowl until they are thoroughly blended. Beat in the egg, then add the flour mixture ½ cup at a time, stirring well after each addition. Beat in the wine and the chopped almonds.

With your hands vigorously knead the dough in the bowl until it can be gathered into a somewhat firm, compact ball. If the dough then seems too soft, knead in up to ¼ cup more flour, adding it a tablespoon or so at a time.

On a lightly floured surface, roll the dough into a rough circle about ¼ inch thick. With a cookie cutter or the rim of a glass, cut it into 2-inch rounds. Arrange the rounds about 1 inch apart on the buttered baking sheets. Then gather the scraps of dough into a ball, roll it out into another circle, and cut out rounds as before.

Press a blanched almond half lightly into the center of each cookie and brush the entire top surface of the cookie with the beaten egg-white-and-water mixture.

A trio of pastries of Dutch ancestry makes unusual Halloween party sweets. The almond-topped wine-and-spice cookies at the bottom of the photograph are rich with lively flavors. The intricately braided crullers at center are glazed with a cinnamon-and-lemon syrup. The crisp figure-eight cookies at the top are dusted with sugar and chopped nuts.

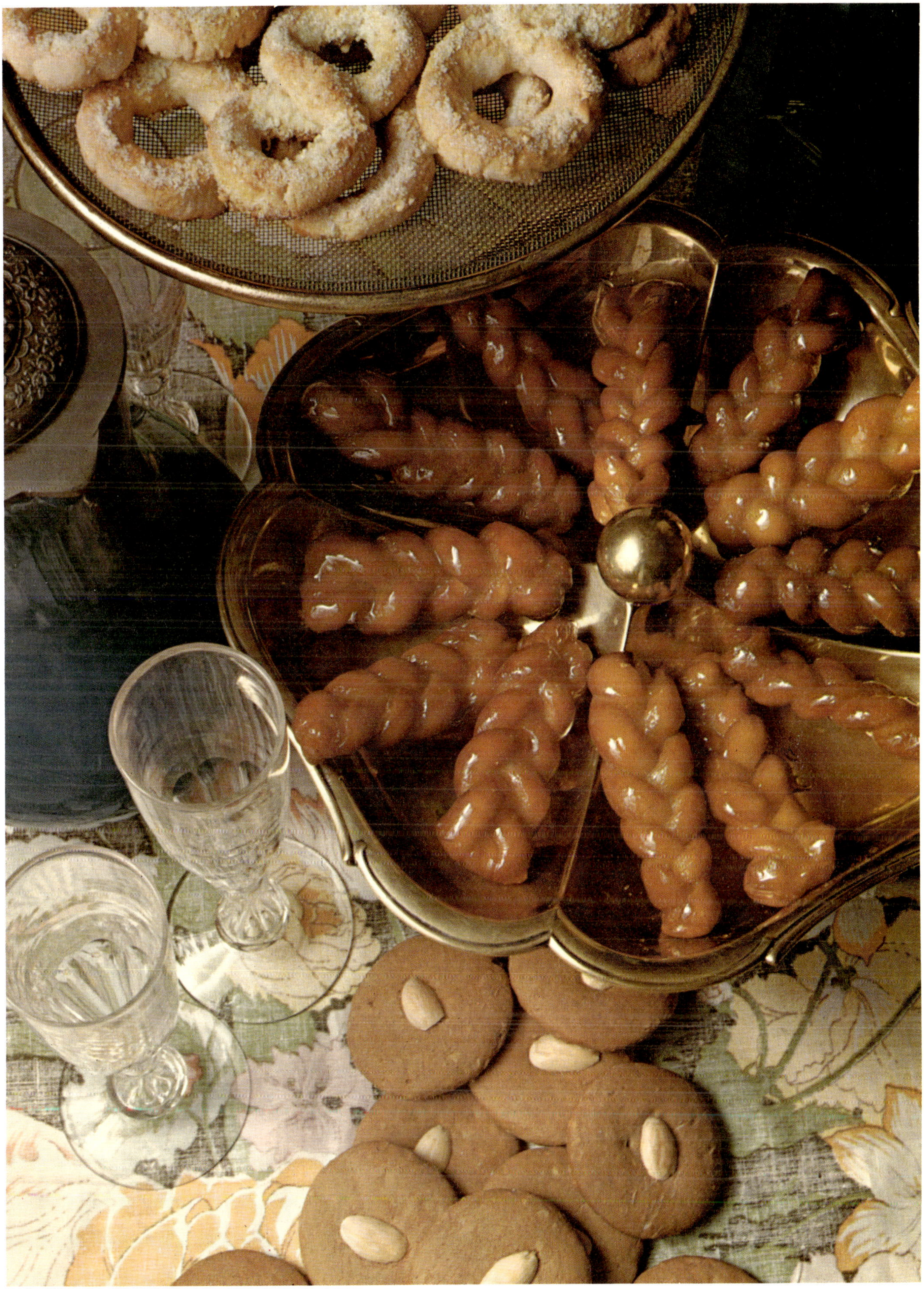

Bake the cookies in the middle of the oven for 15 minutes, or until they are crisp and firm to the touch. With a wide metal spatula, transfer the cookies to a rack to cool. The cookies will keep up to 2 weeks in a tightly covered jar or tin.

Crullers

First prepare the syrup in the following fashion: Combine the sugar, water, stick cinnamon, lemon juice, lemon peel and a pinch of salt in a 2- to 3-quart saucepan. Cook over moderate heat, stirring constantly until the sugar dissolves. Stir in the cream of tartar mixture, increase the heat to high, and cook briskly, uncovered and undisturbed, until the syrup reaches a temperature of 230° on a candy thermometer or a small amount dropped into ice water instantly forms a coarse thread.

Remove the pan from the heat at once and place it in a large pot of ice water. Stir gently until the syrup cools to room temperature. Remove and discard the cinnamon sticks and lemon peel, and refrigerate the syrup for at least 2 hours, or until it is thoroughly chilled.

To make the crullers, sift the flour, baking powder, ground cinnamon, nutmeg and ½ teaspoon of salt together into a deep bowl. Drop in the butter and lard and, with your fingertips, rub the flour and fat together until the mixture looks like fine, dry meal. Stirring constantly with a large spoon, slowly pour in the buttermilk in a thin stream, and continue to stir until all the ingredients are well combined. Then knead the mixture with your hands until it forms a soft, pliable dough. Divide the dough into two balls and drape a dampened kitchen towel over them loosely until you are ready to roll them.

On a lightly floured surface, pat one ball of dough into a rectangular shape about 1 inch thick, then roll it into a rectangle at least 12 inches long and 6 inches wide and no more than ¼ inch thick. With a pastry wheel or small, sharp knife and a ruler, trim the rectangle to exactly 12 by 6 inches. Cut the rectangle crosswise into four 3-inch strips and divide each of these into six 1-inch-wide pieces to make a total of 24 rectangles each 3 by 1 inch.

With a pastry wheel or knife, divide the rectangles lengthwise into three equal strips, cutting from the narrow bottom end to within about ½ inch of the top edge. Starting at the top, interweave the strips into tight three-plaited braids. Pinch the loose bottom ends together and tuck them snugly under each braid. Set the braids on wax paper and cover them with a dampened kitchen towel, then roll, cut and shape the remaining ball of dough similarly.

Pour the vegetable oil into a deep fryer or large, heavy saucepan to a depth of 2 or 3 inches and heat the oil until it reaches a temperature of 375° on a deep-frying thermometer. Fry the crullers 4 or 5 at a time, turning them occasionally with a slotted spoon, for about 4 minutes, or until they are richly browned and crisp on all sides.

As they brown, transfer the crullers to paper towels to drain briefly. While they are still hot, immerse them in the cold syrup for a minute or so. Then, with tongs, transfer them to a wire rack set over paper tow-

---

To make about 4 dozen 3-inch-long crullers

SYRUP

4 cups sugar
2 cups water
3 pieces of stick cinnamon, each 2 inches long
2 tablespoons strained fresh lemon juice
2 pieces lemon peel, each 3 by 1 inch
A pinch of salt
¼ teaspoon cream of tartar combined with 2 teaspoons cold water

CRULLERS

4 cups all-purpose flour
4 teaspoons double-acting baking powder
½ teaspoon ground cinnamon
½ teaspoon ground nutmeg, preferably freshly grated
½ teaspoon salt
2 tablespoons butter, chilled and cut into ¼-inch bits
2 tablespoons lard, chilled and cut into ¼-inch bits
1½ cups buttermilk
Vegetable oil for deep frying

els and let them drain completely. Serve the crullers either warm or at room temperature.

Figure-Eight Cookies

Sift the flour, baking powder, cinnamon and salt together onto a strip of wax paper and set aside.

In a deep mixing bowl, cream together 7 tablespoons of the butter and ½ cup of the sugar, beating and mashing them against the sides of the bowl with the back of a large spoon until they are thoroughly blended.

Beat in the whole egg, then add the sifted flour mixture, about ½ cup at a time, stirring well after each addition. With your hands vigorously knead the dough in the bowl until it can be gathered into a somewhat firm, compact ball.

On a lightly floured surface, roll the dough into a rectangle at least 6 inches wide, 15 inches long and about ¼ inch thick. With a ruler and a pastry wheel or small, sharp knife, trim the rectangle to exactly 6 by 15 inches, and then cut it crosswise into 30 strips each ½ inch wide and 6 inches long.

To shape each figure-eight cookie, gently pinch and fold the long edges of one strip of dough together and roll the strip lightly into a pencil-like cylinder about 6 or 7 inches long and ⅓ inch in diameter. Lift one end of the cylinder in each hand, cross the ends over one another, and loop them together to make a figure eight. Pinch the ends together tightly and lay the cookie on a wire cake rack set over wax paper.

When all the cookies have been shaped, spread the beaten egg white mixture lightly over the tops with a pastry brush. Stir the almonds and the remaining ¼ cup of sugar together and sprinkle the mixture evenly over the cookies.

Carefully transfer the racks of cookies to the refrigerator and chill them for at least 30 minutes, which will firm the dough and set their shape before baking.

Preheat the oven to 400°. With the pastry brush, spread the remaining tablespoon of butter evenly on 2 large baking sheets. Carefully transfer the cookies with a metal spatula to the buttered sheets, arranging them 1 inch apart. Bake the cookies in the middle of the oven for about 12 minutes, or until they are delicately browned.

With a spatula, transfer the cookies to wire racks to cool. The cookies will keep up to 2 weeks in a tightly covered tin.

To make about 30 cookies

1½ cups all-purpose flour
1 teaspoon double-acting baking powder
1 teaspoon ground cinnamon
⅛ teaspoon salt
8 tablespoons butter (1 quarter-pound stick), softened
¾ cup sugar
1 whole egg, lightly beaten
1 egg white combined with 2 teaspoons water and beaten to a froth
½ cup blanched almonds, finely chopped or pulverized in a blender or with a nut grinder

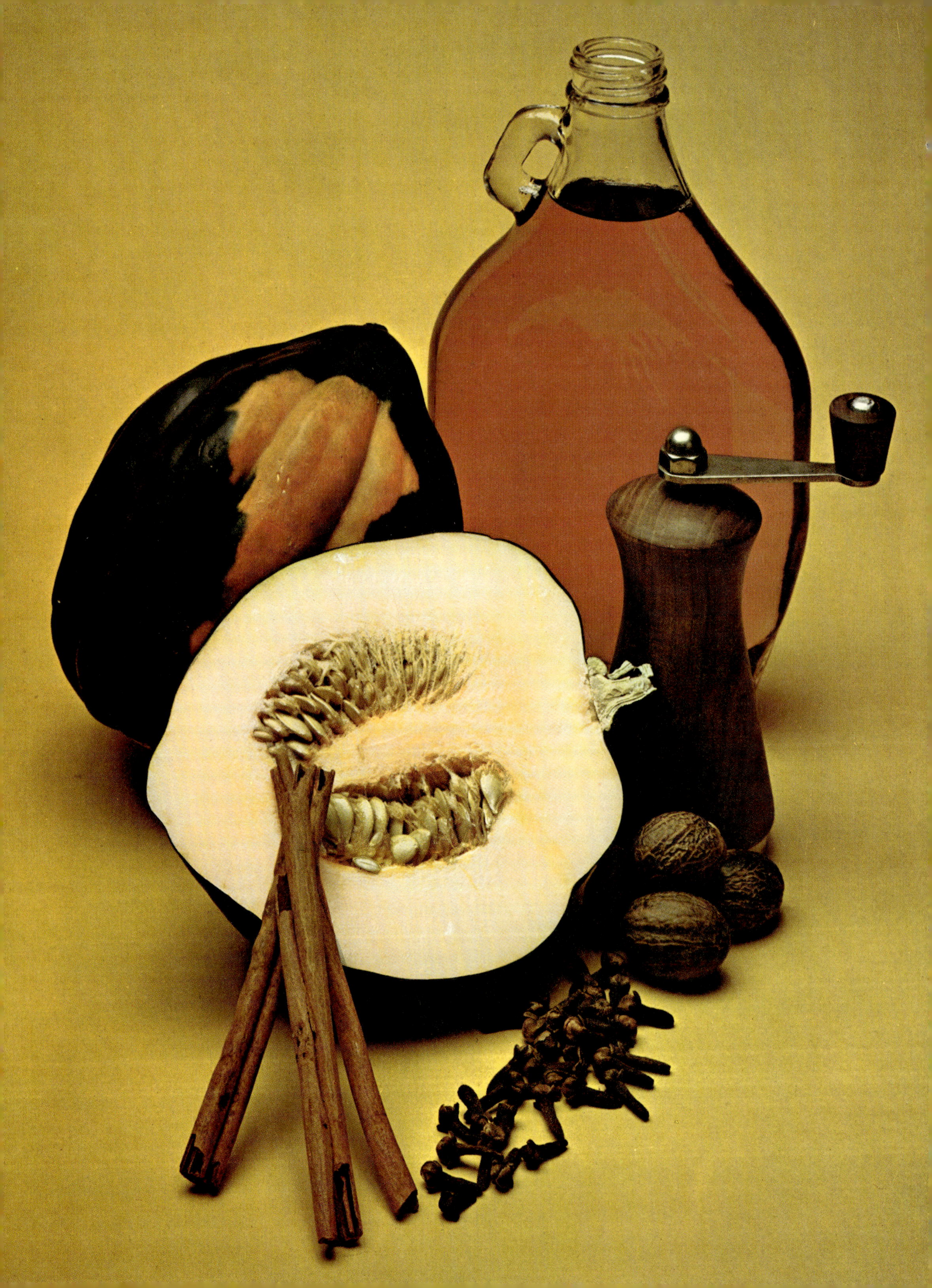

The Thanksgiving Table

Thanksgiving would not seem right, of course, without stuffed turkey, cranberry sauce, a large variety of vegetable dishes and more than one dessert—including the obligatory pumpkin pie. All the essentials for a traditional Thanksgiving dinner are here. But there are also suggestions on the following pages for unusual ways to prepare some time-honored ingredients. Cranberry sauce, for example, is only one of the delicious things that can be made from these tart native American berries; they can also be candied, cooked in muffins, made into a chiffon pie or transformed into a rosy water ice. Sweet potatoes, combined with eggs and corn syrup, make a perfect pie filling, while pumpkins can be baked into a rich bread or simmered with onions and chicken stock to make an unusual hot or cold soup.

Thanksgiving is also a harvest festival, and the seasonal profusion of nuts is celebrated in 10 different recipes, covering every course of the meal. A first course of peanut soup might be followed by turkey filled with sausage, cornbread and pecan stuffing, and accompanied by braised celery and almonds. To assuage any lingering pangs of hunger after a helping of maple-walnut or pecan pie, the family can nibble on toasted, candied or sherried nuts as they linger over a comfortable after-dinner drink.

Acorn squash, an authentic American food, dates back to the pre-Pilgrim Indians. It is an old-fashioned Thanksgiving treat when slowly baked with cinnamon, cloves, nutmeg and maple syrup.

Traditional pumpkin and peanut soups

The succulent roast turkey

Favorite stuffing recipes

A groaning board of autumn vegetables

Cranberry relish, cranberry sauce

Cranberry breads and desserts

Six all-American pies

Postprandial nuts, drinks and coffee

Thanksgiving Recipes
America's National Feast

Pumpkin Soup

In a heavy 4-quart saucepan, melt the butter over moderate heat. When the foam subsides, add the onions and cook for 2 or 3 minutes, stirring, until they are transparent but not brown. Add the pumpkin, chicken stock, milk, the cloves, sugar, lemon juice, Tabasco and salt. Stir thoroughly to blend all the ingredients.

Bring to a boil, then reduce the heat to its lowest point and cook the soup, stirring occasionally, for 15 minutes. Then purée the soup by forcing it through a fine sieve or food mill into a large mixing bowl. Do not use a blender; it will result in too bland and smooth a texture. Stir in the cream. Return the soup to the saucepan and heat it through without letting it come to a boil. Taste for seasoning, garnish with croutons, if desired, and serve hot.

NOTE: This pumpkin soup may also be served chilled. If you serve the soup cold, omit the croutons and garnish each serving with a thin slice of peeled, chilled orange.

To serve 4 to 6

1 tablespoon butter
2 tablespoons finely chopped onion
2 cups cooked pumpkin, canned or fresh, thoroughly drained
2½ cups chicken stock, fresh or canned
2½ cups milk
⅛ teaspoon ground cloves
½ teaspoon sugar
1 teaspoon lemon juice
2 to 3 drops Tabasco
½ teaspoon salt
¼ cup heavy cream

Virginia Peanut Soup

In a heavy 3- to 4-quart casserole, melt the butter bits over moderate heat. When the foam subsides, drop in the onions and celery and cook uncovered, stirring frequently, for 5 to 8 minutes, or until the vegetables are soft but have not yet begun to brown. Stir in the flour with a wooden spoon and, when it is thoroughly incorporated, pour in the chicken stock. Stirring constantly with a whisk, bring to a boil over high heat until the mixture thickens lightly and is smooth. Reduce the heat to low and simmer, partially covered, for 30 minutes, stirring occasionally. Pour the contents of the casserole into a fine sieve set over a bowl, pressing down hard on the vegetables with the back of a spoon before discarding the pulp.

Scrape the peanut butter into a large mixing bowl and whisk in the stock, ¼ cup at a time. After all of the liquid has been added and the soup is smooth, return it to the casserole. Stir in the celery salt, salt and lemon juice, and bring to a simmer over moderate heat. When the soup is hot (do not let it boil), pour it into a heated tureen or individual soup bowls. Present the ground peanuts in a small bowl, to be sprinkled on the soup by each diner.

To serve 6 to 8

8 tablespoons (1 quarter-pound stick) unsalted butter, cut into bits
½ cup finely chopped onions
½ cup finely chopped celery
3 tablespoons flour
2 quarts chicken stock, freshly made or canned
2 cups smooth peanut butter, at room temperature
¼ teaspoon celery salt
1 teaspoon salt
1 tablespoon strained fresh lemon juice
½ cup ground peanuts

The spirit of Thanksgiving is captured in the dining room of Thomas Jefferson's Monticello. The festive groaning board features the rich bounty that comes from the land—Virginia ham, beef, turkey and an array of vegetables and condiments.

Roast Turkey with Cornbread, Sausage and Pecan Stuffing

To serve 8 to 12

A 12- to 14-pound oven-ready turkey, thoroughly defrosted if frozen, and the turkey liver, finely chopped
1½ teaspoons salt
Freshly ground black pepper
1 pound breakfast-type sausage
1½ cups finely chopped onions
½ cup finely chopped celery
5 cups coarsely crumbled, cooled cornbread *(page 305)*
1½ cups (about ½ pound) coarsely chopped pecans
¼ cup pale dry sherry
¼ cup milk
¼ cup finely chopped fresh parsley
½ teaspoon crumbled dried thyme
¼ teaspoon ground nutmeg, preferably freshly grated
12 tablespoons butter, melted
½ cup coarsely chopped onions
3 tablespoons flour
1½ cups turkey stock *(see note at end of recipe)*, or substitute fresh or canned chicken stock

Preheat the oven to 400°. Pat the turkey completely dry inside and out with paper towels. Rub the cavity with 1 teaspoon of the salt and a few grindings of pepper, and set the bird aside.

In a heavy 10- to 12-inch ungreased skillet, fry the sausage meat over moderate heat, stirring frequently and mashing the meat with the back of a fork to break up any lumps as they form. When no trace of pink remains, scoop up the sausage meat with a slotted spoon and transfer it to a fine sieve to drain.

Pour off all but a few tablespoonfuls of the sausage fat remaining in the skillet and add the finely chopped onions and celery. Stirring frequently, cook over moderate heat for about 5 minutes, or until the vegetables are soft but not brown. With a slotted spoon, transfer them to a deep bowl. Add the drained sausage meat, the cornbread, pecans, sherry, milk, turkey liver, parsley, thyme, nutmeg, the remaining ½ teaspoon of salt and a few grindings of pepper, and toss together gently but thoroughly. Taste for seasoning and let the stuffing cool to room temperature.

Fill both the breast and the neck cavity of the turkey with the stuffing and close the openings by lacing them with small skewers and kitchen cord or sewing them with heavy white thread. Truss the bird securely.

With a pastry brush, spread the melted butter evenly over the entire surface of the turkey. Place the bird on its side on a rack set in a large shallow roasting pan and roast in the middle of the oven for 15 minutes. Turn the turkey on its other side, and roast for 15 minutes more.

Then reduce the oven temperature to 325°, place the turkey breast side down and roast for 1 hour, basting it every 15 minutes or so with the juices that have accumulated in the pan. Turn the bird breast side up and scatter the coarsely chopped onions around it. Roast for about 1 hour longer, basting the turkey every 15 minutes or so with the pan juices.

To test for doneness, pierce the thigh of the turkey with the tip of a small sharp knife. The juice that trickles out should be a clear yellow; if it is slightly pink, return the bird to the oven and roast for another 5 to 10 minutes. Transfer the turkey to a heated platter and let it rest for 10 minutes or so for easier carving.

Meanwhile, skim off and discard all but a thin film of fat from the roasting pan. Stir the flour into the fat and cook over moderate heat for 2 or 3 minutes, meanwhile scraping in the brown particles clinging to the bottom and sides of the pan.

Pour in the turkey or chicken stock and, stirring constantly with a wire whisk, cook over high heat until the sauce comes to a boil, thickens and is smooth. Reduce the heat to low and simmer uncovered for about 5 minutes, then strain the gravy through a fine sieve into a serving bowl or sauceboat. Taste for seasoning. Carve the turkey at the table and present the gravy separately.

NOTE: If you would like to prepare turkey stock, start about 2 hours before you prepare the stuffing. Combine the turkey neck, gizzard, and heart, 1 scraped chopped carrot, 1 peeled and quartered onion, 4 fresh parsley sprigs, 1 small bay leaf, 1 teaspoon of salt and 4 cups of water in a saucepan. Bring to a boil over high heat, reduce the heat to low and simmer partially covered for 1½ hours. Strain the liquid through a fine sieve into a bowl and skim as much fat as possible from the surface. There should be about 2 cups of stock.

Roast Turkey with Oyster Stuffing

Pat the turkey completely dry inside and out with paper towels. Rub the cavity with 1 teaspoon of the salt and set the bird aside.

Before making the stuffing, combine the turkey neck, gizzard, heart and liver, the carrot, quartered onion, parsley sprigs, bay leaf, 1 teaspoon of salt and the water in a 3- to 4-quart saucepan. Bring to a boil over high heat, reduce the heat to low and simmer partially covered for 1½ hours.

Strain the liquid through a fine sieve into a bowl and reserve it. (There should be about 2 cups of turkey stock; if necessary, add enough fresh or canned chicken stock for the required amount.) Remove the liver, chop it into ¼-inch dice and reserve. Discard the rest of the turkey pieces as well as the vegetables and herbs.

Meanwhile preheat the oven to 400°. Combine the bread, chopped parsley, lemon peel, sage, 1 tablespoon of salt and the pepper in a large deep bowl and toss with a spoon until well mixed.

In a heavy 10- to 12-inch skillet, melt the ½ pound of butter bits over moderate heat. When the foam begins to subside, add the chopped onions. Stirring frequently, cook for about 5 minutes until they are soft and translucent but not brown.

Stir in the celery and cook for a minute or so; then, with a rubber spatula, scrape the entire contents of the skillet into the bread mixture. Add the oysters and egg and stir the ingredients gently but thoroughly together. Taste the oyster stuffing for seasoning.

Fill both the breast and the neck cavity of the turkey with the stuffing and close the openings by lacing them with small skewers and kitchen cord, or sewing them with heavy, white thread. Truss the bird securely. With a pastry brush, spread the 8 tablespoons of softened butter evenly over its entire outside surface.

Place the bird on its side on a rack set in a large, shallow roasting pan and roast it in the middle of the oven for 15 minutes. Turn it on its other side and roast 15 minutes longer. Then reduce the oven temperature to 325°, place the turkey breast side down and roast for 1 hour. Now turn it breast side up and roast it for about 1 hour longer, basting it every 15 minutes or so with the juices that have accumulated in the bottom of the pan.

To test for doneness, pierce the thigh of the turkey with the tip of a small, sharp knife. The juice that trickles out should be a clear yellow; if it is slightly pink, return the bird to the oven and roast for another 5 to 10 minutes. Transfer it to a heated platter and let it rest for 10 minutes or so for easier carving.

Meanwhile, skim off and discard all but a thin film of fat from the roasting pan. Stir the flour into the fat and cook over moderate heat for 2 to 3 minutes, meanwhile scraping in the brown particles clinging to the bottom and sides of the pan.

Pour in the reserved turkey stock (first skimming it of all surface fat)

To serve 8

A 12-pound turkey, thoroughly defrosted if frozen
2 teaspoons plus 1 tablespoon salt
The neck, gizzard, heart and liver of the turkey
1 medium-sized carrot, scraped and cut into 1-inch lengths
1 small onion, peeled and quartered
4 sprigs fresh parsley
1 small bay leaf
4 cups water
2 one-pound loaves of day-old homemade-type white bread, trimmed of crusts and torn into ½-inch pieces (about 10 cups)
¾ cup finely chopped fresh parsley
2 tablespoons finely grated fresh lemon peel
1 tablespoon crumbled dried sage leaves
½ teaspoon freshly ground black pepper
½ pound butter, cut into ½-inch bits plus 8 tablespoons butter, softened
3 cups finely chopped onions
2 cups finely chopped celery
1½ pints shucked oysters (3 cups) drained
1 egg, lightly beaten
3 tablespoons flour

Roast turkey, packed with savory oyster stuffing, is presented with rich pan gravy, cranberry-orange relish and creamed onions.

and, stirring constantly with a wire whisk, cook over high heat until the sauce comes to a boil, thickens and is smooth. Reduce the heat to low and simmer uncovered for about 5 minutes, then strain the gravy through a fine sieve into a serving bowl or sauceboat. Taste for seasoning and stir in the reserved chopped liver.

Uncooked Cranberry-Orange Relish

To make about 5 cups

1 pound (4 cups) firm fresh unblemished cranberries
2 large thin-skinned oranges, preferably a seedless variety
2 cups sugar

Wash the cranberries under cold running water and pat them dry with paper towels. Cut the oranges into quarters. (If the oranges have seeds, pick them out with the tip of a knife.) Then put the cranberries and the orange quarters (skins and all) through the coarsest blade of a food grinder into a deep glass or ceramic bowl. Add the sugar and mix well with a wooden spoon. Taste and add more sugar if desired.

Cover with plastic wrap and let the relish stand at room temperature for about 24 hours to develop flavor before serving. (Tightly covered, the relish can safely be refrigerated for 2 to 3 weeks.)

Cranberry Sauce

Wash the cranberries in a colander under cold running water. Combine the berries with the sugar and water in a small, heavy enameled or stainless-steel saucepan and, stirring frequently, bring them to a boil over high heat. Then reduce the heat to low and, still stirring from time to time, simmer uncovered for 4 or 5 minutes, until the skins of the cranberries begin to pop and the berries are tender. Do not overcook them to the point where they become mushy.

Remove the pan from the heat and stir in the grated orange peel. With a rubber spatula, scrape the entire contents of the pan into a 2-cup mold or small bowl. Refrigerate for 2 or 3 hours until the sauce is thoroughly chilled and firm to the touch.

To unmold and serve the sauce, run a thin-bladed knife around the sides of the mold or bowl to loosen it and dip the bottom briefly in hot water. Place a serving plate upside down over the mold and, grasping plate and mold firmly together, invert them. The cranberry sauce should slide out of the mold easily.

To make about 1½ cups

2 cups (½ pound) firm fresh unblemished cranberries
1 cup sugar
½ cup water
1 teaspoon finely grated fresh orange peel

Creamed Onions

To peel the onions, drop them into boiling water and let them boil briskly for about 30 seconds. Drain the onions in a sieve or colander under cold running water and cut off the root ends with a small, sharp knife. Slip off the papery outer skin of each onion and trim the top neatly.

Drop the onions into enough lightly salted boiling water to barely cover them. Reduce the heat to its lowest setting, partially cover the pan and simmer the onions for about 20 minutes, or until they show only slight resistance when pierced with the point of a small, sharp knife. Drain the onions in a sieve set over a bowl and set them aside. Measure and reserve 1 cup of the cooking liquid.

In a heavy 3- to 4-quart saucepan, melt the butter over moderate heat. When the foam begins to subside, add the flour and mix well. Stirring constantly with a wire whisk, pour in the reserved cup of cooking liquid, the milk and cream and cook over high heat until the sauce comes to a boil, thickens lightly and is smooth.

Reduce the heat to low and simmer the sauce for 3 or 4 minutes. Then stir in the nutmeg, salt and white pepper and taste for further seasoning. Add the onions and, turning them about gently with a spoon from time to time, simmer for a few minutes longer until they are heated through. Serve at once from a heated bowl.

To serve 8

2½ pounds small white onions
4 tablespoons butter
4 tablespoons flour
1½ cups milk
½ cup heavy cream
¼ teaspoon ground nutmeg, preferably freshly grated
1 teaspoon salt
Ground white pepper

Spiced Acorn Squash

Preheat the oven to 350°. Cut each squash in half and with a teaspoon scrape out the seeds and fibers. In a small bowl combine the brown sugar, cinnamon, nutmeg, cloves, salt and melted butter, and stir them together thoroughly.

Arrange the squash in a shallow ovenproof baking dish that is just large enough to hold them all comfortably. Spoon an equal amount of the

To serve 8

4 medium-sized acorn squash
½ cup dark brown sugar
1 teaspoon cinnamon
½ teaspoon grated nutmeg
¼ teaspoon ground cloves
½ teaspoon salt
8 tablespoons melted butter (1 quarter-pound stick)
½ cup maple syrup
Eight ½-inch pieces of bacon
About 2 cups boiling water

spiced butter mixture into the hollow of each squash and over that pour a teaspoon or so of maple syrup. Top with a piece of bacon. Now add boiling water to the baking dish—the water should be about 1 inch deep. Bake in the middle of the oven for about 1 hour, or until the squash can be easily pierced with the tip of a small, sharp knife. Serve at once.

Creamed Winter Squash

To serve 4

2½ pounds acorn, Hubbard, or butternut squash, peeled, seeded and cut into 2-inch chunks
4 tablespoons butter, cut into ½-inch bits and softened at room temperature
1 tablespoon pure maple syrup
¼ teaspoon ground nutmeg, preferably freshly grated
1 teaspoon salt

Pour water into the lower part of a steamer to within about 1 inch of the top pan and bring to a boil. Place the squash in the top pan and set it in place. Immediately cover the pan and steam over high heat for 30 minutes, or until the squash can be easily pierced with a fork.

(Lacking a steamer, you can easily improvise one by using a large pot equipped with a tightly fitting cover and a collapsible steaming basket on legs or a standing colander. Pour water into the pot to within about 1 inch of the perforated container and bring it to a boil. Place the squash in the basket or colander, set it in place and cover the pot. Steam over high heat for about 30 minutes, or until the squash is soft.)

Purée the squash through a food mill set over a bowl, or mash it smooth with a table fork. (There should be about 3 cups of purée.) Transfer the purée to a heavy 8- to 10-inch skillet and, stirring almost constantly, cook over moderate heat until the purée is dry. Stir in the butter, maple syrup, nutmeg and salt and taste for seasoning. Serve the creamed squash at once from a heated bowl, sprinkled with a little more nutmeg.

Mashed Potatoes

To serve 8

4 quarts water
1 tablespoon salt
4 pounds baking potatoes
½ pound butter, softened
½ to 1 cup cream, preferably heavy
1 teaspoon salt
½ teaspoon white pepper
2 to 4 tablespoons melted butter (optional)
1 tablespoon finely chopped parsley, chives or dill (optional)

Bring the 4 quarts of water to a boil in a 6- to 8-quart pot. Add 1 tablespoon of salt. Meanwhile peel the potatoes, cut them into halves or quarters and drop them into the boiling water. Boil them briskly, uncovered, until they are tender. Test for doneness by piercing them periodically with the tip of a small, sharp knife. They should show no resistance in the center, but they should not fall apart. Drain them at once in a colander.

Return the potatoes to the pan in which they cooked, or transfer them to a large, heavy skillet and shake them over moderate heat for 2 to 3 minutes until they are as dry as possible. Then purée them into a heated mixing bowl either by mashing them with a potato masher, or by forcing through a potato ricer or through a large, coarse sieve with the back of a spoon.

Now, 2 or 3 tablespoons at a time, beat into the purée, either by hand or with an electric mixer, the ½ pound of softened butter. Heat the cream in a small saucepan and beat it into the potatoes a few tablespoons at a time, using as much as you need to give the purée the consistency that you prefer.

Ideally the mashed potatoes should be neither too wet nor too dry,

Creamed winter squash, sweetened with maple syrup, is a contribution from New England to the traditional Thanksgiving Day feast.

and they should hold their shape lightly in a spoon. Beat in the salt and the white pepper, and taste for seasoning. Add more salt if you think it is necessary. Serve at once in a heated vegetable dish. If you like, float the melted butter in a well in the center of the potatoes and sprinkle them with one of the herbs.

Mashed Turnips

Place the turnips in a 6- to 8-quart pot and pour in enough water to cover them by about 1 inch. Add 1 teaspoon of the salt and bring to a boil over high heat. Lower the heat, partially cover the pan, and simmer for 20 minutes, or until the turnips show no resistance when pierced with the tip of a small, sharp knife. Drain in a colander, discarding the water, and return the turnips to the pot in which they were cooked. Slide the pan back and forth over low heat for 2 to 3 minutes, until they are dry. Then, in a heated mixing bowl, purée the turnips either by mashing them with a potato masher or by forcing them through a potato ricer or through a coarse sieve with the back of a spoon. Beat the butter into the purée a tablespoon at a time, then beat in the remaining salt and the pepper, sugar and ¼ teaspoon of the nutmeg. Taste for seasoning and serve at once in a heated vegetable dish, sprinkled with the remaining nutmeg.

To serve 8 to 10

3 pounds yellow turnips, peeled and cut into ½-inch cubes (about 7 cups)
1½ teaspoons salt
4 tablespoons unsalted butter, softened
¼ teaspoon freshly ground black pepper
½ teaspoon sugar
½ teaspoon ground nutmeg, preferably freshly grated

Candied Sweet Potatoes

To serve 6 to 8

1 cup sugar
¼ cup strained fresh orange juice
½ teaspoon ground cinnamon
½ teaspoon ground nutmeg
4 large sweet potatoes (about 3 pounds), peeled, cut in half lengthwise, then cut into ½-inch-thick lengths
1 lemon, thinly sliced
8 tablespoons (1 quarter-pound stick) unsalted butter, cut into bits

Preheat the oven to 350°. In a small mixing bowl, combine the sugar, orange juice, cinnamon and nutmeg. Arrange the sweet potatoes in layers in a baking dish about 15 inches long, 10 inches wide and 2 inches high, moistening each layer with the sugar mixture and a scattering of lemon slices and butter bits. Top with the remaining butter bits and bake uncovered in the center of the oven for 1¼ hours, basting the potatoes with the liquid in the dish halfway through the cooking time.

When the potatoes can be easily pierced with the tip of a knife, serve at once, directly from the dish or on a heated platter.

Braised Celery with Almonds

To serve 6 to 8

2 bunches celery
4 sprigs parsley
1 small bay leaf
2 cups chicken stock, freshly made or canned
1 teaspoon salt
⅛ teaspoon white pepper
3 tablespoons butter
3 tablespoons flour
½ cup heavy cream
¼ cup toasted slivered almonds

Remove the green leaves from the celery, bunch them together with the parsley and bay leaf, and tie them into a bouquet with string. Cut the celery ribs in half lengthwise, then slice crosswise into 1-inch lengths. Wash the pieces under cold running water, drain and drop them into a 2- to 3-quart saucepan. Pour in the chicken stock, add the bouquet, salt and pepper, and bring to a boil over high heat. Cover the pan, reduce the heat to low, and simmer for 15 minutes, until the celery is tender but still slightly resistant to the bite. With a slotted spoon, transfer the celery to a heated platter and drape with aluminum foil to keep it warm while you make the sauce.

Pour the contents of the pan through a fine sieve. Discard the herb bouquet and all but 1 cup of the cooking liquid.

In a 1- to 1½-quart saucepan, melt the butter over moderate heat. Stir in the flour, and mix together thoroughly. Stirring the mixture constantly with a wire whisk, pour in the cream and the reserved cup of cooking liquid in a slow, thin stream. Cook over high heat until the sauce comes to a boil and thickens heavily. Reduce the heat and simmer 3 minutes longer, to remove any raw taste of flour. Taste for seasoning, and pour over the celery. Scatter the almonds on top and serve at once.

Corn Pudding

To serve 6

1 tablespoon butter, softened, plus 4 tablespoons butter, melted and cooled
¼ cup flour
1 teaspoon salt
¼ teaspoon ground white pepper
3 eggs
3 cups fresh corn kernels, cut from about 6 large ears of corn, or substitute 3 cups frozen corn kernels, thoroughly defrosted
2 cups light cream

Preheat the oven to 325°. Brush the tablespoon of softened butter evenly over the bottom and sides of a 1½-quart baking-serving dish.

Combine the flour, salt and pepper and set aside. In a deep bowl, beat the eggs with a wire whisk or rotary beater until they are frothy. Stir in the corn and then, stirring constantly, sift in the combined flour, salt and pepper. Add the melted butter and cream and stir well for 2 to 3 minutes.

Pour the mixture into the baking dish and place it in a large shallow pan set on the middle shelf of the oven. Then pour enough boiling water into the pan to rise at least 1 inch up the sides of the dish. Bake the pudding for 2 hours, or until the top is a delicate brown and a knife inserted in the center comes out clean. (Keep a kettle of boiling water handy, and replenish the water in the pan if it boils away.)

Serve at once, directly from the baking dish.

Pumpkin Bread

Preheat the oven to 350°. With a pastry brush, spread 2 tablespoons of the softened butter over the bottom and sides of two 9-by-5-by-3-inch loaf pans. Sprinkle 1 tablespoon of the flour into each pan and tip it from side to side to spread the flour evenly. Invert the pans and rap the bottoms sharply to remove the excess flour.

Combine the remaining 3 cups of flour, the baking soda, baking powder, cinnamon, cloves and salt, and sift them together onto a plate or a sheet of wax paper. Set aside.

In a deep mixing bowl, cream the remaining 8 tablespoons of softened butter and the sugar together by beating and mashing them against the sides of the bowl with the back of a spoon until the mixture is light and fluffy. Beat in the eggs, one at a time, then stir in the pumpkin. Add about 1 cup of the flour mixture and, when it is completely incorporated, beat in 2 or 3 tablespoons of the water. Repeat two more times, alternating 1 cup of flour with 2 or 3 tablespoons of water, and beating well after each addition. Stir in the walnuts and raisins.

Ladle the batter into the two loaf pans, spreading it evenly and smoothing the tops with a rubber spatula. Bake in the middle of the oven for 50 to 60 minutes, or until the loaves shrink away from the sides of the pans and a cake tester or toothpick inserted in the centers comes out clean.

Turn the loaves of pumpkin bread out on wire cake racks and cool to room temperature before serving.

To make two 9-by-5-by-3-inch loaves

10 tablespoons butter, softened
2 tablespoons plus 3 cups unsifted flour
2 teaspoons baking soda
½ teaspoon double-acting baking powder
1 teaspoon ground cinnamon
1 teaspoon ground cloves
1 teaspoon salt
2½ cups sugar
4 eggs
2 cups puréed pumpkin, freshly cooked or canned
½ cup water
½ cup coarsely chopped walnuts
½ cup finely chopped seedless raisins

Cranberry-Fruit-Nut Bread

Preheat the oven to 350°. With a pastry brush, spread the teaspoon of softened butter evenly over the bottom and sides of a 9-by-5-inch loaf pan. Sprinkle 1 teaspoon of flour into the tin, tipping it to coat the bottom and sides evenly. Then invert the tin and rap it sharply on the table to remove any excess flour.

Wash the cranberries under cold running water and pat them dry with paper towels. Put the cranberries, apple and walnuts through the coarsest blade of a food grinder into a glass or ceramic bowl. Set aside.

Combine the 2 cups of flour, sugar, baking powder, baking soda and salt and sift into a deep bowl. Add the 6 tablespoons of butter bits and, with your fingertips, rub the fat and dry ingredients together until they look like flakes of coarse meal. Stir in the egg, orange peel and orange juice, then add the cranberry-apple-walnut mixture and continue to stir until the ingredients are thoroughly combined.

Spoon the batter into the buttered pan, spreading it and smoothing the top with a spatula. Bake in the middle of the oven for 1½ hours, or until the top is golden brown and a toothpick or cake tester inserted in the center of the loaf comes out clean. Turn the loaf out onto a wire cake rack to cool. Serve cranberry-fruit-nut bread while it is still warm or when it has cooled completely.

To make one 9-by-5-inch loaf

1 teaspoon butter, softened, plus 6 tablespoons unsalted butter, softened and cut into ½-inch bits
1 teaspoon plus 2 cups all-purpose flour
2 cups (½ pound) firm fresh unblemished cranberries
1 medium-sized tart cooking apple, peeled, cored and cut into small chunks
½ cup walnuts
1 cup sugar
1½ teaspoons double-acting baking powder
½ teaspoon baking soda
½ teaspoon salt
1 egg, lightly beaten
1 tablespoon finely grated fresh orange peel
½ cup strained fresh orange juice

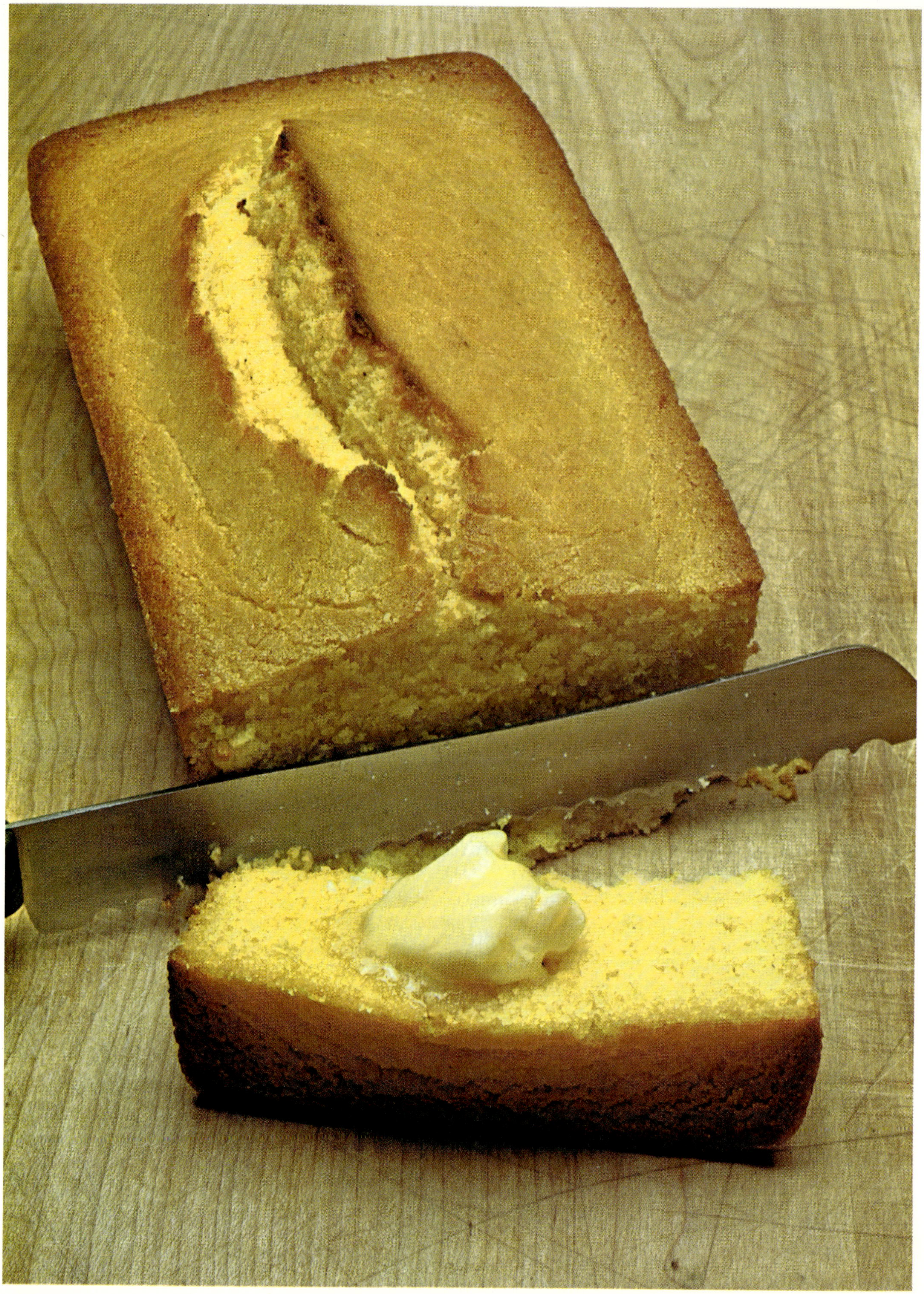

Cranberry Muffins

Preheat the oven to 400°. With a pastry brush, spread the softened butter over the inside surfaces of a medium-sized 12-cup muffin tin (each cup should be about 2½ inches across at the top).

Wash the cranberries under cold running water and pat the berries dry with paper towels. Put them through the coarsest blade of a food grinder into a glass or ceramic bowl and set aside.

Combine the flour, sugar, baking powder and salt and sift into a deep mixing bowl. Stirring constantly with a large spoon, pour in the milk in a thin stream. When the milk is completely absorbed, stir in the egg and the 4 tablespoons of melted butter. Add the ground cranberries and continue to stir until all the ingredients are well combined.

Ladle about ⅓ cup of the batter into each of the muffin-tin cups, filling them about ⅔ full. Bake in the middle of the oven for 30 minutes, or until the muffins are puffed and brown on top, and a cake tester or toothpick inserted in the center comes out clean. Run a knife around the inside of each cup to loosen the muffins, then turn them out of the tin and serve at once, or cool to room temperature before serving.

To make a dozen 2½-inch muffins

1 tablespoon butter, softened, plus 4 tablespoons butter, melted and cooled
1 cup firm fresh unblemished cranberries
2¾ cups flour
¾ cup sugar
4 teaspoons double-acting baking powder
½ teaspoon salt
1 cup milk
1 egg, lightly beaten

Cornbread Loaf

Preheat the oven to 400°. Sift into a mixing bowl the cornmeal, flour, sugar, salt and baking powder. Beat the eggs lightly, add the melted butter and shortening, and stir in the 1½ cups of milk. Pour into the bowl of dry ingredients and beat together for about a minute, or until smooth. Do not overbeat. Lightly butter an 8-by-12-inch shallow baking pan and pour in the batter. Bake in the center of the oven for about 30 minutes, or until the bread comes slightly away from the edge of the pan and is golden brown. Serve hot.

NOTE: If you wish you may bake the cornbread in a 9-by-5-by-3 inch loaf pan. Increase the baking time to 45 minutes.

To make one 9-inch loaf

1½ cups yellow cornmeal
1 cup all-purpose flour
⅓ cup sugar
1 teaspoon salt
1 tablespoon baking powder
2 eggs
6 tablespoons melted and cooled butter
8 tablespoons melted and cooled vegetable shortening
1½ cups milk

Cranberry Ice

Wash the cranberries under cold running water. Combine them and the water in a 2- to 3-quart enameled or stainless-steel saucepan and bring to a boil over high heat. Reduce the heat to low, cover tightly and simmer for 10 to 12 minutes, or until they can be easily mashed against the side of the pan with a spoon.

Purée the cranberries with their cooking liquid through a food mill into a glass or ceramic bowl. Or rub them through a fine sieve with the back of a spoon, pressing down hard on the skins before discarding them. Stir in the sugar and lemon juice.

Pour the mixture into 2 ice-cube trays from which the dividers have been removed. Then freeze the cranberry ice for 3 to 4 hours, stirring and mashing it every 30 minutes or so with a fork to break up the solid particles that will form on the bottom and sides of the trays. The finished ice should have a fine, snowy texture.

To serve, spoon the ice into parfait glasses or dessert dishes.

To make about 1 quart

2 cups (½ pound) firm fresh unblemished cranberries
4 cups water
1½ cups sugar
1 teaspoon lemon juice

This crisp-crusted cornbread, sliced and buttered, is a Southern favorite. The same recipe *(above)* provides a full-flavored stuffing for turkey.

Candied Cranberries

To make about 2 cups

2 cups firm fresh unblemished cranberries
4 cups sugar
1 cup water
A pinch of cream of tartar

Wash the cranberries under cold running water and pat them completely dry with paper towels. With a trussing needle or a small skewer, pierce each berry completely through. Set the berries aside.

In a 2- to 3-quart enameled or stainless-steel saucepan, combine 3 cups of the sugar, the water and the cream of tartar. Stirring constantly, cook over moderate heat until the sugar dissolves. Raise the heat, let the syrup come to a boil, and cook briskly, uncovered and undisturbed, for about 5 minutes more, or until the syrup reaches a temperature of 220° on a candy thermometer. Remove the pan from the heat and gently stir the cranberries into the syrup, turning them about with a spoon until the berries are evenly coated. Set aside at room temperature for at least 12 hours, preferably overnight.

Stirring gently, bring the cranberries and syrup to a simmer over moderate heat. Then drain the berries in a sieve or colander set over a bowl and return the syrup to the saucepan.

Bring the syrup to a boil over high heat and cook briskly, uncovered and undisturbed, until it reaches a temperature of 250° on a candy thermometer, or until a few drops spooned into water immediately form a firm but still slightly pliable ball.

Remove the pan from the heat, drop the berries into the syrup, and stir gently until they are thoroughly coated and glistening. With a slotted spoon, arrange the berries in one layer on a long strip of wax paper. (Discard the remaining syrup.) Let the berries cool to lukewarm; if pools of syrup collect around any of the berries, carefully move the berries to a clean part of the paper.

Two or three at a time, roll the berries in the remaining cup of sugar and transfer them to fresh wax paper. Cool the berries completely to room temperature before serving.

Cranberry Chiffon Pie

To serve 8

CRUST
2½ cups pecans, pulverized in an electric blender or with a nutgrinder
7 tablespoons sugar
4 tablespoons butter, melted and cooled

FILLING
2 cups bottled cranberry juice
1 envelope unflavored gelatin
¾ cup firm fresh unblemished cranberries
¾ cup sugar
3 egg whites
½ teaspoon salt
2 cups heavy cream, chilled
2 tablespoons confectioners' sugar
14 pecan halves

First prepare the crust in the following fashion: Combine the pulverized pecans and 7 tablespoons of sugar in a deep bowl and stir until they are well mixed. Sprinkle the melted butter over them and stir until the butter is completely absorbed. Scatter the mixture into a pie tin 9½ inches across at the top and 2 inches deep. With your fingers or the back of a spoon, press the crust firmly and evenly against the bottom and sides of the tin. Refrigerate for at least 30 minutes.

Preheat the oven to 350°. Bake the crust in the middle of the oven for 10 minutes, or until it browns lightly and is firm to the touch. Remove the tin from the oven and let the crust cool to room temperature.

Meanwhile, prepare the filling. Pour ¼ cup of the cranberry juice into a heatproof measuring cup and sprinkle it with the gelatin. When the gelatin has softened for 2 or 3 minutes, set the cup in a small skillet of simmering water and cook over low heat, stirring constantly, until the gelatin dissolves. Remove the skillet from the heat but leave the cup in the water to keep the gelatin fluid and warm.

Cranberries bring color and piquance to four sweets: cranberry ice, candied cranberries, cranberry-orange sherbet and cranberry chiffon pie.

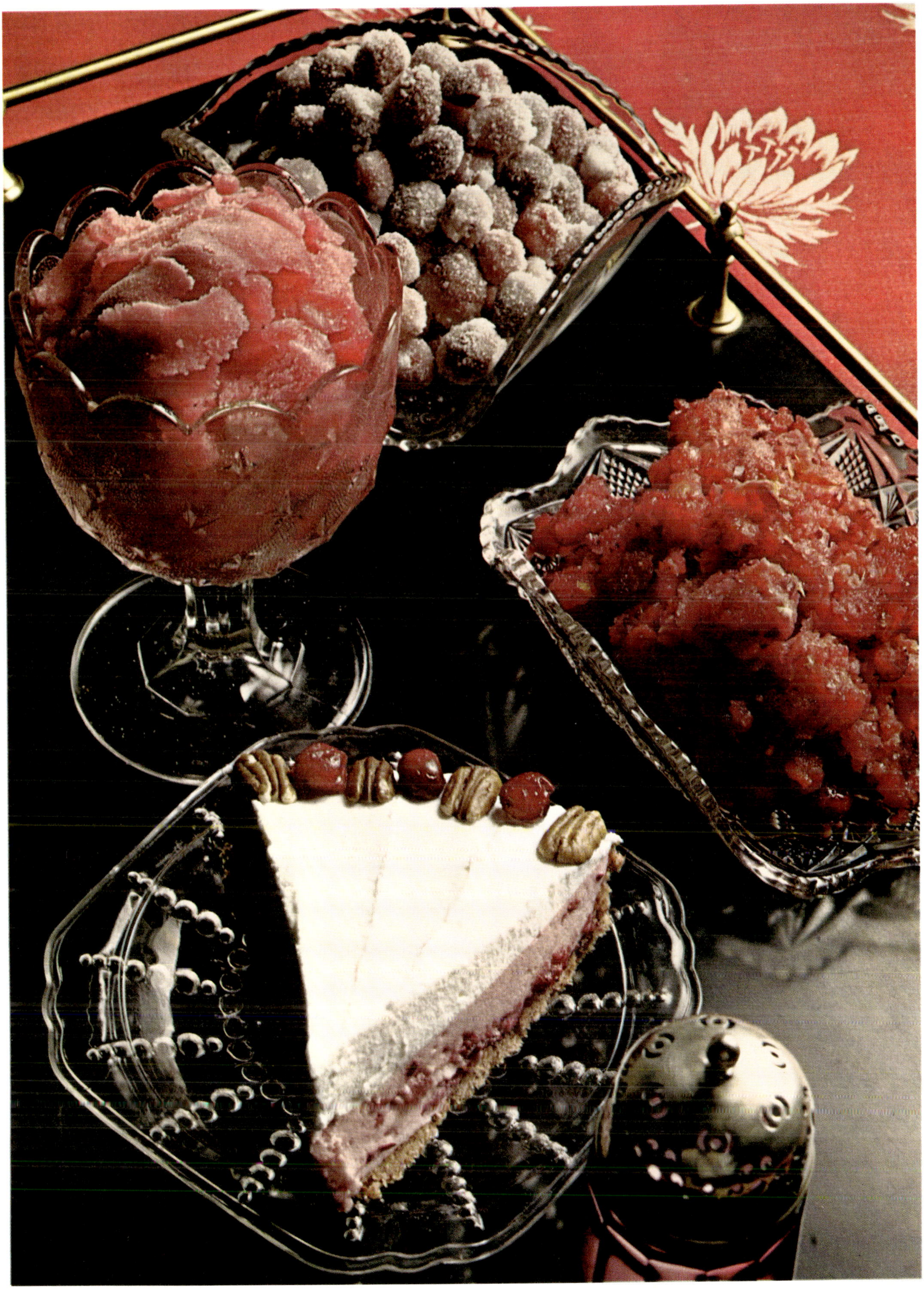

Wash the cranberries under cold running water, drop them into a small enameled or stainless-steel saucepan. Add the remaining 1¾ cups of cranberry juice and the ½ cup of sugar and bring to a boil over high heat, stirring constantly until the sugar dissolves. Reduce the heat to low and, still stirring from time to time, simmer uncovered for 4 or 5 minutes, until the skins of the berries just begin to pop and the berries are tender. Remove the pan from the heat, add the gelatin and stir until dissolved. Then drain the entire mixture through a fine sieve into a large glass or ceramic bowl. Measure the liquid and, if necessary, add enough cranberry juice to make 1½ cups. Set the liquid aside to cool.

Select the 12 or 15 best-shaped whole, cooked cranberries, pat them dry with paper towels and reserve them for use as a garnish. Pat the remaining berries dry and chop them as fine as possible with a knife.

When the cranberry liquid begins to thicken and is somewhat syrupy, beat the egg whites and salt with a whisk or a rotary or electric beater until they are frothy. Sprinkle the remaining ¼ cup of sugar over them and continue to beat until the egg whites stand in soft peaks on the beater when it is lifted from the bowl.

In a deep chilled bowl, whip ½ cup of the cream with a whisk or a rotary or electric beater until it is firm and stands in unwavering peaks in the bowl. Scoop the egg whites over the cream and, with a rubber spatula, fold them together gently but thoroughly, using an over-under cutting motion rather than stirring.

Pour the egg white-and-cream mixture over the thickened cranberry syrup and fold with the spatula until no trace of white remains. Gently fold in the chopped cranberries, distributing them as evenly as possible. Pour the mixture into the cooled pie crust and refrigerate for at least 3 hours, or until the chiffon is firm to the touch.

Just before serving, whip the remaining cream and the confectioners' sugar with a whisk or a rotary or electric beater until the mixture forms unwavering peaks on the beater when it is lifted from the bowl. Spread the whipped cream over the entire surface of the pie, smoothing it with a spatula. Arrange the reserved whole cranberries and the pecan halves attractively on top and serve at once.

To make about 1 pint

1⅓ cups uncooked cranberry-orange relish *(page 298)*
1 cup strained fresh orange juice

Cranberry-Orange Sherbet

Combine the relish and juice in a glass or ceramic bowl and stir until well mixed. With a rubber spatula, transfer the entire contents of the bowl into an ice-cube tray from which the dividers have been removed.

Freeze the mixture for 3 to 4 hours, stirring and mashing it every 30 minutes or so with a fork to break up the solid particles that will form on the bottom and sides of the tray.

To serve, spoon the sherbet into parfait glasses or dessert dishes.

Sweet-Potato Pie

Preheat the oven to 425°. Drop the quartered sweet potatoes into enough boiling water to immerse them completely and boil briskly, uncovered, until they are tender and show no resistance when they are pierced with the point of a small skewer or knife. Drain off the water, return the pan to low heat and slide it back and forth for a minute or so to dry the potatoes completely.

Rub the sweet potatoes through a fine sieve with the back of a spoon or purée them through a food mill. Set the puréed potatoes aside to cool to room temperature.

In a deep bowl, cream the butter and brown sugar together by beating and mashing them against the sides of the bowl with the back of a wooden spoon until they are light and fluffy. Beat in the cooled puréed sweet potatoes and, when they are completely incorporated, add the eggs one at a time, beating well after each addition. Add the light corn syrup, milk, grated lemon peel, vanilla, grated nutmeg and salt and continue to beat until the filling is smooth.

Pour the sweet-potato filling into the fully baked pie shell, spreading it evenly with a rubber spatula. Bake in the middle of the oven for 10 minutes. Then reduce the oven temperature to 325° and bake the pie for 35 minutes longer, or until a knife inserted in the center comes out clean.

Serve the sweet-potato pie warm or at room temperature.

To make one 9-inch pie

4 medium-sized sweet potatoes, peeled and quartered
4 tablespoons butter, softened
¾ cup dark-brown sugar
3 eggs, lightly beaten
⅓ cup light corn syrup
⅓ cup milk
2 teaspoons finely grated fresh lemon peel
1 teaspoon vanilla extract
¼ teaspoon ground nutmeg, preferably freshly grated
½ teaspoon salt
A 9-inch short-crust pastry pie shell, fully baked and cooled (*pages 241-242*)

Pecan Pie

Preheat the oven to 400°. With a wire whisk or a rotary or electric beater, beat the eggs in a mixing bowl for about 30 seconds, or until they are smooth. Beating constantly, pour in the syrup in a slow, thin stream. Then add the cooled melted butter and the vanilla and continue to beat until all the ingredients are well blended.

Pour the egg-and-syrup mixture into the pie shell and scatter the pecan halves evenly over the top. Bake in the middle of the oven for 35 to 40 minutes, or until the filling is firm to the touch.

Serve the pecan pie warm or at room temperature.

To make one 9-inch pie

4 eggs
2 cups dark corn syrup
2 tablespoons butter, melted and cooled
1 teaspoon vanilla extract
A 9-inch short-crust pastry shell, partially baked and cooled (*pages 241-242*)
1½ cups pecan halves (about 6 ounces)

Orange Meringue Pie

In a small heavy saucepan, heat the evaporated milk until bubbles begin to appear around the edges of the pan. Remove from the heat and cover to keep the milk warm.

In a deep bowl, beat the egg yolks with a wire whisk or rotary or electric beater for about a minute. Slowly add ½ cup of the sugar and the gelatin, and continue beating for 4 to 5 minutes until the mixture is thick enough to fall back on itself in a slowly dissolving ribbon when the beater is lifted out of the bowl.

Beating constantly, pour in the warm milk in a slow thin stream. Then pour the custard mixture back into the saucepan and, stirring constantly with a wooden spoon, cook over low heat for about 5 minutes. Do not let it come anywhere near a boil or the custard will curdle. When the custard is thick enough to coat the spoon lightly, remove the pan from the heat

To make one 9-inch pie

1½ cups evaporated milk
4 egg yolks
¾ cup sugar
2 teaspoons unflavored gelatin
⅓ cup Grand Marnier or other orange-flavored liqueur such as Cointreau, Triple Sec or Curaçao
2 tablespoons finely grated fresh orange peel
4 egg whites
A 9-inch short-crust pastry pie shell, fully baked and cooled (*pages 241-242*)

Flaunting their fillings are two single-crust pies to serve on Thanksgiving Day: old-fashioned sweet potato and orange meringue.

and stir in the orange liqueur and orange peel. Transfer the custard to a bowl and let it cool to room temperature.

Preheat the oven to 350°. With a wire whisk or a rotary or electric beater, beat the egg whites to a froth. Add the remaining ¼ cup of sugar and continue to beat until the meringue is stiff enough to stand in unwavering peaks on the beater when it is lifted from the bowl.

Pour the cooled custard into the pie shell and smooth the top with a rubber spatula. Then spread the meringue on top, mounding it slightly in the center and creating decorative swirls with the spatula. Bake in the upper third of the oven for about 15 minutes, or until the meringue is firm and a delicate brown. Cool to room temperature before serving.

Maple-Walnut Pie

Preheat the oven to 400°. With a wire whisk or a rotary or electric beater, beat the eggs for 2 or 3 minutes until they begin to thicken and cling to the beater. Beating constantly, pour in the syrup in a slow, thin stream. Then beat in the cooled, melted butter and the vinegar.

Pour the maple filling into the baked and cooled pie shell and bake in the middle of the oven for 35 to 40 minutes, or until the top is delicately browned. (The filling may appear somewhat undercooked and soft, but it will become firm as it cools.) Remove the pie from the oven and let it cool to room temperature. Sprinkle the walnuts in a circle around the edge of the pie before serving.

To make one 9-inch pie

4 eggs
2 cups pure maple syrup
2 tablespoons butter, melted and cooled
2 teaspoons cider vinegar
A 9-inch short-crust pastry pie shell, baked and cooled (*pages 241-242*)
¼ cup coarsely chopped walnuts

Pumpkin Pie

In a large mixing bowl, combine the flour, vegetable shortening or lard, butter and salt. Use your fingertips to rub the flour and fat together until they look like flakes of coarse meal. Pour the ice water over the mixture, toss together, and press and knead gently with your hands, only until the dough can be gathered into a compact ball. Dust very lightly with flour, wrap in wax paper and chill for at least ½ hour.

Lightly butter a 9-inch pie plate. On a floured surface, roll the dough out into a circle about ⅛ inch thick and 13 to 14 inches in diameter. Lift it up on the rolling pin and unroll it over the pie plate, leaving enough slack in the middle of the pastry to enable you to line the plate without pulling or stretching the dough. Trim the excess pastry with a sharp knife to within ½ inch of the pie plate and fold the extra ½ inch under to make a double thickness all around the rim of the plate. With the tines of a fork or with your fingers, press the pastry down around the rim. Preheat the oven to 350°.

In a large mixing bowl, combine the cream, milk, brown sugar, cinnamon, cloves and ginger. Stir thoroughly, then add the lightly beaten eggs and the applejack. Stir in the 1½ cups of puréed pumpkin. Carefully pour the filling into the pie shell. Bake for 40 to 50 minutes in the center of the oven until the filling is firm and the center of the pie barely quivers when the pie pan is gently moved back and forth. Serve warm or at room temperature with vanilla ice cream or stiffly whipped cream.

To make one 9-inch pie

1¼ cups all-purpose flour
4 tablespoons chilled vegetable shortening or lard
2 tablespoons chilled butter, cut in ¼-inch pieces
⅛ teaspoon salt
3 tablespoons ice water

FILLING
½ cup heavy cream
½ cup milk
¾ cup dark brown sugar
1 teaspoon cinnamon
⅛ teaspoon ground cloves
½ teaspoon ground ginger
3 eggs, lightly beaten
2 tablespoons applejack
1½ cups puréed pumpkin, freshly cooked or canned

Spiced Mixed Nuts

Preheat the oven to 275°. With a pastry brush, spread the tablespoon of softened butter over a large baking sheet. Combine the sugar, cinnamon, cloves, nutmeg, ginger, allspice and salt in a small bowl and mix well. Add the egg white and water and stir until the mixture is a smooth paste. With a table fork, stir in about ½ cup of the nuts and, when they are evenly coated, transfer one at a time to the baking sheet. Coat the remaining nuts by the half cupful and arrange on the sheet in one layer.

Bake the nuts in the middle of the oven for 45 minutes, or until the spice coating is crisp and golden brown. Cool to room temperature and store the spiced mixed nuts in a tightly covered jar until ready to serve.

To make about 1 pound

1 tablespoon butter, softened
¾ cup sugar
1 teaspoon ground cinnamon
½ teaspoon ground cloves
¼ teaspoon ground nutmeg
¼ teaspoon ground ginger
¼ teaspoon ground allspice
½ teaspoon salt
1 egg white, lightly beaten
2 tablespoons cold water
1 cup whole blanched unsalted almonds
1 cup unsalted broken black walnuts
½ cup whole unsalted filberts

Sherried Walnuts

To make about ½ pound

1 tablespoon butter, softened
1½ cups sugar
½ cup dry sherry
½ teaspoon ground cinnamon
⅛ teaspoon ground nutmeg
2 cups unsalted walnut halves

With a pastry brush, spread the tablespoon of softened butter over a large baking sheet and set it aside.

Combine the sugar and sherry in a heavy 1-quart enameled saucepan and bring to a boil over high heat, stirring until the sugar dissolves. Then cook briskly, uncovered and undisturbed, until the syrup reaches a temperature of 240° on a candy thermometer or until about ⅛ teaspoon of the syrup dropped into ice water instantly forms a soft ball.

At once remove the pan from the heat and add the cinnamon, nutmeg and walnut halves. Stir gently for a few minutes, until the syrup becomes opaque and creamy. While the mixture is still soft, spread it on the buttered baking sheet and, with two table forks, carefully separate the candy-coated walnut halves. Set the sherried walnuts aside to cool to room temperature, then store in a tightly covered jar until ready to serve.

Toasted Pecans

To make about 1 pound

6 tablespoons butter, cut into ½-inch bits
1 pound (about 4 cups) whole unsalted pecans
1 tablespoon salt

Preheat the oven to 350°. In a heavy 8- to 10-inch skillet, melt the butter over moderate heat. When the foam subsides remove the pan from the heat, add the pecans and stir until they glisten with butter.

Spread the pecans in one layer in a jelly-roll pan or shallow baking dish. Toast the nuts in the middle of the oven for 15 to 20 minutes, stirring and turning them occasionally. When the nuts are crisp and brown, remove the pan from the oven, add the salt and toss the nuts about gently to season them evenly.

Cool to room temperature and store the toasted pecans in a tightly covered jar until ready to serve.

Mixed-Nut Brittle

To make about 2 pounds

1 cup whole unsalted blanched almonds
1 cup unsalted broken black walnuts
½ cup whole unsalted filberts
1 teaspoon salt
1 tablespoon butter, softened, plus 2 tablespoons butter, cut into bits
1½ cups sugar
1 cup light corn syrup
⅓ cup water
1 teaspoon vanilla extract

Preheat the oven to 350°. Mix the almonds, black walnuts, filberts and salt in a large shallow baking dish. Toast the nuts in the middle of the oven for about 5 minutes, stirring them from time to time. Then turn off the heat, but leave the nuts in the oven to keep them warm.

With a pastry brush, spread the tablespoon of softened butter over a large baking sheet and set it aside. Combine the sugar, corn syrup and water in a heavy 2- to 3-quart saucepan and bring to a boil over high heat, stirring until the sugar dissolves. Then cook briskly, uncovered and undisturbed, until the syrup reaches a temperature of 290° on a candy

An autumn bounty of nuts ends the Thanksgiving feast. At near left are spiced mixed nuts—almonds, black walnuts and filberts that have been dipped in a sugar-and-spice paste and baked to a crisp. The ladle holds crunchy salted oven-toasted pecans. The mixed-nut brittle below the glass of cider is chock-full of filberts, almonds and black walnuts. The basket at the bottom brims with sherried walnuts—walnut halves in a sherry-and-spice syrup.

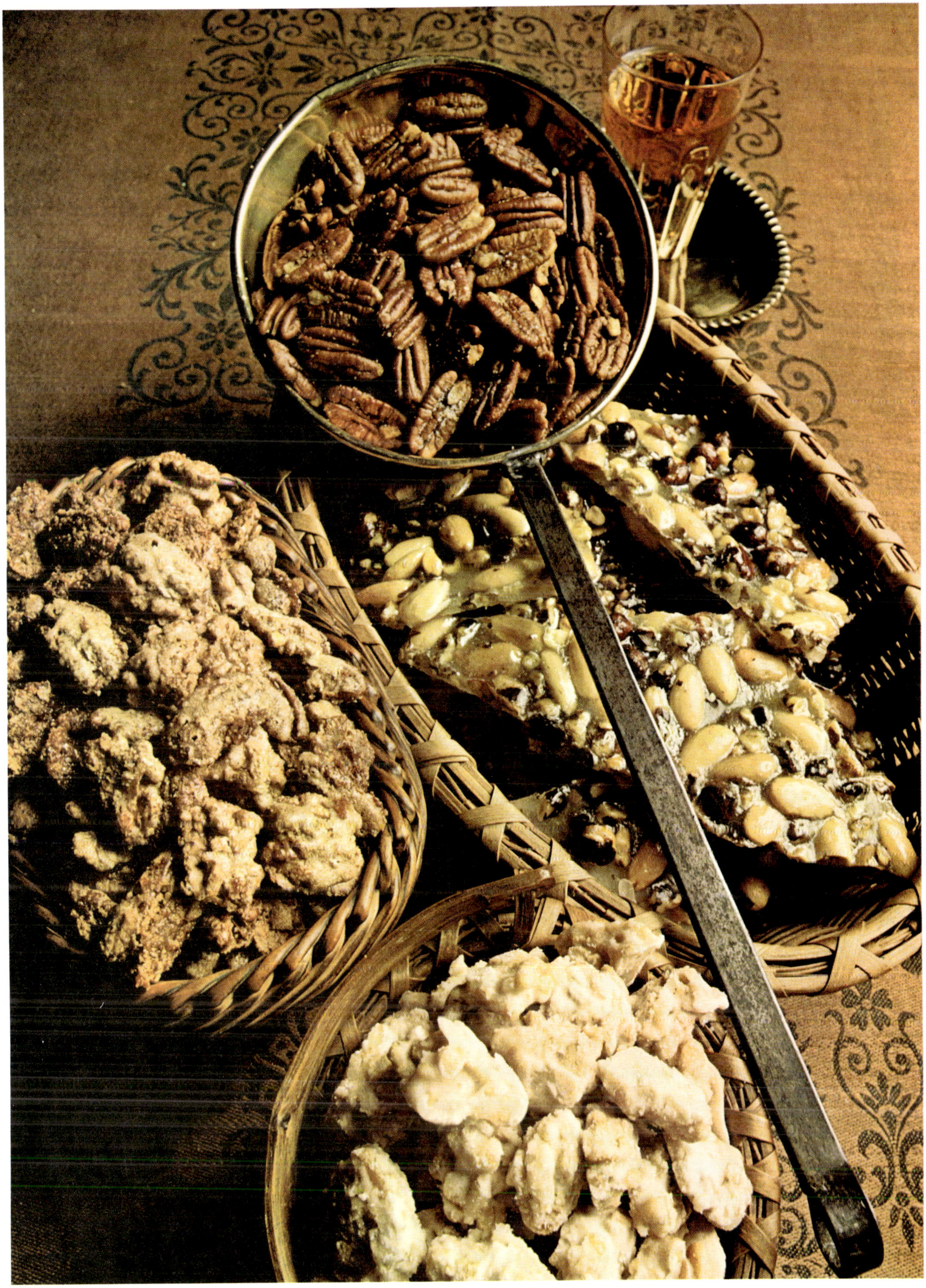

thermometer or until about ⅛ teaspoon of the syrup dropped into ice water immediately separates into hard but not brittle threads.

Remove the pan from the heat and immediately beat in the 2 tablespoons of butter bits, the vanilla and the warm nuts. Pour the candy onto the buttered baking sheet and set it aside to cool to room temperature. Break the mixed-nut brittle into pieces with a kitchen mallet or your hands, and store in a tightly covered jar until ready to serve.

To serve 6

The peel of 1 orange, cut into 1-by-⅛-inch strips
The peel of 1 lemon, cut into 1-by-⅛-inch strips
3 sugar lumps
6 whole cloves
A 2-inch cinnamon stick
1 cup cognac
½ cup curaçao or other orange liqueur
2 cups fresh strong black coffee

Café Brûlot

Assemble the ingredients for the *café brûlot* at the dinner table and prepare it there in the following manner: Light the burner under a *brûlot* bowl or chafing-dish pan and adjust the heat to low. Drop the orange and lemon peel, sugar lumps, cloves and cinnamon stick into the bowl or pan, pour in the cognac and curaçao, and stir to dissolve the sugar. When the mixture is warm, ignite it with a match. Stirring gently, pour in the coffee in a slow, thin stream and continue to stir until the flames die. Ladle the *café brûlot* into *brûlot* or demitasse cups and serve at once.

To make 1 after-dinner drink

3 strips lemon peel
A dish of superfine or confectioners' sugar
½ stick cinnamon
1½ ounces cognac
3 ounces hot coffee

Café Brûlé (or Café Royale)

Rub the cut edge of a strip of lemon peel around the inside rim of an old-fashioned glass and then dip the glass into the dish of sugar so that the sugar adheres to the inside rim. Twist the 2 other strips of peel over the glass to release their oil, and drop them and the ½ stick of cinnamon into the glass. Warm the cognac in a chafing dish or in a deep spoon held over a flame. Set a spoon in the glass to prevent the glass from cracking, pour in the warmed cognac, and set it aflame with a match. Let it burn itself out, then add the hot coffee and serve.

To make 1 after-dinner drink

½ ounce fresh lemon juice
1 ounce brandy
1 ounce Cointreau
1 ounce light rum
3 to 4 ice cubes

Between the Sheets

Combine the lemon juice, brandy, Cointreau, rum and ice cubes in a mixing glass. Place a shaker on top of the mixing glass and, grasping them firmly together with both hands, shake vigorously. Remove the shaker, place a strainer on top of the mixing glass, and pour into a chilled cocktail glass.

To make 1 after-dinner drink

1 lump sugar
1 strip lemon peel
1 strip orange peel
3½ ounces warmed brandy

Brandy Blazer

Combine the sugar, lemon peel, orange peel and brandy in a warmed old-fashioned glass. Mash with a muddler to thoroughly dissolve the sugar, then ignite the brandy with a match.

Angel's Dream

Pour the crème de cacao into a liqueur glass. Drop the dashes of heavy cream into a small demitasse spoon and place the spoon in the glass on top of the liqueur. Let the cream slide off slowly—it must not mix with the liqueur but should float on the surface.

A variation of this drink is the Angel's Kiss, made by preparing the drink as above and then piercing a maraschino cherry with a toothpick and laying the toothpick across the top of the glass.

To make 1 after-dinner drink

1½ ounces crème de cacao
3 dashes of heavy cream

Stinger

Combine the brandy, white crème de menthe and ice cubes in a mixing glass. Place a shaker on top of the mixing glass and, grasping them firmly together with both hands, shake vigorously 6 or 7 times. Remove the shaker, place a strainer over the mixing glass, and pour into a chilled cocktail glass.

To make 1 after-dinner drink

3 ounces brandy
1 ounce white crème de menthe
3 to 4 ice cubes

Grasshopper

Combine the crème de cacao, green crème de menthe, heavy cream and ice cubes in a mixing glass. Place a shaker over the top of the mixing glass and, grasping them firmly together with both hands, shake vigorously 7 or 8 times. Remove the shaker, place a strainer on top of the mixing glass, and pour into a chilled cocktail glass.

To make 1 after-dinner drink

1½ ounces crème de cacao
2½ ounces green crème de menthe
½ ounce (1 tablespoon) heavy cream
3 to 4 ice cubes

Picture Credits

The sources for the illustrations that appear in this book are listed below.
Credits from left to right are separated by semicolons, from top to bottom by dashes.

Front dust jacket—Richard Jeffery—Anthony Blake. Back dust jacket—Eliot Elisofon. 8—Anthony Blake. 12—Arie deZanger. 16—Mark Kauffman. 17—Drawings by Matt Greene. 22—Richard Meek. 25—Fred Lyon from Rapho/Photo Researchers. 28, 29, 33—Anthony Blake. 35—Drawings by Mary Farmberg. 36—Richard Meek. 39—Henry Groskinsky. 41—Fred Eng. 42, 43—Drawings by Matt Greene. 44—Anthony Blake. 50 through 59—Mark Kauffman. 62—Arie deZanger. 66—Richard Jeffery. 71, 74, 75—Mark Kauffman. 78, 79—Richard Meek. 84, 85—Richard Jeffery. 87—Ronald D'Asaro. 90, 92, 93—Arie deZanger. 95—Richard Jeffery. 97—Richard Meek—Ted Streshinsky. 101—Michael Rougier. 104—Mark Kauffman. 106—Richard Jeffery. 112—Fred Lyon from Rapho/Photo Researchers. 117—Richard Meek. 120—Richard Jeffery. 124, 125—Eliot Elisofon. 128—Richard Meek. 131—Fred Lyon from Rapho/Photo Researchers. 133—Richard Jeffery. 136—Constantine Manos from Magnum. 138—Arie deZanger. 140 through 151—Mark Kauffman. 154—Novosti Press Agency. 156, 157—Eliot Elisofon. 160—Richard Meek. 163—Richard Jeffery. 165—Fred Schnell. 168—Mark Kauffman. 170—Fred Lyon from Rapho/Photo Researchers. 174—Sebastian Milito. 179, 182, 183—Mark Kauffman. 186—Arie deZanger. 189—Richard Meek. 192, 193—Richard Jeffery. 198—Fred Lyon from Rapho/Photo Researchers. 203—Richard Jeffery. 206 through 223—Mark Kauffman. 225, 227—Richard Jeffery. 230—Anthony Blake. 232 through 243—Mark Kauffman. 247—Dmitri Kessel. 248—Arie deZanger. 250—Richard Jeffery. 254, 255—Ralph Crane. 259—Richard Meek. 261—Bill Helms. 264—Fred Lyon from Rapho/Photo Researchers. 267, 269—Richard Jeffery. 271—Fred Lyon from Rapho/Photo Researchers. 273—Charles Harbutt from Magnum. 277, 280—Richard Jeffery. 284—Mark Kauffman. 287—Richard Jeffery. 290—Mark Kauffman. 294 through 301—Richard Jeffery. 304—Mark Kauffman. 307—Richard Jeffery. 310—Mark Kauffman. 313—Richard Jeffery. Hand lettering by Raymond Cruz.

Index

Numerals in italics indicate a photograph or drawing of the subject mentioned.

A

Absinthe *Suissesse,* 94, 95
Almonds:
  Macaroons, 163-164
  Nougat, 115
  Rice-and-almond dessert, *22, 23*-24
  Rum layer cake with praline topping, 200-201
Angel's Dream, 315
Appetizers:
  Benne-seed cocktail biscuits, 11
  Caraway twists, 13
  Cheese balls, 15
  Cheese pennies, 14-15
  Fondue *Neuchâteloise,* 11, *12*
  Galantine de canard, 16, 17-20
  Ham balls, 13
  Mushroom caps stuffed with anchovy cream cheese, 14
  Steak tartare balls, 15
  Tomato cheese *croustades,* 14
Apples:
  Fritters, *280,* 281
  Halves stuffed with prunes in port wine, 23
  Red cabbage with, *260*-261
Artichokes:
  Boiled, 147
  Stuffed with shrimp and Green Goddess dressing, 180
Asparagus:
  With egg sauce, 148
  Tips with Chinese-mushroom sauce, 103, *104,* 105
Aspic:
  Boeuf à la mode in, 190-191
  Tomato, 167-168
  Veal in, 180-181
  Vegetable, 238
Avocado and tomato soup, cold, 235

B

Babka—Polish Easter cake, 153-154
Bacardi, 248
Baked Alaska, 202, 204
Bananas flambé, 202, *203*
Basil sauce, Genoa style, 268
Batty cakes, lacy-edged, *165,* 166-167
Bavarois Clermont, 204-205, *206-207*
Beans:
  Black, sea bass with fermented, 105
  Boston baked, 224, 226
  String, plantation, 169
  Three-bean salad, 218, *222-223*
Béarnaise sauce, 148
Béchamel sauce, 196-197
Beef:
  Boeuf à la mode, hot, 188-190
  Boeuf à la mode en gelée, 190-191
  Chili con carne, 220, *222-223*
  Roast, 31, *33*
  Rouladen—braised stuffed steak rolls, 260, *261*
  Sauerbraten, 253, 256
  Steak tartare balls, 15
  Steaks Eszterházy, *198,* 199
  Stroganoff, 199
  Swedish meatballs, 79, 81-82
  -And-sweet-potato stew, 275-276
  T-bone or Porterhouse steak, charcoal-broiled, 218, *219*
  Tongue in sweet-and-sour sauce, 276
Beets:
  Borscht, 26-27, 272
  Pickled, 77
Benne-seed cocktail biscuits, 11
Between the sheets, 314
Beverages. *See* Drinks, after-dinner; Drinks and punches, holiday
Bird's nest soup, 100
Birthday cake with maple-sugar icing, 201-202
Biscuits:
  Beaten, *66,* 69-70
  Benne-seed cocktail, 11
Black bun cake, 88-89
Black Russian, 91, *92*
Blackberry cobbler, 242, 244
Bliny, 123, *125*
Bloody Mary, 90, *92-93*
Blueberries:
  Pie, 241
  Roll, 244-245
Boeuf à la mode, hot, 188-190
Boeuf à la mode en gelée, 190-191
Borscht, 26-27;
  Cold, 272
Boston baked beans, 224, 226
Bourbon balls, *59,* 61
Boxty pancakes, 139
Brandy:
  Blazer, 314
  Butter, *44,* 46
Bratwurst in sour-cream sauce, 258
Breads:
  Beaten biscuits, *66,* 69-70
  Benne-seed cocktail biscuits, 11
  Corn, 226, *304,* 305
  Cozonac—Rumanian Easter, 152-153
  Crackling, 226
  Cranberry fruit-nut, 303
  Cranberry muffins, 305
  Czech Christmas sweet bread, 35, *36*
  Fruit loaf, 37
  Irish soda, 137
  Onion rolls, stuffed, 79, 82
  Poppy-seed roll, 34-35
  Pumpkin, 303

Sauce, 29, 30
Shrove Tuesday buns, 121-122
Sweet, 35, 36
Tsoureki—Greek Easter, 152
Broccoli:
Ham and chicken with, 102-103
Purée, 30-31
Brownies:
Butterscotch, 279
Chocolate, 279
Brussels sprouts with walnuts, 26
Bûche de Noël, 56-57
Bullshot, 91, 93
Burgoo, Kentucky, 167
Butter:
Brandy, 44, 46
Clarified, 177-178
Cumberland rum, 44, 46
Sauce, 268
Butterscotch brownies, 279

C

Cabbage:
Braised red, 21, 22
Corned beef and, 135, 136, 137
Pickled, 134
Red, with apples, 260, 261
Sweet-and-sour stuffed, 275
Caesar salad, 240
Café:
Brûlé (or *Café Royale*), 314
Brûlot, 314
Cakes:
Babka—Polish Easter, 153-154
Birthday, with maple-sugar icing, 201-202
Black bun, 88-89
Blueberry roll, 244-245
Bûche de Noël, 56-57
Cherry, 129
Coconut, with lemon filling, 57, 58, 60
Doboschtorte, 84-85, 86-87
Dresdner Stollen, 38, 39
Dundee, 37
English fruitcake, 46-47
Gingerbread house, 40, 41, 42-43
Gypsy creams, 112, 113-114
Haselnusstorte, 83, 84, 86
Honey, 132-133
Huckleberry, 244
Irish fruitcake, 47
King's, 118-119, 120, 121
Kulich—Russian Easter, 154, 155, 158
Linzertorte, 85, 88
Paskha—Russian Easter cheesecake, 156-157, 158
Rehrücken, 84-85, 87-88
Rum layer, with praline topping, 200-201

Spanish Wind *Torte*, 170, 208-209
Spongecake, with cherries, 129
Strawberry cream roll, 106, 109-110
Strawberry shortcake, 242, 243
Strawberry spongecake, 106, 110-111
White fruitcake, 59, 60-61
Candied cranberries, 306, 307
Candy:
Almond nougat, 115
Bourbon balls, 59, 61
Divinity, 59, 61-62
Maple-walnut fudge balls, 114
Penuche, 114-115
Caraway twists, 13
Carrots, minted, 168
Casseroles:
Cassoulet, 73, 74-75, 76
Hopping John, 70
Jansson's Temptation, 79, 82
Kentucky burgoo, 167
Matzo, chicken and dill, baked, 162
Ratatouille, 220-221
Red cabbage with apples, 260-261
Cassoulet, 73, 74-75, 76
Celery:
Braised, with almonds, 302
Slaw, 237
Victor, 184-185
Champagne:
Pick-me-up, 94
Punch, 65
Punch, Creole, 120, 121
Or Rhine wine cup, 186, 187
Cheese:
Balls, 15
Pennies, 14-15
Quiche au fromage, 70-72, 71
Tomato, croustades, 14
Cherries:
Cake, 129
Cobbler, 127
Jubilee, 127
Pie, sour-, 128
Soup, cold, 130, 131
Spongecake with, 129
Twist, 129-130
Chicken:
And ham with broccoli, 102-103
Kentucky fried, 226, 227
Kiev, 191, 192-193, 194
With kumquats, 276, 277
Matzo, and dill casserole, baked, 162
Soup with matzo balls, 161-162
Chili con carne, 220, 222-223

Chocolate:
Brownies, 279
Mousse, 205, 208
Walnut cookies with, filling, 283-284
Cioppino—California fisherman's stew, 229, 231, 232-233
Clams, steamed, 228-229
Claret cup, 65
Clarified butter, 177-178
Cocktails. *See* Drinks and punches, holiday
Coconut cake with lemon filling, 57, 58, 60
Colcannon, 135
Coleslaw with boiled dressing, 237
Cookies:
Almond macaroons, 163-164
Figure-eight, 287, 289
German, 39
Hamantaschen, 132
Jewish, 22, 24
Joe Froggers—rum-and-molasses, 282-283
Lemon bars, 285
Licorice, 283
Little brown cakes, 22, 24
Moravian sand tarts, 285
Oatmeal, 284-285
Pecan-stuffed date, 279, 281
Toll House, 278-279
Tom Thumb, 282
Walnut, with chocolate filling, 283-284
Wine-and-spice, 286-287, 288
Corn:
Pudding, 302
Sticks, 226-227
Cornbread:
Loaf, 304, 305
Sausage and pecan stuffing, 296
Corned beef and cabbage dinner, 135, 136, 137
Coulibiac—salmon brioche loaf, 173, 174, 175-177
Cozonac—Rumanian Easter bread, 152-153
Crabs:
Shrimp and okra gumbo, 116, 117, 118
-And-sole mousse with shrimp sauce, 181, 182-183, 184
Steamed, 229
Crackling bread, 226
Cranberries:
Candied, 306, 307
Chiffon pie, 306-307, 308
-Fruit-nut bread, 303
Ice, 305, 307
Muffins, 305
-Orange relish, 298
Orange sherbet, 307, 308
Sauce, 299
Crullers, 287, 288-289

Cucumber:
Pickled, salad, 77, 78
Sauce, molded salmon with, 231, 234
-And-sour-cream salad, 187
Cumberland rum butter, 44, 46
Czech Christmas sweet bread, 35, 36

D

Dag Kavush—pickled fish, 274
Daiquiri, 248, 249
Deep-dish peach pie with cream-cheese crust, 245
Desserts:
Babka—Polish Easter cake, 153-154
Baked Alaska, 202, 204
Bavarois Clermont, 204-205, 206-207
Birthday cake with maple-sugar icing, 201-202
Black bun cake, 88-89
Bûche de Noël, 56-57
Doboschtorte, 84-85, 86-87
Dresdner Stollen, 38, 39
Dundee cake, 37
Gâteau Saint-Honoré, 52-55, 54
Gelati—Italian ice creams, 270-271
Ginger peach ice cream, 246
Granité—Italian ices, 270, 271
Haselnusstorte, 83, 84, 86
Honey cake, 132-133
King's cake, 118-119, 120, 121
Kulich—Russian Easter cake, 154, 155, 158
Linzertorte, 85, 88
Maids of honor, 111, 113
Maple-walnut pie, 311
Mousse au chocolat, 205, 208
Paskha—Russian Easter cheesecake, 156-157, 158
Pecan pie, 309
Rehrücken, 84-85, 87-88
Rice and almond, 22, 23-24
Riz à l'Impératrice, 48-49, 50-51
Rum layer cake with praline topping, 200-201
Spanish Wind Torte, 170, 208-209
Spongecake with cherries, 129
Vanilla ice cream, 245-246
See also names of fruits
Divinity candies, 59, 61-62
Doboschtorte, 84-85, 86-87
Doughnuts:
Fasching, 126
Sugar, 250, 278
Dressing. *See* Salad dressing
Drinks, after-dinner:
Angel's Dream, 315

Between the sheets, 314
Brandy blazer, 314
Café Brûlé (or *Café Royale*), 314
Café Brûlot, 314
Grasshopper, 315
Irish coffee, *138*, 139
Stinger, 315
Drinks and punches, holiday:
Absinthe *Suissesse*, 94-95
Bacardi, 248
Black Russian, 91, *92*
Bloody Mary, 90, *92-93*
Bullshot, 91, *93*
Champagne pick-me-up, 94
Champagne punch, 65
Champagne punch, Creole, *120*, 121
Champagne or Rhine wine cup, *186*, 187
Claret cup, 65
Daiquiri, *248*, 249
Eggnog, Southern, *58*, 63
Fish House punch, 89, *90*
Frozen daiquiri, 249
Gimlet, 91, *93*
Gin fizz, 94, *95*
Green Dragon, 91, *93*
Grog, 64
Hot buttered rum, *62*, 64
Hot toddy, 64
Mai-Tai, *247*, 248
Milk punch, 94, *95*
Mint julep, *168*, 169
Peach daiquiri, *248*
Planter's punch, *248*, 249
Sangría, 247
Sauternes cup, 187
Screwdriver, 91, *92*
Silver fizz, 91, *92*
Swedish *Glögg*, 63
Tom and Jerry, *62*, 64
Vin Chaud (or *Glühwein*), *62*, 63
Duck:
Galantine de canard, 16
Peking, 100, *101*, 102
Dumplings:
Bread, *22*, 26
Kreplach—meat-filled, *272*, 274
Potato, 262
Yeast, *256*, *261*
Dundee cake, 37

E

Eggnog, Southern, *58*, 63
Eggs:
In aspic, *140*, 143-144
Derby, 164
-And-ham fried rice, 103
Kentucky scramble, *165*, 166
-And-lemon soup, 144
Rolls with shrimp and pork, *96*, 98

F

Fasching doughnuts, 126
Fettuccine and butter sauce, 268
Figure-eight cookies, *287*, 289
Fillets, rolled stuffed fish, 188, *189*
Fish:
Coulibiac—salmon brioche loaf, 173, *174*, 175-177
Dag Kavuch—pickled fish, 274
Fillets, rolled stuffed, 188, *189*
Gefilte, 159, *163*
German, dish for a hangover, 76
Gravlax—salmon marinated in dill, 78, 80
Herring plate, 77, *78*
Herring salad with sour-cream sauce, *78*, 80
Mackerel, soused, 137
Salmon, barbecued, 215-216
Salmon with cucumber sauce, molded, *231*, 234
Sea bass with fermented black beans, 105
Sole-and-crab mousse with shrimp sauce, 181, *182-183*, 184
Swordfish, grilled, 218
Swordfish shish kabob, 221, *224*, *225*
Fish House punch, 89, *90*
Fondue *Neuchâteloise*, 11, *12*
Frozen daiquiri, 249
Fruitcake:
Danish Christmas fruit loaf, 37
Dresdner Stollen, 38, *39*
Dundee cake, 37
English, 46-47
Irish, 47
White, *59*, 60-61
Fruits. See names of fruits
Fudge balls, walnut-maple, 114
Fumet de poisson, 177

G

Galantine de canard, *16*, 17-20
Game chips, *28-29*, 30
Garlic-and-tomato sauce, 265
Gâteau Saint-Honoré, 52-55, *54*
Gazpacho, 236-237
Gefilte fish, 159, *163*
Gelati—Italian ice creams, 270-271
Gelatin salad, lime, 178-179
Gimlet, 91, *93*
Gin fizz, 94, *95*
Ginger-ale salad, 178, *179*
Ginger peach ice cream, 246
Gingerbread house, 40, *41*, *42-43*
Glögg, Swedish, 63

Glühwein (or *Vin Chaud*), *62*, 63
Goose:
Roasted, with sauerkraut, *25*
Roasted, stuffed with apples and prunes, *21*, 22
Granite—Italian ices, 270, *271*
Grasshopper, 315
Gravlax—salmon marinated in dill, 78, 80
Green Dragon, 91, *93*
Green Goddess dressing, 180
Griddle cakes, 122-123
Grog, 64
Gypsy creams, *112*, 113-114

H

Ham:
Baked, with brown-sugar glaze, 66
Baked bourbon-glazed, 149, *150-151*
Balls, 13
And chicken with broccoli, 102-103
-And-egg fried rice, 103
Hamantaschen cookies, 132
Haselnusstorte, 83, *84*, 86
Hash, turkey, 166
Herring:
Plate, 77, *78*
Salad with sour-cream sauce, *78*, 80
Holishkes—sweet-and-sour stuffed cabbage, 275
Hollandaise sauce, 147-148
Honey cake, *132-133*
Hopping John, 70
Horseradish sauce, *32*, *33*
Horseradish sauce with beets, 159, *161*, *163*
Hot toddy, 64
Huckleberry cake, 244

I

Ice cream:
Gelati—Italian, 270-*271*
Ginger peach, 246
Vanilla, 245-246
Ices, Italian, 270, *271*
Icing, maple-sugar, 201-202
Irish coffee, *138*, 139
Irish soda bread, 137
Irish stew, 134

J

Jansson's Temptation, *79*, 82
Jewish cookies, *22*, 24
Joe Froggers—rum-and-molasses, 282-283

K

Kasha varnischkes—noodles with buckwheat groats, 274

Kentucky fried chicken, 226, *227*
King's cake, 118-119, *120*, 121
Kreplach—meat-filled dumplings, *272*, 274
Kulich—Russian Easter cake, 154-155, 158

L

Lamb:
Chops, sautéed, 197
Crown roast of, with peas and new potatoes, 145, *146*, 147
Leg of, marinated, 145
Shish kabob, 221, *225*
Latkes, potato, 162-163
Lemon bars, 285
Lentil soup, 235
Licorice cookies, 282
Lime-gelatin salad, 178-179
Linzertorte, *85*, 88
Liver *pâté*, *78*, 81
Lobster:
Boiled, *210*, 228
Soufflé with lobster sauce, 195-196

M

Macaroons, almond, 163-164
Mackerel, soused, 137
Mai-Tai, *247*, 248
Maids of honor, 111, 113
Mandarin pancakes, *101*, 102
Maple:
Barbecue spareribs, 215
-Sugar icing, 201-202
-Walnut fudge balls, 114
-Walnut pie, 311
Marzipan, 46-47
Matzo:
Balls, 161-162
Chicken and dill casserole, baked, 162
Meatballs, Swedish, *79*, 81-82
Milk punch, 94, *95*
Mince pies, *44*, 45
Mincemeat, 45
Minestrone, Genoa style, 265-266
Mint julep, *168*, 169
Moravian sand tarts, 285-286
Mousse au chocolat, *205*, 208
Mushrooms:
Caps stuffed with anchovy cream cheese, 14
Chinese-mushroom sauce, asparagus tips with, 103, *104*, 105
Mussels in white wine, 228
Mustard sauce, *78*, 80

N

Noodles with buckwheat groats, 274

Nuts:
 Mixed-nut brittle, 312-313, 314
 Spiced mixed, 311, 313
 See also names of nuts

O

Oatmeal cookies, 284-285
Oeufs en gelée—eggs in aspic, 140, 143-144
Onions:
 Creamed, 298, 299
 Glazed, 32
 Rolls, stuffed, 79, 82
 Soup, 72-73
Orange meringue pie, 309-310
Oyster stuffing, 297, 298

P

Pancakes, 122-123
 Batty cakes, lacy-edged, 165, 166-167
 Bliny, 123, 125
 Boxty, 139
 Griddle cakes, 122-123
 Mandarin, 101, 102
 Potato, with applesauce, 262
Paskha—Russian Easter cheesecake, 156-157, 158
Pasta:
 Dough, 267
 Fettuccine with butter sauce, 268
 Ravioli, 266, 267
Pastry, short-crust, 45, 241-242
Pâté, liver, 78, 81
Peach:
 Daiquiri, 248
 Ice cream, ginger, 246
 Pie, deep dish, with cream-cheese crust, 245
Peanut soup, 293
Peas:
 Black-eyed—Hopping John, 70
 Fresh green, à la française, 148-149
 Split, soup with mint, cold, 235-236
Pecans:
 Cornbread and sausage stuffing, 296
 Pie, 309
 Stuffed date cookies, 279, 281
 Toasted, 312, 313
Peking duck, 100-102, 101
Penuche, 114-115
Pepper and salt, roasted, 99
Pesto—basil sauce, Genoa style, 268
Pheasant, roasted, 27, 28-29
Pie shell. See Short-crust pastry
Pies:
 Blueberry, 241
 Cranberry chiffon, 306-307, 308
 Maple-walnut, 311
 Mince, 44, 45
 Orange meringue, 309-310
 Peach, with cream-cheese crust, deep-dish, 245
 Pecan, 309
 Pumpkin, 311
 Short-crust pastry, 45, 241-242
 Sour-cherry, 128
 Sweet-potato, 308-309
Pilaf, 224, 225
Pizza, 263, 264, 265
Planter's punch, 248, 249
Plum pudding, 49, 52
Pommes soufflées, 197
Poppy-seed roll, 34-35
Pork:
 Loin, roasted smoked, 257-258
 And shrimp, egg rolls with, 96, 98
 Sweet-and-sour, 99
Porterhouse steak, charcoal-broiled, 218, 219
Potatoes:
 Colcannon, 135
 Caramelized, 22, 23
 Dumplings, 262
 Game chips, 28-29, 30
 Jansson's Temptation, 79, 82
 Latkes, 162-163
 Mashed, 300-301
 Pancakes with applesauce, 262
 Pommes soufflées, 197
 Salad, 224
 Salad with bacon bits, 258
 Scalloped, *Dauphinoises*, 149
 Straw, 192-193, 194
 Stuffed baked, with cheese, 216-217
 Sweet, candied, 302
 Sweet-, pie, 308-309, 310
 Sweet-, stew, beef-and-, 275-276
Prunes, apple halves stuffed with, in port wine, 23
Puddings:
 Corn, 302
 Plum, 49, 52
 Yorkshire, 31-32, 33
Pumpkin:
 Bread, 303
 Pie, 311
 Soup, 293
Punches:
 Champagne, 65
 Creole Champagne, 120, 121
 Fish House, 89, 90
 Milk, 94, 95
 Planter's, 248, 249

Q

Quiche au fromage, 70-72, 71

R

Ratatouille, 220-221
Ravioli, 266
Rehrücken, 84-85, 87-88
Red cabbage with apples, 261-262
Relish, cranberry-orange, 298
Rice:
 À l'Impératrice, 48-49, 50-51
 -And-almond dessert, 22, 23-24
 Ham-and-egg fried, 103
 Pilaf, 224, 225
Riz à l'Impératrice, 48-49, 50-51
Roast beef, 31, 33
Rouladen—braised stuffed steak rolls, 260, 261
Roux, brown, 118
Rum:
 Bacardi, 248
 Hot buttered, 62, 64
 Layer cake with praline topping, 200-201
 -And-molasses cookies, 282-283

S

Salad dressings:
 Boiled, 237
 Green Goddess, 180
 Strawberry-and-sour-cream, 178
Salads:
 Caesar, 240
 Celery slaw, 237
 Coleslaw with boiled dressing, 237
 Cucumber, pickled, 77, 78
 Cucumber-and-sour-cream, 187
 Ginger-ale, 178, 179
 Herring, with sour-cream sauce, 78, 80
 Lime-gelatin, 178-179
 Potato, 224
 Shaker, 240
 Spinach, 239
 Three-bean, 218, 222-223
 Tomato aspic, 167-168
 Vegetable aspic, 238
 Water-chestnut-and-watercress, 185, 187
 Yoghurt, vegetable and herb, 240
 Zucchini, cold marinated, 238
Salmon:
 Barbecued stuffed, 215-216
 Coulibiac—salmon brioche loaf, 173, 174, 175-177
 With cucumber sauce, 231, 234
 Gravlax—salmon marinated in dill, 78, 80
Salsa di pomodori—tomato sauce, 268
Salsa pizzaiola—tomato and garlic sauce, 265
Salt and pepper, roasted, 99
Sangría, 247
Sauces:
 Béarnaise, 148
 Béchamel, 196-197
 Bread, 29, 30
 Butter, 268
 Chinese-mushroom, 103, 104, 105
 Cranberry, 299
 Cucumber, 234
 Hollandaise, 147-148
 Horseradish, 32, 33
 Horseradish, with beets, 159, 161, 163
 Lobster, 195-196
 Mustard, 78, 80
 Pesto—basil sauce, Genoa style, 268
 Red, 213, 214
 Salsa di pomodori—tomato, 268
 Salsa pizzaiola—tomato and garlic, 265
 Shrimp, 182-183, 184
 Sour cream, 78, 80, 188, 189, 258
 Sweet-and-sour, 277
 Sweet or spicy, 213
 Veloutée, 177
Sauerbraten, 253, 256
Sauerkraut, steamed spiced, 257
Sausage, cornbread and pecan stuffing, 296
Sauternes cup, 187
Screwdriver, 91, 92
Sea bass with fermented black beans, 105
Seafood:
 Cioppino—California fisherman's stew, 229, 231, 232-233
 Clams, steamed, 228-229
 Crab-and-sole mousse with shrimp sauce, 181, 182-183, 184
 Crab, shrimp and okra gumbo, 116, 117, 118
 Crabs, steamed, 229
 Lobster, boiled, 228
 Lobster soufflé with lobster sauce, 195-196
 Mussels in white wine, steamed, 228
 Seasoning, 229
 Shrimp, barbecued, 216
 Shrimp and Green Goddess dressing, artichokes stuffed with, 180
 Shrimp balls, deep-fried, 98-99
 Shrimp curry, 194-195
 Shrimp and pork, egg rolls with, 96, 98
Seasoning, seafood, 229

Shaker salad, 240
Sherbet, cranberry-orange, 308
Short-crust pastry, 45, 241-242
Shrimp:
    Artichokes stuffed with, and Green Goddess dressing, 180
    Balls, deep-fried, 98-99
    Barbecued, 216
    Crab, and okra gumbo, 116, *117*, 118
    Curry, 194-195
    And pork, egg rolls with, 96, 98
    Sauce, *182-183*, 184
Shrove Tuesday buns, 121-122
Silver fizz, 91, *92*
Sole-and-crab mousse with shrimp sauce, 181, *182-183*, 184
Soups:
    Avocado and tomato soup, cold, 235
    Bird's nest, 100
    Chicken, with matzo balls, 161-162
    Cold cherry, 130, *131*
    Egg-and-lemon, 144
    Gazpacho, 236-237
    Lentil, cold, 235
    Minestrone, Genoa style, 265-266
    Onion, 72-73
    Peanut, 293
    Pumpkin, 293
    Spinach, 144-145
    Split pea, with mint, cold, 235-*236*
Sour cream:
    Cucumber-and-, salad, *187*
    Sauce, *78*, 80, 188, *189*, 258
    Strawberry-and-, dressing, 178
Spanish Wind *Torte*, *170*, 208-209
Spareribs:
    Barbecued with red sauce, 213, *214*
    Barbecued with sweet or spicy sauce, 213, 215
    Maple barbecue, 215
    Stuffed, 259
Spätzle, 256-257
Spinach:
    Gnocchi, 269
    Salad, 239
    Soup, 144-145

Split pea soup with mint, cold, 235-236
Squash:
    Acorn, spiced, *290*, 299-300
    Creamed winter, 300, *301*
Steak:
    Eszterházy, 198, 199
    Rouladen—braised stuffed, rolls, 260, *261*
    T-bone or Porterhouse, charcoal-broiled, 218, *219*
    Tartare balls, 15
Stew:
    Beef-and-sweet-potato, 275-276
    Cioppino—California fisherman's, 229, 231, *232-233*
    Irish, 134
Stinger, 315
Stocks:
    Fumet de poisson, 177
    Turkey, 296-297
Stollen, Dresdner, 38
Strawberries:
    Cream roll, *106*, 109-110
    Flummery, *106*, 110
    Shortcake, 242-243
    -And-sour-cream dressing, 178
    Spongecake, *106*, 110-111
String beans, plantation, 169
Stuffings:
    Apple and prune, 21, *22*
    Cornbread, sausage and pecan, 296
    Oyster, 297, *298*
    Sauerkraut, 25
Sucre filé—spun sugar, *54*, 55-56
Sugar:
    Doughnuts, *250*, 278
    Spun, *54*, 55-56
Swedish meatballs, *79*, 81-82
Sweet-and-sour pork, 99
Sweet bread, 35, *36*
Sweet potatoes:
    Beef-and-, stew, 275-276
    Candied, 302
    Pie, 308-309, *310*
Swordfish:
    Grilled, 218
    Shish Kabob, 221, 224, *225*

T

T-bone steak, charcoal-broiled, 218-*219*

Tarts, maids of honor, 111, 113
Toll-House cookies, 278-279
Tom and Jerry, *62*, 64
Tom Thumb cookies, 282
Tomatoes:
    Aspic, 167-168
    And avocado soup, cold, 235
    Cheese *croustades*, 14
    And garlic sauce, 265
    Sauce, 268
Tongue in sweet-and-sour sauce, beef, 276
Tsimmes—beef-and-sweet-potato stew, 275
Tsoureki—Greek Easter bread, 152
Turkey:
    Hash, 166
    Roasted, with cornbread, sausage and pecan stuffing, 296-297
    Roasted, with oytser stuffing, 297-298
    Stock, 296-297
Turnips, mashed, 301

V

Vanilla ice cream, 245-246
Veal in aspic, 180-181
Vegetables:
    Artichokes, boiled, 147
    Artichokes stuffed with shrimp and Green Goddess dressing, 180
    Asparagus tips with Chinese-mushroom sauce, 103, *104*, 105
    Asparagus with egg sauce, 148
    Aspic, 238
    Beans:
        Boston baked, 224, 226
        Salad, three-bean, 218, *222-223*
        Sea bass with fermented black, 105
    Beets, pickled, 77
    Broccoli, ham and chicken with, 102-103
    Broccoli purée, 30-31
    Brussels sprouts with walnuts, 26
    Cabbage, braised red, 21, *22*
    Cabbage, corned beef and, 135, *136*, 137

    Cabbage, pickled, 134
    Cabbage, sweet-and-sour stuffed, 275
    Cabbage with apples, red, 260
    Carrots, minted, 168
    Celery, braised, with almonds, 302
    Celery slaw, 237
    Celery Victor, 184-185
    Colcannon, 135
    Cold marinated, 185
    Cucumber salad, pickled, 77, 78
    Onions, creamed, *298*, 299
    Onions, glazed, 32
    Peas, fresh green, *à la française*, 148-149
    Ratatouille, 220-221
    Spinach salad, *239*
    Squash, creamed winter, 300, *301*
    Squash, spiced acorn, *290*, 299-300
    String beans, plantation, 169
    Turnips, mashed, 301
    Yoghurt and herb salad, 240
    Zucchini, cold marinated, 238
Veloutée, sauce, 177
Vin Chaud (or *Glüwein*), *62*, 63

W

Walnuts:
    Cookies with chocolate filling, 283-284
    Maple-, fudge balls, 114
    Maple-, pie, 311
    Sherried, 312, *313*
Water-chestnut-and-watercress salad, 185, 187
White fruitcake, 59, 60-61
Wine-and-spice cookies, 286-*287*, 288

Y

Yeast dumplings, 256, *261*
Yoghurt, vegetable and herb salad, 240
Yorkshire pudding, 31-32, *33*

Z

Zucchini, cold marinated, 238

Printed in U.S.A.